EXPRESSION
IN
AMERICA

THE WORKS OF
LUDWIG LEWISOHN

Criticism

THE MODERN DRAMA[1]
THE SPIRIT OF MODERN GERMAN LITERATURE
THE POETS OF MODERN FRANCE
THE DRAMA AND THE STAGE
THE CREATIVE LIFE
CITIES AND MEN[1]
EXPRESSION IN AMERICA

Autobiography and Public Affairs

UP STREAM[2]
ISRAEL[1]
MID-CHANNEL[1]

Fiction

THE BROKEN SNARE
DON JUAN
ROMAN SUMMER[1]
THE CASE OF MR. CRUMP[3]
THE ISLAND WITHIN[4]
STEPHEN ESCOTT[5]
THE LAST DAYS OF SHYLOCK[6]
THE ROMANTIC[7]
THE GOLDEN VASE

Drama

ADAM: A DRAMATIC HISTORY

Selections from the Works

VÉRITÉ ET POÉSIE. TRADUCTION DE RÉGIS MICHAUD ET F. L. SCHOELL
A JEW SPEAKS. EDITED BY JAMES WATERMAN WISE

[1]*Also published in England.* [2]*Published in England and translated into German.* [3]*Published by E. W. Titus of Paris and translated into German, French, Dutch, Italian, Swedish, Spanish, and Dano-Norwegian.* [4]*Published in England and translated into German, French, Dutch, Swedish, Dano-Norwegian, Hungarian, Polish, and Rumanian.* [5]*Published in England and translated into French, German, Dutch, and Spanish.* [6]*Published in England and translated into German and French.* [7]*Published by E. W. Titus of Paris.*

EXPRESSION
IN
AMERICA

BY
LUDWIG LEWISOHN

*All men live by truth and stand
in need of expression. . . . The
man is only half himself, the other
half is his expression.*—EMERSON.

Harper & Brothers, Publishers
NEW YORK AND LONDON

2362

CONTENTS

The author's grateful acknowledgment is due to all writers and publishers whose copyrighted works are referred to in the course of these pages. In particular for the quoted passages from the works published by the following firms:

HARCOURT, BRACE AND COMPANY
> Carl Sandburg

HARPER & BROTHERS
> Edna St. Vincent Millay
> William Dean Howells
> Mark Twain

HENRY HOLT & COMPANY, INC.
> Carl Sandburg
> Robert Frost

HOUGHTON MIFFLIN COMPANY
> Amy Lowell
> William Vaughn Moody

ALFRED A. KNOPF
> Stephen Crane
> Elinor Wylie

LITTLE, BROWN & COMPANY
> Emily Dickinson

HORACE LIVERIGHT, INC.
> Hilda Doolittle
> Ezra Pound
> T. S. Eliot
> Hart Crane

THE MACMILLAN COMPANY
>William Cullen Bryant
>Vachel Lindsay
>Edgar Lee Masters
>Edward Coote Pinkney
>Edwin Arlington Robinson

THE PRINCETON UNIVERSITY PRESS
>Philip Freneau

CHARLES SCRIBNER'S SONS
>George Santayana

THE VIKING PRESS
>William Ellery Leonard

PREFACE

Indirect preparations for this book were begun when, in early youth, I was a member of the seminar in American literature conducted by Professor W. P. Trent at Columbia University; the plan to write it took definite shape in 1927 and has since, despite the intervention of other tasks and duties, never been far from my mind. In sending it at last from the study into the world a few observations may be made. The book is not, in any hitherto accepted sense, a history of literature. Scholars who look in vain for a name, a date, a work, are asked to believe that these were not slighted but eliminated. For what is here attempted is a portrait of the American spirit seen and delineated, as the human spirit itself is best seen, in and through its mood of articulateness, of creative expression. To this end selection under the appropriate guiding principle was inevitable. It was equally inevitable that I use the organon or method of knowledge associated with the venerated name of Sigmund Freud. The portrayer of any aspect of human life or civilization who does not do so today will soon be like some mariner of old who, refusing to acknowledge the invention of mathematical instruments because their precision was not yet perfect, still stubbornly sailed his vessel by the stars. That both under my principle of selection and in my use of the psychological method I have committed many errors was unavoidable and

vii

human. Nor is it grave, since time is sure to correct them. I venture, nevertheless, to entertain the hope that this book will coöperate with the creative forces in American life and that it will, in the words of Sainte-Beuve, "advance the question and not leave things hereafter quite as they were before."

LUDWIG LEWISOHN.

PARIS, *Autumn*, 1931

INTRODUCTION

I

Wherever thoughtful people gather today in the Western World their talk, leaving sooner or later the vexing questions of war and peace or food and oil, drifts toward books. Except among the technically lettered this talk will rarely deal with methods or forms or kinds. Æsthetic considerations may arise. But readers, wiser in this than critics, stick to the work of art in its totality as substance, as life projected and interpreted by a significant personality. They seek in books both light and guidance, both precept and example, not after the way of old seekers for exact laws in a fixed and finished world, but as inquirers and fellow workers, as themselves creators in this vast and intricate business of human experience. Sometime near the middle of the nineteenth century an old crack in that rigid shell which was supposed to represent the universe suddenly burst and vistas opened racing into the infinite past and the infinite future. Space joined time in being unimaginable. Authoritative wisdom became as dust. What Lucretius suspected and Goethe prophetically saw was revealed to thousands; within the past three-quarters of a century it has been revealed to millions. A new type of reader arose—one to whom literature was no longer an elegant diversion or an illustration of the foreknown and fixed, but moral research, a road to salvation, the bread of life.

In all matters of this sort practice comes before either theory or conscious knowledge. The process is slow. It must have been very gradually that men and women, their faith in scripture and churchly tradition beginning to be shaken, came to expect of secular literature more than the amusement of an idle hour or the agreeable confirmation of what they already knew and believed. A strong minority, to be sure, had always sought instruction in books; a few readers here and there must, since the days of Montaigne, have approached creative literature in an inquiring temper. Broadly speaking it remains true that the modern attitude to the written word could not and did not arise *until scripture had become literature and literature scripture.* It is undeniable that numerous classes of readers still regard books as either a pastime or as an illustration of their antecedent certainties. For these classes it is not illogical to demand that a censorship suppress or an Index condemn books which, conflicting with their antecedent certainties, they must conceive of as false and therefore harmful. Nor are there lacking other survivals: the æsthetes, descendants of the "amateurs of elegant composition," who dislike plays and novels of ideas; the rhetoricians whose verbal games recall the feeble dabbling of the Byzantines and the later builders of acrostics. But the serious modern artist writes neither for Fundamentalists nor for the elegant and trivial. He addresses himself to that reader to whom the creative records of the human spirit are a religion, a new binding of himself to his kind through the intercommunication, the enlargement and clarification of experience that are offered by the written word.

The change which has come over the attitude of intelligent people to literature is of great, of ultimate importance. Yet much criticism and all of literary history is written as though we still lived in the tight and thoroughly explored little cosmos of our ancestors and as though the psychology of the writer were still that of the minstrel, the purveyor of information or the adorner of pious legend. The minstrel is still with us. But his name is Edgar A. Guest; so is the writer of pious legends and his name is Harold Bell Wright. These names and the qualities that they recall suffice to illustrate how enormous is the cleavage between the past and the present. The difference between the ox-cart and the aeroplane is not as great nor as fundamental as the difference between the peasant listener to a border ballad of revenge and blood or a reader of Robert Service on the one hand, and on the other, one who absorbedly ponders "Of Human Bondage," "An American Tragedy," "The Magic Mountain."

Wherein does that vast difference primarily reside? In this: that in every age previous to our own there was supposed to exist a body of knowledge, whether recorded or traditional, whether legal or revealed, which was assumed to be closed, final and infallible. Greece and Judæa were exceptions. There the human spirit went through a development analogous to our own and Plato and Euripides, Amos and Isaiah were, the former intellectual, the latter moral revolutionaries. But the Latin Christian tradition knew no exception until the coming of the scientific age. All that man needed to know of metaphysics or morals, all of speculation concerning vital and final issues was fixed and closed. Hence literature was by the very nature of things confined to the tale and the homily, to providing a pastime or a lesson. This limitation favored the art of poetry which is unapt at inquiry; the Divine Comedy is as perfect and complete as a Cathedral, as rounded and seamless as the Christian universe which it illustrates; Faust is like a series of granite boulders strewn on a plain that melts into an infinite horizon. Between the days of Dante and Goethe the great and unparalleled change had come. Tradition and authority had broken down; slowly, painfully science was striving to rebuild a forever imperfect cosmos on an inhuman and unimaginable scale. This is forgotten by the æsthetes who yearn feebly for great works in verse. Those works were not accidents. They grew out of a world of their own, a world that is forever gone.

The writers of the Christian centuries, even of the Renaissance and beyond, were entirely conscious of their situation and even the most enlightened among them gave to this situation their intellectual assent. Sidney, of course, defended poetry as being "a treasure-house of science" and as fit to commemorate the deeds of one's ancestors and the praises of one's gods. But the classical passage on the whole matter, a passage quite neglected hitherto, is to be found in Bacon's "Advancement of Learning." Creative literature, Bacon writes, "is nothing else but feigned history, which may be styled as well in prose as in verse. The use of this feigned history hath been to give some shadow of satisfaction to the mind of man in those points wherein the nature of things doth deny it, the world being in proportion inferior to the soul. . . . History propoundeth the successes of issues and actions not so agreeable to the merits of virtue and vice, therefore Poesy feigns them more just in retribution and more according to revealed Providence . . . for that *tendeth to demonstrate and illustrate that which is taught or delivered.*" Surely there is no more brilliant and telling commentary upon the history of civilization than that the best mind of the English renaissance, the founder of the inductive sciences is, in his demands upon literature, precisely at one with the Babbitt and the shopgirl of today: he wants happy endings and life with moralistic sugar-coatings in order that plays and stories may feign life to be what, according to tradition and convention, it ought to be. Literature in brief was neither to teach nor to deliver; it was to "illustrate that which is taught and delivered." But the enlightened and seeking modern reader has no "revealed Providence" to fall back on. Literature must teach and deliver in a new and flexible sense or it is meaningless. Scripture, I may repeat, having become literature, it was necessary for literature to become scripture.

Doubts of that older theory of letters struck sensitive and disillusioned minds from time to time. There is an unconscious pathos in that sentence of La Bruyère: "A man born a Christian and a Frenchman finds himself constrained in the matter of satire; the great subjects are forbidden him." But the overshadowing right wing was struck by no doubts and impeded by no hesitations. As late as 1820 no less a man than Walter Scott could write these words: "The best that can be hoped is that novels may sometimes instruct the youthful mind by real pictures of life, and sometimes awaken their better feelings and sympathies by strains of generous sentiment and tales of fictitious woe. Beyond this they are a mere elegance, a luxury contrived for the amusement of polished life . . . . and are read much more for amusement than with the least hope of deriving instruction from them." Amusement or instruction! Scott even when contemplating the works of Fielding could get no further than the Horatian tag:

> aut prodesse volunt aut delectare poetæ.

Of the free creative process by which the poet sees and re-interprets the universe anew for his contemporaries Scott had no inkling. Tory and Christian, all that is greatest in litera-ture was antecedently tied up and completed for him in law, tradition and scripture. Minstrelsy was left him, tales to illus-trate what he accepted as "taught and delivered" concerning the traditional virtues and gallantries of men. It would have been inconceivable to him to inquire what, in a bound-less and changing world, was the nature of true virtue and gallantry. Minstrelsy and historical information. In the creation of character he occasionally transcended his own views. Reflectively he never wavered from the mediæval no-tion of secular literature as consisting of the tale and the homily alone.

III

Yet the old bondage of literature to authority had been attacked long before. It was in 1759 that Edward Young wrote his astonishing "Conjectures on Original Composition" and announced to an unhearing world the organic character of the work of art: "It grows, it is not made," and the true relation of the writer to his great predecessors: "The less we copy the renowned ancients, we shall resemble them the more." The implications of which Young was not always clearly conscious are obvious: from the whole body of human experience the writer absorbs, forms and transmits as art to the reader what he has seen and felt and known. Literature, in other words, has become more and more lyrical and subjective in both origin and appeal. The Renaissance impulse, the Protestant and democratic revolutions all tended to make a separate entity of the individual, to differentiate man from man, to create individual impulse and need and vision. What troubled the classicists and conservatives throughout that long romantic period in which all our modern origins are rooted was the question: if literature is so personal in source and character what becomes of its appeal to mankind? If it clings wholly to the concrete, how shall it express the typical and the universal? In a hundred sayings in verse and prose Goethe answered this question with sovereign finality. He who was scientist as well as poet, the first great poet to see the universe as free and becoming, solved that difficulty in theory as all good modern literature solves it in fact: "True symbolism arises wherever the particular represents the general, not as dream and shadow, but as a living and instantaneous revelation of the inscrutable." The thing is so self-evident, once it is expressed. If the individual phenomenon did not lead to all things cosmos would be chaos, science would be impossible, the sum of things a discontinuous heap. The poet in his most intense subjectivity speaks for and to his fellows and his equals. The novel, the typical modern art-form, is exactly what Goethe called it, "a subjective epic"; yet no form in any age has spoken to men so widely and so profoundly. It was Goethe who also defined poetically but exactly the relation of the modern reader to the maker of literature: "Even at the moment of our highest happiness or of our deepest wretchedness we stand in need of the artist." And it is abundantly clear that this need could not have arisen until men began to seek in secular literature that inspiration, life and light which once they had sought in scripture and authoritative tradition alone.

Amid an hundred critical battles and reactions that have taken place since Goethe's day the deep sense of the difference between modern literature, in its broadest meaning and that of the past, between the modern reader and the reader of earlier ages has never been lost and rarely blunted. From Goethe one proceeds easily to Sainte-Beuve's definition of the "passion and the seriousness which consecrate" a genuine work of art, and to the same critic's conviction that the "study of literature leads naturally to moral inquiry." One proceeds, above all, to those extraordinary intuitive sayings of Emerson which he was not always able himself to apprehend or to establish intellectually. "All men live by truth and stand in need of expression." In other words, the modern reader craves vicarious inquiry into the truth through the expression of which, by one who can speak, he must try to live. "The experience of each new age requires a new confession." Literature is no longer an art of fixed forms or contents or appropriate imitation, but an endless, ever-changing scripture and revelation, the scripture and revelation of the life of man. Deeper still and of quite ultimate significance is Emerson's remark that the poet "uses forms according to life, and not according to the form." Experience creates substance and substance creates form. The poet no longer chooses the ballad meter for a balladesque subject nor blank verse or hexameter for an idyll. He literally did that once; only the surviving purveyors of the flattest mob-amusement do it now. The source of literature is, in the memorable words of Thomas Mann, "that mysterious blending in which suffering and the instinct for form (Leiden und Formtrieb) have become one."

Are such considerations difficult and intricate? Perhaps. But it is by avoiding them that criticism and literary scholarship and literary history are among us so often puerile and vain. We operate with concepts from before the Flood. We act as though literature, the fullest and most continuous expression of the totality of man's life, had stood still in all but outward fashion, while philosophy and statecraft and science had been wholly transformed in the ever swifter torrents of time. Literature is no more what it was than the modern industrialized state is like the self-sustaining agrarian kingdoms of long ago. Man both as a living and experiencing creature and therefore as a listener or reader has undergone changes which have transmuted the very groundwork of his character and outlook. . . . One more simple and yet very significant illustration may further clarify the differences here pointed out. In his mellow and eloquent defense of literature and philosophy Cicero, among many equally fine ones, has this passage: "Many who have been in the power of enemies and tyrants, many who have been in chains and many who have been in exile have eased their grief through the study of wisdom." What kind of wisdom was that? The grief of these men was eased by lovely and dignified maxims concerning the brevity of life and the inevitableness of evil and the dignity of bearing misfortune with courage and serenity. But modern man, who does not accept but inquire, would hardly be eased by such wisdom. For he asks: Must there be enemies? Dare there be tyrants? Has any the right to chain his fellowman? May freedom abroad not be less exile than slavery at home? He asks. He proceeds from facts to the supposed laws of those facts and questions the laws themselves and destroys, if only by the hardihood of impassioned thought, a world and a universe in which such things can be. Stoic maxims in well-wrought verse will seem feeble and trivial and impertinent to him. The poet who speaks to and for him must have grasped with a superior power of experience and of speech the high and difficult problems of his world. Mind must touch mind and deep answer unto deep.

IV

The error that the reader of the scientific age is identical with the listener to old lays and sermons, or with the mere student or with the amateur of polite letters, has its counterpart in the graver error that the psychology of the modern poet[1] has not changed from that of his predecessors. From

[1] I shall use the term poet, as the Elizabethans did and the Germans and Scandinavians (Dichter, digter) have always done as applicable to the creative artist in letters irrespective of external form. The distinction based upon the mere use of prose or verse has always been dangerous and confusing; how much more so is it today when imaginative prose is assuming nearly all the functions of verse and when the boundaries between the two forms are becoming more and more obliterated. The poet—the maker or creator—is such by virtue of his inner character.

this error arises the manifest nonsense still heard from critics and reviewers, that a play or novel involving moral or economic or metaphysical notions is the less a play or a novel on that account, or that there is a subtle indecency in the poet's drawing upon his intimate experience of life or that the poet, abstracting himself from his total human self, shall project æsthetic values into a void. Since useful literary history cannot be written while this mistaken notion is entertained but will remain an enumeration and description of documents without regard to their true character or value, I shall proceed first to the difficult but grateful task of clarifying the nature and the methods of the poetic or creative mind.

The history of letters, which is the deepest and most significant part of the history of civilization, reveals clearly enough three types of the poetic mind. Each of these types corresponds to a phase and to an epoch of human development. To a phase rather than to an epoch. For human development is evidently not uniform. Each period is thronged with survivals from former periods, and throw-backs will occur from time to time. Ox-carts, to use that illustration again, are found in country lanes a hundred miles from the great flying-fields, faith-healers flourish under the shadow of institutes for medical research, Robert Service and Edwin Arlington Robinson, Zane Grey and Margaret Deland and Theodore Dreiser all co-exist in time. War comes, in addition, and reduces intelligent modern poets to the level of medicine-men and tribal bards. Allowing for this chronological confusion it remains true that we have knowledge of three types of the poetic mind which, corresponding to three phases of particular civilizations as well as to three phases of civilization as a whole, may usefully if not altogether happily be called the bard, the artificer or verse-smith and the poet.

The bard is the earliest articulate man, differentiated from his fellows by nothing but that articulateness. When terror or triumph shake the tribe that terror or triumph finds in him a direct and immediate voice. He is an improviser; he is inspired by what he believes to be the god and what is in reality a surge of group emotion. Not always clearly differentiated from the medicine-man and the soothsayer, the bard is found among all primitive peoples. But we need not turn to the anthropologists for evidence. "Tragedy as well as comedy," Aristotle tells us, "derives from improvisation; the former going back to the precentors of the dithyramb, the latter to the precentor of the phallic songs, as both are still practiced in many cities." Primitive societies have their proper developments too and the bard does not remain wholly the voice of the tribe. He tends to acquire the skill of the artificer or verse-smith and develops that vocabulary of stock epithets which we find in the Homeric poems, in the Beowulf, in the Nibelungenlied, in balladry and folk-song. But his psychology remains the same and can be admirably studied in such modern war-poetry as the *Serment* of Henri de Régnier and the *Hassgesang* of Ernst Lissauer. Both of these extremely sophisticated modern poets momentarily lost their differentiated selves in a great up-rush of group passion. They were no longer themselves; they became the voices of their frightened and infuriated tribesmen. The spirit of the tribe improvised through them. Their subject, a common and immediate passion, clutched them; experience and expression were one and simultaneous.

The guess may be hazarded that the bard tended to become the artificer in periods of peace and stability. The gods demanded praise and the chiefs flattery and entertainment. Now the poet, uninspired by an immediate tribal passion, began to look for subjects from without, to select his "matter" and to present and to adorn it in a fashion to please his hearers. In societies still more complicated the artificer assumes the character of a didactic poet. He tells of olden wars and of saints' lives; he edifies and instructs and pleases. His personality counts for little or nothing and so there arises no sense of property in the products of the mind. Mediæval writers of romance copy and translate each other; they draw upon a common substance of Christian tale and legend and motive. They go about writing in the fashion of craftsmen. They select their subject-matter from without at the dictates of custom or fashion and experience and expression are wholly divided.

Modern poets, as we have seen, can lapse back into the tribal bard. The artificer, however refined and sophisticated when compared to his mediæval prototype, is always with us. It was he who wrote the didactic poems of the eighteenth century; it is he who, in a thousand guises but chiefly as a novelist, clutters the literature of the nineteenth century. As a poet he can rise as high as Longfellow or even as William Morris; as an essayist he can cut as creditable a figure as the late Hamilton Wright Mabie; as a teller of tales he can deceive the half-educated into thinking him spontaneous and original, like O. Henry when he is only tricky and sentimental. His constant mark is that expression in him has little to do with experience, that he chooses his subjects from without and that he strives to please or to edify, never to disturb or to arouse. He accepts all current values in politics and thought and morals. In fiction or the drama he deals uncritically with the contemporary modes of behavior and treats life as though it were a game with rules to be kept or broken. As a critic he is fond of what he calls technical considerations, unable to conceive of the creative oneness of substance and form and thus reducing the great poets to artificers in his own image. He is never influenced by the creative mind, for he does not understand its workings. But he is a great imitator and copier of meter or structure or external method or stylistic mannerism. The bard uses a common spontaneous form, the artificer a common traditional or conventional form. He multiplies enormously with the spread of education; he crowds the popular magazines; his are the chief outer successes of the market-places of literature—the bookshop and the popular stage; he rules the trade of letters and darkens council, for he is often in the editorial office and the professor's chair. It is he who writes the far too many books which will flood and blind us one day and disgust us with literature itself. He is inevitable; he has his uses as an entertainer and a popularizer of knowledge. But no sound history of literature can now or hereafter be written that does not recognize and know and exclude him and fix its attention wholly upon the products of the creative spirit.

Of that creative spirit or eternal poet isolated examples have arisen whenever in an age or land authority was broken or transcended, personality emerged, literature became scripture and first-hand experience could project a vision which was to remould and save the world. Euripides and Plato and the Prophets of Israel belonged to that company of poets; Catullus and Lucretius belonged to it and then no one again until the early humanists began to turn their eyes from a rule and a ritual to nature and their own hearts. And even they rarely saw life at first hand but rather through the eyes of the recovered ancients and we must wait for the appearance of Montaigne to observe, though in so prosaic an example, the free play of the creative mind.

Now it is clear to everyone, except to the professed students and critics of literature, that the time from the Protestant Revolution to the Industrial Revolution, even though it is probably only the dawn of a still longer and stranger age, is the longest continuous period of intellectual liberty and flexibility, of the possibility, therefore, of direct and fresh human experience, in all the long annals of the race. Freedom of thought, moreover, was accompanied by freedom of movement; the machine which, today, threatens to enslave us anew, broke the hard castes of feudalism. The townsman insisted upon his human rights, next the agrarian slave. The ancestors of Keats and Hebbel were serfs sold with a parcel of land. Economic flexibility and the gradual breakdown of dogma and churchly authority were accompanied by a slow growth of moral freedom. The varieties of human experience increased in number, and heresy and travel and love and speculation became vivid possibilities to ever widening classes and groups. Hence while, for reasons I have pointed out, the number of artificers has increased in modern society, the number of true poets necessarily shows a comparable growth and many an intense small novelist today has more to communicate concerning man and nature and human life than Gottfried von Strassburg or even the great Dante. It is a question not of dimension but of quality and character, and this small heresy of mine will be the commonplace of day after tomorrow.

Let anyone examine, with a mind unclouded by the traditions of the schools, two anthologies of verse: one of the Elizabethan and Jacobean lyric, one of verse in any modern language selected from the poetry of the past thirty years. The advantage of mere beauty, of piercing simplicity or hieratic splendor of speech will be clearly with the former. The advantage of subtlety and interest and significance of subject-matter will be overwhelmingly with the latter. In the former will be found a few stately or joyous or melancholy commonplaces about honor and mutability and chivalric love and the changing seasons and the doom of death; in the latter all that deep and intricate research into the soul and the world and the relation of the two and of men to each other which has been released by the destruction of dogma and the economic and moral flexibility of our age. Yet this comparison is manifestly unfair to the moderns. For verse is not their characteristic form. Their best is found in the essay, the novel and the prose play.

Human life, in brief, has made more and more for the appearance of the creative spirit, the poet who is neither bard nor artificer. This poet who may correctly enough be called the modern poet, starts not like the tribal bard with a group passion that chooses to speak through him nor, like the artificer, with a subject which, under certain rules and accord-

xxiv

ing to certain traditions, he chooses deliberately and from
without. He starts from an inner fact of his individual consciousness. Out of that consciousness, which is both perceiver
and thing perceived, both container and content, there arises
the impassioned need for the release and the communication
of experience, for the liberation from that experience and its
projection for the contemplation and salvation of his fellows. In the modern poet, as in the bard, experience and expression are one. But his experience is not tribal; it is wholly
individual; it tends more and more to have, as one important
element, a revolt from the tribal. Above all, experience and
expression though indissolubly one in him *are not simultaneous*. Weeks, months, years will intervene between experience
and expression, between what was once called inspiration and
execution. For the modern poet has not chosen a subject,
grateful or ungrateful, which he can determine to treat in
this or that fashion. He and his subject are one. He has de-
scended to the depth of his soul and so to the core of the
world whence, if the world is organic or even continuous, all
roads must be roads to God. And now he must wait in quie-
tude to see whether the experience which has come to him as
a communicable one will grow and weave between him and
the world, between subject and object, a body and a form
which will leave it utterly his own and yet make it a possession of his fellowmen. During this period of gestation processes take place which can be roughly defined as the processes of condensation and of heightening. Experience is
diffuse; life lags and halts; its direction is veiled to us while
we are in its midst and its crucial moments can be lost to us
under the attritions of our common day. Thus the creative

mind condenses time and space and action and speech and gesture until experience is purged of the apparently accidental and aimless, until there arises the substance of art which is truer than what we call truth to life and more real than reality and yet unfathomably rooted in both. This process of condensation is accompanied by that heightening which makes all things and actions and thoughts clearer and intenser, which brings out their inherent significance both for the self and for the world. Thus experience assumes form, a form now at last liberated from kinds and genres and truly incomparable and unique. Under what law do these processes take place, under what informing principle, loosely analogous perhaps to that unknown principle according to which a thousand substances will crystallize in forms equally exquisite but each different from every other? Plainly under the informing law of the individual creative mind, conformable to its innermost nature, which has its special personal relation both to all concrete things and to their sum. No wonder that Aristotle called poetry, by which he too meant imaginative creative literature, more serious and philosophical than history. It is the core and spirit of both history and philosophy. For the poet lives with the highest awareness his day in human history; unconsciously or consciously he shapes his experience into a work which implies such a universe as he dreams or can endure, or else implies the repudiation of the world and the triumph, however pessimistic, of man's spirit over the hostile gods. Amusing criticasters who blame the modern poet for being autobiographical and philosophic! What else, not being a bard and disdaining to be a mere artificer, can he be? Out of his experience, out of suffering and vision he rebuilds the world; he needs to wring its secret from it for his own release and for the salvation of his fellows. He is the poet, whether his outer form be novel, play or lyric, whom the thoughtful and instructed modern reader seeks out to experience for him, to interpret for him, to illuminate and to guide him, to face for him the inscrutable from which all older and once apparently certain messages have fallen silent.

v

A certain poet being spoken of, Goethe quietly remarked: "He can help us no more." The saying has been called crudely utilitarian. Quite wrongly; for it is the mark of the essential poet that he continues to help us across ages and across revolutions in morals, religions, economic systems. That a given writer was fashionable in his own day or brilliantly entertained his generation continues to be interesting in the antiquarian study of that day and that generation. In the history of literature conceived of as the ultimate articulateness and intercommunication of man concerning himself and his fate the works of such writers have no place. It will be found, too, that the writers who can help us no more lack the true marks of the creative spirit. The story is well known of how accidentally, in his mature manhood, James Fenimore Cooper drifted into writing. And his strong point, quite as one should expect, is invention. But there is nothing more certain than that invention is never a mark of the creative mind and that the poets and dramatists and novelists who can still help us have relied upon common myths for the projection of their sense of life or upon the observation that is borne of suffering from the world or upon the direct expression of their personal experience. Invention is the dross in writers as eminent and different as Balzac and Wassermann. Neither Euripides nor the author of Job nor Lucretius nor Shakespeare nor Molière nor Fielding nor Goethe nor Wagner nor Flaubert nor Whitman was strong in invention. Literature is expression, not tribal formulation nor an entertaining and inventive adornment of the known, the accepted, the believed. Cooper can help us no more.

I have, then, it is clear, a kind of history of literature in mind that shall limit itself to the record of essential expression of the spirit of man. What figures such a history of literature will choose out of the past and what figures neglect is plain enough. The scholar will at once querulously ask, however, by what process of selection the history of literature so conceived and practiced will deal with the present and the immediate past. The answer is that, though there can be in the nature of things no rigid standard or sure criterion, the test I propose to apply has its peculiar chances of use and fruitfulness. The character of the poet is a thing known and ascertainable under all variations of age and form. I shall be deceived by no specious success or outer brilliancy of execution. But a concrete example is worth a page of theory. Other critics beside myself have had their obscure doubts in contemplating a talent so magnificent and so expert as that of Mrs. Edith Wharton. Especially her earlier works seem in their structural completeness and fine intelligence of detail as though they might be built for perpetuity. Yet those obscure doubts linger and grow less obscure as one considers the sources from which all lasting art has always risen. Mrs.

Wharton has never wholly liberated herself from the illusions of the world which she portrays. Her constant play of irony is a defensive gesture; her intelligence has transcended her special group and tradition and society; her heart and her instincts are with them. If the deeps arose and this social structure were to topple Mrs. Wharton, for all her wit and insight, would take her station with these snobs and wasters and players of a social game. She is above them but of them. Her tribe has never let her go. As during the war, so on some day of judgment, she would adopt the superstitions of her clan and group and prefer society to the kingdom of God. One cannot be an artist and a lady. Thus her works share, as they need not have shared, the perishableness of the society which she has chosen to portray. Let it not be objected that this judgment is moral and philosophical in character. Morals and metaphysics are only learned names for reactions that are identical with personality, character and talent. An artist's *Weltanschauung* is both the man and the style.

From this apparent digression I may return to what in my attempt to disengage the essentials of literature from its accidents is directly applicable to America. The history of our national expression differs from that of any other people in that our folk or bardic periods lie far away and long ago in other lands and have never been a living force among us. Men came to America bearing with them the narrow Protestant culture of the post-Renaissance period. The Puritans in Massachusetts, Pastorius and his Germans in Pennsylvania and the Southern colonists to a greater extent than the Cavalier legend admits were at one in their adherence to a view of the world according to which nearly the whole of human conduct was prescribed by dogmatic authority and all the expansive forces of life, except war and trade, identical with the realm of Satan and of sin. The margin left for art was the sermon, the chronicle and the elegy. Nor must it be forgotten how large a portion of earlier and later colonists consisted of indentured servants, of fugitives and of petty criminals. How were creative values in life or literature to be expected of people who had not been able to reach conformity with the average *mores* of their day? They strove, naturally, after the normal respectability of the Puritan view of life. Thus the leveling and hardening of American civilization began early. And all these people were not only largely isolated from the developmental forces of the civilization that had originally produced them; they had in their isolation and their necessary moral rigidness to confront and to live the dangerous, wild, cruel, drunken life of the wilderness and of the frontier. The life that had actually to be lived was often terribly at variance with the moral theories not insincerely professed. Thus there was added to the original opposition between the life of grace and the life of sin another and all but unexampled division between the ideal and the real, precept and practice, expression and reality, literature and life. From this division sprang the self-righteous Christian rum-merchant and slave-trader, the ancestor of the charitable business magnate of a later day. All life being in theory governed by the most stringent rules but the life of war and trade being left by tacit and universal consent in an outer wilderness, this society set up its strongest defenses against all those varied experiences in thought and action from which art springs. From the Colonial laws which punished incontinence by brands and lashings and public confessions to the latest experiments in Prohibition enforcement, American society, true to its origin, has compensated itself for its fierce sinning against the Indian, the slave, the business competitor, by bearing down with unparalleled harshness upon all the more amiable and expansive forces of human nature. What tempted men most sorely they avenged most cruelly. Hence there arose in the course of time the pornography that justified Anthony Comstock, and on the other hand the spirit in himself and the rich men who abetted him that could not distinguish between pornography and the expressiveness of art. Any attempt to speak out was felt during the greater part of the American past to be a danger and a betrayal. Nowhere else has the integration of literature with life been so suspected and feared. The only artist tolerated was the artificer who observed the rules of the social and moral game, glorified fighting and stealing and represented life as emptied of both reflection and desire. An unbalanced sense of sin soaked through the whole of existence and letters remained polite letters unintegrated with life until almost the other day. Men wrote not what they thought or believed or experienced but what, according to Puritan business morality a good and respectable man ought to experience and to believe. All books so written can help us no more; they are the monotonous documents of an age that is passing and that is not likely ever to be reborn.

Fortunately the human spirit has in it something of an undying flame. The true history of literature in America is the history of those poets and thinkers who first in mere theory, later in both theory and practice, denied the Puritan

xxxi

division of experience from expression, broke the moulds of the artificer, and brought their countrymen first freedom of perception and of thought, next flexibility of conduct in pursuit of each man's idea of the good life. The story of our literature is the story of successive moral revolutions, nor has the time for severe and serene masterpieces come to us yet. The revolutions are far from won. Great masses of the American people have felt and still feel the reintegration of experience and expression to be a godless and un-American attempt to destroy their cherished tradition of the division between life and art, their frontier sense of the sinfulness of the natural and have in a hundred ways tried to tighten defensively the fighting solidarity of that degenerate Puritan view of life which has gathered power and pride from its successes in the material world. No, the revolutions are not yet won. But the story of them is the best record of our past and the happiest omen of our future.

BOOK ONE

Beginnings

I

Let us disturb once more, if but for a moment, the dust on the works of the New England Puritans. Their flat and crabbed or extravagant seventeenth-century prose has scarcely a moment of expressiveness or warmth. But their long shadow falls upon us to this day. For these dark Calvinists drove God out of the world and intensified unbearably the opposition between a small and artificial realm of grace and the boundless wilderness of sin. By consigning nine-tenths of human life to the devil, they withdrew it from cultivation and control. The American folk-beliefs that men are either total abstainers or drunkards, either monkish or libertine, either hustlers or idlers, either political and economic conformers or enemies of all social order, derive straight from the doctrines of the Separatists. To an increasing number of American minds this view concerning the fatal division of the universe remains unintelligible. Among great masses of the people its attractiveness is still felt and its power persists. To it, rather than to the harsh but not ignoble struggles of the wilderness and the frontier, is to be attributed all that is unlovely and cruel and grotesque in the life of the American people. Hysterical religiosity without charity or sweetness, dullness alternating with vulgar or trivial amusements, the intolerance that stamps any moral non-conformity with the ugliness of vice and any rational enlargement of human experience with the reproach of license—all these phenomena issue, as a matter of necessity, from the doctrine that in God's house there is but one narrow mansion and that the entire realm of nature is corrupt and damned. The Whigs of the revolutionary period fought this doctrine; the Transcendentalists of New England fought it; Whitman fought it and Mark Twain writhed under it; the whole of our modern literature is a single act of rebellion against it and its consequences. Its gaunt wall still looms over us, cracked but not crumbling yet.

The early village theocracies of Massachusetts upon the dark edge of the unknown and perilous forest held this doctrine of theirs not without dignity or a touch of somber grace. A part, at least, of their age was with them. Its examples supported them; its learning provided justification and defense. But the current of human civilization soon changed its direction completely and American Puritanism became the doctrine and the mode of life of great masses of rude and unlettered provincials. The fire and fury of Geneva had burned themselves out. Europe set its face toward the century of prose and reason. In that very century Jonathan Edwards, last of the eminent divines of the original order, a sick soul but a scholar and a man of high spiritual dignity, approved and supported the "great awakening" of his time. With what eyes would a man of his tastes and temper have viewed the teeming sects of later days, the orgiastic camp-meetings, the strange Mormon revolt, the coarsely seductive anti-Mormon literature which filled the peasants in a thousand villages with envy and hatred, the preaching and the grotesque pamphlets of Mason Locke Weems, the roaring crusades against liquor, against vice, against literature, against science which, from the post-revolutionary reaction against Deism to the days of the Volstead Act, the Mann Act, the activities of the Watch and Ward Society, and the Dayton trial have solidly united the rival churches of Protestant America by their common expression of the undying Puritan conviction that man and nature and man's instincts are from the beginning evil and without hope.

The history of American civilization and hence the history of American literature must be conceived and imagined and written against that background of dualistic doctrine—against that metaphysic of the folk which, like the fundamental metaphysic of every folk or group, is an expression of immemorial instincts of the blood. It is beyond explanation and withdraws itself from all judging why the Anglo-American people, kindly, affectionate, hospitable, truly desirous of justice and political freedom, has been swept again and again into every conceivable folly and cruelty by its inexpugnable terror of those instincts and appetencies which have marked humankind from the beginning. Need I rehearse the thousand proofs? But they are in the consciousness of every American, in his memories of his native town or village, in his experiences of all that concerns love, free-

3

dom, knowledge, art. Nor need I foreshadow here the thousand shapes which this terror at worst, this profound ambivalence at best, has assumed in the expressive life of America: the flight from reality which made our earlier letters seem so strangely feeble and trivial to all who expected power and light from this new eagle nation; the suppressions and substitutions and enforced insincerities that meet us in the lives and works of some of our chief men of letters; the unheroic attempt of pragmatism to gild and justify the prevalent metaphysics upon another ground; or, deeper and more significant than all, the turmoil and the roar of business and belligerency by which so many of the best Americans in commerce and in the liberal professions seek to palliate the ache and hunger of their souls. . . . A saving remnant has always, or nearly always existed. Since the World War that minority has grown in numbers, in articulateness, in courage. It has created a literature upon which the eyes of the world are beginning to turn. But this generation and this literature no more than any other in the annals of America can be understood or interpreted without a glance at those heroic and terrible villages that once clung to the Massachusetts coast.

II

It is a mistake to begin with the swelling imperialist note of John Smith. "What so truly suits with honor and honesty, as the discovering things unknown, erecting towns, peopling counties . . . Rome, what made her such a Monarchess?" For good or evil, this note did not affect American destiny. But in William Bradford's *History of Plymouth Plantation*

4

we find at once, at that far threshold of American affairs, familiar notes of which the echoes are daily with us still. Protestantism oppressed, in exile, in danger, conscious of its feigned or real kinship with the apostles and the early church, has always been capable of a sincere and moving gesture. The Separatists prepared to leave Leyden to fare across that monstrous ocean to a land which was to be even harsher than they dreamed. They "left that goodly and pleasant city, which had been their resting-place near twelve years; but they knew they were pilgrims and looked not much on those things, but lifted up their eyes to the heavens, their dearest country, and quieted their spirits." One catches that note still in white village churches in summer at love feasts and on communion Sundays. But soon another note, an ominous and resonant one, is sounded by Bradford. Whether dug into caves of the earth for a habitation or living on mussels and mildewed corn, these Pilgrims had become masters. On an early Christmas sundry colonists remembered in the wilderness the sports and amusements of that merry England which was perishing under the Puritan revolt. Governor Bradford's whip cracked. The "dearest country" was not thought upon. There was to be no merry-making in Plymouth. The people could "work or pray." No wonder that Thomas Morton and his band went farther into the wilderness and changed the name of Mount Wollaston, at least according to Bradford, to Merry Mount and erected a May pole, consciously innocent, of course, of its phallic symbolism, and disported themselves, again according to Bradford, "as if this jollity would have lasted forever." The Plymouth men put a stop to it and we shall never know whether

5

Morton and his fellows were really guilty of selling arms to the Indians and teaching them how to make powder and were thus the "gain-thirsty murderers" of Bradford's description. What is certain is that the arming of the Indians for gain did not, as all Colonial history shows, stop there. The trade must have been continued by the righteous Pilgrims themselves. And Morton wrote a defense of himself and his friends called "The New English Canaan" which was printed in Amsterdam in 1637. The book, attacking their rule and conduct, was declared "scandalous" by the authorities of the villages and Morton was imprisoned in Boston for a year. He may have been a rogue, though the testimony of his persecutors is quite without weight. He speaks in his book in a strain as familiar to us as the righteous wrath and accusation of his judges, of "harmless mirth much distasted by the precise Separatists that kept much ado about the tithe of mint and cumin, troubling their brains more than reason would require about things that are indifferent, envying the prosperity and the hope of the plantation of Ma-re Mount." No wonder that the far pathos of this story touched the imagination of Hawthorne. Is it not almost a symbol and a prophecy?

The truth of history is pragmatic. The legend of the conqueror prevails. His seed reports. Strange secrets concerning the theocratic villages of Massachusetts might be revealed could we summon to the bar of history a certain Philip Ratcliff, a servant of a Mr. Cradock who "being convict *ore tenus*, of most foul scandalous invective against our churches and government, was censured to be whipped, lose his ears, and be banished from the plantation, which was presently executed." There was a finality in this manner of disposing of your critics: to drive them bleeding, mutilated, crippled into the bleak, trackless forests. Ratcliff was no more heard of, nor a certain Hugh Bewett who was banished for maintaining "that he was free from original sin." These are specimens out of the History of New England, written by the famous John Winthrop, who was no arbitrary tyrant and inquisitor in his own conceit, but practised this sort of government upon learnedly supported philosophical principles. There exists, according to him, a twofold liberty. First there is the liberty of nature, which man shares with the beasts. This is an equal liberty toward good and evil and is to be rooted out. Civil liberty "is the proper end and object of authority, and cannot subsist without it; and it is a liberty to that only which is good, just and honest." How familiar that psychology is! What I consider good, just, honest, is liberty; what you consider so is license and sin. In spite of whippings and mutilations and exile John Winthrop was concerned over the fate of the settlements because "authority was overmuch slighted, which, if not timely remedied, would endanger the commonwealth, and bring us to a mere democracy." This authority of the clerical governors of men's minds and bodies knew and dictated what was fit for each human soul. A Mrs. Hopkins lost her mind, poor woman. She had been much given to reading and writing according to John Winthrop. "If she had attended her household affairs and such things as belong to women, she had kept her wits." One can see behind this anecdote the possibility of a sensitive and aspiring spirit driven mad, despite attempts at sublimation, by the repression, the harshness and the unbearable dullness of life. She was no truly virtuous woman. Such an one was the eldest daughter of the famous and saintly Mr. Hooker, married to the Reverend Thomas Shepard. She died young, worn out with child-bearing. She limited her reading to her husband's notes for his sermons "which she had to muse on every week." She had—terrible woman—"an excellency to reprove for sin, and discern the evils of men." She was above rubies.

The self-righteous authoritarianism of John Winthrop is shared by his two eminent contemporaries, John Cotton and Thomas Hooker. There was a touch of disease, of megalomania in this doctrine as held by these particular men. For they were, in their time and place, the sources of authority, the vicegerents of God, divines, magistrates, judges, executioners. Their authoritarianism was no academic doctrine. The ministers came out of their studies and witnessed the whippings, the cuttings of ears, the boring of tongues with red-hot irons, the scourgings and the hangings which they had ordained. Whether their delight in cruelty, in sadistic power over the flesh and blood of fellow-creatures came first or sprang from a previous and ready-made rationalization— this is a subtle but a minor point. The rationalization was complete and left no place for any human faltering. "To excommunicate an heretic," John Cotton wrote, "is not to persecute; that is, it is not to punish an innocent, but a culpable and damnable person, and that not for conscience, but for persisting in error against light of conscience." You assume, in other words, that your truth is the only truth and that hence any resistance to it is not rational but plainly wicked. That psychological process, too, is not wholly un-

8

familiar in America to this day. A more intimate and sinister element is added to Puritan doctrine and practice by the Reverend Thomas Hooker, a man sincerely beloved by his colleagues and a saint according to his lights. "Christ has appointed church-censures as good physic to purge out what is evil." It were useless to inquire by what strange process of thought a rigorous and disciplinary institutionalism could be derived from the sayings or the example of Jesus, as it would be unprofitable to inquire into the sources of the effrontery by which the Puritans, with the agreement and consent of their modern historians, attributed their most repulsive doctrines and practices to the religion of ancient Israel. It is the human element that I seek, the human element, above all, that has not quite perished from American thought and American practice. And so I let the Reverend Thomas Hooker significantly continue: "All men are made watchmen over the welfare of their brethren, and by virtue of their consociation and combination have power over each other and a judicial way of process against each other in case of any sinful aberration." That is a sufficiently dangerous doctrine of moral and physical lynch-law in itself. It becomes appalling in its working-out. Any brother in the church may "by reason of another's obstinacy be constrained to tell it to the Church." And the "sinful aberrations," be it remembered, were not confined to crimes against society, but to the most intimate details of opinion and personal living. The labor spy, the liquor spy, the Ku-Klux guardian and whipper of his fellows, the wartime informer or, rather, the patience with which these are endured, proves that this doctrine of

9

Hooker, too, is based upon a permanent element in the psychology of American Protestants.

Slightly older than his colleagues, not wholly subdued to the seemliness of seventeenth-century divinity, Nathaniel Ward, for a few years minister at Ipswich, conserved even in his old age something of the quaint and vivid speech of the Jacobeans. Hence in his "Simple Cobler [sic] of Aggawam in America, Willing to Help Mend His Native Country" (1647) he expresses with a delightful frankness principles and prejudices which in other forms and sometimes directed against other subjects are with us still. He is prophetic of the very phraseology of certain patriotic organizations that flourished two-hundred and seventy years later: "All Familists, Antinomians, Anabaptists and other enthusiasts, shall have free liberty to keep away from us." Among the "four things" which his heart "hath naturally detested" are "Foreigners dwelling in my country to crowd our native subjects into the corners of the earth." He sees astutely enough a spiritual dilemma that has clearly or obscurely troubled his intellectual descendants ever since: "The state that will give conscience in matters of religion, must give liberty of conscience and conversation in moral laws, or else the fiddle will be out of tune." He is the forerunner of the advocates of long skirts and opaque bodices. There were, one is glad to learn from him, five or six women in the Colony who tried to dress charmingly. As for such a woman, Ward exclaims, "I look at her as the very gizzard of a trifle, the product of a quarter of a cipher, the epitome of nothing, fitter to be kicked, if she were of a kickable substance, than either honored or humored." Far more frank, pathetic and naïve is Ward's comment on his indignation than any expressed by his more knowing descendants. "If I see any of them accidentally, I cannot cleanse my fancy of them for a month after. I have been a solitary widower almost twelve years." Poor old man. The suppression of natural instinct prevented him from seeing a comely woman without indecent fancies and was sublimated, as it was often in our own day, in blood-thirstiness and unmotivated rancor. "Cursed be he that holdeth back his sword from blood: yea, cursed be he that maketh not his sword stark drunk with Irish blood, that doth not recompense them double for their hellish treachery to the English, that maketh them not heaps upon heaps and their country a dwelling place of Dragons." At least one anecdote of the acidulous wit of Ward survives and in his more amiable moods he could even write verses in commendation of Mrs. Anne Bradstreet, that tenth Muse lately sprung up in America and, according to him "a right Du Bartas girl." But his unconscious exposition of the moral pathology of Puritanism is complete.

III

A light breaks suddenly in upon the Puritan darkness. A man of the same age and origin as the others proclaims and unforgettably establishes the faith which, despised and rejected from age to age, is the faith that alone justifies the American hope. The man is, of course, Roger Williams, the only Christian of his day in America. He was, as every schoolchild knows, driven into the wilderness by the tyrannical zealots of Massachusetts. What is not so generally known is that the fury of that old controversy lasted so

11

long that, a century after the death of Williams, the commonwealth he founded was still held by the conventional and orthodox to be a den of thieves and cut-throats. The character of that century of moral propaganda is preserved in the pages of "The Anarchiad."

> Hail! Realm of rogues, renown'd for fraud and guile,
> All hail! ye knaver'ries of yon little isle . . .
> The wiser race, the snares of law to shun,
> Like Lot from Sodom, from Rhode Island run.

Such is the common treatment and such the common slanders that followers of Jesus have always met with in Christian commonwealths. Of that small and illustrious company of libertarians and pacifists Williams was the first American member. He wrote to Endicott: " 'Tis impossible for any man or men to maintain their Christ by their sword." As early as 1644 he destroyed in a few final phrases the superstition of the authoritarian State: "The original and foundation of civil power lies in the people . . . A people may erect and establish what form of Government seems to them most meet for their civil condition. . . . Such governments have no more power nor for longer time . . . than the people shall betrust them with." I must add that Williams meant what he said, since in a later America these phrases have become a nerveless litany. From the bottom of his pure and troubled heart he "plead the cause of truth and innocence against the bloody doctrine of persecution for cause of conscience." He knew that "two mountains of crying guilt lie heavy upon the backs of all that name the name of Christ in the eyes of Jews, Turks and Pagans," namely, "idolatrous inventions" and "inhuman oppressions." His hope of melioration was small. "Yet"—his resonant and sweet and tragic cry comes as the most living voice of his time across the years—"yet *liberavi animam meam*, I have not hid within my breast my soul's belief." Williams was not a good writer, though what indeed constitutes a good writer is an ill-understood question that will be met with and discussed more than once in these pages hereafter. But there are moments in "The Bloudy Tenent of Persecution" when an impassioned experience creates its body of words: "Having bought truth dear, we must not sell it cheap, not the least grain of it for the whole world . . . for a little puff of credit and reputation from the changeable breath of uncertain sons of men; for the broken bag of riches on eagles' wings, for a dream of these—any or all of these— which on our deathbed vanish and leave tormenting stings behind them."

Williams being driven forth into the wilderness, the Puritan régime continued its accustomed course. Eliot, the apostle to the Indians, took every possible "occasion more fully to teach" the poor savages "original sin and the damned state of all men." He reports with satisfaction the remarks of the Indian Cutshamaquin, one of the few who accepted the white man's teaching: "Before I knew God I thought I was well, but since I have known God and sin, I find my heart full of sin, and more sinful than ever it was before, and this hath been a great trouble to me."

This trouble, this profound malady of the soul darkened more and more the lives and minds of the New Englanders, until in the second generation we find something akin to both individual and group madness. It is not wholly unjust that

13

the names of Increase and Cotton Mather are largely connected with the witch-trials in the last decade of the seventeenth century. Man and nature and human life had become utterly drained of God and good. An English traveler reports that in the day of the Mathers men were whipped "for kissing a woman in the street, though in the way of civil salute" and had their tongues bored with a hot iron for "cursing and swearing." These ferocities of punishment were, of course, in direct proportion to the smothered rebellion of the natural passions of humanity. Barring the universal crimes against life and property, a society will bear down most heavily upon those actions toward which its members are most vividly drawn, but which some ghostly superstition causes them to fear. This fierce ambivalence, this terrible alternation between attraction and repulsion, pollutes and sickens the soul from age to age. A way out is sought—a way out of this unbearable contradiction. An enemy is invented, an evil one, one upon whom both guilt and punishment can be rolled, who is both instigator and sacrifice, who both explains the moral torment in which men find themselves and expiates it for them. This method of finding for an irresolvable moral conflict an outer instigator and sacrifice is as old as the world. Under this pretext Jews have been burned and heretics massacred from age to age. But in wave after wave this sickness of the soul with all its violent consequences has rolled over Puritan America. Periodic outbursts of terror and hate have been directed in the course of our history against Mormons, Irishmen, the Latin immigrants, the free Negro, the German people, Catholics, foreigners once more, Communists, unbelievers. Political and, above all, economic causes have contributed their share. But always, from the witch-hunts in seventeenth-century Massachusetts to recent whippings and shootings of the Ku-Klux Klan, these outbursts have been characterized by a hectic torment, a sexual symbolism and ambivalence that stamp them with the unmistakable stamp of the Puritan conflict. The beginnings of this process are always the delusions of a plot whereby a strange sect, or the Pope or the Jews or a foreign power are about to overthrow the native civilization. Such a delusion had fastened itself upon the Mathers. "At prodigious witch-meetings," Cotton Mather writes, "the wretches have proceeded so far as to concert and consult the methods of rooting out the Christian religion from this country, and setting up instead of it, perhaps a more gross diabolism than ever the world saw before." It is, as recent investigators have suspected, not impossible that small and stealthy groups of men and women had determined to break through the taboos and, sunk in superstition themselves, naturally believed themselves dedicated to Satan. But facts had little to do with the convictions of Cotton Mather. He carried his devils in his heart. "Are we at our boards? There will be devils to tempt us unto sensuality. Are we in our beds? There will be devils to tempt us unto carnality. . . . I am verily persuaded that there are very few human affairs whereinto some devils are not insinuated." This is the uttermost depth of moral pathology. It is no wonder that, as the diarist Samuel Sewall informs us, during the witch-trials "Mr. Mather said they all died by a righteous sentence." The poor sick man had his dreadful compensations. One can imagine the estate of the unmarried mother in that place

15

and time. A tragic girl was to be executed for killing her child. Another had been appointed to preach the execution sermon and Cotton Mather wondered what would "become of his particular faith of her condition being so ordered in the providence of God that it should furnish me with a special opportunity to glorify him." The execution date was changed; Mather had his special opportunity. "For near two hours together," in the presence of that "miserable Malefactor" he was enabled to utter "the most awakening things." A disease of the moral nature, scarcely distinguishable from hard depravity, has not often in history assumed a more repulsive form.

We shall never know the story of that girl who went out after the sermon to die. But the humane Judge Sewall who even "essay'd to prevent Indians and Negroes being rated with horses and hogs," tells us, among many others, an illuminating anecdote concerning the special forms which life took in his day. A youth named Dwight swooned after prayer; he kicked; he sprawled; he seemed distracted by all the normal symptoms of religious mania. He was put to bed and plentifully prayed over and declared that he was the last of sinners and that "his day of grace was out." Gravely Sewall finishes the narration: "Notwithstanding all this semblance of compunction for sin 'tis to be feared that his trouble arose from a maid whom he passionately loved: for that when Mr. Dwight and his master had agreed to let him go to her, he eftsoons grew well."

How healing after that is the tone and substance of William Byrd of Virginia. Light and sanity break in and one gets a brilliant glimpse not only of the then Carolina frontier but of lives which, hard and superficial enough, were at least human. Byrd was invited by friends to stay at a handsome estate. He was taken through the grounds and "made to drink some very fine water that issued from a marble fountain, and ran incessantly. Just behind it was a covered bench where Miss Theky often sat and bewailed her virginity." After the "miserable malefactor" and young Dwight, how grateful one is for that vision of Miss Theky!

But there is scarcely enough of that note for contrast and relief. Doubtless as population increased and affairs expanded the Puritan control of human life lost something of its stifling ferocity and people not quite corrupted by it from within discreetly took such seemly liberties as they needed to exist. But the last and latest of the eminent Puritan divines, Jonathan Edwards, whose brief life falls wholly within the eighteenth century, reiterates with a superior power and eloquence all the old terrible doctrines which had now come to be an inexpugnable part of the American consciousness. It has recently become a fashion to speak of Edwards as a man of commanding intellect. He was not that. He was a baffled poet and stylist, baffled by the moral pathology of his kind. The logical web he wove in his treatise on the Freedom of the Will was tight and tense. But his absurd assumptions invalidate all of his logical processes. Great minds, Spinoza, Locke, Hume, begin by breaking with the vulgar errors and delusions of their time. The faint popular memory and tradition have done quite right in neglecting Edwards' logical prowess and recollecting the sermon called "Sinners in the Hands of an Angry God." There are early entries in his diary that have a mystical sweetness; there are others that

17

show a quite enlightened psychological curiosity; there is his lovely and touching, though quite morbid description of Sarah Pierrepont, his future wife. These things fade. He fought his parishioners, determined to prevent the reading of fiction; he fed his sick soul on the eerie and ghastly conversion of little, neurotic children; he became convinced that the hysteria of the "great awakening" was a sign that the world's conversion to Calvinism "may begin in America." The sadism of the earlier divines rises in him to a wild and poetic intensity: "The bow of God's wrath is bent and the arrow made ready on the string, and justice bends the arrow at your heart, and it is nothing but the mere pleasure of God . . . that keeps the arrow from being made drunk with your blood." One remembers Nathaniel Ward's "sword stark drunk with Irish blood." The image was a favorite one among the Puritans. Edwards marshalls the creation itself against the corruption of man. "The sun does not willingly shine upon you to give you light to serve sin and Satan; the world does not willingly yield her increase to satisfy your lusts." A baffled poet, a sick and corrupted soul. In the eleventh sermon comes the last touch of all: "The sight of hell torments will exalt the happiness of the saints forever."

In spite of the fact that Calvinism with its central tenet of the corruption of the natural is one of the most dangerous among the many superstitions of mankind, it must not be supposed that the New England Puritans were either worse or better than an hundred other earlier and later groups recorded by history. Nor shall I prove unmindful of the moral idealism of isolated groups of their descendants from Robert Gould Shaw to Roger Baldwin. Were it not for the

18

fact that they implanted the undying seed of their central doctrine into the very blood and consciousness of a great nation, one might well forget today all but their unfaltering heroism and blend that with their quaintness in ballad or in tale. It is because the fortunes of men and women in America today are still at the mercy of laws, customs and opinions that grew out of the Manicheism of the Puritans; it is because the youngest writers of the twentieth century are still, through infection or resistance, warped by its fears and hates, that this account of its expression became imperative.

IV

It is clear enough that imaginative literature had no place in the New England colonies. Not because the settlers lacked leisure. In proportion to population and cultural opportunities the amount of actual writing was large. But the sources of imaginative literature were sealed from the start. Human experience being wholly evil, its interpretation in verse or prose was held to be so no less. Elegies of clerics on clerics from Cotton's on Hooker to the younger Mather's laments over his colleagues constitute the bulk of formal early verse. This verse is cold and crabbed in the second-rate mid-seventeenth-century manner. Its substance is even feebler than its form. Academic critics have found a superiority in an elegy on the Reverend Thomas Shepard by President Urian Oakes of Harvard. I am unwilling to contend with them.

> A friend to truth, a constant foe to error,
> Powerful i' th' pulpit, and sweet in converse,

19

To weak ones gentle, to th' profane a terror—
Who can his virtues and good works rehearse?

The only lay poet was the once-renowned Mrs. Anne Bradstreet, who succeeded in combining with the mothering of eight children the composition of four hundred pages of verse. A human note flickers briefly in a set of verses written to her husband in absence. The rest is empty, artificial and turgid. It has the swelling quality of the Jacobeans without the inner lift:

O Time the fatal wrack of mortal things,
That draws oblivion's curtains over kings.

It is not necessary to waste words on "The Bay Psalm Book" nor on Michael Wigglesworth's "The Day of Doom" with its often quoted episode of the "reprobate infants." One comes with a sense not unlike relief upon the wooden doggerel of Peter Folger, the maternal grandfather of Benjamin Franklin. The early verse is nearly all doggerel; here there is at least a human hope:

I am for peace and not for war
And that's the reason why
I write more plain than some men do
That use to daub and lie.

But the verse of the New Englanders was not the only verse of Colonial America nor was Calvinism the only, though by far the most powerful metaphysic, that went toward shaping the character of the future nation. William Penn brought his colony of Quakers to the state that bears his name in 1682 and one year later Franz Daniel Pastorius and the German pietists founded Germantown. Penn wrote in a humane and Christian spirit to the Indians and paid them for their lands. Religious toleration was really practiced, though neither Jews nor Catholics were permitted to vote. The Quakers were not an articulate people. It was far otherwise with the Germans. Except Pastorius himself, they wrote no secular verse. But their mystical hymns which express in an hundred fashions the yearning of man for union with the divine, constitute a body of verse which, monotonous in substance, is of the gentlest Christian temper and of extraordinary smoothness, melodiousness and variety of execution. Pastorius himself was a scholar, a Christian, a good man and in his hushed and modest way a poet. He was a lover of gardens and of bees. In his garden he found the similitude of that peace which ought to obtain among God's creatures:

> Ich finde in der weiten Welt
> Nichts denn nur Aufruhr, Krieg und Streit,
> In meinem engen Gartenfeld
> Lieb, Friede, Ruh und Einigkeit.
> Mein Blümlein fechten nimmermehr,
> Was alles ihnen auch geschieht:
> Sie wissen nichts von Gegenwehr,
> Kein Waffen man da jemals sieht.
> Drumb acht ich ihr Gesellschaft hoch,
> Und bin bey ihnen gern allein,
> Gedenke offt, dass Christi Joch
> Will ohne Rach' getragen seyn.

These verses and many others equally agreeable, written by a man twelve years older than Cotton Mather, are evidently the expression of a civilized and not unmelodious soul. Johannes Kelpius, the hermit of Wissahickon, disciple of Boehme and mystic adventist, is not humanly as attractive

21

as Pastorius. But his correct alexandrines and elegant dactylic measures show a degree of literary taste and perception hitherto unknown in America.

In 1721 a company of Anabaptists, under the leadership of Johann Conrad Beissel, settled in Lancaster County and established the once famous Ephrata Community. The special tenets of these sectaries and their founding of a Protestant cloister are of little interest today. What is of first-rate interest is that not only the leader, but many of the brothers and sisters of the community were skillful versifiers and musicians. The three earliest hymnals of the community were printed by Franklin. The final and complete collection, the "Paradiesische Wunderspiel," was printed by the Ephrata people themselves. So great was the Christian humility of these men and women that all verses except Beissel's appear anonymously. There were then in the Pennsylvania forest a group of people, dedicated by their beliefs to peace and love and humility, who possessed a uniform degree of literary culture and skill. The more than half a thousand hymns use every known measure and stanzaic form with fluidity and ease, and rifle the world of man and nature for images wherewith to body forth a profoundly sincere conviction of the nothingness of the phenomenal world and the reality of the divine:

> Der tiefe Fried aus Gottes reinem Wesen
> Nimmt unser Hertz und gantze Sinnen ein—
> Und weil wir also sind in Gott genesen:
> So werden wir auch ewig bei ihm seyn.

It is needless to say that in this huge collection of sacred verse the names of hate or hell or vengeance or enmity are never named. The German settlers were Christians and had music in their souls. At Germantown in 1688 the first public protest against slavery was issued; all during the Colonial period men came on foot and in wagons over the rude roads to listen to the choral singing of the brothers and sisters of Ephrata. The Bach festivals at Bethlehem still bear witness to this beautiful tradition. Why has the tradition of the Germans and of the Quakers who, during the lifetime of Franklin, preferred to abstain from public office rather than be implicated with the countenancing of hate and war and violence—why has this noble twofold tradition of Pennsylvania had so little power upon the development of the nation? History stamps these *ex post facto* questions as futile. The tragic fact remains. But a younger America, seeking a usable tradition in its past, may yet turn its face from the Calvinist zealots of New England to the Germans and Quakers who make the early story of Pennsylvania a story of benevolence and peace.

V

It was a wise instinct, at all events, that guided the feet of the young Benjamin Franklin to Philadelphia. This little town was the only one in the America of its day for the expansion of a spirit at once enlightened and practical. And the son of the Boston soap-boiler was by every instinct and from the beginning a typical child of the eighteenth century: industrious apprentice, proud bourgeois, worldly philosopher. Fittingly then in Philadelphia there took place the first known and recorded instance of one of the essential legends of America, a legend told again and again in forms as varied

23

as the newsboys' stories of childhood and the novels of Theodore Dreiser: the legend of the poor boy who comes to the city and succeeds. Franklin walking along Market Street with his penny buns or, on a higher plane, Franklin sent for by the Governor of New York because a youth who possessed so many books must be a rare and admirable person; Franklin the once poor and unlettered lad, self-made, self-taught, literally standing before kings and later the first and most illustrious ambassador of his country in Europe—this man and his story have all the marks of that sober and prosaic romanticism, the romanticism of self-help and success that has become more and more the single ideal of millions of Americans. No "go-getter" of the contemporary business scene could fail to appreciate the story; no Y. M. C. A. secretary but could use it—with proper expurgations—to edify his audience of clerks aspiring to be merchant-princes, of telegraph-operators nursing a dream railroad kingship.

Luckily the expurgations would be necessary. Franklin was the typical American. That alone would give him the importance of a prophetic influence. But he was much more. He had a strong and acute instinct for literary form. The often-cited passage of the autobiography concerning the "Spectator" and the lonely, astute training in expression does not tell the whole story. Within the strict limits of the Enlightenment, pedestrian at its best, Franklin developed his prose with a dignified and affectionate care until, in certain letters of his extreme old age, he adds to sobriety and elegance and dignity an almost creative touch. That aspect of him transcends the legend. What also transcends the legend is the freedom of his mind. He had only in his adolescence to read Locke and Shaftesbury to leave permanently behind him the grosser delusions and superstitions of his time. Thus his youth escapes the legend by its intellectual flexibility; his extreme old age escapes it by the almost "prophetic strain" of the profound "Parable against persecution," the ultimate saying that "there is no good war and no bad peace" and by the mellow urbanity and grace of the letters to Mme. Brillon.

The many active middle years of his manhood, rich as they were in admirable practical results from the remarkable inventions to the founding of the University of Pennsylvania, are less amiable and more prophetic of the *moyen homme sensuel* of business of later and latest days. It was during this long period that Franklin developed his doctrine of physical and moral thrift. The first with its terrible sayings: God helps them that help themselves; keep thy shop and thy shop will keep thee; the sound of your hammer at five in the morning or nine at night heard by a creditor makes him easy six months longer—this first doctrine is creeping and corrupting enough. It becomes unbearable when transferred to higher and more vital spheres of action. The biographers and historians who have tried to hide or gloss over Franklin's so-called "sexual irregularities" see them from an even lower point of vision than he did himself. It is not the irregularities that matter. It is that they were never, from all the evidence of Franklin himself, impassioned or beautiful. Laxness is neither inner liberation nor active flexibility; it breaks no false principle and introduces no new note into the moral world. Laxness countenanced for practical purposes—Franklin's "venery for health" or his letter of advice on the choice of a mistress—secures more powerfully than ever adherence to evil and oppressive moral conventions by setting the example of their easy and successful breach. Laxness is thoroughly orthodox. And Franklin's advice against it, that it does not pay, is on precisely the same level as his practice. "Nothing is so likely to make a man's fortune as virtue." He never dreamed of questioning the values involved in these concepts of either virtue or fortune. There is no beauty in this virtue and no splendor in this fortune. It is the doctrine of success, of training for competition, of never inquiring after fundamental values but winning in the "game," which dominates contemporary meetings of business associations and vice crusaders. Franklin himself is, of course, a far less ignoble figure than his moral descendants. He was a child of his century, a contemporary of the poet who wrote:

> All vice is dull,
> A knave's a fool,
> And virtue is the child of sense.

What makes Franklin's eighteenth-century shop-keeping attitude toward the moral life significant is that that doctrine has survived in America and in America alone. The drop of poison in the cup of each newly elected member of the French Academy is that he may sometime be forced to make the traditional report on virtue. The poet Henri de Régnier, falling victim to this tradition, declared that he had tried to avoid the duty "by the feeling of a certain unworthiness and even incompetence"; he felt himself to be rather a "neutral" in regard to virtue which he had never looked at, so to speak,

26

"except through a keyhole." The clean, clear-cut American leader of men, college dean or business-convention orator, has no such difficulty. Virtue and wealth, in the precise sense of Franklin, are still prized in America. Abstention for material profit is still among our quainter mottoes.

On Franklin himself the last word cannot be negative. The autobiography is not only a piece of writing permanently valuable and agreeable because it communicates adequately and frankly genuine human experience. It remained for longer than is commonly remembered or remarked unique in its realism and honesty. The poets and romancers of the earlier republic did everything except grapple interpretatively with the realities of their mortal lot. Flight and evasion mark American literature for several generations after Franklin. The student of our letters looks back again and again with longing and admiration toward a personality and a book so frank and genuine and earth-rooted. Nor must it be forgotten that, from an American point of view, Franklin was a contemporary of Jonathan Edwards. He was thirty-five years old when Edwards delivered before a convinced and quaking congregation his sermon on "Sinners in the Hands of an Angry God." Thus it is clear that Franklin not only wrote the first American book which belongs permanently to literature but was beyond all question and all criticism, however just, what his most recent biographer has called him: the first civilized American.

VI

The Revolution left no creative record of itself. The generation that brought it forth was somewhat dry of heart and

27

far more conscious of the economic causes of the conflict than romanticizing historians have since assumed. It had, like Washington, strength without warmth and was spiritually parsimonious even in its excesses. These belated Colonials copied the style of Johnson, but could rise neither to his rich melancholy nor to his human sagacity. The eighteenth century at its most arid seemed to have stagnated in their hearts. The Federalists, representing the dourly conservative, violently anti-democratic propertied classes were servile copyists in prose and verse. A few foreign-born Whigs caught a faint flush of the great dawn in France.

"The Federalist," kept artificially alive by successive generations of the academic is, even as a treatise on the technique of government, of merely historical value. Alexander Hamilton and his associates were not only Calvinists, but aristocrats. They assumed not only the initial corruption of human nature, but were persuaded that this corruption was especially hopeless and unmitigated among the lower, by which they meant, the poorer classes. "The people!—the people is a great beast!" To this notorious saying of Hamilton's two others may be added: "That power which holds the purse-strings absolutely, must rule," and the chief magistracy "ought to be hereditary." Samuel Adams alone, of all the regnant gentry, was wholeheartedly on the side of popular rule. Hamilton and John Adams frankly dreamed of a capitalistic oligarchy as the inevitable aristocratic check upon popular institutions. In spite of the fact that their dream has come true, their political philosophy is wholly outmoded. The old struggle has changed its conditions and its terms; the industrial revolution has left not a shred of the moral,

28

the political or even the economic concepts of that day. As a piece of writing "The Federalist" is dignified and sound. But such a sentence as the following, written in 1787, adds nothing to the history of human experience and expression: "Law is defined to be a rule of action; but how can that be a rule which is little known and less fixed?"

I have been deliberately unchronological in order to exhibit the opinions and sentiments of the gentry who supported the revolutionary severance from England, but had no sympathy with the principles of revolution as such. It is no wonder that during the struggle itself they were active but silent. They objected to British taxes, but they objected to liberty at least as much. They and their class and clan pursued with unmeasured slander and contempt, with every mark of indecency and violence, the clearest and most resonant spirit of the American Revolution—"the filthy Tom Paine," of John Adams's well-known characterization.

Paine is still extraordinarily readable. There were that heat and urgency in his mind that belong in a greater or less degree to the minds of all the prophetic friends of mankind. They possess a passion which, by both its nature and its power, makes for that type of expression that is literature. Despite the obloquy from which Paine's reputation has suffered from all the vested interests and official orthodoxies, phrases of his survive—phrases that have both eloquence and glow and struck at the root of some dangerous and cherished fallacy. "A new method of thinking has arisen," he declared; by the use of this new method he stamped his personality upon truths of the last importance. Nor let it be supposed that these truths of the ragged philosopher have lost their

29

use. Lip-worship has been paid to them for a century and a
half; never were they less taken to heart than toward the
end of this period. It is most true that "government even in
its best state, is but a necessary evil," that its sole purpose
is to guard the "freedom and security" of the individual
citizen; it is not yet negligible to observe that "mankind
seems to have stood still at individual civilization, and to retain as nations all the original rudeness of nature," nor that
"he that would make his own liberty secure, must guard even
his enemy from oppression; for if he violates this duty, he
establishes a precedent that will reach to himself." Are not,
in fact, these last two observations the most profound and
prophetic made in the whole of revolutionary America?

Paine's doctrine of the natural rights of man and his
Deism were not of course his own. And eighteenth-century
Deism is in his case as in Franklin's an unlovely thing. To
the post-romantic mind it must always seem shallow and
hard. But this Deism, it should be remembered, was not held
in opposition to philosophers and saints, but was a reaction
against the type of dogma and religiosity which Matthew
Arnold was to call long afterwards the "lowest form of in-
telligential life" that one can conceive of man as leading.
In fundamentalist villages and towns, hag-ridden by hate,
hell-fire, intolerance and property-worship one can still see,
as I have seen, some untutored man of sense instructed, enlightened and civilized by reading "The Age of Reason."
As unlovely to the philosophic mind as Tom Paine in his
guise of a religious thinker are also his intellectual descendants from Robert Ingersoll to the members of "free-
thinkers'" and "Atheists' clubs." But they, like himself,

fought dark and cruel superstitions. It is not the least of Tom Paine's claim upon posterity that he fathered a crude but continuous protest in American life against the prevalent bibliolatry and kept alive, among common men, a sporadic passion for reason and for thought.

An evil sophistication seeks once more to tarnish that doctrine of the natural and inherent rights of man which Paine expressed more effectively than anyone else in America. But this doctrine that "every civil right" is but a natural right exchanged, and that all power exerted by man over man is but a delegated and revocable power, does not need the historical or sociological defense required by his Deism. In the defense of the basic liberties of mankind Paine's shrewdness, informed by a passion of the mind, lends him occasionally a deep and imaginative touch. "Those who lived a hundred or a thousand years ago, were then moderns, as we are now. They had *their* ancients, and those ancients had others, and we also shall be ancients in our turn." That is no shallow argument against the force of mere tradition and precedent. And it is far from the only instance of Paine's rising from the brisk effectiveness of the pamphleteer to something like an imaginative and philosophic vision of the truths and causes that were dear to him.

The few sentences I have quoted make it clear enough that Paine came nearer that transmutation of experience into expression than anyone else writing in America in his day, except Franklin. And he had a vividness and passion that Franklin lacked. It is scarcely necessary to recall the famous opening passage of "The Crisis": "These are the times that try men's souls." It will be useful to quote more

31

fully than is commonly done the really great phrases that describe the pass to which Burke's mind had been brought by either "the ingenuity of his hope or the malignancy of his despair." "He is not affected by the reality of distress touching his heart, but by the showy resemblance of it striking his imagination. He pities the plumage, but forgets the dying bird." Who did not think of that passage when rustling ladies in college towns wept over the sufficiently pitiful taking off of the family of the Czar? The adequate expression of a sincere passion of the mind or the heart has its continuing chance of coming home once more in unheard-of years to the business and the bosoms of men.

Thomas Jefferson, the other great liberal of the Revolution, had not Paine's gift of memorable speech. He was equally sincere, far more profoundly instructed and by virtue of his original social position and his participation in the affairs of the nation far better able to transcend mere revolutionary fervor and address himself to the great and hopeless task of preventing the Republic from becoming but another rigid state machine, primarily concerned with the preservation of property and based upon the old wicked opposition of masters and men. From the dry and strawy autobiographical fragment one gains little insight into Jefferson's force, the emotional force that must have been behind his steady and untiring devotion to the unpopular principles he had embraced. During the Revolution itself all classes assented to his formulation of these principles. So soon as the Republic was established the propertied and "aristocratical parties" sought to undo internally the work of the Revolution and Jefferson led the first of those movements which, at various times since and in forms ever cruder and less philosophical, have sought to assert the rights of the agrarian interests and of the common people against the hardening capitalistic oligarchy. It is but natural that we should owe the "Declaration of Independence," now discountenanced and, at times, forbidden to be read, to Jefferson; to his adoption of the principle of fundamental liberty proclaimed in France we owe the profoundly philosophical phrasing "life, liberty, and *the pursuit of happiness*." It is equally natural that Jefferson's colleagues struck out the word *inherent* in his first formulation, "inherent and inalienable rights," and that they suppressed two of his accusations against the British Government, one, that it was "obstructing the laws for the naturalization of foreigners," and two, that it seemed "determined to keep open a market where men should be bought and sold." Thus early Anglo-Saxon nativism was faintly conscious of itself, as it had already forced the definite declaration from Paine: "Not one-third of the inhabitants of Pennsylvania are of English descent. Wherefore I reprobate the phrase of Parent or Mother country applied to England only, as false, selfish, narrow and ungenerous." Thus also in the Declaration as later in the Constitution slavery was silently admitted as part of the American scheme.

The remarkable thing about Jefferson is that he had the power of thinking through to their ultimate conclusions the principles he had adopted. No statesman of Versailles had so clear an idea of what the "total extinction" of international morality really meant, an extinction which Jefferson exemplified by the conquests of Alexander, of the successors of Cæsar, and by the merely predatory politics of his own age: the partition of Poland, Britain burning the Danish fleet, Bonaparte partitioning the earth and the "blasphemous Holy Alliance" immediately doing the same thing. With equal clarity his mind drives through to ultimate issues in the Act for Establishing Religious Freedom which he drafted in 1785. He pled for no pale and kindly tolerance but announced: "God hath created the mind free. All attempts to influence it by temporal punishments or burdens, or by civil incapacitations, tend only to beget habits of hypocrisy and meanness." Some day the officials of the United States and its lawmakers and those that abet them may come once more to know as much as Jefferson knew.

This great philosophical libertarian was, in his private character, a cultivated country-gentleman of the eighteenth-century type. Delightful and amusing are his directions to his daughter Martha at boarding school. He tells her to mind her mistress for though her obedience and acquirements "cannot increase his love, they will prevent its diminution." He draws up a schedule for her which shows that the "elegant female" of the day was not supposed ever to sniff fresh air and was to indulge in no exercise except indoor dancing, and ends with the delightful admonition: "It produces great praise to a lady to spell well." He takes a loftier tone to his young nephew Peter Carr, draws up for him a magnificent course of classical reading, adds "Shakespeare, Ossian, Pope and Swift," indulges, as a matter of form, in certain moral maxims that he can hardly have taken seriously, but also illustrates in small things as in great his power of reaching the core of a subject: "Games played with a ball stamp no character on the mind."

Like Franklin he grows more attractive with the lengthening years. The sage of Monticello deserved that name. The letters of his old age are precise without coldness and betray to the very end the far-reachingness of his philosophical vision. The well-known character of Washington is too much of a set piece addressed to posterity. Far more profound and memorable is a passage of a letter written in 1813 to his old friend and political opponent, John Adams: "The *summum bonum* with me is now truly epicurean, ease of body and tranquillity of mind; and to these I wish to consign my remaining days. Men have differed in opinion, and been divided into parties by these opinions, from the first origin of societies, and in all governments where they have been permitted freely to think and to speak. The same political parties which now agitate the United States have existed through all time. Whether the power of the people or that of the αριστοι should prevail, were questions which kept the states of Greece and Rome in eternal convulsions, as they now schismatize every people whose minds and mouths are not shut up by the gag of a despot. And in fact the terms of whig and tory belong to natural as well as to civil history. They denote the temper and constitution of mind of different individuals." He was above all battles now and able to recognize the ultimate psychological source of political views. He was not on that account stagnant or false to his long convictions. As late as 1820 he wrote in a letter to William Short a passage which throws its light far into the past of American history and far into the future, and was, in its essential meaning, never more important than it is today: "The . . . clergy are loudest; the most intolerant of all sects, the most tyrannical and ambitious; ready at the word of the lawgiver, if such a word could now be obtained, to put the torch to the pile and to rekindle the flames in which Calvin consumed the poor Servetus because he could not find in his Euclid the proposition which has demonstrated that three are one and one is three, nor subscribe to that of Calvin, that magistrates have the right to exterminate all heretics to the Calvinistic creed. They pant to reëstablish by law that holy inquisition, which they can now only infuse into public opinion."

The last and in some respect not the least memorable writer of the revolutionary period who has a claim upon our memory is the Norman gentleman, Hector St. Jean de Crèvecœur, first of the many continentals to enrich American literature and, as befitted his origin, far more of an artist in letters than his American contemporaries. Not that the author of the "Letters from an American Farmer" was not politically and philosophically minded too. More than that: he was a close thinker on economic subjects and a practical agronomist in addition. He wrote his book, as most important books are written, with a purpose. But that purpose blended with a larger vision—the vision of the early French romantics of a world liberated, like Shelley's, from crippling and dusty institutions, simple and free in its development, unparalyzed by the dead hand of history and tradition. It was the world of that hope which Crèvecœur

36

sought and persuaded himself to have found in America. He rose to an even higher stage in his thinking. He was a pacifist and paid dear for his sentiments. But the mob-rule and the violence that blotted the Revolution, as they do every appeal to force, did not quench Crèvecœur's essential hope and vision. It is in the light of his anterior sentiments that the Letters must be viewed. They give, as Hazlitt said of them, "not only the objects but the feelings of a new country." These feelings, however, were largely subjective on Crèvecœur's part. Much of simplicity and hope there no doubt was in that early America. But the idylls of Crèvecœur owe at least as much to the idealizing imagination as they do to fact. Though fully conscious of the actual workaday America in which he lived, he was more profoundly moved by the belief that he had indeed found a country

> In happy climes the seat of innocence,
> Where nature guides and virtue rules,

and it is this country, half real, half ideal, which he set out to describe. He was, in brief, the first to give literary expression to that great hope of a new start for mankind which has again and again in the course of time fired the hearts of thousands of immigrants and which our generation has done its best forever to destroy. It was this hope that endeared America to the wisest and most generous minds of Europe; it was this hope that the aged Goethe too expressed in memorable gnomic verse:

> America, thy fate is kinder
> Than that of our old continent,
> No ruined keeps are thy reminder
> Of ages mis-spent.

37

Thy soul is not shaken
As thou buildest thy life
Because there awaken
Vain cries of old strife.

Use then thy fortunate present so
That when thy children come to write
A kind fate guide them to forego
The false romance of ghost and knight.

Though he did not learn English until he was sixteen, Crèvecœur became something of an artist in his adopted language. With a skill approaching subtlety he strikes and sustains the idyllic note in his early chapters, especially in those on Nantucket and Martha's Vineyard. In the chapter on Charleston and Negro slavery he succeeds in creating a hushed and sultry atmosphere, while the terrible description of the tortured Negro in the half-tropical forest and the exquisite and brilliant picture of the humming-bird are quite simply the most artistic bits of writing that had yet been done in the New World.

VII

In the popular songs and ballads of the revolution there is nothing of the generosity of sentiment or the rhythmic ardor that marked so many of the verses of the Civil War. The doggerel is dry, gritty, vulgar. The ballad of Nathan Hale is the single, faint exception. There is no note of the folk-song. It is all brash and ugly from the early defiance:

Proud George, you are engaged
All in a dirty cause,

through the conventional Liberty Song:

> Come join hand in hand, brave Americans all;

or it is foolishly artificial, like the Virginian tea verses:

> Begone, pernicious baneful tea,
> With all Pandora's ills possessed,

or the very rinsings of the old ballad manner:

> 'Twas on a pleasant mountain
> The Tory heathens lay,

or smug and shockingly vulgar, like the Thanksgiving hymn of 1783:

> Industry and frugality
> Will all our taxes pay;
> In virtuous ways we'll spend our days
> And for our rulers pray.

Little can be said for the formal verse of the revolutionary period. Were I to adhere strictly to my principle of omitting the mere document and speaking only of what is still alive, this entire section would have been suppressed. It is a concession to the public appetite for useless information. Even so a few words will suffice for the verse of the declining eighteenth century in America. Quarles and Du Bartas had at last given way to Waller, Dryden and Pope. The smooth and mechanical couplet was written. The long didactic and descriptive poem had come into fashion in England and was dutifully copied here. Timothy Dwight, Federalist and Calvinist, an early example of college presidential mentality, damned all who differed from him in "The Triumph of Infidelity," gave sound practical advice as well as a few

39

mildly pleasing descriptions of nature in Greenfield Hill, aimed at grandeur and achieved empty pompousness in "The Conquest of Canaan." Joel Barlow, a mild, well-meaning liberal, is still faintly remembered for his once amusing "Hasty Pudding" and his dull and formidable "The Columbiad," as is John Trumbull for his "Hudibras"-like "M'Fingal," a pre-Whig satire, not wholly without neatness or the salt of wit. None of these versifiasters had, of course, the slightest notion of the character of the creative process but wrote verse as a by-product of their more serious occupations of theology, law or diplomacy. This applies equally to Lemuel Hopkins and David Humphreys who, once known with Trumbull and Barlow as the Hartford Wits, produced from their circle "The Anarchiad," the typical manifesto of the capitalistic Federalists scared out of their wits lest the new Republic fail to belong entirely to their class and raising, in familiar fashion, the cry of anarchy and even, curiously enough, of the ruin of the Western World:

> See, from the shades, on tiny pinions swell
> And rise, the young DEMOCRACY of *hell*;
> The forms of government in ruin hurl'd,
> Reluctant empire quits the western world.

Historians of the period have recently made a considerable literary figure of Philip Freneau. He is excellent, alas, only in comparison with his dreadful contemporaries. And in literature the historical estimate is an academic delusion. Mankind cannot be expected to drag on through the ages an ever-mounting ballast of mediocre books on the amusing principle that the contemporaries of their authors wrote

40

books that were even worse. I have every desire to be generous to Freneau, for his character was most amiable. He shared the more liberal vision of America with Paine and Crèvecœur and was an impassioned friend of the humble and the oppressed. In satires and lampoons he belabored the Federalists and took the part of the people. But these verses are without true life today. It is also possible that in a less turbulent age and in a more cultivated society he might, as he himself rather touchingly pleaded, have been a poet. That, too, is a futile reflection. He is, as things stand, a very minor eighteenth-century writer, more agreeable than his contemporaries because mildly but genuinely touched by the early and restrained romanticism of, let us say, Akenside. He did at least see somewhat poetically the wild honeysuckle and hear the honeybee and the katydid and in "The House of Night" feel for himself the gloom of the Graveyard school of poets. He also wrote blank verse which, fed by the same influences, is not unprophetic of Bryant:

> The Ohio then shall glide by many a town
> Of note: and where the Mississippi stream
> By forests shaded now runs weeping on,
> Nations shall grow and states not less in fame
> Than Greece and Rome of old.

He wrote, finally, the not unimaginative "Indian Burial Ground" and I can do no better for him than to quote the agreeable and obligatory stanza:

> By midnight moons o'er moistening dews,
> In habit for the chase arrayed,
> The hunter still the deer pursues,
> The hunter and the deer—a shade!

It was from the urban and urbane tradition of "The Spectator" and "The Rambler," the familiar essay merging gradually into the sketch and the story, that the first considerable American man of letters arose. Imitations of the British periodical essayists had naturally been attempted again and again in the various centers of American culture: in Boston, Philadelphia, and Charleston. None was comparable to its original in grace of manner or interest of substance until James K. Paulding and Washington Irving published in New York from 1807 to 1808 the twenty numbers of their "Salmagundi"; or, "The Whim-Whams or Opinions of Launcelot Langstaff, Esq., and Others." The place and the time and the talent at last coincided. "When 'Salmagundi' appeared," Bryant said in his memorial discourse on Irving, "the quaint old Dutch town in which he was born had become transformed to a comparatively gay metropolis. Its population of 20,000 souls had enlarged to more than 80,000, although its aristocratic class had yet their residences between the Battery and Wall Street. The modes and fashions of Europe were imported fresh and fresh. Gay equipages dashed through the streets. A new theater had risen in Park Row. The churches had multiplied faster than the places of amusement. Our present City Hall had been erected. Tammany Hall, fresh from the hands of the builder, overlooked the Park. The rooms of Michael Paff, the famous German picture dealer in Broadway, were a favorite lounge for such connoisseurs as we then had." Here was a self-conscious and lively community that evidently welcomed satire not too sharp and relished the humorous characterization of recognizable types. Paulding and Irving were applauded as are the "columnists" of a later day and Bryant was quite right in doubting certainly whether Paulding, possibly whether Irving, ever wrote thereafter with more freshness or verve. For, in addition, the *genre* suited Irving perfectly. A gentleman in easy circumstances, he sedulously avoided all his years any thinking on fundamental subjects; a man either timid or cool, he let all the major experiences of life escape him. He studied, traveled and observed. This elegant writer was a strange enough product for a country and a polity supposedly new. But the Federalist gentry, no more than their present descendants, shared that vision of a renewal of life in a New World which, then as now, dwelt forlornly enough in some immigrant breast. It was always libertarian poets and philosophers in Europe or else immigrants who were astonished at the tepidness and derivativeness that, with definite exceptions, marked American literature until what is almost the other day. These dreamers and thinkers were deceived by the romance of discovery and the physical vastness and grandeur of the new continent. With this romance and this grandeur the descendants of the Puritans who alone or almost alone possessed the means and leisure for the cultivation of the mind, toyed idly. Important to them, as to their kind everywhere, were property, respectability, the education by which the gentleman withdraws himself from the mob. Deprived of class distinctions by the revolution, they invented new ones based upon a brief priority of settlement or some alliance, by culture, taste or blood, with Britain. The idea of America as a new and better and freer place and way

43

of human life touched them lightly and only in the narrower sphere of politics. The idea glowed in the hearts of common men. But the multitude was inarticulate and rude. The gentry, and all American writers before Whitman either belonged to that class by birth or sought, like Poe and Simms and Timrod, to identify themselves with it—the gentry drew more closely than elsewhere about itself the garments of a starched respectability and discretion for fear of being identified with the vulgar, surging, raw-tongued masses of wild villages and frontier settlements. The cultivated American became the most proper of men and, from Washington Irving to Brander Matthews, feared nothing so much as any idea, gesture, sentiment or mannerism that might fundamentally differentiate him from the upper middle class of England. He preferred in the course of time to present an analogy to that class rather than to be identified with it. At best he rarely lost an uneasy inner monition of the insecurity of his social and cultural position. This insecurity accounts both for his passionate snobbishness and for his occasional passionate but never fundamental Americanism. His spiritual civilization, which should be like a man's skin, had become to him like a garment. He worried about its fit and style. How could such a being produce or bear the ardor of the creative vision? No genius towering enough to transcend these conditions and this fate was born. Hence literature was graceful, imitative, superficial and sought not life and reality, but an escape from these. To the Puritan distinction between the realm of grace and the realm of sin was added, to be at times identified therewith, the distinction between what was refined and what was vulgar. In view of these combined forces of Puritan morals, snobbishness and refinement, the wonder is not that so much of American literature has lacked vigor and originality, but that there was any at all. For creative experience must precede creative speech, and such experience was precisely what the American gentry could not afford.

It is no wonder then that the first important American man of letters was a writer of elegant conventional prose, who never departed in thought or form from patterns that were approved and recognized by the best people. Significant for himself and his artistic posterity is his treatment of the Dutch settlers and their history in his native state and section. In the discourse from which I have already quoted Bryant tells how Irving in his youth wandered about the beautiful shores of the Hudson. "He made acquaintance with the Dutch neighborhoods of Nyack, Haverstraw, Sing Sing and Sleepy Hollow. . . . A ferry-boat took him to Brooklyn, then a cluster of Dutch farms." In this Dutch life Irving had an entirely fresh subject for English writing. He used it, because it dwelt with him and haunted him, but his use of it was always humorous and satiric or fantastic. "I remember," says Bryant, speaking in 1860, "that twenty years since, the market people of Bergen chattered Dutch in the steamers which brought them in the early morning to New York." Bryant was a dignified and humane man, a man of greater liberality of thought than Irving. His easy and instinctive use of the word "chattered" is enormously significant. To the Yankee gentry Dutch was a language that was "chattered;" the Dutch could at most be funny or amusingly quaint. It is not now remembered that the "Knickerbocker History of New

45

York" gave offense to people of Dutch extraction on its publication in 1809. That attitude, taken by a group which was trying to establish a special little aristocracy of its own, and in fact succeeded, was trivial and foolish too. It remains true that all of Irving's literary dealings which the life and history of the Dutch settlers were characterized by kindly condescension. No English peasants "chattered" to his ear.

These observations are psychologically important and interesting for the light they throw upon other years and other things. Within the limitations of mind and temper and outlook as defined, Irving's talent was far from negligible. He begins in "Salmagundi" those character sketches that are both sharp and clear and humorous. He is a confirmed aristocrat, of course. "To rise in this country a man must first descend"; he must plunge "into that mass of obscenity, the mob." Then follows the sketch of Timothy Dabble, the low politician. Happier and kindlier is the character of Aunt Charity, and there are others not below these. In "The Sketchbook" character and landscape are permitted to build legend; the prose is mellower; the two subdued but still unfaded little masterpieces "Rip Van Winkle" and "The Legend of Sleepy Hollow" come to enrich, in their minute degree, the imagination of the world. With them, whether he knew it or not, Irving had hit not only upon the happiest vein of his own talent but upon a *genre*, the fantastic, legendary tale, which was to employ nearly all the strongest American talents for many years to come. The romantic tale with its flight from present reality suited the temper of the American gentry. How ably Irving could deal with a scene of the actual and the present is illustrated by the excellent sketch, "The Stout

Gentleman," in "Bracebridge Hall." But he chose to do so rarely. His other successes: "The Bold Dragoon" in "Tales of a Traveller," "The Devil and Tom Walker" in the same collection, the rather charming tale of Peregil, the water-carrier, from "The Alhambra" are all in that manner and spirit of German romance as practiced by Fouqué and Hauff, against which Goethe warned America in the verses I have quoted. What has not been sufficiently noted is Irving's more than ordinary ability in the delineation of actual scenes. The inn, the parlor and the inn yard in the rain in "The Stout Gentleman" and the interior of the Flemish inn at Bruges in "The Bold Dragoon" are concrete, colorful and rich. But the romantic flight from reality intensified in his later years. He plunged into romantic history and Spanish romance, wrote his elegant, dreamy, languid books on Columbus and the Alhambra—"an elegant memento of a brave, intelligent and graceful people, who conquered, ruled, flourished and passed away"—and lived long enough to protest from the depth of his genteel, romantic absorption and enchantment against the mild realistic trend of the mid-century. In Spanish romance, he wrote in 1855, "the chivalric virtues were refined upon to a degree sometimes fastidious and constrained; but at other times inexpressibly noble and affecting. . . . In the present day, when popular literature is running into the low levels of life and luxuriating on the vices and follies of mankind, and when the universal pursuit of gain is trampling down the early growth of poetic feeling and wearing out the verdure of the soul, I question whether it would not be of service to the reader occasionally to turn to these records of prouder times and loftier modes of thinking, and to steep himself to the very lips in old Spanish romance." Have we not here the significant temper and program of American romanticism which always turned backward with Scott, never toward the future with Shelley, and which later skipped immediately from Scott to Tennyson? And have we not here also the root and core of what has happily been called the genteel tradition in American literature—the tradition, namely, of the Puritan gentry who excepted themselves, tacitly and unconsciously to be sure, from the corruption of human nature and concentrated that corruption in the lower classes and in the present? Irving wants no delineation of low life; the vices and follies of mankind are absolute and hopeless. Then why contaminate the mind with them? He and his class were materially at ease. The pursuit of gain on the part of others offended him. I am aware of the fact that the passage on Spanish romance represents the sentiment of a testy old gentleman. It happens also to represent nearly the whole of American romanticism which lingered almost to the world war, which lingers still here and there among "refined" people in Southern cities and academic communities.

IX

It is easy to smile at the folk-poems that arose in the early years of the Republic. They persist. They still express the sentiments of millions. There is nothing in them of yearning or passion, nothing of parting; there is no tragic note. They are domestic and religious; the common people were unromantically sentimental. The patriotic songs are in a class apart. Far more significant is the rise and persistence of Samuel Woodworth's "The Old Oaken Bucket," of John

Howard Payne's "Home, Sweet Home," of George P. Morris' "Woodman, Spare that Tree," of Emma Hart Willard's "Rocked in the Cradle of the Deep." The pioneer was happy to have settled, to have a home, to be at home. He did not, like the peasant's son in the old world, yearn to wander to other lands from the patch of earth that his people had tilled for generations. The American clung to the ground and hearth he may have gained and to the sentiments that gathered about it. He had fewer material traditions against which to revolt and became passionately domestic. A new conservatism of folkways and sentiments developed, which is still expressed by these old American songs. It must not be forgotten in any account of the nation's civilization or its literature.

The formal poetry of the period may, save that of Bryant, be treated briefly. Most of it is never read and does not deserve to be. Fitz-Greene Halleck's four pathetic lines in memory of Joseph Rodman Drake are worth all of his Byronizing; Drake's "Culprit Fay" is feebly fanciful. Slightly younger was the other New Yorker, Nathaniel Parker Willis, who cut a great figure in his day as journalist, poet and man about town. His fundamentally insincere "The Death of Absalom" lingered in school readers till the other day. His "Unseen Shadows," quoted by Poe in one of Poe's many accesses of Southern romantic and chivalric sentimentalism is the conventional gloating of the "pure" over the "impure" which is half envy and half cruelty. Charles Fenno Hoffman's "Monterey" has a rhythmic compactness that is grateful amid so much nerveless writing and Daniel Webster in

49

the lines to his dead son touched for one moment that grandeur which he strove for in his endless rhetoric in vain:

> Thou art my ancestor, my son,
> And standst in Heaven's account the oldest.

The Southerners had more of an inkling of what poetry is like when it exists. Richard Henry Wilde had a shadow of this insight; the young Edward Coate Pinkney more than a shadow. His is the earliest lyric voice in America. He wrote what he felt, not what a respectable gentleman was expected to feel. His few frail songs do faintly record a genuine emotion of that kind which experience has shown to be central to literature and life. Such a stanza as this, by no means soaring in itself, was in its acceptance of the tragic beauty of life a thing new and unheard of and, of course, unregarded in American letters:

> And still the old impassioned ways
> And habits of my mind remain,
> And still unhappy light displays
> Thine image mirrored in my brain.

A great contemporary has half-humorously applied to personality the term "format." What, in this precise sense, distinguishes William Cullen Bryant from his contemporaries was not so much fineness of quality as the far greater "format" of his personality both as a writer and as a man. He had the good fortune too to live to a very great age and the merit of measurably supporting during his long editorship of the "New York Evening Post" all good and among them not a few liberal causes. His poetry is limited in flexibility and glow by his own excessive temperateness of nature; it is limited in subject-matter and crippled in method by the conventions of his class and kind. He seeks the forest because he will find nothing there of what "pained him in the haunts of men," namely "guilt and misery," or, in other words, these great and haunting varieties of human experience which literature exists to express. But these belong to the realm of sin, rigidly and Puritanically conceived, and genteel literature must limit itself to the expression of what falls within the realm of grace, of what is "sinless," like the entirely abstract and non-existing rural maid:

> The forest depths by foot unpressed
> Are not more sinless than thy breast.

This attitude sincerely and instinctively embraced would have reduced to modest achievement a far more powerful poetical temperament than Bryant's since it prevents the channeling into poetry of all that is most poetical. What is left is mild reflectiveness and mild moralizing, those moralistic tags at the end of poems which, in their peculiar American unashamedness, Bryant seems to have invented and passed on to Longfellow and many others. Thus he starts out with "The Yellow Violet" and ends with the remark that they

> who climb to wealth forget
> The friends in darker fortunes tried;

he starts out with "The Fringed Gentian" and ends with

> Hope blossoming within my heart,
> May look at heaven as I depart.

Now philosophical reflection deeply rooted in the clarification of mortal passion and dismay and aspiration is, of course, an organic part of poetical expression. But from such reflection, too, Bryant is cut off by his initial Puritanical exclusions. All he can offer is a shallow and shabby moral tag. Once or twice he strikes a more personal and therefore a deeper and sincerer note in the lyrical pieces, but only once or twice. There is a wistfulness in the final stanza of "The Waterfowl" which for a moment redeems the bad method; there is genuine elevation in a few lines of "The Past":

> Thou hast my better years;
> Thou hast my earlier friends, the good, the kind,
> Yielded to thee with tears—
> The venerable form, the exalted mind.

The famous or once famous blank-verse pieces, beginning with "Thanatopsis," are solemn rather than elevated, for while the mood is high, the thought is feeble and the emotion cool. In "Thanatopsis" there are moments of strong visual imaginativeness:

> Pierce the Barkan wilderness
> Or loose thyself in the continuous woods
> Where rolls the Oregon and hears no sound
> Save its own dashings.

But the conclusion, "yet the dead are there," is lame. The famous final verse-paragraph, "So live that when thy summons," has dignity without persuasiveness; it soothes the ear; it does not reach the heart. The admiration with which the poem was greeted in its day is thoroughly comprehensible. It was again that question of "format." No blank verse as accomplished had yet been heard on this side of the Atlantic; no American poem had yet so convincingly gone through the gestures of nobility. In "Thanatopsis," too, Bryant achieves a genuine sobriety of diction. The later blank-verse pieces are full of the withered *clichés* of Young and Blair. *Clichés* of words, distressing *clichés* of imagery:

> This mighty oak
> By whose immovable stem I stand and seem
> Almost annihilated—not a prince
> In all that proud old world beyond the deep
> E'er wore his crown as loftily as he
> Wears his green coronal of leaves.

No comparison could be less just or less happy, more tawdry or incongruous. To write thus is to have given up all attempt at first-hand feeling and visualization and to be carried on by a mere hypnosis of sonorous verbiage. It is useless to multiply instances. No wonder that Bryant, like all artificers, naïvely and sincerely in his youth "worshipped the visions of verse and of fame." Poetry is suffering and servitude; the god has a lash. Fame is a mortal accident.

I am aware of the slight revulsion which many thoughtful and cultivated Americans will feel at this analysis of Bryant. I am aware of it and understand it. The standard American poets are interwoven with my memories of childhood and boyhood too. At thirteen, having few books, I pored over the quotations in Lockwood's school rhetoric and, from constant re-reading, memorized hundreds of lines of Bryant and Longfellow, which I find it hard to disassociate from a period of life so instinct with poetry and poetical feeling that it can make the woodenest verses seem refulgent with creative glow. But it is precisely this act of disassociation which must be accomplished. If this record of creative expression in America is to contribute to the clarification of our past and the enrichment of our cultural atmosphere, it must keep itself clear of all those considerations of either sentiment or decorum that vitiate the conventional histories of literature.

x

Our fiction began well with Hugh Henry Brackenridge's picaresque and satiric "Modern Chivalry," on many pages a sharp, realistic record of the rude, turbulent life of the early Republic. It dropped again almost at once with Mrs. Rowson's "Charlotte Temple," the first of that host of maidens whose seduction has, from that time almost to this, produced oceans of easy tears. But the romantic movement was too imminent for either the picaresque or the eighteenth-century sentimental to prevail. Godwin and Scott were the rising masters. Our first truly equipped and professional novelists were romanticists of horror or of adventure and history: Brown, Cooper, Simms.

It has often been remarked that Charles Brockden Brown borrowed the central device of his few best books from Godwin's "Caleb Williams." Brown added here and there the horrors of "Gothic" romance, but preferred pseudo-scientific to supernatural explanations to undo the intricate knots which he had tied. At his best, as in "Wieland," he has a pedestrian but somber energy of manner. In "Ormond" and more especially in "Arthur Mervyn" he produced an account of the yellow-fever epidemics which, for terrible detail and cumulative physical and moral terror, rivals Defoe on the plague in London and Heine on the cholera in Paris. But both Brown's aims and methods belong hopelessly to tastes and

54

preoccupations that have long and permanently faded from civilized consciousness.

The next quarter of a century, if not this day and this year, will pass a similar judgment upon the romances of James Fenimore Cooper and William Gilmore Simms. Let it be remembered that for many years past physical suspense, pursuit and capture, sheer combat and the savage prejudices of warfare have faded from serious literature and been confined to periodicals of the "Argosy" type and to the raw melodrama. But even these types of popular entertainment are yielding to others: to the "confession" magazines, to slightly salacious plays which, vulgar as they are, represent a higher or, at least an other kind of human interest. Now the mind will always delight in combat, suspense and physical heroism as these are delineated in saga, ballad or primitive epic. For in these records and expressions of barbarous but not ignoble ages theme and spirit have a profound harmony and the hearts of heroes obey an *ethos* that justifies their deeds. Cooper and Simms are so alien to us precisely because they are too near. They are hopelessly prosaic and civilized. Hence they are never strong but only violent and even intelligent and well-bred children of today find their stories inconceivably tedious. The suspense of pursuit no longer delights; it only teases, because we have lost all interest in the event. Thus things invented always fade, for the preoccupations that are eternal and that are expressed in all permanent literature exist from the beginning and cannot be invented, only creatively illustrated. But invention in regard to pursuit and capture and physical combat are all that Cooper has to offer. His books are redeemed by no beauty of style, no

55

depth of characterization, no sense of his standing above the silly illusions which he chronicles. He has vast, undisciplined energy; he has a deep feeling for the majesty of the forest and of the sea. That is all and it is not enough. It has long been conceded that his civilized characters are wooden and insipid. Critics have taken up the last line of Cooper's defense at the side of Natty Bumpo. But a careful rereading of the Leatherstocking series will but too clearly reveal the fact which Cooper himself rather proudly admitted, that Natty Bumpo was neither observed nor remembered but invented. He is well and vigorously and feelingly invented. But the bundle of congruous qualities never, at any moment, fuses into a human soul. Nor will any but the most primitive-minded be able to avoid the conclusion that Bumpo's long career of murder is based upon prejudices as vulgar and cruel as those of his foes, and will take no more pleasure in a Mohican scalping a Huron than in a Huron scalping a Mohican. Harvey Birch in "The Spy" is both more sympathetic and more human. But the method of the revolutionary stories and the namby-pamby unreality of speech and characterization are the same as in those of the frontier and the sea. It is of the last significance that neither Cooper nor Simms had an ear for human speech, which is almost the unerring test of the novelist whose work is likely to have a permanent appeal to mankind. No, Cooper can help us no more. Neither his early popularity nor the fact that in editions abbreviated for children the Leatherstocking tales still have a considerable sale in Europe need alter our attitude. That attitude is, indeed, fixed. Intelligent people find they can no longer read Cooper. The trouble is that even enlightened historians of literature have lashed themselves into an historically minded enthusiasm and so have given the timid pause. What those historians say concerning Cooper's energy, inventiveness, knowledge, priority in the treatment of the sea and other subjects is admirably true. Only these things do not make for permanent appeal which, luckily, is the reward of profound and rich humanity, creative vision and moral insight alone. The schoolboy who loathes having to read "The Last of the Mohicans" shows his civilized instinct and his good sense; the pedagogue who insists on that reading, only his timidity and his conventional-mindedness.

The case of Simms is practically identical with that of Cooper. Though he was an even ruder and more careless improviser than the former, he too delighted his generation. His facts and interests were its own; he had no ability of raising these facts or interests into the permanently valid sphere of the human spirit. Yet he was a far more impassioned lover of letters than Cooper. He edited many periodicals, wrote many volumes of verse and was the center and informing spirit of the Charlestonian group of writers. One or two of his poems exhibit a delicacy of feeling and of vision which was beyond Cooper's reach or perception. Yet this did not avail him. Nothing avails except stringent veracity or the sovereign creative imagination. And for these America had yet long to wait.

BOOK TWO

The Polite Writers

I

In this book I purpose to examine that entire group of writers, from Longfellow to Brander Matthews, which created what has come to be known as the genteel tradition in American letters. This somewhat unchronological procedure is justified by the remarkable homogeneity of the group. Men born into it by their antecedents or by the natural climate of their minds resisted and still resist all disturbing influences. The latest members of the group are at one with the earliest. Neither talent nor reading nor travel nor even experience of great affairs can change the polite mind. Its mark is that two-compartmental arrangement of the psyche which keeps the major and intenser experiences of life from spilling over into that compartment whence the substance of the genteel writer's product is dipped. Polite criticism is, of course, rationalization after the fact. The genteel mind is, however wanly in later and latest days, a Puritan mind, that is to say, a mind whose picture of the universe reserves the old division into a narrow sphere of grace and an almost boundless sphere of sin. To save sin from its sinfulness, to humanize and mold into harmony the whole of experience—this is a concept of which it is not capable. It is not so much concerned with conduct, as all literature must be, as with one specific and unhealthy kind of conduct. It has neither the vigor nor the convincedness of its ancestors; it substitutes decency and refinement for righteousness; it finally takes a half-shamed refuge in the merely technical; it is a mind often nimble but always afraid and ashamed. The world is too rough for it, thought too athletic, man too human. It had its one great moment during the anti-slavery struggle when a high and arduous and impassioned idea happened by good fortune to arise within the narrow circle of its approbation. With the emancipation of the slaves its degeneration promptly set in. There was, from the point of view of the polite mind, nothing that mattered left to write about. The World War found it totally emasculated: even its anglophilism was largely money interest or sentimental snobbishness. It rose to a last apotheosis and suffered a final eclipse in the character of Woodrow Wilson, who mouthed all the idealisms of his tradition and, lacking all contact with reality, all power of coordinating the ideal with experience, feebly consented to a world of chaos and distraction.

The day has happily passed when history or criticism need take an acrid or a controversial tone in regard to the writers of the genteel school. What is needed is definition and description. For the issues that are concerned have been badly confused, first by the polite critics, secondly by echoes that are still with us of that earlier opposition which talked about art for art's sake in one decade and about pure art in another. The trouble with the polite writers was not that they were moral; they were not moral enough. The substance of art is life; life means human experience and human conduct; to write at all without introducing explicit or implicit judgments of value in respect of conduct is wholly and forever impossible. But the range of experience to which the polite writers applied their judgments of value was so narrow, and the judgments themselves were so feeble, so parochial, so unintegrated with the central tendencies of human civilization, that it is no paradox to declare them to have been, first of all, lacking in moral vitality. Nor is this all. After the Civil War the sap slowly oozed out of the stock. Even the values they upheld were no longer part of a deep inner monition. Feeble flight from reality and elderly querulousness alone were left. It is easy to forgive the aging Lowell for his refusal to entertain new ideas; within his tradition he had had his high and intrepid period between the Mexican and Civil Wars. Degeneracy was complete and hopeless when, in 1902, Mr. Bliss Perry declared that "although American fiction may not be national and may not be great, it will have at least the negative virtue of being clean." For by "clean" Mr. Perry and his contemporaries did not mean either an achieved asceticism, the asceticism of the saint or the scholar, which is a comprehensible ideal, nor did they mean an orientalizing transcendence of the world of matter including the body. No, they consented unctuously to the gross and roaring materialism of an industrial and commercial civilization of unexampled power and pride; they consented practically to that older, ruder, perhaps in a subtle sense more joyous and decent America which is clear in the memory of all but the youngest: the America of four bar-rooms at every intersection of streets, of raucous evangelists and flaring prostitution, of Peruna in every cupboard and the old "Police Gazette" in every barber-shop, of the "Fireside Companion" in the home, dancing girls at city-fairs, show-boats on the great rivers and old Dr. Grindles peddling their wares in the daily press. And to the terrible but magnificent aliveness of their world the genteel writers offered as an ideal the parlor-stuffiness of "clean," of not mentioning things that were not nice nor decorous. And in this category of the indecorous they included not only the life of their age and country but, like their ancestors, the life of nature as well. Things amusing, saddening, next door to unbelievable issued from this complete repudiation of experience and the consequent divorce between experience and expression, things that are still with us in the shape of censorships, certain types of commercialized fiction, correspondence courses to produce makers of imaginative narrative, dramaturgic workshops to supply our stage with dramas, distinguished classical scholars who, recording themselves as of the Presbyterian faith, are capable of declaring: "Civilized man is the only creature whose necessary state is war upon himself." With this sentence by Mr. Grant Showerman written and printed in 1922 we have come full circle and integrated the work of the polite writers of America with the Puritan doctrine of the corruption of the natural.

The necessary interdependence of the various literary phenomena to be recorded in this book may require a further word of elucidation: If the major part of human nature and experience is repudiated *ab integro* as ungovernably sinful and unworthy of expression in art, it follows that literature, thus impoverished in its sources, thus limited in its aims, will degenerate into a game and a trade. Experience being so largely excluded, invention will take its place: for passion and wisdom we shall be given ingenuity and adroitness, for the spiritual triumph of form, the nimble manipulation of forms, and the art of letters will become more and more a base or shallow mechanic exercise. The reign of the artificer will be complete; the poet will be held to be a gross and immoral fellow; Mr. Walter Pitkin will teach the confection of stories, Mr. G. P. Baker that of plays, Mr. Brander Matthews that of *vers de société* and the roaring presses of the cheap magazines will be glutted with an article as standardized and as unrelated to creative expression as Boston garters and Community silver. Of this development the earlier and finer spirits of the genteel school, men like Longfellow or like Aldrich could not possibly be aware. But in a great industrial civilization in which all men can read the practice and the theory of polite Puritanism in letters could lead to no other end. Neither Hawthorne nor Thoreau nor Whitman nor Mark Twain could influence or retard the inevitable degeneration of literary practice and literary theory; Howells took refuge in a troubled and broken conformity; Henry James, man of genius that he was, carried with him through all the pageantries of European life the burden of his inhibited and genteel soul. Nor has the great modern revolt in American life and letters done much more than sear the edges of that neo-Puritan reduction of literature to a pleasing artifice, of that doctrine of the necessity and decency of the divorce between experience and expression which, still promulgated in a thousand schools and colleges, newspapers and periodicals, determines the character of the more visible cultural landscape of America to this day.

II

Far in an unimaginable future lay this world of the "Saturday Evening Post" and the "Pictorial Review," of the dramatic theories of Brander Matthews and their practice by David Belasco, of the correspondence course and the kisses cut out of the moving-picture film, in those idyllic and aspiring days when the young Henry Wadsworth Longfellow went to Europe to fetch home learning and romance for his future students at his college in the forests of Maine. But the seeds of that future were definitely present in the young man of good Federalist antecedents who was to become the most popular of American poets. He had from time to time fleeting intuitions of what it means to be a poet. He had one early in that prelude to his first volume in which the verses are not without an agreeable and liquid cadence:

> Look, then, into thine heart and write!
> Yes, into Life's deep stream.

He had a clearer one much later in lines on Gaspar Becerra with their wooden trip:

> O thou sculptor, painter, poet!
> Take this lesson to thy heart:
> That is best which lieth nearest;
> Shape from that thy work of art.

Or, since he never dreamed of following this monition, perhaps the lines of neither poem express an inner experience or personal conviction but are a mere repetition of a sentiment old enough and repeated in literature often enough to have seemed to Longfellow both respectable and poetic. And that doubt sums him up—him and his kind and his intellectual descendants. The doubt has nothing to do with Longfellow's position as an educator, as an able and influential pioneer of modern language scholarship in America. As such his reputation is quite secure. But the academic critics have tried to make his services to scholarship count as poetic achievement. And that is absurd. For even in his character of a translator of verse and a transmitter of poetic culture he showed himself fundamentally unrelated to the possessors of creative vision. He was in earlier years not tempted to translate anything but the third-rate, not Goethe, not Heine, not even Schiller, not even the lyrical Uhland, but Tiedge, Müller, Mosen and Salis-Seewis. The "Coplas de Manrique" have a touch of solemn eloquence. But their content is wholly commonplace. Later he used Dante as refuge and defense from the turmoil and agony of the Civil War. And Dante, as he explained in the sonnets on the "Divina Commedia" which speak more beautifully for him than anything else— Dante was to him in truth a Cathedral at whose altar he could re-dedicate himself to the traditions of Christendom. Thus the artificer always treats or leans upon the common stock of existent ideas and emotions. But since ideas and emotions do not become common and traditional until they have all but lost their edge and glow and saving power, the artificer is the comfortable repeater, safe to himself and others, of what has long been believed and approved and can no longer stir or wound or awaken. Of himself he has little to add, nor does he feel the need of addition and personal flavor, since he has no thought beyond that of edification and entertainment.

Am I slaying the thrice slain? Who, except wretched schoolchildren, now reads Longfellow? But people until but the other day read the verses of Henry van Dyke and thousands are still reading those of Robert Service. The thing to establish in America is not that Longfellow was a very small poet, but that he did not partake of the poetic character at all. For minor poets have this in common with major poets —so far as such distinctions of magnitude are not in themselves absurd—that their business and function is the transmutation of impassioned experience into intelligible personal form. Such was evidently not the business and the function of Longfellow. Twice he came near poetic speech, once in the pathetic sonnet on his dead wife, once in "The Warning"— "There is a poor blind Samson in this land"—when the anti-slavery struggle roused even him. The ballads and the moralizing lyrics are all written from without, are all lacking the organic connection with one shaken soul and are therefore outside of the soul of the world. He can fall as low as Ella Wheeler Wilcox in "The Rainy Day"; he can rise as high as Webster in the final lines of "The Building of the Ship." He never touches poetry. He borrows form and accepts content from without. The longer works are all strictly patterned upon the works of others. The plays are weary imitations of the Elizabethans; "The Building of the Ship" and "Keramos" lean almost slavishly on Schiller's "Lied von der Glocke," itself hardly a poetic masterpiece, nor has it been

65

sufficiently observed how almost to the point of the popular and of course absurd notion of plagiarism "The Golden Legend" copies "Faust." When Longfellow turned to native subjects he told pleasing or pathetic or picturesque anecdotes in forms borrowed whole. "Evangeline" and "Miles Standish" are imitations rather of the "Luise" of Voss than of Goethe's "Hermann und Dorothea"; for "Hiawatha" he borrowed with his most striking lapse of even the scholar's insight the measure of the Finnish folk-epic, "Kalewala." For the "Tales of a Wayside Inn" he used a framework that is, in the good and high sense, common property. But in the elaborate "Musician's Tale," "The Saga of King Olaf," he again borrowed the very measures, devices and mannerisms of the rather jejune "Frithjof's Saga" of the Swedish poet Tegner. He was really not unlike those minstrel artificers of the middle ages who borrowed freely from each other methods of dressing up a common substance and had not yet risen to the notion of expression as an individual act and therefore of literature as individual property. Doubtless this large body of narrative verse as well as certain lyrics of pleasant sentiment and easy rhythm still give pleasure to a subliterary public. But men are not contemporaries though the same decades embrace their lives. To minds concerned with the imaginative interpretation of man, of nature and of human life, Longfellow has nothing left to say.

I find John Greenleaf Whittier a far more respectable and memorable figure. Earth clung to the man from hardship and bleakness, and love and spiritual courage were his Quaker inheritance. One smiles at his naïve and trashy ballads; one is oppressed by Longfellow's gentlemanly stuffiness.

One has no doubt of the truth of Margaret Fuller's assertion that Longfellow's social position and his publisher's sumptuous bindings were factors in his excessive reputation. About Whittier there is something clear and authentic, something of brooks and trees rather than of horse-hair furniture and antimacassars.

He knew the ways of both genius and taste and was aware of the fact, unlike Longfellow in this, that he probably possessed neither. But this insight itself rendered the character of the creative process far more accessible to him than it ever was to his gentlemanly contemporary. With a precision excellent and even melodious for his time and place, he stated his case:

> Nor mine the seer-like power to show
> The secrets of the heart and mind;
> To drop the plummet-line below
> Our common world of joy and woe,
> A more intense despair or brighter hope to find.
>
> Yet here at least an earnest sense
> Of human right and weal is shown;
> A hate of tyranny intense
> And hearty in its vehemence
> As if my brother's pain and sorrow were my own.

True to his training and to the examples about him, tempted also by the necessities of production and later by his popularity, Whittier remains an artificer in ballad, anecdote and occasional poem throughout nine-tenths of his work. But wherever human liberty, wherever a brother's pain and sorrow are his theme, profound experience does become fused with expression and the result is poetry, true if neither high nor deep. Nor is this all. He had the sagacity to know whence the creative sources probably rise. He failed in the "Songs of Labor"; he did not wholly succeed even in "The Barefoot Boy" or in "Snowbound," interesting and agreeable as those pieces are. He wanted the intensity that, as he himself knew, raises the concrete into the permanently significant. But he had a perception of the character of the poetical process however rarely he himself reached it.

A good deal has been made of the slipshodness and vulgarity of form which he himself admitted. That slipshodness belongs to the wholly negligible nine-tenths of his work. In the small but definite remainder his form is tighter than that of his contemporaries and more at one with the substance of the poem. This is true of "Ichabod"; it is true of "Astræa," of the untitled prologue to the "Home Ballads," of "The Rendition," of that single classic which has come out of the huge body of American religious verse, "The Eternal Goodness." Not equally well-wrought but approaching the nature of creative literature are also "Skipper Ireson's Ride" and "Brown of Ossawatomie." And not infrequently amid verses otherwise quite flat and external, Whittier has moments in which he perceives and reacts poetically—"the sea's long level dim with rain"—that is, sees both passionately and precisely, although his power of creative speech is short-breathed and faltering. It is a pity that stupid anthologists and pedagogues keep alive the memory of "Maud Muller" and "Barbara Frietchie." Vulgar triviality can go no farther than in those pieces. Longfellow never fell so low. But Longfellow never reached the spiritual strength and distinction which at rare, brief moments glow in the work of the Quaker peasant.

What is one to say today of Oliver Wendell Holmes? A snob, though a not unamiable one, he had nevertheless a remarkably free mind for one of his generation. His hostility toward the ancestral Calvinism of New England was, due to his scientific training, not only sincere but sane and well-grounded. "Anything that assumes the necessity of the extermination of instincts which were given to be regulated—no matter by what name you call it—no matter whether a fakir or a monk or a deacon believes it—if received, ought to produce insanity in any well-regulated mind." Many other remarks in the "Autocrat" series are almost as good and not a few are as good in substance and wittier in form. There was a time when Holmes seemed a bold blade enough; he may still seem so in remote levels of the population. From any permanent point of view his prose has the fatal defects of knowingness, of feeble jauntiness, of a total lack in depth of tone. It has lightness and brightness but no body. It is ingenious and adroit. There is a high polish, but the polish is on tin. If there was one quality after which Holmes aimed, it was distinction. Yet distinction is what he inveterately misses. Like higher qualities, which commonly include it, distinction evidently cannot be summoned or sought. Nor has it anything to do, as Longfellow and Holmes illustrate, with conventionally gentle birth and breeding. Conscious fastidiousness, such as Holmes', is wholly alien to it. All through the polite period it escaped, significantly enough, the scholarly, the well-bred, all who by their careful selectiveness in both life and literature seemed, from a superficial point of view, to be entitled to distinction, if to little else. The quality belongs, like all other high qualities, to intensity and veracity and to these alone. Here is, if anywhere, the secret of the hopeless withering and wilting of the prose of Holmes. He declared himself a Brahmin; he had light without fire; but his light, too, was not permitted either to blaze or to glow; it only glinted. Distinction of thought and manner should have saved him and it was distinction that he hopelessly missed. Of the verse nothing, by fairly common consent, remains but the amusing "One Hoss Shay," the ingenuous and mildly tender "Last Leaf," the vapid if not unmelodious "Chambered Nautilus." And the last remains, as it were, by sentimental courtesy. One records this extinction of a figure once as eminent as that of Holmes without regret. Amiable and clear-minded up to a certain point that he was, there was so little literary virtue, *virtus,* in the man's make-up. Literature never cost him a pang nor life apparently an ache. He lived blamelessly and delightfully and wrote easily and achieved an enormous reputation without a struggle. But you cannot set fire to the city of time with a rocket, only with the flame of the much-enduring soul.

One cannot deal so summarily with the youngest of the famous original New England group. It is again, as with Bryant, a question of "format," of dimension. But in the case of James Russell Lowell the dimension is much greater and the interior force much higher. Lowell is not likely to be much read in the future. He can never fade as hopelessly as Oliver Wendell Holmes. A man and a man of letters is behind those largely tiresome volumes, one who loved freedom, within the limits of his conception, to the point that he would, like Garrison, have been willing to suffer for it; one who loved poetry so well that he almost attained it; one whose pursuit of the critical Muse failed not through narrowness of sympathy or feebleness of speech but through the ancestral Puritan aversion from dealing with ultimate questions in any field except theology and politics. During his best years, in a word, a strong, aspiring, not unimpassioned soul.

The anti-slavery struggle was the experience that saved him. At the touch of the intimately human he was, like all of his kind, feebly moral or, as in "The Changeling," downright false and maudlin. The Puritan cannot face love or death; he substitutes what he calls reverence and heaven. He cannot, in reality, ever learn to face nature either. He has to prettify and falsify and personify. Nature has to be like good people. Thus Lowell wrote in "The Vision of Sir Launfal":

> Then Heaven tries earth if it be in tune,
> And over it softly her warm ear lays.

He cannot face the dandelion without a "thou teachest me to deem"—it doesn't matter what. No manner of either feeling or writing can be worse or more alien from literature. But the anti-slavery struggle released a passion which, luckily, was no less strong for being proper; it made those especially who, like Lowell, had the grace to enter it early, partakers of that third experience which, with love and death, almost completes the list of the supreme experiences of the human heart, the experience which Lowell himself has recorded if not in essential poetry then at least in powerful and still memorable verse:

Then to side with truth is noble when we share her wretched
    crust
Ere her cause bring fame and fortune and 'tis prosperous to
    be just.

Or again and more succinctly:

> They are slaves who dare not be
> In the right with two or three.

The great central experiences save not only the heart and inspire the tongue; they enlarge the mind. They transform the gentleman into the man. His own brought Lowell not only face to face with stripped truth; it brought him back to the people of his native section. It enabled him to write in "The Biglow Papers" many homely verses that are not likely to lose their pungency:

> Ez for war, I call it murder,—
> There you hev it plain an' flat.

It let him put in the mouth of Birdofredom Sawin the observation as pertinent to the Nicaraguan muddle of 1928 as it was to the Mexican situation of his day:

Our nation's bigger'n theirn an' so its rights air bigger,
An' thet it's all to make 'em free that we air pullin' trigger.

These verses, pertinent as they are, illustrate, of course, the great inequality of "The Biglow Papers." First one must strip off the once doubtless amusing but now tiresome editorial apparatus; next a careful selection is still necessary. What remains is small in bulk; it slides back at almost any moment, despite the dialect, into artifice. It is, for all that, closer in character to creative literature than anything, except a few verses of Whittier, written by anyone of the strictly polite New England tradition. "The Courtin'" is one of the earliest altogether genuine things in American verse, "What Mr. Robinson Thinks" is satire that rises above its place and time into the domain of the universal and long enduring. The second set of "The Biglow Papers" is upon the whole inferior to the first. But it contains "A Yankee Idyll" with its delightful opening lines:

> I love to start out after night's begun
> An' all the chores about the farm are done,
> The critters milked and foddered, gates shet fast,
> Tools cleaned against tomorrer, supper past,
> An' Nancy darnin' by her ker'sene lamp—

and with that other less perfect but more ambitious passage into which Lowell put all that was best and most poetical within him:

> O strange new world that yit was never young,
> Whose youth from thee by gripin' need was wrung,
> Brown foundlin' of the woods whose baby-bed
> Was prowled roun' by the Injun's cracklin' tread,
> An' who grew'st strong through shifts an' wants an' pains,
> Nussed by stern men with empires in their brains,
> Who saw in their vision their young Ishmael strain
> With each hard hand a vassal ocean's mane.
> Thou skilled by freedom and by great events
> To pitch new states as old World men pitch tents,
> Thou taught by fate to know Jehovah's plan
> That man's devices can't unmake a man,
> An' whose free latch-string never was drawed in
> Against the poorest child of Adam's kin—
> The grave's not dug where traiter hands shall lay
> In fearful haste thy murdered corse away.

73

I have said that Lowell slides back at almost any moment into artifice. He does even in this short passage. The last couplet is sheer balderdash. And yet the passage, to borrow that useful phrase of Jules Lemaître, "exists"; it exists; it is not likely to fade wholly from the memory of America.

The slaves emancipated and the Civil War over, Lowell as a poet was finished. Other experiences were not for him. On the "Commemoration Ode" his own remark in a letter to Miss Norton four days after its delivery suffices: "Like a boy, I mistook my excitement for inspiration, and here I am in the mud." As the great experience that had once widened his mind faded into the past, he lapsed back more and more into polite, Puritanical gentility. He was horrified at Swinburne in 1866 and emphasizes his complete agreement with the silly principle, silly both as from the man and for the daughter, that no man should "write a line that he would not have his daughter read." He would not entertain the thought of evolution; the dawning signs of the industrial revolution scared him into uneasy conservatism and almost into doubting the wisdom of that "free latch-string." He went the way of his kind, writing to Leslie Stephen, of all people, in 1876: "I continue to shut my eyes resolutely in certain speculative directions," and adding querulously; "When they tell me that I can't *know* certain things, I am apt to wonder how *they* can be sure of that." His later verse is of no importance. The pathos of the situation lay in the fact that he loved poetry sufficiently to understand its nature and to realize that he had no creative share in the secret known, according to his overstatement "since the world was by scarce two or three." Out of that pathos came his brief and most genuine lyric utterance. He feared the cessations of even such poetic visitings as were his:

> My heart, I cannot still it,
> Nest that had song-birds in it.
>
> Had they been swallows only,
> Without the passion stronger
> That skyward longs and sings—
> Woe's me, I shall be lonely
> When I can feel no longer
> The impatience of their wings.

Lowell's critical works that once seemed so solid and commanding have failed and faded from the intellectual horizon largely because Lowell, like his own dull reviewer in the "Fable for Critics," was "at sea without compass or chart." His speculative incuriosity left him without a method. Now there are almost as many critical methods as there are first-rate critics. But certain large and not indefinite tendencies are discernible. There is Sainte-Beuve's natural history of souls; there is the attempt after a coherent *Geistesgeschichte* of the best German criticism; there is Arnold's use of literature as both test and tool in the study of perfection; there is the rhetorical approach, the mere study of outer forms or techniques which, being the easiest and entailing no speculative commitments, has been very popular; there are, finally, the two extremes of pure philology and the purely æsthetic disengagement and reproduction of an author's aroma or "bouquet." Now Lowell used none of these methods; he shows no awareness of their existence. His equipment was considerable; his philological comments are often close and minute enough, as in his strictures on Masson's "Milton," for use in a technical journal. But his criticism has neither starting-point nor direction; the essays have no structure. Occasional *obiter dicta* are both sagacious and pungent; but they are accidents. Except for these he tells us nothing in either the Dryden or the Lessing, the Milton, the Spenser or the Dante which cannot be found better organized if not as warmly written in a dozen text-books. Not in Lowell's day, it may be truly objected. Then these essays have a place in the technical history of education, with which I have here nothing to do. They are in brief able professorial exercises for undergraduates. The "Fable for Critics," composed in earlier years out of a far greater freshness of spirit is also far more memorable. The well-known and often quoted sketches of his contemporaries, including especially the rather neglected sketch of Cooper, are witty and agreeable in themselves and welcome infractions of the academic law concerning the necessary futility of the criticism of contemporaries. Yes, the "Fable for Critics" is still alive. But it was written in the great days of the anti-slavery struggle before Lowell had become a professor, an ambassador, a pillar of society. The ardor of a great inner experience saves even the remotest by-products of the experiencing mind. That is the kind of thing which Lowell, the professional critic, never permitted himself to know. Hence his formal criticism is justly forgotten.

III

Except for Simms the South had been very nearly inarticulate. There had been writing enough. The various periodicals from "The Southern Review" in 1828 to "Russell's

Magazine" in 1857 had never lacked for contributors. But all that can be said for even the best contributions is that their authors gave evidence of a genuine appreciation of the successive phases of English poetry. If there is a distinguishing mark of all earlier and, in fact, not a little later Southern writing, it is a pervasive melancholy, a preoccupation with the tomb and the charnel-house. For all the bravery and handsome gestures and often enough true elegance of mind and life which characterized the Southern gentry, slavery and typhoid fever, the stricken charm of the landscape and hard drinking in a sub-tropical climate all had their devastating effects. True expression of the individual in literature was even more dangerous than in the Puritanic North. The group spirit was of great ferocity, because the group profoundly, though unconsciously, felt its position to be precarious. The "peculiar institution" was pride, menace, perversion, all in one. Hectic orations on the glory of the South and its institutions, fiery reassertions of the group-spirit or quite imitative exercises in verse were all, or almost all, that the situation permitted. In the earlier days of, let us say, Hugh Swinton Legaré, a calmer temper prevailed. But from the days of Nullification to the Civil War and far beyond to the end of the Reconstruction period the South was in its psychical character an armed camp in which any expression deviating from the strictest group conventions was held the last and foulest of disloyalties. As late as 1880 the editor of the Charleston *News and Courier,* deploring the death of an excellent citizen in a duel and appealing to the public and the courts to uphold the anti-dueling laws on the statute-books of the State, felt impelled to add: "We cast no stones at those who consider 'The Code' a necessity or a shield, although in our judgment it is morally wrong and socially indefensible." It is significant that the writer of these words was assassinated by a Charleston physician nine years later under circumstances that were never cleared up. If such were the conditions in Charleston in the last quarter of the nineteenth century, it is an easy and correct inference that in the Old South creative living and creative speech were alike impossible. Small towns only punctuated this great agrarian territory; there were no cities in which any protestant could have taken refuge and lived his own life. But it is safe to assume that there were few such. The poor whites were ignorant and degraded; the gentry lived lives of high physical and physiological expansiveness, of authority and pleasure. The accident of flaming genius did not happen. Men bred in Oxford and Heidelberg returned home to their plantations or to the honored practice of the law or of medicine, wholly content with their position and their institutions and ready to subordinate any individual protests or stirrings to the strengthening and perpetuation of their group. Heretics were rare and all creative spirits are necessarily heretics. The literary sterility of the South ceases, like many other problems, to have any problematic character so soon as we attain to the true conception of literature as, on its lowest terms, the expression of an experience that is differentiated from the experience of the social or tribal group. But since it was held dishonorable and disloyal in any Southern gentleman to differentiate himself in any manner from the experience, opinion, emotion, of his dominant, aristocratic and yet subtly menaced group, it is clear that there was no place for art in this society. Culture was highly prized. A gentleman could quote his Horace. If he could compose an oration and write an agreeable copy of verses on the death of some sweet, pure woman or of some gallant gentleman or in praise of his State or section, he was honored for having added the agreeable to the useful. But any special absorption in literature, even upon the mildest terms led, like James Matthews Legaré's, to failure and obscurity. Legaré's talent was thin and his verses imitative. But he wanted to be a poet. He was forgotten. If ever there was a note of the slightest intensity, it was, like that of Catharine Gendron Poyas, sounded by a woman and was religious in character. William John Grayson's defense of the "peculiar institution" in Popean couplets, "The Hireling and the Slave" represented as late as 1854, what were considered the legitimate uses, except orations, elegies or complimentary verses, of literature in the South. Good literature was widely read, Tennyson was adored; the suggestion that the sources of literature existed here, too, in these towns, on these plantations, would have been regarded as a subtle impropriety. But this is an attitude common to aristocracies from the Junkers of East Prussia to the Charlestonian gentry of the old régime. It belonged to the nature of things that the writers produced by the Old South should have been assimilationists: Simms the son of a frontiersman, Timrod the grandson of a German immigrant, Poe the waif of strolling players.

The war came and the Southern people arose to defend with the sincerest ardor, even with a somewhat Roman sense of dedication, their frontiers and what they regarded as their rights. I have used the word Roman advisedly. The sentiments involved were all aristocratical and pagan sentiments. Of course the common people fought with their masters. When have they, alas, not done so? The pagan and chivalric loyalties, the feudal virtues, are not yet wholly extinct. But even 1861 was a late year for them. The Northern poets had two initial advantages over their Southern colleagues: they had enjoyed, as Abolitionists, the supreme Judæo-Christian experience of being in the minority for the sake of the oppressed; they were, by virtue of the character and quality of that experience, not only in harmony with their ancestral faith at its best but also prophetic of the immediate humanitarian future. There could be no John Brown, new embodiment of the eternal Christian symbol, in the South; there could not be the spiritual rapture that throbs in Julia Ward Howe's "Battle Hymn of the Republic." The Southern sentiments were, of necessity, all pagan sentiments and it is but natural that the most perfect stanza of the most gifted of Southern poets should have the carved and cool completeness of Latin verse:

> In seeds of laurel in the earth
> The blossom of your fame is blown,
> And somewhere, waiting for its birth,
> The shaft is in the stone.

Old irritations in the South over the neglect of Henry Timrod by Northern critics and historians of literature throng my memory. For all I know these irritations may still exist. Wholly detached from these far-off things I can today hold the balance utterly level. It is most true that as an artificer—and except for isolated hours all the poets

80

discussed in this Book were artificers—Henry Timrod was easily the superior of all his contemporaries. An immediate disciple of Tennyson, a close and sensitive student of the great renaissance tradition of English poetry, he knew, with both skill and ardor, what such poetry should be like. With a half-pathetic sense of amusement I can join the comrades and teachers of my youth in challenging the North to produce a passage from Longfellow or Lowell or Whittier that goes through the gestures of the lofty imagination according to the strictest traditions of English poetry as well as this passage from "The Cotton Boll":

> As men who labor in that mine
> Of Cornwall, hollowed out beneath the bed
> Of ocean, when a storm rolls overhead,
> Hear the dull booming of the world of brine
> Above them, and a mighty muffled roar
> Of winds and waters, yet toil calmly on,
> And split the rock and pile the massive ore,
> Or carve a niche, or shape the archèd roof;
> So I, as calmly, weave my woof
> Of song, chanting the days to come,
> Unsilenced, though the quiet summer air
> Stirs with the bruit of battles, and each dawn
> Wakes from its starry silence to the hum
> Of many gathering armies.

Nor is this by far the only passage that I might have chosen. The whole of "The Cotton Boll," of "Ethnogenesis," of "Caroliana," of "Spring," of "Charleston," of half a dozen lyrics and sonnets, of the well-known "Magnolia Cemetery Ode," is as firmly wrought, as smoothly accomplished, as conventionally noble and imaginative as these lines. There is no slackness of execution, no lapse from taste. This small body of poetry is correct, sonorous, firm. How were the friends of my youth to know that, in a very few years as history goes, the very tradition of English poetry in which Timrod wrote would begin except in its highest and freshest and oldest examples, to seem itself outworn and inexpressive and especially in America no longer adequate to clear and human and important speech? What can save a Timrod in the decline, to be corrected but never undone, of a Tennyson's reputation? Whitman was a contemporary of Timrod's! The Southerner's smooth verses and Roman sentiments belonged to the irrecoverable past even as they were being written. He missed a brief period of over-valuation such as Longfellow, for example, enjoyed and still enjoys. A hundred years hence he stands a better chance of amusing and interesting the curious student than the New Englander.

Not so much can be said for Paul Hamilton Hayne, though he, too, being a Southerner, may be said to have missed the brief period of national approval enjoyed by artificers no more accomplished and varied than himself. His level of traditional poetic workmanship is, in fact, higher and steadier than has commonly been admitted. Living much longer than poor Timrod he passed from the influence of Tennyson under that of William Morris and wrote a series of romantic tales in verse—"Daphles," "The Wife of Brittany," "The Story of Glaucus the Thessalian," —that have not a little of the liquid flow and sunset shimmer of his model. That is the least that can in justice be said for Hayne. How little it is and how unavailing! Neither Timrod nor Hayne nor, except on that one matter of slavery, their Northern contemporaries, had anything to *say*. Artificers are less like poets than like those carpet-weavers whom I have seen crouching in shady courtyards in walled Tunisian towns and repeating with variations themselves traditional and common the patterns invented by their ancestors a thousand years ago. . . . Need I add that in Simms' "War Poetry of the South" there is, by the side of much empty truculence and sheer balderdash, as in all warlike verse, a moment here and there of bardic ardor, but that the most agreeable, living and human verses in that collection are those in which Joseph Blythe Allston and John Dickson Bruns express the grief, the resignation and the dignity of the defeated?

IV

I proceed to complete this survey of polite writing in America, of literature according to the standards of the American Academy, in order to pass on, as rapidly as may be, from document to expression and from artifice to art.

After the Civil War the genteel writers turned their eyes more sedulously than ever from both the interior life as it is really lived and from the life of their time and country. An age, terrible and heroic at once set in, an age of great affairs, great passions, grotesque contrasts, epic despite its sordidness. The West was settled and the frontier pushed to the ultimate sea; the Indians were beaten into final submission and landlessness in a thirty years' conflict; the cattle-rangers drove their innumerable herds from Texas to Wyoming and were themselves driven from the great grazing lands by millions seeking farms and homes; the railroads crossed the continent and opened new empires and the great, astute, unscrupulous founders of the trusts, the concentrated money-power, the most efficient and gigantic machinery for the production and distribution of goods that the world has seen, urged on and welcomed those quiet, massive streams of immigration first from the North, next from the East and South of Europe, that have changed and are still changing the very face and character of American civilization itself. Millions of black freedmen in the South struggled from utter helplessness and ignorance into self-consciousness, both racial and cultural; new religions were born from the bosoms of the native Protestant masses: Prohibitionism and Christian Science; new surges of self-protective fear arose and the American Protective Association took the place of the older Know Nothing or American Party, to be itself duplicated in later years by the Ku-Klux Klan. Wealth assumed unheard-of proportions and was spent with unheard-of extravagance and display in the Gilded Age and the workers and the disinherited became conscious and crystallized that consciousness in a growing demand for social and economic justice. And side by side with that conflict grew another, more silent but in the end equally significant one between the sense of life and civilization of the native Anglo-American people and a divergent sense of life and scale of values brought by the yet inarticulate masses of later immigrants. An age of a thousand conflicts, dramas, adventures, heaven-storming hopes and ice-bleak tragedies. And the poets played hymn-tunes on a village parlor melodeon or tinkled pseudo-oriental ditties on a borrowed mandolin; the essayists and critics made a cult of cleanness and propriety and the novelists wrote tight little stories to illustrate the efficacy of some silly moralistic saw. I am not, of course, forgetting those greater and lesser figures from Emerson and Whitman and Mark Twain on with whom the larger part of this history is to deal. They neither touched nor expressed effectively the thoughts of any considerable groups of Americans until the other day. To the vast majority of readers in American homes, to pupils and students in numberless schools and colleges poetry meant, so far as it was read at all, Stoddard and Aldrich and Gilder, serious prose meant Donald G. Mitchell and George W. Curtis and Thomas Wentworth Higginson and William Winter and Brander Matthews and Hamilton Mabie and Henry van Dyke and Agnes Repplier; fiction, when it did not mean the works of the Reverend E. P. Roe or "St. Elmo" or "Ben-Hur" or "Little Lord Fauntleroy," meant either such vapid stuff as Aldrich's "Marjorie Daw" or Stockton's feeble cleverness and more genuine fun or such vigorously executed yet melodramatic exoticism as the Italian novels of Francis Marion Crawford or such warm sentimentalities or whalebone apologues as the stories—again able in technique—of Margaret Deland. Finally, toward the end of the century, when life and nature and creative energy were already asserting themselves in the forerunners of the moderns, the great public, with the approval of the polite critics, indulged a brief but excessive orgy of flight into a superficially romanticized past with Paul Leicester Ford, Mary Johnston, S. Weir Mitchell or went on equally romantic modern adventures with the smart and shallow Richard Harding Davis.

It is not necessary and would not be fruitful to examine in detail the documents of this huge mass of second-rate and hardly memorable literature. It lacked almost wholly the background of creative experience; it either did not understand or, as in the case of the critics, blankly repudiated the necessity for such a background. The closer student of the vagaries of the human mind will, for instance, find no more curious example of smug or strident limitedness than in American dramatic criticism from, let us say, William Winter to Brander Matthews and their colleagues and disciples. In the face of Euripides and Shakespeare and Molière and Hebbel and Ibsen, it was asserted and taught by these critics that the drama is and should be a hard and ingenious artifice guided by technical rules growing out of the mechanism of the theater and illustrating in substance and purpose the excellence and permanence of the fleeting *mores* of its hour in history. It was, in brief, to be ingenious and clean, adroit and agreeable, neat and shrewd. It was to be everything that a genuine piece of literature never has been nor could be. For the high poet may be God's fool; he can never be an empty technician or a professor of dramatic literature.

This is but one of the dozen different points of view from which one could illustrate the character of the degenerate genteel tradition which was in complete possession of the field of American letters well on into the first decade of the twentieth century and whose standards, taste, influence, power have not yet wholly disappeared from our literary scene. One might illustrate that character from the editorial policies of the great magazines and publishing houses, from the quality and substance of literary teaching and research in the universities, from lectures and newspaper reviewing, from conversation and from anecdotes of the literary life.

Wherever one turns one finds the same conscious or unconscious theory of literature as a device of elegant amusement or conventional moral edification constructed wholly from without according to rhetorical rules as plain and as communicable as those that govern a plumber's or a joiner's trade.

Poetry from the Civil War to the publication of "The Lyric Year" in 1912, omitting such gifted and memorable forerunners of later developments as Richard Hovey and especially William Vaughn Moody, offers the most significant illustration of the methods of the polite writers—a significance borne out and heightened by the fact that the revolution in modern American literature began with that lyrical movement which restored reality to verse and so verse to the renewal of its function in literature and life.

There is an almost symbolical pathos about Bayard Taylor. So much ardor, ambition, knowledge and a product so diffuse and faded. It cannot be said of him, as of most of his contemporaries, that he did not know what poetry was. His profound and excellent devotion to Goethe, the years he spent on his version of "Faust," by far the best in English, must have taught him that. Yet he never achieved poetry— never came near its necessary depth of tone, concentration, inner reality. The same cannot be said of Thomas Bailey Aldrich, who is likely to come to stand out slightly above his contemporaries. Unconsciously enough, Aldrich made a virtue of his weakness and necessities. Instead of going feebly through grandiose poetic gestures, the commonest and worst fault of the polite poets, he read Tennyson *and* Théophile Gautier and practiced a tight and precise little art whose deliberateness saved it from the immediate suspicion of flight from the realities of the poet's life. At least a dozen of his pieces are excellent and complete of their kind. A well-carved bead is better than a smudged and smeary statue. Nor can it be said of Aldrich that he did not have more poignant moments of the inner life than those recorded in the mass of his verse. Once, at least, in "An Untimely Thought" he expressed one of those moments. But the polite writers had persuaded themselves or had been hypnotized into believing that all reality is low. So Aldrich writes querulously and disdainfully:

> Today we breathe a commonplace
> Polemic, scientific air:
> We strip Illusion of her veil;
> We vivisect the nightingale
> To probe the secret of his note,

and turned to "Bagatelle" and "Cloth of Gold" and Tennyson and, at his highest and best, to

> the changing pageantry
> The fading alps and archipelagoes
> And spectral cities of the sunset sea.

A Federal prison, poverty, disease, Beethoven—these were some of the realities which Sidney Lanier, only six years younger than Aldrich, encountered. And there are, in fact, true and exact perceptions and thoughts in the "Poem Outlines" published by his son. "A man does not reach any stature of manhood until like Moses he kills an Egyptian, i.e., murders some oppressive prejudice of the all-crushing Tyrant Society or Custom or Orthodoxy, and flies into the desert of his own soul." And better still: "It is but two years since Boston burned me for witch-craft. I wrote a poem which

88

was not orthodox: that is, not like Mr. Longfellow's." Best of all: "Every rule is a sign of weakness." The poems themselves are unluckily quite orthodox in substance and temper to the very minutiæ of polite and Southern modes of thought and feeling. Such lyrics as "Into the Woods my Master Went" and "The Stirrup Cup" and even the fantastic evening song have a touch of imaginative energy that was rare in those flat days. That is all. More can undoubtedly be said for the long odic poems on which Lanier's reputation rests. Their orthodoxy is almost careful and precise. But their rhythmic movement and contour, despite the untenable theory that guided Lanier, are fresh and stirring. If he did not succeed in getting the best part of his mind into his finished work, he gave the evidence of a seeing eye. Amid the verbalized and conventionalized poetic landscapes of his period, it is refreshing to come upon sharp details actually observed and expressed in verse:

The creeks overflow: a thousand rivulets run
'Twixt the roots of the sod; the blades of the marsh-grass stir;
Passeth a hurrying sound of wings that whir;
Passeth and all is still; and the currents cease to run;
And the sea and the marsh are one.

Little can be said of or for the many ambitious verses of Edmund Clarence Stedman or the false energy and labored eloquence and conscious grandiosity of Joaquin Miller or the neat little fantasies of John Bannister Tabb or the stucco sonnets of Lloyd Mifflin or the moralizings of Edward Rowland Sill or the blurred idealisms of George Edward Woodberry or the labored wit or conscious wistfulness of Henry C. Bunner. It was an age not of silver but of tin.

89

The blight of politeness and false dignity or false homeliness, of correct sentiments and nerveless meter let no one escape. Emma Lazarus, a Portuguese Jewess, wrote as pseudonobly and conventionally as the other sonneteers and odic gesticulators; Paul Laurence Dunbar, a Negro and far younger, wrote purely or playfully or with humble pathos. The stream of verbiage went endlessly on and has not yet been wholly dried. Rose Terry Cooke wrote:

> O God, how cold
> It must be in that wintry mold!

and William Winter:

> Say, if thy spirit yet have speech
> What port lies hid within the pall;

and Helen Gray Cone:

> Spirit supernal, splendor eternal: England,

and Louise Imogen Guiney, who had other almost human moments, "the moth's auroral wing," and Richard Burton:

> May hath her own blithe beauty nor doth need,

and Madison Cawein issued the information that Earth

> robes herself in raiment green of love and laughter spun;

and Julian Hawthorne, carefully personifying for decency's sake, relates how

> All that deep noon of day
> Heart to beating heart we lay,
> And oh, love had his way,

and Clinton Scollard announced:

> Let there be dreams, one said. I answered: Yea,
> Let there be dreams today.

If I dwell for another moment on one more poet of the age of tin, it is to illustrate still further two matters of the last importance: one, how completely without influence upon their time and country were the notable spirits who had arisen in America since Emerson, a phenomenon not unknown in the histories of other literatures; and, two, the necessity and the splendor of that modern revolt in American letters which re-allied itself in spirit with Thoreau, with Whitman, with Mark Twain on his realistic and his somber side, with Emily Dickinson, with whatever the nineteenth century offered of reality, poignancy, freedom of mind, and swept like a cleansing wind through the wilted and withered forest of the genteel tradition.

The poet I select is Richard Watson Gilder. He was no better than several of his contemporaries and certainly no worse. There have been, despite the gods according to Horace, mediocre poets before. What makes Gilder significant is the discrepancy between the quality of his work and his standing and reputation. These did not come wholly from his poetry. For more than twenty-five years he was the editor of "The Century Magazine." He was, too, according to his lights, an honorably public-spirited citizen of New York. But the poet and the editor were one. The tastes and mentalities of Gilder and Henry Mills Alden and, let us say, Hamilton Wright Mabie, though I use these names as symbols rather than as the names of men, determined what was and what was not to get a hearing in American literature. And the literary aspirant received a friendly and a courteous welcome in those old "Century" offices on the north side of Union Square from Gilder and Robert Underwood Johnson.

But that aspirant had no chance if the tonic weather of reality had touched his work, if it was the expression of any but correctly traditional sentiments swathed in a pseudo-Tennysonian wool of words, if it did not conform to Sill's extraordinarily typical demands upon a poem, that it was to be full of "lovely images," not pertinent or precise or stirring or illuminating, but lovely, and that, above all, it was to "bring about us troops of high and pure associations." One had to be, especially if one was an American, high and pure. Englishmen were permitted to take liberties. Thus Gilder refused the early naturalistic work of Stephen Crane but accepted the stories of Arthur Morrison. Gilder's poetry is the image of the man, the age, the literary taste that had to be rudely attacked and shown up if America was ever to express itself in prose or verse. Gilder—and he was not alone —had lost all sense of anything but idealistic verbiage. Whatever sounded high and pure was poetry, was literature. He wrote:

> Thou art so used, Love, to thine own bird's song,
> Sung to thine ear in Love's low monotone,
> Sung to thee only, Love, to thee alone
> Of all the listening world.

And years later he wrote:

> There are four sisters known to mortals well,
> Whose names are Joy and Sorrow, Death and Love.

On the death of Tennyson he grew cryptic:

> When that great shade into the silence vast
> Through thinking silence past.

92

The war with Spain elicited from him the following agreeable and melodious comment:

> He shows the gentlest mercy
> Who rains the deadliest blows;
> Then quick war's hell is ended,
> And home the hero goes.

The attitude of himself and of his group to the new literature of his later years he summed up in a quatrain called "Sacrilege":

> Wed, thou, with sweet and silent Death,
> Rather than join the prurient throng
> Would soil, with foul, empoisoned breath,
> The sanctity of song.

He expressed it once more in another quatrain, "To the Hero of a Scientific Romance":

> If you wish, go be a pig,
> In and out of season;
> But do not bore us with a big
> Philosophic reason.

v

It is clear that the polite writers left no more memorable work in the essay and the novel than in verse. For the essay requires mental flexibility and the novel, at least as its starting-point, a pure absorption in the concrete. Enormous antecedent exclusions, an unwillingness to observe except within the narrowest range, the determination that every inquiry into literature or life shall issue in foreknown results and foregone conclusions—these attitudes and qualities rob prose of any chance of being a creative or interpretative record of the world. The technique of American fiction improved rapidly and notably between the Civil War and the end of the century. The purely genteel novelist came to offer as smooth a surface as the more hopeful novelists of the soil —the *Heimatskünstler*—or as the forerunners of the modern national movement. Writers like F. Hopkinson Smith or Robert Grant or, on an even higher plane of accomplishment, like Alice Brown and Margaret Deland, produced stories and novels that had all the superficial marks of good literature. But these books, and a thousand other similar ones, that were so gallant or so earnest in aspect were incurably frivolous in substance and drift. They narrowed the world of nature and experience to the confines of a stuffy spiritual parish; their authors were determined that men should be angels, and at the same time choked uneasily over the secret of a dark conviction that men were mammals. It never occurred to them that the biologic character has been infinitely transformed, while it has been definitely retained. He who is forced to examine this specific Puritan tradition from without is often inclined to wonder by what observation of gross animalism intelligent people were driven to opposite extremes so faded, tasteless and unproductive in themselves.

Definitely divided from the Puritan chroniclers on the one hand and from the later rococo romanticists on the other stands the most gifted as well as the most popular novelist of the later nineteenth century in America. The phenomenon of Francis Marion Crawford will long remain a good illustration of the ultimate futility of high talents unaccompanied by brains. "We are nothing more than popular amusers," Crawford wrote of himself and his fellow novelists in his absurd little treatise: "What Is the Novel?". The result of this conviction was that he sedulously observed all the taboos of his class and country, shrank from no melodramatic device in bringing his fables to astonishing and satisfactory conclusions, falsified character and concentrated his gifts at no point. In view of these facts which render each of his books as well as his work in its totality ephemeral, it is astonishing how many faces and scenes and gestures survive in the memory from the long pageant of Crawford's stories: the *Gigerl* and the dark man at his trade in "A Cigarette-maker's Romance," the English countryside in "A Tale of a Lonely Parish," Katherine Lauderdale and Jack Ralston and their elders and the Washington Square of their day, the two young men and the girl in a boat on the lapis-blue sea in "Children of the King" and scene after scene, full of high lights and sharp dark shadows, from the novels of the "Saracinesca" series. Crawford had, if no more, a seeing eye, a high sense for the passion and the pageantry of life, an inventiveness which, up to a certain point in each story, caught enough of the rhythm of reality to create a momentary illusion even in not wholly uncritical minds. But his essential frivolousness of temper and intention is the worm within this large and once lustrous body of work which is swiftly eating out its core and will soon have wholly reduced it to dust.

Of the miscellaneous prose-men of the polite group— familiar essayists, nature writers, critics—little that is profitable can now or hereafter be said. Formally their prose was never less than competent; it attained its moments of elegance or even warmth. It has ceased to "exist." They were and are

far enough from being bad writers, these Higginsons, War-
ners, van Dykes. But the student of literary history must
remember that the nineteenth century came very near eliminating the bad writer, the incompetent, crabbed dullard,
in an older and now perished sense. It is no longer remarkable, as it was in earlier ages, to write merely correctly or
agreeably or even with superficial elegance. We take for
granted all that. It is, as in no previous period of history,
the mind and the vision that count. The modern writer stands
or falls by an infinitely higher, more exacting, more flexible
standard than his predecessor. Where every high-school
teacher and every reporter on a provincial paper can, with
some pains and training, write tolerable prose or traditionally
correct verse, only he can hope to be even briefly saved from
oblivion, who in the solitariness of some creative hour has
added a new and personal note or perception or thought or
vision to the sum of what mankind already knows and feels.
The intellectual foundations, as Rémy de Gourmont pointed
out long ago, must be deeply and solidly sunk. Works without such foundations crumble. Nor must another circumstance be forgotten. We are still very near the writers discussed in this Book. A new collected edition of the works
of Henry van Dyke is even now in process of publication for
some of those great masses of men who are not truly contemporaries of their own age, as that age is expressed in the
works and ways of its high and scrupulous and even prophetic spirits. But *fugaces labuntur anni.* How long will it
be in the cycle of history before our now middle-aged chiefs
of the modern revolt in American letters will be old and the
youngest insurgents of today the mature leaders of tomor-

row? And these generations too will vanish and other men with other thoughts and other achievements and still newer aspirations will crowd the scenes from which we have passed, and what then will be the aspect of the polite Presbyterianism in verse and prose of a Henry van Dyke or of the critical patter about perished techniques of a Brander Matthews? Oblivion so sure may be anticipated.

These men failed, finally, in an ultimate and telling test. Emerson, with whatever reservations, fluctuations, doubts, did befriend and acknowledge Whitman. Longfellow, Holmes and Lowell—of which more hereafter—were wholly blind to their great contemporary. Even so the surviving prose men of the polite tradition set their faces resolutely and blindly against that creative change which conforms to the character of the universe itself. Their portentous flaring up during the World War was no accident. What they could not foresee was that despite victory in arms their moral and intellectual world was to suffer final defeat on every field from Flanders to the Polish plain. Toward the heralds of a newer America they were peevish from the first. "True to life it undoubtedly is," Professor Fred Lewis Pattee wrote of the work of Frank Norris. "But to what end?" The beginnings of an American drama rose faintly on a dim horizon. These critics continued to babble of William Dunlap who had once adapted Kotzebue, of Augustin Daly who, among his numerous adaptations, had never blundered upon a sound work, of the theatric slush and clap-trap of Dion Boucicault and Bronson Howard. Their very prose, which had commonly been at least correct, broke down and disintegrated and Professor Brander Matthews wrote and proofread this sentence on the prose of Holmes: "Despite its acuteness, its liveliness, its briskness, its vivacity, it never lacks seriousness, without ever becoming ponderous," and this other sentence on the verse of Eugene Field: "His feeling is more spontaneous, his sentiment more abundant and finer in feeling." The epilogue of the polite mind and tradition in American letters was written, unconsciously enough, by Professor Henry Augustin Beers of Yale in the "New York Evening Post" of February 3, 1923: "The present reviewer, who belongs exclusively to the nineteenth century, has not read the writings of Messrs. Lewisohn, Mencken, Cabell, Dreiser, Sandburg, *et al.*, and is therefore in no position to judge of the question at issue. There is a new reading public, a new set of novelists, poets, and critics in this country who strike no root in the native soil, who are neither in the English nor in the older American tradition. They are not of Colonial stock. They are Italians, Russians, Jews, Irish, Germans, Slavs or descendants of such.

> These all in sweet confusion sought the shade
> And filled each pause the nightingale had made.

The Yankee nightingale, it must be owned, has made frequent pauses and long ones. But whether those pauses were not better filled by silence than by the notes of these foreign song-birds?" I need not point out that I quote these sentences of Professor Beers' without any touch of malice, but to record for the present and explain for a future day why the academic critics of the genteel tradition fell into such complete disrepute. They were wholly confused on their own ground; they were wholly unaware of the mad arrogance of desiring those immigrant stocks that had been invited to America on both idealistic and practical grounds to remain inarticulate helots; no gleam of the true character of the issues between literature narrowed and drained by Calvinist metaphysic and literature in its eternal aspect ever entered their minds. By the blindness of their resistance they invited the full violence of jeering and revolt.

I point out furthermore that I have reserved for future Books all writers whose works either retain a spark of vitality or whose influence made, however mildly or indirectly, for the future creation of vital literature. Thus I have reserved the novelists of the soil from Edward Eggleston on. Many of them were minor artificers. But the very impulse to study closely the concrete phenomena of sectional life was a saving and hopeful one. I have reserved the humorists and the "columnists" from Eugene Field on, because the former were the forerunners of Mark Twain, the latter of a new species of entertainment and social criticism which has become a part of our cultural scene. I have reserved, in addition, a critic like Mr. Paul Elmer More. A reactionary temper and a refusal to yield to the drift of the cosmic forces may have a greatness, even a majesty of their own. A man of Mr. More's stature and philosophic power must not, despite superficial agreements, be grouped with the mere empty and querulous babblers of the dying genteel tradition. I have tried to describe and define that tradition and to explain how its resolute determination to divorce expression from experience brought American literature to that pass which confronted in their youth all men who have now reached their middle years, and how it created the dilemma between a complete extinction of literary expression and a ruthless revolution which went beyond forms, moods, methods to the very groundwork of both the individual and the national life.

VI

Literature never perishes wholly. Were it ever to do so the artificers would be right in their theory of art as decoration or entertainment or edification. No, expression is part of the biologic process. Man is, to put it on the humblest plain, a speaking and singing animal and he speaks and sings, whenever he is not corrupted by professors and politicians, of what stirs his heart or touches his vital interests without regard for propriety or genteel morality or decorum. Only, since the preservation of written records is in the hands of the intimidated and polite, this folk-expression is often either lost or preserved in emasculated forms. In the very years when timid and scholarly and polite literature had none to resist or criticize or gainsay, the folk was imagining, singing, speaking. Among the lumberjacks of the far West arose the legend of Paul Bunyan and that cycle of grotesque and humorous and, undoubtedly, ribald tales which add the forests of the New World to the realm of the human imagination. And in the great days of the cattle-trails cowpunchers and frontiersmen and gamblers and booze-fighters spoke out. A good many of those anonymous confessions have over them the film of popular sentimental balladry. But the best have a direct, harsh, melancholy contact with life as lived. Sadly the cow-punchers started on the long trail from Texas to the North West:

> Whoopee ti yi yo, git along little dogies,
> It's your misfortune, and none of my own.
> Whoopee ti yi yo, git along little dogies,
> For you know Wyoming will be your new home.

The gold-hunters warned others of disasters scarcely escaped:

> Don't go away, stay at home if you can,
> Stay away from that city, they call it Cheyenne,
> For big Walipe or Comache Bills
> They will lift up your hair on the dreary black hills.

These rude men were not the smiling gentry taken over by the films from the rosy Western tales of genteel novelists. They had a bleak and stinging sense of what made up so much of their lives:

> I'd rather hear a rattler rattle,
> I'd rather buck stampeding cattle,
> I'd rather go to a greaser battle,
> Than to fight the bloody In-ji-ans.

No wonder that, from time to time, they wanted to forget and chanted their drinking-songs in the flaring, sordid bar-rooms of the frontier settlements:

> Whoop-ee! drink that rot gut, drink that red nose,
> Whenever you get to town;
> Drink it straight and swig it mighty,
> Till the world goes round and round!

The harsh verses of rough, undisciplined men, nameless men huddled away at last somewhere in the West they helped to conquer. Yet these verses have the quality unattainable by any expression that is not brought to the lips by the experience of the heart.

And while the polite writers were scribbling inutilities and the cow-punchers mourning the harshness of their lot, the black slaves were singing. They built their songs upon African rhythms and used the African refrain. But the substance of their songs was transmuted into the terms of the white man's religion and their heavy fate was lightened to them by the reflection that the chosen people of the white man's God had also been slaves and oppressed in a foreign land. One cannot, of course, disassociate the words of the Negro Spirituals from their music. But the words exist as literature, as poetry, too. All moods are there: the true folk-song sadness of "Sometimes I feel like a motherless child," which destroys by contrast a whole century's sentimental home-and-mother balladry; there is the mystic gravity of "Deep River," the restrained, majestic indignation of "Go down, Moses," the delicate symbolism of "All God's Chillun Got Wings," the stricken, laconic tenderness of "Crucifixion." There are those strangely swift rhythms with their tragic undertones and their touch of mystic whimsicality, like "Joshua fit de battle of Jericho" or "Little David, play on yo harp," or "My father took a light and went to heaven." There are still other moods and rhythms in this astonishing literature of poetry and music to which must be added, too, the words of the Blues and of the Working songs. And were there not, amid a people so impassioned and so free of the self-tormenting somberness of the white tribes from under the Arctic Circle, songs of love and human delight which their leaders and men of letters, intimidated or even corrupted by the polite tradition, have not yet added to the music and literature of America?

Directly, then, the Negroes created the only body of fine

folk-poetry in America and the only body of permanently valuable music; indirectly they were responsible for that only moment in which the writers of the New England tradition, Harriet Beecher Stowe, Whittier, Lowell, stopped weaving artificial patterns and spoke out. Only one Yankee of a humbler stripe wrote a book in the high days of the New England pseudo-classics which also belongs to the folk-literature of America. That book was, of course, the autobiography of Phineas T. Barnum. . . . Many years ago a boy about twelve years old, belonging to what is now known as an alien race, found on a bookstall in the old market in Charleston where the turkey-buzzards flown in from the bay strutted with a strange gravity, two old books at a nickel apiece. They were Ik Marvel's "Reveries of a Bachelor" and "The Life of P. T. Barnum Written by Himself." The boy in question read the first book not without emotion, not without pleasure. Early youth is sentimental and easily stirred. But having read the book he forgot it and lost it. Not so with "The Life of Barnum." He read that with a severe absorption and in the course of the next few years returned to it again and again and carried throughout many succeeding years with him a hundred images and incidents from that homespun narrative which communicated somehow the very tone and taste and tang of American life. And it was not long before the boy was astonished that he was told and taught concerning a hundred books that seemed empty and artificial and meaningless and never heard anyone mention the book of which the reality and concreteness had so absorbed him for reasons that he could in those years not have explained. But he learned those reasons later and with him his whole generation learned them. Donald G. Mitchell wrote what was proper and polite and sentimental and false. Barnum, rogue and vulgarian, wrote out what he thought and saw and dreamed and knew. I tell this anecdote, impossible and unbelievable of any other country, for its symbolic significance. Only today are Americans realizing that Mitchell is trash and Barnum literature, because only today does the genteel tradition show signs of loosening its long grip upon our civilization and our life.

BOOK THREE

The Transcendentalist Revolt: Emerson and Thoreau

I

The strong rationalistic movement of the eighteenth century left deep marks upon the New England mind. But it left its marks only upon the minds of the descendants of the Puritans. No part of the discipline of Calvinism was discarded; there was no relaxation of opinion in the practical field of morals or politics. These people were by nature hostile to the revolutionary expansiveness of the Deists of the great days of France. In as quiet and seemly a fashion as possible they dropped the theological doctrines that seemed to them untenable. As early as 1785 the liturgy of King's Chapel began to omit the dogma of the Trinity; in 1815 the Trinitarian and Unitarian churches divided and theological liberalism had won its first great victory on the American Continent. But it was a victory of abstract opinion alone. Life and religion continued to be dry and meanly proper and William Ellery Channing declared only four years after the formal schism between the Churches that the philosophy upon which

Unitarianism was based was enough to wither the heart. He meant, of course, only the religious emotions. He had read both Rousseau and Godwin, yet it never in reality occurred to him that a stream of fresh ideas had been turned upon the whole of life. The Puritan distinction between the realm of grace and that of sin persisted in almost its full rigor. It was the realm of grace which the Unitarians sought first to render rational, next to sweeten and to warm. It is not without significance for the whole history of New England liberalism nor for the light it sheds upon the not unenigmatic Emerson, that an eminent cleric of our own day who wished to extend liberalism from theology to the practice of life, from the realm of grace to that of sin, was early forced to sever his connection with the Unitarian Churches. The Unitarians had no doctrine except that of the Fatherhood of God, the brotherhood of man and the leadership of Jesus. The trouble was that, according to them, man could so easily cease to be a brother if he did not live the unchanged life of Puritan propriety. The forms and molds of conduct remained quite rigid. One has the suspicion indeed that, both in the past and in the present, not a few Unitarians have felt it necessary to compensate for their heresy of thought by an anxious and eager conformity of action. I emphasize this process because it is vital to any understanding of two eminent and brave spirits: Emerson and Thoreau. It is implicated with their origins, their character, with an element of ultimate ineffectualness or, rather, of disproportion between power and result, between intellectual intrepidity and temperamental lack of vitality that marks them both. Two archers in the sun and the glittering arrows soar and hit their marks and drop without penetrating. The tips were blunted from the beginning. Opinions infinitely less subversive of both the moral and the political order than Emerson and Thoreau held with a profound sincerity have again and again brought men into cruel disrepute, into disgrace, poverty, exile. I need not recall the warmth and security of Emerson's life; Thoreau's was bleaker by choice and shorter by fatality. It was no less secure; it was hardly less respectable. Was that a golden age of freedom in which men could preach anarchism from Lyceum platforms and be heard with reverence and assent? But is not Emerson still read in schools and colleges whose administrators would take instant and violent fright at the shadow of a Wobbly across the outmost gates? Or did Emerson and Thoreau at least not attack the sacred institution of property? But was not their whole activity directed toward a radical criticism of all institutions? Does not that phrase indeed sum them up? Here, then, is an enigma. By stating it, by gradually throwing light upon it, we may come upon the precise qualities of Emerson and Thoreau and succeed in giving a clearer definition to their characters and works and influence.

II

There was insanity in the Emerson family. "The constitutional calamity of my family," the young Emerson calls it and adds: "I have so much mixture of silliness in my intellectual frame that I think Providence has tempered me against this." There was consumption in every second New England family of the period. Emerson's brother died of it and his first wife and later Thoreau. His own lungs were never strong. As early as 1827 he sought warmth and healing in a trip to Florida and South Carolina. Children, like Emerson's own small son Waldo, died in great numbers. There was a good deal of wiry resistance; there was no robustness at all. Two centuries of Puritan morals and hard living amid the New England winters on that rocky soil had thinned the blood of a race. The finest spirits were the wanest. A febrile atmosphere, hot heads and cold extremities, hangs about the whole Transcendentalist group. They were great walkers, all of them, even in rain and snow; they got drenched and chilled and came home into houses imperfectly heated and with the most primitive conveniences. Of visible beauty, except as it existed in nature, they had none. Ecclefechan was, no doubt, even more barren. But both Thomas and Jane Carlyle had an inner fire. Emerson, Thoreau, Alcott had light. But the light was almost polar. It gave no warmth.

Emerson recognized the character of his temper and situation in very early years. There was indeed little that Emerson did not mark and recognize. A few things he would not wholly admit, since the admission would have destroyed more than he could afford to see destroyed. But his mind and his perceptions were among the most lucid and unerring in the world. When he was summing himself up at the age of twenty-one he speculated whether there was not in him "a signal defect of character which neutralizes in great part the just influence my talents ought to have." And finds that defect "in an absence of common sympathies." "So cold a being," he calls himself soon thereafter. But this coldness did not issue from the heart. It reached the heart and the senses from otherwise. It was a matter of vitality, of the soil, blood, tradition, earth and sky. "I was born cold. My bodily habit is cold. I shiver in and out; don't heat to the good purposes called enthusiasm a quarter so quick and kindly as my neighbors." That self-critical plaint continues through the years. There is "a want of sufficient bottom to my nature. . . . What is called a warm heart I have not." . . . "I have not the kind affections of a pigeon . . . a barren and desolate soul. . . . I have no animal spirits; therefore, when surprised by company and kept in a chair for many hours, my heart sinks, my brow is clouded and I think I will run for Acton woods, and live with the squirrels henceforward." Nearly twenty years pass and the old plaint is the recurrent motif. "The capital defect of my nature for society is the want of animal spirits. . . . Even for those whom I really love I have not animal spirits. . . . I have so little vital force that I could not stand the dissipation of a flowing and friendly life; I should die of consumption in three months. But now I husband all my strength in *this bachelor life I lead*; no doubt I shall be a well-preserved old gentleman. . . . I think I have not the common degree of sympathy with dark, turbid, mournful, passionate natures." There were whole ranges of experience to which, thanks to the "native frost" of his soil and kind he had simply no access. "Goethe fell in love in his old age, and I would never lose the capacity of delicate and noble sentiments." One thinks of Marienbad and Ulrike. No doubt, Goethe's sentiments were delicate and noble too. But what a description of that high impassioned effort of nature to transcend itself and actually once more lighting the creative torch on the brink of mortality! But imagination can only follow the hints of experience.

There were things Emerson could not imagine. When he traveled in America the people in the hotels oppressed him "with their excessive virility." No wonder, seeing that, though married to a charming and sympathetic woman, he had to lead a "bachelor life" in order "not to die of consumption." And so it is with complete sincerity, for he was utterly honest and clear-sighted so far as his vision went, that he wrote: "There is no greater lie than a voluptuous book like Boccaccio. For it represents the pleasures of appetite, which only at rare intervals, a few times in a lifetime, are intense, and to whose acme continence is essential, as frequent, habitual and belonging to the incontinent." Since I shall be accused of indelicacy even for selecting and grouping these statements from the "Journals," I leave to the reader the easy task of analyzing in terms of fact and evident experience this finally symptomatic statement. I content myself with saying that Emerson's low vitality which he calls absence of animal spirits affected his love life from the beginning. Passionate ardor, plastic vision, high intensity of speech, the somber and triumphant glow of life as tragic and yet as infinitely precious and significant—all these things were not for him. For him and his fellows were light, high intellectual courage, hopefulness, serenity. He suspected that something kept him from still other goals. Happily for himself his insight could not pierce to the ultimate cause. "A cold mechanical preparation for a delivery as decorous—fine things, pretty things, wise things—but no arrows, no axes, no nectar, no growling, no transpiercing, no loving, no enchantment. And why? I seem to lack constitutional vigor to attempt each topic as I ought."

He was lonely by reason of his coldness. You cannot lay hold of life without passion and passionate attachments. He consoled himself with feeble rationalizations. "Love is temporary and ends with marriage . . . which dwarfs love to green fruit." He is a little of a stranger under his own roof and ruefully says: "I was a little chubby boy . . . spouting poetry from Scott and Campbell at the Latin school. But time has taken out of his vest pocket a great, awkward house . . . some acres of land, several persons full-grown and several very young persons." Sometimes he is almost blunt. "I guard my moods as anxiously as a miser his money. . . . I think then the writer ought not to be married; ought not to have a family." Other writers have said this. From how different a point of view! You cannot imagine Emerson choosing a Continental artist's alternative. He needed neither the one thing nor the other. So at moments, only at moments when the conventional conscience was asleep, he felt burdened. Nor was there comfort in friendship. "How insular and pathetically solitary are all the people we know." They all, alas, shared that lack of warmth. "I spoke of friendship, but my friends and I are fishes in our habits. As for taking Thoreau's arm, I should as soon take the arm of an elm-tree." There was no geniality, comradeship, relaxation. The merely formal and social inhibitions never lost their tenseness. "It is a pity that meetings for conversation should end as quickly as they ordinarily do. They end as soon as the blood is up and we are about to say daring and extraordinary things. They adjourn for a fortnight." One can see those meetings, for these habits and traditions have persisted in American life: the tepidness, the hesitations, the eager avoidance of impassioned statement or conviction, the constant preference of propriety to sincerity, of politeness to truth. The alternative to such contacts was social ceremony. "If Socrates were here we could go and talk with him; but Longfellow we cannot go and talk with; there is a palace and servants, and a row of bottles of different colored wines, and wine glasses, and fine coats." He comes back repeatedly to the need of a *café* of the European kind where people may sit and talk and be at ease. Friends came. But usually with the same result: "whom I freeze and who freezes me to silence, when we seem to promise to come nearer." He had his fleeting perceptions of what would ease the strain and thaw the frost. "I think wealth has lost much of its value, if it have not wine. I abstain from wine only on account of the expense." Love, friendship, and so passion and creation being inaccessible to them, Emerson and Thoreau took to nature and metaphysics and morals. Not consciously nor as a *pis-aller* or second choice. But because by their very constitutions these were their only possible objects of intense preoccupation, of experience and of expression. I am not seeking to belittle them. That they were chilled under-sexed valitudinarians, deprived of helpful and sympathetic social and intellectual atmosphere, renders their achievements only the more remarkable. But only an exact vision of them will define and explain the character of their work and influence.

High and clear souled, needing a little sunlight all the more sorely for the lack of warmth within, Emerson sought from the beginning some substitute for that faith "bare and very cold" which was all that the axes of the reformers had left. He wanted something "equi-distant from the hard, sour, iron Puritan on one side and the empty negation of the Unitarian on the other." He talks, in early entries in the "Journals," a small amount of the conventional verbiage of a young man about to enter the ministry. But these phrases about "the service of God and the war against sin" are few and sound hollow. He was on the other side, in a beyond, as far as the conventional Christian ministry went from the start and his resignation of his pastorate in 1832 on the ground that he could not administer the Communion in any mystical sense was so quiet and undemonstrative because the issues involved had never had any reality for him at all. He didn't want to be a minister anyhow—"a minister, plainest prose, the prose of prose. He is a warming-pan, a night-chair at sick-beds and rheumatic souls." In that description there comes out again, of course, the lack of inner warmth. "I like man, not men." He was aware of the higher ground: "To be a good minister it was necessary to leave the ministry." He set up, in a word, as a minister at large, determined to bring "men to God by showing them that he is, not was, speaks, not spoke." But both the entering and the leaving of the ministry were gestures dictated by the New England environment and tradition. Emerson was moralist and man of letters and like all important men of letters something of a prophet in the original Hebrew sense of a critic and a judge of his civilization and his age. In his ultimate most sober and private conclusion he was at one with all prophets past and present, prophets differing from each other only through the means by which they hope to change the stubborn heart of mankind. "All the people we see want the things we now have, and not better things. It is very certain that they will, under whatever change of forms, keep the old system. When I see changed men, I shall look for a changed world."

Plain as the fact is from the history of every literature and necessarily true if writing is not to be reduced to the level of a superior sort of clowning or acrobatic display, it is still too often forgotten that the superior man of letters is always a prophet, always exercises the precise function of the historical Hebrew prophet and is not less but more a true man of letters for that reason. Paradoxical and even confused as it may seem, it remains true—symbolically but profoundly—when I say that Emerson was the Jeremiah, the Juvenal, the Voltaire, or, if one prefers, the Shaw or Mencken of his day: man of letters and therefore reformer and prophet. Not less I repeat but more the man of letters on that account. This is nowhere clearer than in his literary judgments and perceptions. They drive powerfully to the center and have been neglected too long.

"Poetry must be as new as foam and as old as the rock." He knew what was wanted in the higher, in the highest and deepest sense. American literature he saw clearly to be "respectable, not valid. Irving thin, and Channing thin and Bryant and Dana; Prescott and Bancroft . . . Longfellow, Holmes, Lowell; all excellent in their way." He knew what was forgotten then and later that none of these writers stirred any depths. "Lowell's new poems . . . rather express his wish, his ambition, than the uncontrollable interior impulse." The amusing professors who have treated that literary group as a group of authentic poets needed only to have gone to Emerson. "We have not had since ten years a pamphlet which I have saved to bind." There came Thoreau; later, with whatever reservations, Whitman. That was all. Everywhere he saw "the insanity that comes of inaction and tradition." His vision was quite incorruptible. Amid the high years of supine Tennyson worship he wrote: "Tennyson is a beautiful half poet . . . I think he got his inspiration in gardens. . . . Many of Tennyson's poems are only the sublime of magazine poems . . . the poetry of an exquisite . . . prettyness carried out to the infinite. . . . He is content to think and speak a sort of king's English, embodying the sense of well-bred successful men, and by no means of the best and highest men: he speaks the sense of the day, and not the sense of grand men, the sense of the first class, identical in all ages." His instinct for the valid, the permanent, the central never wavered. Thus he perceived rather than knew that "Goethe is the pivotal man of the old and the new times with us. He shuts up the old, he opens the new. He was the cow from which all their milk was drawn." I say he perceived rather than knew this because his actual contact with Goethe's works was small. He knew "Meister" in the Carlyle translation; many years after Goethe's death and so after the publication of the second part of "Faust" he still speaks of the "Helena," showing that he never got beyond Carlyle's account of the fragment. He betrays almost no knowledge of the poetry. But his instincts, which he had learned to trust, were trustworthy. "Life consists in what a man is thinking all day." That is prophetic of the theories of the latest school of fiction. And: "These novels will give way, by and by, to diaries or autobiographies—captivating books, if only a man knew how to choose among what he calls his experiences that which is really his experience, and how to record truth truly."

A great critic, evidently, when he is not preaching or trans-cendentalizing or slumping into a silly weakness for Sweden-borgianism. So great a critic, at least fragmentarily—but then, he is a man of fragments like Novalis—that he knew not only what ailed American literature but knew, trans-cending the very make-up of his body and his temperament, what ailed himself: the lack of intensity, of severity, of ab-sorption in the concrete coil of things. "A currency of words is accepted. I suppose the evil may be cured by this rank rabble party, the Jacksonism of the country, heedless of Eng-lish and of all literature—a stone cut out of the ground with-out hands: they may root out the hollow dilettanteism of our cultivation in the coarsest way and the newborn may be-gin again to frame their world with greater advantage. . . . What a pity that we cannot curse and swear in good society! Cannot the stinging dialect of the sailors be domesticated? It is the best rhetoric and for a hundred occasions, those for-bidden words are the only good ones. . . . This profane swearing and bar-room wit has salt and fire in it. . . . One who wishes to refresh himself by contact with the bone and sinew of society must avoid what is called the respectable portion of his city and neighborhood. . . . Dante knows 'God damn' and can be rowdy if he please, and he does please." These passages add a welcome shadow to the tire-less metaphysical optimism of Emerson's more formal works and sayings. He must have had moments in which that ever-lasting brightness and high, piping note of his wearied him. But low vitality, custom and habit, origin and expectation kept him publicly on his rarefied heights, willing to do with-out "salt and fire."

His practical opinions, too, have in the "Journals" a sting and edge which his public utterances lack. Very early he declared himself suspicious of the cleanness of hand and purity of heart of "a whole nation roaring patriotism at the top of its voice." He wished that "non-resistance" might be tried fairly; he considered soldiers "an offensive spectacle" and a ridiculous one; he declared war to be "unmanlike" and exposed the "vulgar error that a gentleman must be ready to fight." In regard to the Fugitive Slave Law he has for once the "salt and fire" of speech. "This filthy enactment was made in the nineteenth century, by people who could read and write. By God, I will not obey it. . . . An Infamy has fallen on Massachusetts, that clouds the daylight and takes away the comfort out of every hour. . . . All I have and all I can do shall be given and done in opposition to the execution of this law." He went to an anti-slavery meeting and was howled down by the mob. But there was, alas, too little that could cloud the daylight for him. He is magnificent on the broadest of issues. "Do not be too timid and squeamish about your actions. All life is an experiment." But his brother died "pure, almost untempted." And "there can be no high culture without pure morals." What a word: pure! Not intense or brave or holy or fruitful or creative or enriching or wise or compassionate. Pure—the negation of negations, the most stripped and meaningless of concepts. Yet the keyword that unlocks the mystery of this intrepid, sagacious, first-rate mind, a mind that had no commerce with deep, primordial, tragic, human things, an almost abstract, disembodied mind, fine but thin, bloodless and so unclouded, never somber, almost never troubled to its depth because it had no direct contact with the problems and conflicts—nine-tenths of human life—which spring from human passions, relations, longings, triumphs, despairs.

III

He was born to be a Transcendentalist. It was the philosophy that he needed. He understood perfectly the doctrines on which it was based without much contact with the documents composed by its originators. Much trickled through Wordsworth, more through Coleridge. How much Kant Emerson actually read for himself is not quite clear. There is a note concerning his having read Hegel, but the note is without precision. Nevertheless his central statement in a lecture delivered in Boston in 1842 is not only exact but full. He begins with the necessary questioning of the phenomenal world as anything but phenomenal, a world, then, of mere appearances and leaps rather blithely but logically enough to the extreme conclusion that "it is always our own thought that we perceive." Nature, literature, history are thus subjective phenomena, rank and value are assigned by the mind alone. This Subject, this almost Fichtean man respects nothing, labor, government, the law, the state except in so far as these "reiterate the law of his mind." This is, of course, Germanic Protestantism or, as Mr. Santayana has called it, philosophic egotism raised to the highest power. "I—this world which is called I—is the mold into which the world is poured like wax." A happy image by which to body forth the character of the Kantian categories which, toward the end of the lecture in question, he explains with technical accuracy: "imperative forms" which, anterior to all experience

118

and preëxistent in the mind, mold and shape the formless chaos of whatever external reality does exist into the world we know. Starting with Kant, but not following him to the "Critique of Practical Reason," Emerson goes to the extreme lengths of romantic idealism and uses phrases dangerously like those that were later to be used by the Christian Scientists.

This fact, that Emerson starts with a definite, above all, with this definite metaphysic is of the utmost importance. His extreme revolutionary utterances, precious to us only through our hardier and more realistic use and interpretation of them, are in him and his Transcendentalist contemporaries, the utterances of a metaphysically creative Subject, not of an ethically or politically active man. The followers of Fichte, declaring the creative freedom of the individual, took their philosophy in a practical sense. There was romantic vagabondage, there were queer marryings and unmarryings and givings in marriage among them. Not so in New England. The inner light can bear witness to what it pleases and the creative Ego can shape the world in its own image. And so the New England Transcendentalists projected a world in which everything was intellectually dared but in which practically (except in the matter of anti-slavery), nothing was done. On one whole important side of life or, rather, on all aspects of life save one, the creative Ego of New England projected over again the world that already was and the pronouncement of doctrines that should have rent civilization like the temple's veil were accompanied by lives of the utmost conformity. Only extreme shallowness would utter the word hypocrisy here. I have already explained how, as a matter of mere physiology, Emerson and Thoreau were so divided from the normal average of mankind, not to speak of genius or exorbitance, that they had no inner reason to use their intuitive re-creation of the world to any more unconventional purposes than they did. Nor was this all. The New England mind clung to its God. Calvinistic dualism was abolished at least in theory. God remained. Souls rose from the infinite Oversoul "within which every man's particular being is contained," within that eternal One "the act of seeing and the thing seen, the seer and the spectacle, the subject and the object" are identical. The One who, through the organs of individual souls, creates the world is good, tends wholly toward wisdom, virtue, beauty, power. Thus evil is either a figment or a thing wrongly interpreted, something "whose poetry is not yet written." "The simplest person who in his integrity worships God, becomes God." The universe is unshadowed. A cosmic optimism bathes time and eternity in its equal glow.

Angry Dualists, like Mr. Paul Elmer More, have blamed Emerson for neglecting so wholly the evil that is under the sun. And it is indeed in the long run profoundly irritating and his great defect that he wholly neglects human suffering. But that is not what the Dualists mean. They are thinking of sin and morals and laws and prisons, of repentances and punishments, of judging and being judged. It is Emerson's precise virtue, the virtue of his mystical idealism, that he omits evil in the Puritanic sense. If ever there was a civilization in which evil, in the utterly questionable sense of sin, had been emphasized to a destructive and corrupting extent, it was and is America. Emerson missed the inherent and unescapable tragedy of man: suffering and aspiration beyond the possibilities of mortality; injustice and disease and death with life unfulfilled. He missed that, as Thoreau missed it and Whitman missed it and all the earlier proclaimers of the ultimate democratic hope. But that he dropped sin from his vision of things is all but his highest claim as a prophet and a teacher of his time and folk. He was not heeded. He has, in this respect, never been heeded. The forces arrayed against his spirit were and are too dark, massive, turbulent. And they have in their primitive and dreadful way what he lacked in his lucid and saving one—intensity. The voice of so virginal a spirit does not penetrate the brawlings of the world. Innumerable adolescents have found their first liberation through the pages of Emerson. But his teachings have slipped from them and they have become sinners and conformers. It takes a sharper monition to cleave through. The arrows, as I said, were blunted from the start.

IV

It is against the background of Emerson's very special temperament and of the philosophy which that temperament so inevitably adopted that his works as a whole must be regarded. I say: as a whole. Yet wholeness of any kind is precisely what Emerson lacks. He is a man, not of fragments but of aphorisms. It is a reflection on the unskillfulness of our literary scholarship that there does not exist a volume of aphorisms in prose and verse drawn from Emerson's writings. Such a volume would bring the core and true character of both his mind and style far closer to succeeding generations than those wavering and discontinuous discourses. It would set into the highest relief, stripped of its mystical swathings, that doctrine of the free creative individual which is Emerson's great gift to his civilization. And that gift is more sorely needed than ever. The dark, unindividualized mass, rolling nearer and nearer to the few embattled heights on which freemen hold out, threatens to engulf us all.

The doctrine is fully implicit if not fully expressed in that early and memorable discourse "The American Scholar," which is referred to as a declaration of independence from literary Colonialism—its least important aspect—but which if read and taken to heart on any American campus today would cause an intellectual riot and extra meetings of solemn trustees. "Each age must write its own books. . . . The books of an older period will not fit this." What a truth, partial but profound and necessary, for a class-room in English. "The guide is a tyrant. . . . Only so much do I know as I have lived." The concept of literature as expression, fought by all moldy pedagogues to this day is announced here in 1837. I say this not out of unnecessary rudeness, but because the pedagogues, even the nobler kind, feign to revere Emerson and mis-report him. You will find neither his fiery individualism nor his teaching concerning the creative processes of the mind set down in Paul Elmer More's chapter in the "Cambridge History of American Literature." Emersonianism is there defined as "a volatile and heady liquid." This liquid, closely examined, turns out to be a solid as impenetrable as the rock. "Is it not the chief disgrace in the world, not to be an unit . . . not to yield that peculiar fruit which each man was created to bear, but to be reckoned in the gross, in the hundred or the thousand, of the party, the section, to which we belong?" But this rock is a danger and an offense now as it was then to "meek young men who grow up in libraries," to "the scholars" who are "addressed as women" and do not hear "the rough, spontaneous conversation of men." Either Emerson was too hopeful or else things have grown worse since his day. For the rough, spontaneous conversation of men in America is usually a herd-growling as that of the scholars is a herd-bleating and youth seeks as vainly for council from either kind. But Emerson is still there: "In yourself slumbers the whole of reason; it is for you to know all, it is for you to dare all."

The early essays on Nature are too entangled in idealistic metaphysics to sound very clearly across the years. I do not mean that the problem of appearance and reality is settled or that the Kantian analysis is either false or unimportant. But that particular problem is not ours; it is not a problem of this age. Also in "Nature" there are still strictly clerical vestiges. "What is a farm but a mute gospel? . . . Beauty is the mark God sets upon virtue." We can make nothing of that. Emerson dragged his feeble teleology along with him to the end. But in the greater "Essays" we can forget and dismiss it. From time to time Emerson was always tempted to declare: "I believe in Eternity." The irresponsible verbiage fades under the fire, under, at least, the brilliant light of the central and memorable passages concerning the individual and the individual's creative function.

Those central passages are in the essays on "Self-Reliance" and on "The Poet." Successive Young Americas in search of a native tradition, of a usable past, will find both here. For the recurrent and incessant danger of civilization is the hardening of its forms and processes into empty tyrannies that throttle and do not sustain or nourish the soul. Salvation comes from the individual who breaks these forms, re-envisages ultimate reality, creates first his own autonomy, then freedom and flexibility for his fellows. It is that individual, that savior and renewer, needed at all times and in all lands, needed, above all in American life as a revolutionary, in American letters as a poet and not an artificer, whom Emerson describes and foretells:

> Cast the bantling on the rocks,
> Suckle him with the she-wolf's teat;
> Wintered with the hawk and fox,
> Power and speed be hands and feet.

I shall quote largely from the essay on "Self-Reliance." It is known; it is neither heeded nor heard. Its great sayings are hushed in the context and the book by Emerson's lack of structural emphasis, his lack of sustained intensity, the metaphysical implications, the very title. The title is out of Samuel Smiles or Y. M. C. A. discourses. The essay is, for its length and non-technical nature, the most revolutionary document in modern literature. Here, then, is the American charter, the unbinding and not binding creed of the libertarian: "Imitation is suicide. . . . The virtue in most request is conformity. . . . It loves not realities and creators, but names and customs. . . . Society everywhere is a conspiracy against the manhood of every one of its members . . . a joint stock-company, in which the members agree, for the better security of his bread to each shareholder, to surrender the liberty and culture of the eater. . . . Whoso would be a man must be a non-conformist. He who would gather immortal palms must not be hindered by the name of goodness, but must explore if it be goodness. Nothing is at last sacred but the integrity of your own mind. Absolve you to yourself. . . . No law can be sacred to me but that of my nature. Good and bad are but names very readily transferable to that or this; the only right is what is after my constitution, the only wrong what is against it. . . . I am ashamed to think how easily we capitulate to badges and names, to large societies and dead institutions. . . . What I must do is all that concerns me, not what the people think. . . . Is it so bad, then, to be misunderstood? . . . Let us affront and reprimand the smooth mediocrity and squalid contentment of the times. . . . Our housekeeping is mendicant, our arts, our occupations, our marriages, our religion— society has chosen them for us. . . . Insist on yourself; never imitate. . . . The reliance on Property, including the reliance on governments which protect it, is the want of self-reliance. . . . A cultivated man becomes ashamed of his property . . . he hates what he has, if he see that it is accidental, came to him by inheritance or gift, or crime. . . . It does not belong to him, but merely lies there, because no revolution or no robber takes it away."

Did Emerson mean all that? The answer to that question should by now be clear. He meant it within his temperamental limitations of an essential chill of nature on the one hand, of religiosity channeled into a mixture of Platonism and Kantianism on the other. To save him for the present and the future we must dismiss the wilted verbiage about "the resolution of all into the ever-blessed one," as well as the parochial limitation: "The bold sensualist will use the name of philosophy to gild his crimes." The descendant of the Puritans could not write "bold murderer" or slanderer or bearer of false witness or practicer of cruelty; he could not name the name of anyone who is a menace. He had to defend himself from the suspicion of lending support to any variety or freshness or freedom in the life of the senses. These things, to keep Emerson alive and usable, we must dismiss; we must treat the great sayings and doctrines as though he meant them in a universal and permanent sense. He is memorable for the creative boldness and flexibility of his intuitions which he himself was unable to integrate with the life either of thought or of action. Thus in this same astonishing essay he becomes for five fiery and then forgotten minutes a forerunner of Nietzsche. "Do not tell me of my obligation to put all poor men in good situations. Are they *my* poor? I grudge the dollar, the dime, the cent, I give to such men as do not belong to me and to whom I do not belong. There is a class of persons to whom by all spiritual affinity I am bought and sold; for them I will go to prison, if need be; but your miscellaneous popular charities: the education of college fools, the building of meeting-houses . . . alms to sots. . . . I sometimes succumb and give the dollar; it is a wicked dollar which bye and bye I shall have the manhood to withhold." This is far more questionable and one-sided and limited than Emerson's individualism. But for ten minutes he had the intuition of an ethic wholly divorced from his race, tradition, personal temper. That, too, is something, is much and is another element in the portrait of one whose intuitions always went far beyond either his power to think or his power to act.

126

A lazy and probably not always candid tradition has assigned to other essays an importance they do not possess. In "Compensation" Emerson plays with questionable fancies; the optimism becomes false and pink. There are great flashes here, as everywhere: "The history of persecution is a history of endeavors to cheat nature, to make water run up hill, to twist a rope of sand. . . . Every burned book or house enlightens the world." They are only flashes. The doctrine of Compensation in itself is an attempt to cheat nature, too, to avoid the acceptance of life as tragic. The essay on "The Over-Soul" reaches an almost Christian Science or New Thought depth; a beautiful spirit is behind it; Emerson never has less than that. But the ideas are without fortitude, edge or any conformity with the nature of things. "Spiritual Laws," "Friendship," "Heroism," "Circles," and various other of the essays contain isolated aphorisms that are memorable. As wholes they are part of that same flight from the core and kernel of human experience, the tragic character of which Emerson could not face.

The essay on The Poet completes the portrait and doctrine of the individual by adding the necessity of expression to the fact of being. As the former is a charter for American life, the latter may be a charter for American literature. It begins lamely enough. Those who pretend to "an inclination for whatever is elegant" are found to be "selfish and sensual." That is profoundly true. But one suspects Emerson's use of those words. They represent the Puritan *clichés* of thought. All men are self-regarding. He is the good man whose self cannot be at peace while others suffer pain or injustice. All normal men are sensual. He is the good man who instinctively integrates the free play of the senses with love, beauty and loving-kindness. But soon Emerson settles down to his real subject and is magnificent, epoch-making, for several pages. With his thoughts, as we know from the "Journals," shrewdly enough upon his contemporaries, including Tennyson, he dismisses the artificers: "Even poets are contented with a civil and conformed manner of living, and to write poems from the fancy, at a safe distance from their own experience." But he proceeds almost at once to the root of the matter. The Poet "is isolated among his contemporaries by truth and by his art, but with this consolation in his pursuits that they will draw all men sooner or later. *For all men live by truth, and stand in need of expression.*" Here is the foundation of all art, a foundation to which no æsthetic theories reach. And since it is by truth that men live, the expression they ask of the poet must be rooted in experience. "The sign and credentials of the poet are that he announces that which no man foretold. . . . He is the only teller of news, for he was present and privy to the appearance which he describes. . . . For we do not speak now of men of poetical talents, or of industry and skill in metre, but of the true poet." From the utterance of these sentences on there should have been little or no debate in America concerning the character of literature; there should have been little opposition to either realism or naturalism when these appeared and the academic swingers of critical yard-sticks should have been silenced. Here again Emerson was not heeded because he did not heed himself, because he did not himself know the differences in value between his great sayings and his maunderings about "Orpheus, Empedocles . . . Swedenborg." The great sayings were wrapped in cotton-wool; their impact was blunted. But they are final. Emerson knew the character of the creative mind. He was also acquainted with its processes: "The thought and the form are equal in the order of time, but in the order of genesis the thought is prior to the form. The poet has a new thought; he has a whole new experience to unfold; he will tell us how it was with him and all men will be the richer in his fortune. *For the experience of each new age requires a new confession, and the world seems always waiting for its poet.*" The confession of the new ages from Whitman to Dreiser was resisted. Yet America pretended to have listened to Emerson. Readers clung to his questionable and unfruitful metaphysics: "The Universe is the externisation of the soul," and erected inner defenses against his integration of literature with life: "The chief value of the new fact is to enhance the great and constant fact of life, which can dwarf any and every circumstance. . . . *Expression is organic,* or, the new type which things themselves take when liberated." In brief, Emerson set forth unmistakably the still neglected but inevitable notion of literature as a continuous interpretation of experience in a dynamic world. As early as 1836 he had written:

> Striving to be man, the worm
> Mounts through all the spires of form.

Hence he knew that "the quality of the imagination is to flow and not to freeze." And as though to rob American criticism of any excuse for repeating its old preceptist errors held within a supposedly static, stratified and rigid world, he added: "I look in vain for the poet whom I describe. We do not with sufficient plainness or sufficient profoundness address ourselves to life, nor dare we chant our own times and social circumstance." He went beyond this, grasping the autobiographic character of great literature by his declaration that it was "Dante's praise that he dared to write his autobiography in colossal cipher, or into universality." In one of his sudden blazes of intuition he ends with a maxim quite worthy of Goethe: "Art is the path of the creator to his work."

Emerson did not add to his stock of ideas in later works or years. Occasionally as in the "I must absolve me to myself" of "Representative Men" he repeats not only the same thought, but uses the same formula. His criticism of the undifferentiated democratic mass is implicit in his individualism; the precious doctrine of the necessary flexibility of life and art in a dynamic universe receives confirmation but is not extended in the later writings. There are sharp and memorable sayings—"All conservatives are such from personal defects"—in the "Conduct of Life"; there are curious prophetic glimpses of the industrial revolution; there is, of course, a reiteration of the mysticism of the over-soul and compensation doctrines. He becomes more and more strictly a Kantian on one side, and expresses his complete agreement with the categorical imperative as a sufficing guide of action in "Society and Solitude." There is the same mingling as in the great central essays of prophetic and revolutionary individualism with relapses into New England primness at its wanest. The thing to do to save Emerson is, as I have sufficiently pointed out, to strip the chief doctrines of the great essays from the mysticism and relapses into conventional modes of feeling, to gather from the other works earlier and later all that confirms and fortifies those central and saving doctrines and thus to liberate in Emerson that element of the permanent which he undoubtedly possesses. "Duration," writes André Gide in a fine passage, "is promised only to those writers who can offer new nourishment to successive generations; for each generation brings with it a hunger of its own." By that test Emerson can be made to endure; he can be made to relive; he can be made to reach the ears of men. His low vitality and lack of intensity, his consequent exclusion of both passion and the tragic—all that accounts for his too respectable status—can be gradually eliminated from his work. Into his magnificent and liberating central doctrines new American generations can pour their ardor and their hope. From this coöperation there can arise an authentic and perdurable classic whose name is Emerson.

V

The re-creation of that classic is made easier by the existence of "English Traits" and of the verses. The book on England and the English adds a touch of manly strength and human shrewdness to the image of Emerson. Reading it one forgets that he is capable of much in his work that is feeble and vaporous. One forgets the mutually repellent particles out of which the essays are built. Emerson shows himself a sagacious judge of men, of historical experiences, of national characteristics; he shows himself capable of writing with continuity, sobriety, precision. There is an unexpected touch of satiric wit in many of the observations; all of them are so sound, so full of a classical balance and propriety of judgment that more than seventy years with their vast changes and cataclysms have left their truth and pertinence untouched. Away from Concord, freed from the inhibitions and atmosphere of the ancestral scene, Emerson loses much of both his feeble and his febrile aspects; he takes on intellectual vigor and tone. His most precious qualities are absent from "English Traits," but also his most irritating ones. The book is a refreshing and memorable corrective to an impression of the looser and less well-knit qualities of his mind and work.

Turning to the poems we are back with the more familiar Emerson, with his gold and his dross. By dross I do not mean the defective measures, the gritty rimes, the sediments of a blank and conventional diction in the earlier poems. In the mass of his better work in verse these things are wholly negligible. The dross in the verse as in the prose is the vague mysticism, the feebly stubborn optimism, the frequent lack of even intellectual edge and fire. But when all this dross is simply neglected and put out of mind there remains a small body of verse not yet perhaps quite equaled by any formal poet in America. Highest among the verses stand "Days." These eleven lines are unique in American literature, which has all qualities save sublimity and severity. Here both are found. Nor has it been sufficiently noted that Emerson approaches the severity of these verses not a few times in the blank-verse pieces, as in the closing lines of "Sea-Shore":

> Planting strange fruits and sunshine on the shore,
> I make some coast alluring, some lone isle,
> To distant men, who must go there, or die.

Lines like these throw a light upon his great desire in Europe to see not only Wordsworth and Coleridge and Carlyle but also Landor. He had a Landorian taste for lucid serenity and severity. And he had isolated moments when he went beyond Landor in that he treated with that high, cool lucidity the homely scenes and subjects of the New England countryside. I wonder whether Mr. Robert Frost has not at some time deeply pondered the blank-verse portion of "Hamatreya" with its astonishing opening lines:

> Minott, Lee, Willard, Hosmer, Merriam, Flint,
> Possessed the land which rendered to their toil
> Hay, corn, roots, hemp, flax, apples, wool and wood,

and its severe and somber ending:

> Ah, the hot owner sees not Death, who adds
> Him to his land, a lump of mould the more.

"The Snow-Storm" is better known and so is the beautiful "Forbearance" with its softer and more romantic touch. Comparatively neglected are "The Day's Ration," "Blight" and "Musketaquid," pieces of uneven execution but each containing lines which have that rare and refreshing note of severity:

> To our sick eyes
> The stunted tree looks sick, the summer short,
> Clouds shade the sun, which will not tan our hay,
> And nothing thrives to reach its natural term;
> And life, shorn of its venerable length,
> Even at its greatest space is a defeat,
> And dies in anger that it was a dupe.

The more visionary pieces in rime are more accessible in their beauty. Of these the most perfect is, of course, "The Problem" with its magnificent restatement of the character of the creative process and the passage from "Not from a

133

vain or shallow thought" to "With Andes and with Ararat" which, to speak on the manner of the old-fashioned critic, is probably the high-water mark of American poetry prior to the work of the present generation. Linked with it is the exquisite "Rhodora" with its amusingly disputed passage:

> Tell them, dear, that if eyes were made for seeing,
> Then Beauty is its own excuse for being,

the plangent "Good-bye, proud world," the only one of Emerson's strictly personal poems that at all succeeds in convincing the mind and the heart, and single passages of a memorable sort from the harsh, tonic and veracious:

> 'Tis the day of the chattel,
> Web to weave and corn to grind;
> Things are in the saddle
> And ride mankind,

to the more mystical

> The hero is not fed on sweets,
> Daily his own heart he eats,

and the more purely gnomic verses which, at their best, have a large and sustaining quality:

> Though love repine, and reason chafe,
> There came a voice without reply—
> " 'Tis man's perdition to be safe,
> When for the truth he ought to die."

Nor does Emerson lack the touch of magic which the poet needs. He has it in:

> Over me soared the eternal sky
> Full of light and of deity,

134

and in

> And the poor grass shall plot and plan
> What it will do when it is man,

and in

> Flowering April cools and dies
> In the insufficient skies

and in dozens of other passages. Needless to say, there are
no poems of a fundamentally personal, passionate and lyrical
nature. But such poetry or, in fact, such prose, did not belong
to the America of his section and his age. But if, during the
greater part of the nineteenth century, there had not been
an almost complete absence not only of poetry but of poetical
taste in America, it could never have occurred to anyone
to question the preëminence of Emerson as a poet, not only
in quality but in kind, over all American poets save Whitman alone. What, in fact, astonishes the modern critic is the
treatment that Emerson as a whole has received at the hands
of his conservative predecessors. They accepted Emerson's
works as all equivalent, which is absurd; they exercised no
analysis upon his personality; they treated him with a certain awe. Yet you will never get from them the patent fact
that of all the New England group he alone has a self-
sustaining and permanent existence, that Longfellow, Whittier, Holmes, Lowell, are underbrush about this single soaring tree. He was a man among Babbits and a musician among
the dumb. I am assuredly not blind to his limitations: the
cool and sluggish blood with its consequent old maidenish-
ness of attitude; the exclusion from his vision of suffering
and so of life as tragic; the lack of self-critical intellectual

steadiness, so that he can talk almost like Goethe and almost like Mary Baker G. Eddy on the same page. Yet I have written to no purpose if it is not clear that he is, in his minor and limited way, a classic. For what is a classic? Not a perfect writer. The day, I hope, is past when people out of a sense of duty struggle through "Love's Labour's Lost" or "Two Gentlemen of Verona" or the minor plays of Goethe or the slap-stick farces of Molière. A classic is simply a writer who has left certain works or even pages which the youth of each generation can and does by some instinctive and passionate reinterpretation make its own. This mark of the classic will increasingly belong to Emerson as his terrible Collected Works in I do not know how many hideous volumes are sedulously neglected and a volume containing the greater part of the essays on "Self-Reliance" and "The Poet," a thousand aphorisms from the "Journals" and the formal writings and a handful of verses is put into the hands of sophomores and juniors of both sexes, not as a part of "required reading" but as a summons away from the timid, the mean, the conventional, the imitative and toward creative living and creative speech.

VI

There is a hard pathos about Thoreau, the wanness of a stripped, unblossoming tree against a gray sky. He was intellectually one of the bravest men that ever lived, and also a clammy prig. He was a prose-stylist of singular and signal excellence and left no complete book behind him. The highest austerity assumes an inner fire; Thoreau did not even, like Emerson, recognize the necessary existence of warmth by regretting his want of it. He was wholly unaware of his human limitations, a bachelor and bachelor of nature from beginning to end. "He was a protestant," Emerson wrote of him after his too early death, "à l'outrance, and few lives contain so many renunciations. He was bred to no profession, he never married, he lived alone, he never went to church, he never voted, he refused to pay a tax to the state, he ate no flesh, he drank no wine, he never knew the use of tobacco, and, though a naturalist, he used neither trap nor gun." This is the portrait—is it not?—of a great sage. But a moment later Emerson, continuing the praise of his friend, goes on: "He had no temptations to fight against,—no appetites, no passions, no taste for elegant trifles. . . ." Well, if that was true, where were his renunciations? The picture of a great sage instantly changes into that of a subnormal valetudinarian. Strike the descendants of the Puritans where you will; as soon as they touch the moral life they talk nonsense. They can attain insight into politics, philosophy, even beauty. In regard to all matters of personal character and conduct, they babble formulas and contradictions. Hence they never produce great drama or great fiction; they are confined to the essay and to verse.

   Which is the true Thoreau, the strong man curbed or the defective man? Thrice in the "Journals" and the "Letters" Thoreau speaks of sex. . . . Yes, excellent reader, I have to "drag in" sex here as I shall do again and again. God dragged it in from the beginning of things, and even in New Hampshire and Alabama and Kansas the common instinctive good sense of mankind has not been so wholly warped that people do not recognize a man unmanned and a barren woman as tragic figures—tragic as a matter of spiritual experience and not only of physical fact. . . . Thrice, then, in his "Journals" and "Letters" Thoreau spoke of sex. "I would preserve purity in act and thought, as I would cherish the memory of my mother. A companion can possess no worse quality than vulgarity. If I find that he is not habitually reverent of the fact of sex, I, even I, will not associate with him. I will cast the first stone. A man's speech on this subject should, of course, be ever as reverent and chaste and simple as if it were to be heard by the ears of maidens." Now Rabelaisian speech is characteristic of the weak or ill-mated, not of the strong and well-mated. But that was not the distinction in Thoreau's mind. To him interest in sex was unnatural and repugnant in itself. For it is evidently impossible to say anything true or pertinent on sex in terms chaste and simple enough for a New England maiden of, say, 1840. His repugnance is complete. The fearless anarchist soul faced by this subject cringes and flees. Once in his "Letters" Thoreau launches forth upon an almost formal discourse on love and marriage. And this is what he produces: "If it is the result of a pure love, there can be nothing sensual in marriage. Chastity is something positive, not negative. It is the virtue of the married especially. All lusts or base pleasures must give place to loftier delights. . . . Virginity, too, is a budding flower, and by an impure marriage the virgin is deflowered. Whoever loves flowers, loves virgins and chastity." Seriously questioned by a physician I do not suppose Thoreau would have been prepared to maintain that positive chastity is the special virtue of marriage within which the wife must continue a virgin. The extinction

138

of the race was not among his doctrines. I suspect that he did not, in fact, mean anything. He was hopelessly inhibited, probably to the point of psychical impotence or else physiologically hopelessly undersexed and simply on this subject made the conventional pseudo-idealistic noise. The third passage, which is also from the "Letters," has a touch of the grimly farcical. "I have had a tragic correspondence, for the most part all on one side, with Miss ———. She did really wish to—I hesitate to write—marry me. That is the way they spell it. Of course I did not write a deliberate answer. How could I deliberate upon it? I sent back as distinct a *no* as I have learned to pronounce. . . . I wished that it might burst, like hollow shot, after it had struck and buried itself." The point of this quotation is not, of course, in Thoreau's horror at such a suggestion from a particular individual, but in his horror of the suggestion being made at all. To these three passages another, an entry made by Thoreau in his Journal at the age of thirty-four, should be added. "The society of young women is the most unprofitable I have ever tried. They are so light and flighty that you can never be sure whether they are there or not there. I prefer to talk with the more staid and settled, settled for life, in every sense." I think it is clear from this quotation that young women faintly troubled him, but that this faint emotion turned into strong repulsion, because he was aware of the fact that nature had somehow excluded him from all those appetences and activities with which youth is concerned.

The reason for these quotations and for this analysis is not far to seek. Sex, contrary to the common uninstructed opinion, is not peripheral and localized, but pervasive. It is like one drop of the most powerful coloring matter in the world dropped into a great jar of colorless water. It tinges every atom of the water. All that a man is, does, thinks, says, produces is, consciously or unconsciously, tinged by that all-powerful element. Now Thoreau is a man and a writer, so to speak, in black and white. There is no color in him. A man like an etching. Nature had forgotten her drop of color in the jar. In one of his happiest critical moments Lowell spoke of Thoreau's style: "The language has an antique purity like wine grown colorless with age." Only this wine had not grown colorless; it was so from the beginning. And that is probably the reason why Thoreau's style, for all its crystalline purity and lucidity, its happy balance, its exquisite moderation, does not continuously hold the reader. It is perhaps the best style yet written by an American. It slips from one's psychical grasp and is best tasted in single passages. It is the style of a great writer but of a defective man.

Nor is this all. How could Thoreau, once more, in his age and land, have become and freely have been a complete philosophical anarchist, a total negator of the absolute value of the institutions of society? How could he have escaped jail except for that one voluntary night in it? Because his arrows, too, were blunted from the beginning. He was able to exclude from his life and so from his teaching the most burning of issues. He neither burned within nor set other hearts on fire. And so one let him be. He was queer but not dangerous. He could announce the doctrine of Civil Disobedience from the Lyceum platform. Massachusetts knew that he was pure and harmless. He offended no deeply cherished prejudices and integrated his doctrine of non-coöperation exclusively with that doctrine of abolitionism which even its enemies came gradually to resist with a bad conscience. Imagine him announcing his doctrines with the ardor of a normal man of high talent, extending his denial of institutions to that of marriage, preaching civil disobedience for any cause less strictly ethical in New England eyes than that of freeing the slaves! Draft-dodgers in '61 were not gently handled, conscientious objectors in 1918 were suspended by their wrists in foul dungeons. There is scarcely a country today in which men are not in prison for speech far less incendiary in appearance than was Thoreau's. But Massachusetts knew that he was pure and a gentleman of Concord. His name was neither Sacco nor Vanzetti and the industrial revolution had not yet reached an acute stage and the masters were not yet nervous. Even more truly than in the case of Emerson we must abstract the teaching from the man and his age in order to save it for ourselves and for the future.

His great and central and tonic doctrine of independence of the material and of the machinery of civilization must be tested quite apart from himself. For him it was easy; for him it was a temerity of thought but not of action. A man can live in the woods easily enough if he have no passions, affections, no human cares and solicitudes; if he desires neither the love of woman nor the hope of posterity nor friendship nor hospitality nor the human cheer of morning or of evening fire. Such a man's renunciations are few and others can learn but little from his doctrine. It must cease almost to become his before it can be effectual. This is not to say that Thoreau is not admirable in himself. There is something high and severe, like a mathematical passion, about him and his life. His simplicity and courage have a faint icy pathos. Alone, almost unfriended, except for those months of his youth in Emerson's house, he walks the woods and winter uplands, chatting detachedly with wanderers and laborers, or else, especially in the early years, drifts about in Concord, content to be the queerest of yokels, sent on errands by the jailer, grimly hugging to himself this obscurity and lowliness as a patent of freedom. He goes to New York, but the city has no lure for him who is almost disembodied and strikes him as simply sordid and useless and noisy. The disease that killed him must have clung to him for years with its fevers, cold and hot, its weakness, its languor. He disdains to make a note of his suffering. He dies as he has lived with a cold, abstract cheer and wintry courage. He had acquired neither love nor obligations in the world; he left no one and nothing but himself. Time shrank. But he who has nothing to regret nor to leave except the hills and woods is not time's fool. "I *suppose* that I have not many months to live: But, of course, I know nothing about it. I may add that I am enjoying existence as much as ever, and regret nothing." These words are from his last letter. A wraith-like man. A man possible only in New England. Men have gone into the desert and crucified the flesh for years or, like the Hindoo ascetics, crippled their bodies by long slow torture and have not attained that frozen freedom from all human longings, temptations, exultations, despairs that was the birthright of Thoreau. His doctrine is very great but also infinitely more difficult and intricate than he dreamed. It is, of course, still a convention, though a fading one, in certain circles in

America to pretend that men are all either New Englanders of the Thoreau type or else not quite decent. Luckily the not quite decent prevail. It is to them that literature is addressed. It is they who must be able to make something of Thoreau, to establish a personal relation to his spirit and his teaching, if either is to survive.

VII

They can establish that relation. There is this much concrete truth in the transcendentalist doctrine of the over-soul that it is the happy fortune of the highest sincerity to utter truth from a greater depth than the depth of its awareness and to promulgate doctrines that another age, accepting them in its own and special sense, can make profitable to purposes beyond the original prophet's dreams and hopes. There was, so far as one can tell, a minimum of material entanglement in Thoreau's Concord. People lived very hardily. Farmers may have added to their acres, shopkeepers put a few dollars in a bank. No doubt even these little triumphs and economies involved an element of meanness and unfreedom. But what a simple scene it was. Not only Concord. Even New York. One time Thoreau climbed the stairs of strangers in the city. The manager of the greatest American publishing-house told him that, since the business was making $50,000 a year, he was inclined to let well enough alone. All this was before the Civil War, the winning of the West, the Gilded age. But even then it seemed to Thoreau that men were become the slaves of things. Not only of institutions. The latter doctrine he held in common with all the romantic revolutionaries. But slaves of a daily entanglement with the very

143

means of life. "There is little or nothing to be remembered on the subject of getting an honest living. Neither the New Testament nor Poor Richard speaks to our condition. I cannot think of a single page which entertains, much less answers, the questions which I put to myself on this subject. . . . How to make the getting our living poetic; for if it is not poetic, it is not life but death that we get." In this entry in the "Journals" is the kernel of Thoreau's freshest contribution to living and to thought. For he is quite right in saying that the New Testament offers no help. The Gospel bids men disregard the question of work and material existence. But in cold climates and industrial civilizations they simply cannot do that. Unable to heed a quite impracticable counsel, they submit wholly to the material elements of civilization and become literally the slaves of houses, cars, garments, food, drink. For these things acquire symbolical values; they cater to pride, security, self-importance. The result is Babbit who in all his life has never done a single thing he really wanted to do. The result is, on a higher plane, men and women throwing away their better part for unnecessary things made of wood or stone or glass or silk or wool. The process is infinitely insidious. It is as close to us as our own breathing and so it does not often come into consciousness. But Thoreau's voice is an arousing one, quiet though it be. "To have done anything by which you earned money merely is to have been truly idle or worse. . . . You must get your living by loving. . . . Cold and hunger seem more friendly to my nature than those methods which men have adopted and advised to ward them off." I have fully explained how Thoreau did not himself meet the problem normally. Nothing is easier than to risk cold and hunger for oneself; risking cold and hunger for others is a graver and more complicated matter. Thoreau should be read by women whose influence, for both biological and social reasons, is commonly on the side of an increasing servitude to material things. His solution of the problem, which he himself, in his solitariness and coldness, and also in his place and time, was able to apply practically was, as is well known, to strip living of unnecessary desire, to reduce material needs to their true minimum, to withdraw for all satisfactions to the spiritual center of life. Since those satisfactions are, after all, the only true ones, since, in fact, all others leave a faint tinge of bitterness behind them, why do we sacrifice freedom, dignity, health to idols of wood and calves of gold? There is one reason of which Thoreau was wholly unaware: most men are afflicted with a troubling or sometimes crushing feeling of inferiority. From this feeling arises most so-called ambition, all vulgar eagerness, all striving for material success. It is success that most men want far more than its fruits; it is the sense of having added a new value to the self which cringes in the cavern of the undeveloped soul. The clerk wants to be boss, the teacher principal, the professor dean, the laborer foreman, the average author a writer of best-sellers, the manufacturer head of a trust—partly to buy luxuries for their wives and children, the natural male being a simple creature content with little, partly in order to flee from that initial sense of inferiority. In brief, the whole problem is infinitely more complex than Thoreau dreamed. But of these complications he, being what he was, could not possibly be aware. We must, be it said once more, abstract his ideas from his

145

personality and limited experience and apply them in a new sense to ourselves.

Thoreau cultivated a material austerity or life for itself and its essential satisfactions. He cultivated it also for the flexibility that it gives man in the political and social sphere. A man who owns much, houses, lands, shops, can be attacked and enslaved by majorities, legislators, officials. Now Thoreau held with absoluteness the doctrine that all governmental power is delegated power, delegated not only by the people as a group—that is conventional democracy—but delegated by the individual who may withdraw that delegated power, that voluntary surrender of a part of his liberty whenever those to whom the power is delegated use it to foolish or to wicked ends. This is his great doctrine of civil disobedience— a doctrine that has in fact been practiced by all the highest spirits in human history, by all redeeming personalities, that is sometimes even practiced by groups of people—as today in America in connection with the Eighteenth Amendment— but which fills the average, timid, propertied man with terror. "I think that we should be men first, and subjects afterwards. It is not desirable to cultivate a respect for the law, so much as for the right. The only obligation which I have a right to assume is to do at any time what I think right." To this as a theoretical statement most liberal-minded people might assent. They come, however, with various practical arguments, especially with one which Thoreau has answered in a great and final passage of the discourse on Civil Disobedience. "Unjust laws exist: shall we be content to obey them, or shall we endeavor to amend them, and obey them until we have succeeded, or shall we transgress them

146

at once? Men generally under such a government as this think that they ought to wait until they have persuaded the majority to alter them. They think that, if they should resist, the remedy would be worse than the evil. But it is the fault of the government itself that the remedy is worse than the evil. It makes it worse. Why is it not more apt to anticipate and provide for reform? Why does it not cherish its wise minority? Why does it cry and resist before it is hurt? Why does it not encourage its citizens to be on the alert to point out its faults, and do better than it would have them? Why does it always crucify Christ and excommunicate Copernicus and Luther and pronounce Washington and Franklin rebels?" "The authority of government," he adds, "can have no pure right over my person and property but what I concede to it." And in the "Journals" there are two private notations which complete directly and indirectly but magnificently first the austere inner earnestness with which Thoreau held his doctrine and secondly the ultimate implication of men's present inability to accept it. "I had never respected this government, but I had foolishly thought that I might manage to live here, attending to my private affairs and forget it." Then came the Fugitive Slave Act and forgetting would have meant participation in evil. Thoreau did all that, given the circumstances, he could do to withdraw the power which he, like every other individual, had delegated to a government which was no longer worthy of his coöperation and support. And if all men did that? There is no hope that they will. But if they did the greatest of all evils and barbarisms, war itself, might disappear. Alas, "nations are thus ready to talk of wars and challenge one another, because they are made up to such an extent of poor, low-spirited, despairing men, in whose eyes the chance of shooting somebody else without being shot themselves exceeds their actual good fortune." In brief: the man not too deeply entangled with dead, material things can in truth afford to be a free man to the extent of defying the wickedness of governmental machines and saving himself from the degradation and slavery of war. Such is the central thought and teaching of another American classic. No wonder they teach Longfellow in the schools.

VIII

I have defined a classic as one whose vision the youth of successive generations can make its own. Thoreau meets that test. He meets another and a commoner one, the test of form, of style. He meets this test better perhaps than Emerson, though like Emerson the highest or structural achievements of form were beyond his grasp. Even "Walden," for all its oneness of impression, is only a series of essays, descriptions, reflections held together by a unity of thought and tone. The excellence of Thoreau's prose does not commonly extend beyond the paragraph. But within that unit it is complete and high. It avoids the excess which he disliked in many prose-writers of his time. It has constantly the "moderation and sententiousness" which he praised and is full of sentences "concentrated and nutty. Sentences which suggest far more than they say, which have an atmosphere about them, which do not merely report an old but make a new impression, sentences as durable as a Roman aqueduct—to frame these, that is the art of writing." That is probably the finest as well as the soundest passage on style in the whole of American literature. Thoreau took the Horatian advice literally, turning over the pages of the Greeks by day and by night. He has something of their limpidness, severity, color of dawn and dusk. In this one respect his lack of human passion furthered his special end. At his worst it leaves him flat, dull, pedestrian; at his best it saves him from adornment, excess, Corinthianism in all its phases. He is, as a mere writer, the soundest as model and influence among American men of letters. He has, in fact, had little influence hitherto. But that, too, in our revaluation of our national past, is likely to change.

The nature writings, special in interest, belonging to a mood that had its year and date, need not detain one long. They will always have their quiet lovers, people who dwell in a lovely but confined region of the human spirit. It suffices to speak of "Walden," a book like those Thoreau himself described as desirable and admirable. "Books, not which afford us a cowering enjoyment, but in which each thought is of unusual daring, such as an idle man cannot read and a timid one would not be entertained by, which even make us dangerous to existing institutions—such I call good books."

"Walden" is one of the most tonic and heartening books in all literature. I cannot imagine young people reading it and ever thereafter consenting as easily as before to the mean conventions of the world. "Man's capacities have never been measured; nor are we to judge of what he can do by any precedents, so little has been tried." He did not, of course, mean those mechanical inventions which are in his own final words only "improved means to an unimproved end." He meant

149

the molding of life. "The greater part of what my neighbors call good I believe in my soul to be bad." He means the necessary and constant revaluation of values without which life stagnates. "One generation abandons the enterprises of another like stranded vessels." Seeing this to be so, he set out on his great experiment of living, really living the philosophic life of simplicity, magnanimity, non-conformity. "The cost of a thing is the amount of what I call life which is required to be exchanged for it." This was the essential point. For "lo! Men have become the tools of their tools." He was determined to serve neither government nor tool and, achieving that freedom, looked not only upon the present but upon the past with purged and magnificent eye. "As for the Pyramids, there is nothing to wonder at in them so much as the fact that so many men could be found degraded enough to spend their lives constructing a tomb for some ambitious booby, whom it would have been wiser and manlier to have drowned in the Nile." He wants no more of such dull, supine masses and anticipates the great Nietzschean monition: "Werde der du bist!" "I desire that there may be as many different persons in the world as possible; but I would have each one be very careful to find out and pursue *his own* way, and not his father's and his mother's and his neighbor's instead." He has more amazingly prophetic moments than even this, anticipating the psycho-analyst's explanation of the American moral reformer's fiery and tyrannous zeal. "I believe that what so saddens the reformer is not his sympathy with his fellows in distress, but, though he be the holiest son of God, is his private ail." He returns again and again to the necessity of all necessities, that of creative living. "Commonly men will only be brave as their fathers were brave or timid." Finally, in the stirring conclusion, he drives home his essential thoughts in sentences that have a concentrated and cleaving strength. "The universe is wider than our views of it." Homelier but even deeper is this other expression of the same truth: "The surface of the earth is soft and impressible by the feet of men; and so with the paths which the mind travels. How worn and dusty, then, must be the highways of the world—how deep the ruts of tradition and conformity! . . . If a man does not keep pace with his companions, perhaps it is because he hears a different drummer. Let him step to the music which he hears, however measured and far away." It is the great virtue of "Walden" that it is the record of the experience of a man who followed the music that he heard. Thoreau left the woods as freely as he went to them. He never, so far as his temperamental limitations permitted, followed the worn and dusty paths. He sums up the result of his central experiment in simple but infinitely memorable words: "I learned this, at least, by my experiment: that if one advances confidently in the direction of his dreams, and endeavors to live the life which he has imagined, he will meet with a success unexpected in common hours."

Is "Walden" then a great and complete book? And if it is not, why was it necessary to begin by discussing Thoreau's defective nature? Unfortunately "Walden" contains a chapter called "Higher Laws" which, in the accustomed Puritan way, blunts all the arrows, retracts all the brave and lofty sayings of the earlier and later chapters and makes it necessary for Thoreau to be saved, as by fire, for our uses and the uses of posterity. That chapter is full of the Puritan's cheap unfairness to the senses, his complete unwillingness to bring the whole of human nature under creative and significant control. "There is never an instant's truce between vice and virtue. . . . We are conscious of an animal in us, which awakens in proportion as our higher nature slumbers." Ah, no, good Puritan, *we* are not; you are. We are not conscious of any inner division and have long integrated all aspects of our nature upon the highest or, rather, the most significant and fruitful plane that is attainable by us. Chastity is not "the flowering of man"; it is possible to "eat, or drink, or cohabit, or sleep sensually" and yet nobly. For who told you that the senses are necessarily ignoble? They are ignoble only when, as in yourself, they are abstracted and divided from the faculties of the mind and the soul. But in us they are not; they have never been. We do not have to "overcome nature," for nature is not something outside of or below us, but has long been conquered and cultivated and embodied in the total harmony of life. Our purity is not one of abstention, but of fitting and beautiful use. . . . Yes, Thoreau, like Emerson, must be saved in spite of his limitations; he must be thought of as meaning what he said without Puritan reservations, without excluding the richer half of life. That will be accomplished if a sufficient number of Americans are determined to live a civilized life—a life that includes a national past as well as a present and as the best part of that past prophetic and poetic voices that may be heeded now and in future days.

BOOK FOUR

The Troubled Romancers

I

The years between 1840 and the Civil War were rich years.
One might, though not without an hundred reservations
and even with a touch of irony, call these decades an Augustan
age. Gentlemen pursued literature in a seemly fashion;
even the transcendentalist revolt did not forget what was due
to birth and breeding; a frugal literary summer brought to
New England the reward of her long, tenacious culture of a
stony soil. From the artificers and essayists, from Emerson,
the philosophic lyrist, came no discordant note. Nor was the
thin harmony broken by those members of the gentry who,
like Prescott and Motley, made the past their refuge and
history their theme. But there appeared three creative temperaments,
three "problematic natures" who were at last impelled
to transmute experience into expression and at once
flight and sickness and sorrow break in upon the serenity of
the literary scene. "Creative substance," said Goethe, "is the
substance of the artist's life." That saying, which propheti-

153

cally anticipates the last results of modern research, states the problem, the woe, the difficulty of Poe and Hawthorne and Melville.

Accident is a word by which we conceal our ignorance of the causes of things. Was it the quality of American life or was it wholly their own natures which drove these three into expression that has the structure of a neurosis? They saw the life of their age and country. Hawthorne, as his "American Notebooks" prove, saw it acutely and closely; Melville touched it concretely at a thousand points; Poe's absorption of definite elements in his Southern environment has never been adequately noted. Yet all three chose flight and fantasy. Hawthorne, the best-balanced of them, attempted in certain tales as well as in "The Blithedale Romance," to embody his creative impulse in the present, the concrete and the exist- ent. Yet under his touch reality always turns into legend and fact into fancy. He knew himself with that detached insight which he alone of the three possessed to be fatally a weaver of romance. Poe's work was genetically a defense-neurosis; the stormy and troubled Melville fled to Paradises in which he never wholly believed, projected the malevolence of the universe, which rose to him from his hopeless inner conflicts, in a vast and ghastly symbol and finally, still uneased of his pain, poured forth in "Pierre" the confused contents of his aching soul. No, the quality of American life had little or nothing to do with the character of the work of these ro- mancers, any more than the quality of German life had to do with that of Hoffmann or the quality of French life with the torments and visions of Baudelaire. In the study and inter- pretation of the arts we can dismiss in respect of the indi-

154

vidual's possibility of expression and his special approach to it, the pressure of environment. Every age and land is the right age and land for creative expression. The man may starve. He will speak if he can. Thus our romancers, belated in the age of Dickens and Thackeray, of George Eliot and Flaubert, were romancers because they were hopelessly imprisoned in their unconscious conflicts. They could not pour these into real experience which they never reached. Unable to face life, they built structures of dream and phantasmagoria in which to dwell, into which to flee from the intolerable exactions of the normal world. They feared death and yet dwelt upon it without ceasing. "The fever called 'Living,'" low in Hawthorne, high and throbbing in Poe and Melville, was all they knew of life.

Two warnings must be sounded: Firstly, The environment, age, country, culture, climate, has everything to do with determining the existence and the entire character of the work of both the bard and, above all, the artificer. Without the printing-press and large masses of semi-literate readers neither Dr. William Lyon Phelps nor Mr. Calvin Coolidge would have adopted the device of public communication with their fellows. Edgar Allan Poe would have been driven to express himself in any age. The poet must speak—whether as primitive mythmaker, anonymous mediæval sculptor or singer or as modern writer of words that are printed. He must speak because he cannot endure life without the exercise of that creative faculty which is, on various levels and with varying values to mankind, first of all his personal substitute for lacks and defeats that are otherwise insupportable. Hence the genesis of art, of all inevitable expression, is in the poet's soul; age, country, fortune, do but determine method and convention—the common denominator of all communication.

The second warning is this: the genesis of a thing does not necessarily tell us anything concerning the thing's value. It may indeed, as we shall see, help us to define and delimit value. The music of "To One in Paradise" has an enchantment that no analysis can deaden or destroy. But a knowledge of the sources of Poe's art can instruct us with complete finality concerning the strict limits of his appeal and the wrong-headedness of those foreign critics who make of the so-called neglect of Poe a reproach against American culture. "Hamlet" expresses supremely a conflict common, in a greater or less degree, to all men—a conflict also embodied in myth, legend and religion. "Berenice" expresses a rarefied but definite tendency to necrophilia. Excessively few men, luckily, share that tendency. But the tale can appeal profoundly only to those who do. It speaks for them and releases them from a portion of their mortal burden. To all others, to the vast majority of mankind, "Berenice" can be but as a curiously woven tapestry, the intricate pattern of which corresponds to nothing that they have known or felt. In brief, the romancers with which this Book deals, as this extreme example illustrates, were men who from the character of their inner constitution and its peculiar conflicts, missed both the deepest and the broadest motives of art. They were, upon the whole, not human enough. It is clear that this limitation was not an American limitation; it is equally clear that these inquiries into the genesis of works of art dispose of many futile controversies that have filled the world with clamor.

Of these controversies the most persistent concerns itself
with the work of Edgar Allan Poe. It was but the other day
that M. Paul Valéry spoke again of the "world-wide glory"
of Poe and added: "This Anglo-Saxon poet is strangely
slighted by his own peoples." Nor was M. Valéry thinking
primarily of the "Tales" and "Poems" but of Poe's critical
theories. "A man arose," he writes, "who considered the
things of the mind and, among these, the production of literature, with an exactness, a sagacity, a lucidity, which had
never before been found in a mind endowed with poetic inventiveness." There is much more in the same strain. It
suffices to add M. Valéry's declaration that Poe "analysed
the psychological conditions" under which a poem comes into
being. In a sense of which M. Valéry does not dream that is
true. Poe's critical theory is a defensive rationalization of his
instinctive and inevitable practice, a justification, a glorification of his own lack of passion, humanity, ethical perception,
continuity of power, imaginative sympathy, knowledge of
man and of human life—of all the capacities and qualities, in
brief, that give substance and import to a writer. Poe, like all
persons whose inner self-esteem is abnormally low, needed to
build a legend of greatness for himself. He made his own
limitations the laws of art. Hence writers like Baudelaire,
stricken by similar neuroses and driven to similar compensatory gestures, accepted his critical theories with profound
satisfaction. Baudelaire, a psychical and physical masochist
with the mentality of a monk of the dark ages records in his
diaries his determination to let no morning pass without pray-

ing for the intercession of his father, his sister and of Edgar Allan Poe. Whenever we seek closely the sources of the continental glory of Poe, we fall upon this atmosphere of the cloister and the sanatorium.

It is needless to say that I feel no moral disapprobation toward such psychopathic types as Poe and Baudelaire. On the contrary: the single criticism that might fairly be made against Joseph Wood Krutch's brilliant and definitive biography of Poe is that he shows an insufficient sympathy for the blind and bitter suffering that must have afflicted the poet. Hopelessly crippled in the most vital and pervasive of human functions by a trauma sustained in infancy, a pseudo-aristocrat of Virginia and an outcast, a prey to poverty and all its worst humiliations, greatly gifted, insanely sensitive, driven into the temporary release of intoxication by that first and most insupportable of human ills—Poe is worthy of tears and not of taunts. What probably irritated Mr. Krutch, as it must every rational mind, are the claims made for Poe, both man and writer, by certain circles both at home and abroad. Yet these special estimates are recurrent and explicable. Thus, for instance, homosexual readers and critics have contributed to the absurdly inflated reputations of Oscar Wilde, André Gide and even of Miss Radclyffe Hall and exhibitionists have contributed to the atmosphere of awe that surrounds the intricate dullness of Mr. Joyce and the pornography of the late Mr. Lawrence. Now all types of human character and experience have a right to their poets and spokesmen. But the British and American estimate of Poe as a writer of narrow and special appeal and therefore of strictly secondary importance is not a matter of opinion, but of demonstrable fact. The great writer, however narrow his immediate and conscious purpose may seem to be, involuntarily injects into his work those elements of the broadly and profoundly human that ultimately find and reach the heart and the instincts of mankind. He may begin, like Milton, by justifying a perishable and dusty theological system; he ends, as Milton did, by expressing the universal virile instinct in love, the universal Promethean protest with both its fire and pride and its deeply troubled conscience. . . . He may, as a lyrist or autobiographer, speak of the intimate and apparently unique. He will be seen to have unwittingly raised the concrete to the universal and to have uttered some truth that comes ultimately home to all.

For perceptions of this order Poe had no instinct. The critical theory which M. Valéry admires has little relation to the character either of the creative process or of the work of art. Poetry, Poe declared, has nothing to do with Truth; it is the creation of supernal Beauty, the rhythmical creation of Beauty, having no concern with intellect or conscience. Hence it is the duty of him who "claims the sacred title of poet" to create novel moods of beauty. Both the lyric and the tale, the only two kinds that "best fulfill the demands of high genius" should aim at a unique and single effect, a coldly preconceived effect, which is then wrought out by the invention and combination of incidents in the tale, of imagery and rhythmic structure in the poem. The tale may indeed deal with Truth. "Some of the finest tales are tales of ratiocination." There are also tales of "terror or passion or horror." Thus Beauty or Beauty and Truth are to be embodied in compositions that can be read "at one sitting," since otherwise there is lost the sense of totality, from which the mind derives its highest satisfaction.

It has been customary to grant Poe's critical theories a limited validity, largely, no doubt, because his opponents were extremely dull and given to moralistic and didactic clap-trap. It has been customary to represent him as an apostle of the beautiful in an environment smitten with æsthetic blindness. It has become something of a convention to make of him a banner and a war cry in the fight against dullness and neo-Puritan resistance to art. In the light of the change-less character of sound literature none of these claims and uses can be allowed. For even the didactic is closer to the root of the matter than the so-called æsthetic, since the didac-tic is sincere and seeks to deal sincerely with man and na-ture and human life on its own level. Nor is a great didactic poem unthinkable, as witness the "De Rerum Natura," nor one so sagacious and brilliantly wrought that it survives successive and fundamental changes in taste, as witness Pope's "Essay on Criticism." The so-called purely æsthetic, on the other hand, is always a hypocritic gesture. Form with-out substance and content exists neither in art nor in nature. The æsthetic writers express themselves like all others. They feign literature to be less than expression because they are commonly impelled to express appetencies or sexual habits which are repulsive to the majority of their fellows. I do not for a moment defend the legal pursuit of "Les Fleurs du Mal" or the hounding to death of poor Oscar Wilde, or the cold-ness and contempt visited on a man as cruelly ill in soul and as gifted as Poe. It is the intolerance of the mob which, here as elsewhere, darkens council. It evokes a natural and generous resistance; it is highly creditable to the craft of letters that those have been overestimated who have had to suffer from the fury of fools. But the time has come when the intellectual character and the works of Poe can be objectively examined.

The childish confusion at the heart of his critical theory is to be found in his use of the word truth. He uses that word as though it meant proposition, scientific statement, maxim or saw. With these forms of intellectual expression literature has in fact little to do. But Poe pretended to himself, for unconscious reasons of his own, that he was fighting a mean didacticism, when he was declaiming against the necessary and eternal content of literature, which he himself was incapable of achieving. That content can, of course, be summed up under the word truth—truth to the human vision of the universe, to the struggles, agonies, hopes and aspirations of the heart of man, truth to consciousness, to character, truth, above all in the sense that the artist seeks to apprehend reality, whether to accept or repudiate or transform it. It was Poe's pathological flight from the realities of his own constitution and character and thus from all reality that blinded him to the confusion of his thinking and to the nature of the books which he evidently read. No, Griswold and the "North American Review" were more at the center of the so-ness of life and literature than Poe. They were right even in certain details in respect of which Poe jeered most harshly. Thus they were right in making "sustained effort," that is, creative wealth and architectonic talent, among the chief marks of truly notable works.

Having emptied literature of "truth," Poe declared its

aim to be "beauty." The distinction itself is, of course, inadmissible. Form and substance are simultaneously conceived, develop as two aspects of the same entity and are born together. If Poe's account of his composition of "The Raven" were literally true, the poem would not even possess the modicum of somber charm and rhythmic quaintness that half offset its emptiness and hard artifice.

His best poems were, of course, produced in the quite normal manner. He conceived of them as expressions of pure beauty, of "supernal beauty." What he called beauty was, in sober fact, the only kind of truth he had to offer—the truth of his own inwardness and sickness and pain. He declared that a "certain taint of sadness is inseparably connected with all the higher manifestations of beauty." And this is profoundly true, because life is tragic and all beauty transitory. But Poe did not mean that at all. He meant the "taint"—significant word!—of a melancholy devoid of moral energy or human contemplation or resistance or power. He meant, in brief, the substance of his own defensive and compensatory reveries. These were the reveries of a man whose stricken spirit cringed despairingly within its earthly tenement and who was incapable of human love. Hence he dreamed of himself as the gloomy but high-born and exalted lover of a woman who was "pure," that is passionless, in the good old-fashioned foolish, Southern sense; next of a pure woman stricken with a deadly malady, finally of a dead lady, since such an one was wholly incapable of suddenly becoming less pure and demanding what he had not to give. It is in the light or rather in the gloom of these considerations that the famous passage in "The Philosophy of Composition" is to be reread. "Of all melancholy topics, what, according to the *universal* understanding of mankind, is the *most* melancholy? Death—was the obvious reply. And when, I said, is this most melancholy of topics most poetical? . . . When it most closely allies itself to *Beauty*: the death, then, of a beautiful woman is, unquestionably, the most poetical topic in the world." This passage is of the highest psychological and literary interest in that it illustrates in an extraordinarily clear and special instance how subjective criticism can be. No reader of the "Tales" and "Poems" could have failed to observe the inner compulsion of Poe to create a situation in which love must be frustrated by death. It does not speak well for the intelligence of eccentric and æsthetic critics that they have taken Poe's theories to be more than the rationalization of his own practice and have assigned to them any validity in the world of thought. Nor should it have escaped their attention that Poe, in his essays, his reviews, his *obiter dicta*, always preferred the second-rate, the sentimental and the melodramatic. His highest praise, with the single exception of Hawthorne, is given to sentimental female versifiers, to Tennyson at his feeblest, to Bulwer Lytton, Tom Hood, Fouqué's "Undine." Even of Shelley he quotes a slightly perfumed poem. He dismissed Wordsworth with contempt and was ecstatic over R. H. Horne's "Orion." He had his moments of insight, however troubled, as when he defined originality in literature as the ability to bring out "the half-formed, the reluctant, or the unexpressed fancies of mankind." He had another such moment when he wrote: "To appreciate thoroughly the work of what we call genius, is to possess all the genius by which the work was produced."

But such moments are rare and brief. To a sensitive and instructed ear the harsh, declamatory tone of his critical prose would in itself have betrayed Poe's melancholy purpose: to aggrandize himself at the expense of others and to justify by a pseudo-universal critical theory his own narrow and tortured practice.

III

As a critic he does not exist. Nor was he a child of light battling the Philistines in a dusty and clamorous age. But he was an artist, intense though narrow, expressing his self, which is all that any artist can do, excessively limited through the maladies that dictated the character of his inner life and prevented him wholly from facing and absorbing reality into the substance of his soul and therefore of his art. Like his own Politian in the early dramatic fragment

a dreamer and a man shut out
From common passions,

he was confined in his choice of subjects to a few compensatory fantasies. Type and most perfect embodiment of these fantasies is "The Fall of the House of Usher." There is the gloomy, heart-sick, terror-stricken splendor as of sable velvet blood-flecked; there the compensatory vision of high birth, vast wealth and curious learning; there, above all, the stricken lady loved but forever removed from human passion and implicated with the fear-neurosis of premature burial and with the terror of and yet longing for dissolution. Tale after tale and poem after poem are but as a musician's variations upon this thematic material. The tales of perverseness or rather

164

perversion represent variations from this theme that are slight enough: visions, namely, of cruelty which is always very close to frustrated desire. Such are "The Black Cat," "The Cask of Amontillado," "The Pit and the Pendulum." Finally there is, as in the work of every ultra-romantic, the unconscious confession in the form of the *Doppelgänger* fantasy— "William Wilson." The real "I," crushed by a sense of guilt, unable longer to bear the burden of its sins and weaknesses, invents a malevolent double to be at once monitor and indirect author of all ill. This double personifies the "I's" terror of itself and contempt for itself, comes between the "I" and the object of its passions and thus liberates that "I" from the consciousness of both impotence and guilt. It is at once conscience tempter and scapegoat, a combination not unknown in myth and in mass psychology. The same escape from the too heavy burden of the "I" is found in Musset's "Nuit de Décembre," in Chamisso's "Peter Schlemihl" and Wilde's "Picture of Dorian Gray."

There are, in addition, the tales of imaginative science and the tales of ratiocination. It is from these tales that Poe's widest influence and glory, if one likes, are derived. Perhaps both Jules Verne and H. G. Wells, assuredly the whole company of detective-story writers from Gaboriau and the author of "Nick Carter" to Conan Doyle and S. S. Van Dine owe the method by which they hold their vast audiences to certain of Poe's stories. The reason is not far to seek. Poe liked to fancy himself as the possessor of strange and esoteric knowledge and also of a naked intellectual power of analysis by which he could unravel mysteries and detect crime. These two fancies happen to be of a kind that great masses of men can share. Who, in that adolescent stage of mentality which in most people lasts till death, would not desire imaginatively to identify himself with the cool and superior detective, the unraveler of plots, the guardian of society against those crimes which he himself desires unconsciously to commit, but which, being ethically inhibited from committing, he desires the more ardently to see discovered and punished? This compensatory fantasy which Poe invented for narrow and luckily rare reasons of his own, holds elements of human ambition and desire that are common to great masses of men. It satisfies the desire for self-aggrandisement on a plane conceivable to the ordinary reader; it gives harmless release to his aggressive propensities; it permits him to be "master-mind" and lyncher, vicarious committer of crimes and stalwart citizen at the same time. Through the tales of ratiocination Poe has indeed reached huge audiences of which he did not dream and which the better part of him would have despised.

Poe's fame, then, can receive no aid from either his critical theories which are objectively considered absurd or from his technical inventiveness. It must continue to rest upon a handful of fantastic tales and poems and must, from the psychical origin and character of these tales and poems, remain narrow. Having no commerce with either the human affections or the passions, sharing no fundamental instinct or concern or hope of the spirit of man, what is there left him but the faltering attention of some twilit hour? This hour and its mood are recurrent, especially in youth. In the reveries of late adolescence, which often have a touch of passing malady and perversity, the gloom and abstract cruelty of certain tales will probably always have their share. The maturer mind finds even these difficult to relish on account of their pretentious phrasing, their moments of tawdry melodrama, their constant use of the magniloquent *clichés* so familiar to all who know the older tradition of Southern eloquence. "Classical head," "snow-white and gauze-like drapery," "marble hand," "tumultuous vultures of stern passion," "fair England," "her lofty, her ethereal nature," "menials prepared her for the tomb," "yet I should fail in any attempt," "the fair page need not be sullied," "the wine flowed freely"—it is difficult to keep within the mood of stories broken by these phrases that smack of the provincial society column and of public celebrations of the fair Southland and its pure women. It has never been sufficiently observed how intimately of his time and section—even to the declamatoriness of tone—was both the critical and the imaginative prose of Poe.

A small group of poems, to which belongs neither "The Raven," nor "Lenore" nor probably "Ulalume," is quite free of the pretentiousness, the shabby phrasing, the melodrama of even the best tales. Above all are these verses free from the harsh assertiveness of tone that disfigures not only the essays but the stories. Writing verse Poe was able to listen to his own troubled soul alone and to extract therefrom his one pure gift—the gift for verbal music. This music is not wholly without discord or slightly base intrusion in the more or less "set" pieces, such as "The Conqueror Worm" or "The Haunted Palace." Its moments of high enchantment occur where those qualities of his nature which Poe esteemed the intellectual and consciously artistic were wholly in abeyance.

So soon as he tries to *say* anything, the result verges on melodrama or nonsense. Only where he yields quite passively to a mood is his accent pure and probably immortal. It is so in

> Resignedly beneath the sky
> The melancholy waters lie,

and in

> Of a water that flows
> With a lullaby sound,
> From a spring but a very few
> Feet under ground—
> From a cavern not very far
> Down under ground,

and assuredly in

> And all my days are trances,
> And all my nightly dreams
> Are where thy dark eye glances
> And where thy footstep gleams—
> In what ethereal dances,
> By what eternal streams.

Here is the Poe who counts and will last, here only. Were these few verses and their continued echo in the ears of men reward for those brief years so shattered by frustration and by pain? What is known as art is evidently no happy subject to contemplate. Humanity yields richer fruitage—even as art. Poe was not capable of knowing that truth. His ignorance of it was his tragedy.

IV

A close absorption in the work and personality of Poe has this advantage: it throws into high and bright relief the normal processes of life. Hawthorne was not the healthiest of creatures. But after his marriage there were hours in his life that are like sunlit upland meadows after the dank chambers in the charnel-house of Poe. Guests came to the Hawthornes on August 15, 1842, and Hawthorne writes in his notebook: "It was a sort of acknowledgment and reception of us into the corps of married people—a sanction by no means essential to our peace and well-being, but yet agreeable enough to receive. So we welcomed them cordially at the door, and ushered them into our parlor and soon into the supper-room." On September 17 of the same year Hawthorne and Emerson took a walk. It was a fine day and Emerson records in the "Journals": "We were both in excellent spirits, had much conversation, for we were both old collectors who had never had opportunity before to show each other our cabinets." Here we have, soon after his marriage to Sophia Peabody, a picture of Hawthorne's life that accounts for the creative energy he was to display for over twenty years. Though he remained aloof even in that innermost circle, it warmed and sustained him. Children came who lit a glow in his heart and Mrs. Hawthorne had the power of making to a nature like his the most fruitful of gifts—an adoration that was its own reward. "If I can only be so great," she writes in the eighth year of their marriage, "so high, so noble, so sweet as he in any phase of my being, I shall be glad." He needed to be so sustained. For that aloofness and reserve of his, that unconscious fear of touching life, of giving himself to life is witnessed by all his contemporaries, is admitted over and over again by himself and accounts for the character and quality of his work. The love of his wife and children to which he wisely withdrew was his only source of human power and creative energy. It never touched the otherwise determined substance and quality of his work. The Brook Farm experience in the year before his marriage alone did that. Though he declared later that "the real Me was never an associate of the community" and that it was a spectral self of his who toiled with those comrades in the sun, yet "The Blithedale Romance," written ten years later and written significantly enough in the first person, remains the least spectral of his works, the fullest of concrete characterization and the tang of nature and of life. Here, for once, he had been taken a little out of himself; here a powerful ethical motive—but in the high artist ethics and æsthetics are one—had brought him closer to his kind and time. Nor was he ignorant of the brief liberation that Brook Farm had given him. Wistful enough is his retrospective cry, yet none knowing Hawthorne and his other works and ways can fail to hear in that cry beyond the meaning of the words and context a nostalgia for the brief release from the prison of his darker self which Brook Farm brought him: "Whatever else I may repent of, let it be reckoned neither among my sins nor follies that I once had faith and force enough to form generous hopes of the world's destiny,—yes!—and to do what in me lay for their accomplishment."

What made Hawthorne a romancer of the twilight instead of a novelist of human heart? What within him accounts for the peculiar character of his work? It may be said that an analogous question can be asked concerning every writer and his work. And that is quite true. Nor are we without the beginning of an understanding of the inner character of the creative impulse, of subject choice, even of execution—an understanding, by the way, that leaves wholly untouched the mystery and the splendor of genius. But this understanding of the connection between personality and work, this insight into the necessary oneness of the artist and his art, is more easily come by when the work deals, however intricately or disguisedly, with universal passion or aspiration, with the large and common problems of mortality or else with definite neurosis. There is no difficulty in integrating Milton with "Paradise Lost," Goethe with "Faust," Poe—as we have seen —with both his "Tales" and his critical theory, Theodore Dreiser, to come forward and nearer home, with "Sister Carrie" and "The Genius." The expression of Hawthorne was the excessively indirect expression of an excessively fine but troubled and obscure and stripped and shivering soul. I have not the skill wholly to integrate experience with expression in his case. I must content myself with an intelligent statement of the problem.

He lost his father in his fourth year. His widowed mother withdrew wholly from the world. He passed his childhood and adolescence secluded with his family in the old Manse at Salem. When he was fourteen he spent a year in utter loneliness in the Maine woods. "It was there," he wrote later, "I got my cursed habits of solitude." It takes no analyst to see the defensive nature of this statement. He sought an even deeper solitude than that of Salem because he was impelled to do so, because he could not otherwise have endured it. His flight from life and from himself was fixed at fourteen. At seventeen he entered Bowdoin College. At twenty-one he graduated and returned to that somber Salem house where he spent twelve dusky years, unknown to his fellowtownsmen, rarely going out except at twilight, pursuing his fancies and daydreams, composing the greater number of the "Twice-Told Tales." Nor did he for many years, if ever, conquer his ambivalent feeling toward Salem and the ancestral home from which he fled first at fourteen, but to which he continually returned. "My doom was on me. It was not the first time nor the second that I had gone away—as it seemed—permanently—but yet returned like the bad halfpenny; or as if Salem were for me the inevitable center of the universe." His native city was to him like a scene of guilt. He recognized dimly the quality of his feeling and attributed it, at least half-seriously, to the sins of his ancestors, to that original founder of his stock in America who was a bitter persecutor of Quakers. "I take shame upon myself for their sakes, and pray that any curse incurred by them . . . may be now and henceforth removed." He also knew, in the same dim fashion, that there was an explanation behind this explanation and that in discussing his dislike of his native city and his enforced attachment to it, he was still keeping "the inmost Me behind the veil."

That "inmost Me," which he kept behind such iron reserve, was haunted by a sense of guilt. The phenomenon is an extremely common one. No human soul, in fact, is quite free of that *Schuldgefühl*, which is a constant factor in the neuroses and which is always among the impelling forces toward the self-justificatory process of artistic communication. The difference between Hawthorne and the more normal artist is this, that the latter dwells upon the process of creative justification of himself and, as Thomas Mann has pointed

172

out, hence of mankind. Out of his need to justify himself he becomes servant and savior of his race and seeks constantly "to justify the ways of God to man." Hawthorne, on the contrary, was imprisoned with his feeling of guilt and impelled to state and restate it in tale after tale and romance after romance. Guilt is the subject of nearly all the tales, as well as of "The Scarlet Letter"; guilt as the consequence of a curse is the subject of "The House of the Seven Gables" and nature caught in the snare of guilt is the subject of "The Marble Faun." He did not flee from the varieties of living experience and from the world about him by choice. He was impelled to choose subject-matter, easy enough to find in the history and character of New England, with which he could integrate and through which he could express again and again the feeling that overwhelmed and shadowed his whole soul. Comradeship in a good cause and love released him for a brief period, from April, 1841, when he went to Brook Farm, to the autumn of 1842, from his darker preoccupation. By April, 1843, we find him on a visit to Salem. His wife had gone to Boston to attend the marriage of her sister. He was not entirely the man he had been. He knew that love and marriage had saved him. "At last I had caught hold of a reality which never could be taken from me. It was good thus to get apart from my happiness, for the sake of contemplating it." Yet the temptation to sink back into the gloomy reveries in which ten years of his "youth flitted away like a dream" was as strong as the neurotic's temptation is to flee from life, even from its happy aspects, into the protective neurosis, into the feigned substitute for the mother-womb. No wonder that Hawthorne sought under these circum-

173

stances to explain and justify himself to himself. "A cloudy veil stretches over the abyss of my nature. I have, however, no love of secrecy and darkness. I am glad to think that God sees through my heart, and, if any angel has power to penetrate into it, he is welcome to know everything that is there. Yes, and so may any mortal who is capable of full sympathy. . . . But he must find his own way there. I can neither guide nor enlighten him. It is this involuntary reserve, I suppose, that has given the objectivity to my writings; and when people think I am pouring myself out in a tale or an essay, I am merely telling what is common to human nature, not what is peculiar to myself. I sympathize with them, not they with me." This passage could be analyzed at great length. It will suffice here to give the conclusions of such an analysis: Hawthorne's reserve was his instinctive desire to keep from the world as well as to isolate for his own uses the feeling of guilt which was the core of his psychical life. His writings were the reverse of objective. He integrated with his feeling of guilt and its expression all happenings and persons whether of history, legend or life with which he dealt, and substituted for the various experiences of human nature a single one, because it loomed so large in his own soul. Thence arises the half-ghostly character of all his personages, thence the monotony of their preoccupations, thence the subdued and melancholy images and the unemphatic murmur of his style. But though his writings were so subjective in origin, he reached his audience because the feeling of subconscious guilt dwells in a greater or less degree in every human soul. The old and trite image of the answering chord is vivid and exact. It is the echo in the human heart that gives power to the lyre of the poet. All artistic expression is subjective at its source; it becomes objective because the poet is a man and his hearers are men and by speaking of himself he speaks to and for them. What limits a writer's power and range is not the fact but the character of his subjectivity. Since few human beings are as absorbed as Hawthorne was in the feeling of guilt or sin from which none is wholly free, his work will always seem pale and secondary—as he himself well knew—beside that of richer, more various, more impassioned and more daring natures.

Wise and profound, like all his remarks on his contemporaries are the lines that Emerson, returning from Hawthorne's funeral, wrote in his journal. "Clarke (James Freeman) in the church said that Hawthorne had done more justice than any other to the shades of life, shown a sympathy with the crime in our nature. . . . I thought there was a tragic element in the event, that might be more fully rendered —in the painful solitude of the man, which, I suppose, could no longer be endured, and he died of it. I have found in his death a surprise and disappointment. I thought him a greater man than any of his works betray, that there was still a great deal of work in him, and that he might one day show a purer power. . . . It was easy to talk with him—there were no barriers—only, he said so little, that I talked too much. . . . He showed . . . at one time, a fear that he had written himself out. One day, when I found him on the top of his hill in the woods, he paced back the path to his house and said: 'This path is the only remembrance of me that will remain.' Now it appears that I waited too long."

He underestimated the permanence of his work; he perceived, truly enough, that that single theme of his had already
been elaborated almost beyond endurance. He saw so clearly
that "we are not endowed with real life till the heart be
touched," and he could endow nothing with such life or
touch the heart. For we watch even Hester Prynne and Dimmesdale with a remote and dreamy sympathy; their woe
is but a legend and their passion but as the gestures in a
dream dreamed long ago. But Hawthorne was resignedly
aware of his limitation from the first. It was not merely a
retroactive perception that informs his description of the
"Twice Told Tales": "They have the pale tint of flowers
that blossomed in too remote a shade . . . the author's
touches often have an effect of tameness." He took pains to
explain that his ambition was never the novel which aims at
the "probable and ordinary course of man's experience," but
the romance which is a thing of "atmospherical medium,"
"a legend," with circumstances "of the writer's own choosing and creation," with personages of the author's own
"making or, at all events, of his own mixing." He knew, in
brief, that his stories were reveries and inward fancies in their
essence; he called even "The Blithedale Romance" "essentially a day dream," wherein "the creatures of his brain may
play their phantasmagorical antics, without exposing them
to too close a comparison with the actual events of real
lives." He complained, toward the end of his life, of the
"difficulty of writing a romance about a country where there
is no shadow, no antiquity, no mystery, no picturesque and

gloomy wrong." But this complaint came evidently from the fear he had of having, as Emerson records "written himself out." During the greater part of his career his self-knowledge was remarkable and his resignation to his inner limitations without querulousness. He seemed to know or, at least, to suspect the truth that his inward broodings were never or almost never wholly projected as art, wholly set out in the world of objective things. Creation was never complete enough to liberate him. His preoccupations remained the same. In 1842 he jots down the notion: "To trace out the influence of a frightful and disgraceful crime . . . the guilty person being alone conscious of the crime." He jots down the notion, extremely revelatory in its form: "A man to swallow a small snake—and it to be a symbol of a cherished sin." Eight years pass and he twangs the same string: "The print in blood of a naked foot to be traced through the street of a town." Three more years pass. He is about to set out for England and burns great heaps of old letters. "What a trustful guardian of secret matters is fire! What should we do without fire and death!" Guilt haunted his mind. Not, as critics have hitherto averred, the problem of human sin. The guiding motive of an author's work is never taken from without himself. It is the inner need and urgency that chooses subjects through which to express itself. His own feeling of guilt, whether precipitated, as so often occurs, by the incest wish of infancy or not, haunted him, tortured him, nor did he ever quite achieve a creative liberation from it in some concrete and final and objectified work. And that failure of his is the limitation of the power and reach of his romances. They have a dimness of aspect, an evanescence of

177

atmosphere, a level depressedness of tone. No pulse throbs in any save that one masterpiece "The Scarlet Letter," conceived and executed in the years following his marriage. Hence there is in that one book, too, less of the self-exculpatory commenting which was observed by Emerson. "Hawthorne invites his readers too much into his study, opens the process before them. As if the confectioner should say to his customers, 'Now let us make the cake.' "

A brief survey of the principal works will bear out these various observations. The "Twice-Told Tales," written during his years of isolation in Salem all have that "subdued tinge of the wild and wonderful," of dreariness and dread, which requires, as critics have strangely enough not seen, a special explanation in the work of a man who was young, well-born, healthy, comely, cultivated and not harassed by material need. He delved into the history of his city and section, selecting from that history nothing of its elements of the robust, the valiant, the shrewd or the virile, but like every artist, those happenings and details that answered his inner need and could be steeped into the colors of his soul. Since his soul held few or none of the ordinary interests of mankind his historical touches even in the "Legends of the Province House" are but the echoes of his inner malady: embodied guilt in the form of pestilence stalks in and the inevitable *Doppelgänger* fantasy appears in "Howe's Masquerade." The pages of all the tales are peppered with images of the dark storm, the unearthly wail or shriek, the funeral knell. Phantoms and wraiths pursued by guilt do duty for characters; only or almost only in "The Gentle Boy" is there a delineation of humanity in any truly recognizable aspect. Into two sketches, finally, he poured uninhibitedly the pain and dread of that ultimate preoccupation of a nature "too sensitive to endure the dust"—"Fancy's Show Box" and "The Haunted Mind." The first of these sketches contains an almost clinical delineation of a soul haunted by a sense of guilt as a residuum of repressed anti-social wishes. With deep unconscious insight Hawthorne marks the analogy between wish-fulfillment and art "Thus a novel-writer or a dramatist, in creating a villain of romance and fitting him with evil deeds, and the villain of actual life, in projecting crimes that will be perpetrated, may almost meet each other halfway between reality and fancy." He hopes that the "consequences of sin will not be incurred, unless the act have set its seal upon the thought," but dwells finally upon the universal guilt of man whose heart, although his hand be clean "has surely been polluted by the flitting phantoms of iniquity." Even more revelatory is "The Haunted Mind" through which flit images and wishes un-controlled, to which comes early sorrow "wearing a sister's likeness of first love," and shame, the shadow of what would cause you to blush "even in the remotest caverns of the earth," and remorse "in woman's garments, with a pale beauty amid sin and desolation" or "in the likeness of a corpse with a bloody stain upon the shroud." There is a "wintry gloom about the heart" in the depths of which "there is a tomb and a dungeon." Let it be remembered that in the psychical life, as in the physical order, phenomena are not spontaneous; they are caused. Hawthorne wrote these sketches not by accident but to ease his troubled soul. A purely empirical or descriptive criticism stands barren and baffled before the oneness of experience and expression, which it is forced superficially to recognize but is wholly powerless to interpret. Breaking my rule to remark upon no previous critics or historians of our literature I think it but just to say that empirical criticism is least admirable when it makes a virtue of its impotence. Thus the late Professor V. L. Parrington, analyzing the "Note Books" of Hawthorne remarked, as every observer must, upon their emptiness of either philosophical ideas or human interests and upon the constant recurrence in them of such suggestions as this: "A snake taken into a man's stomach . . . tormenting him most horribly. A type of envy or some other evil passion." Professor Parrington goes on to say that the character of these jottings "offers food for speculation" and adds that "after his marriage they are much less frequent and become more normal—a change which the Freudians, no doubt, would be ready enough to explain." The empiric critic, in brief, after drawing from a dim understanding of Freud's discoveries his one sound observation, adds a cheaply unfair and slighting remark concerning the principle he has just used. Doubtless there were late Ptolomæans who, having solved a problem according to the heliocentric theory, added a belittling observation on Copernicus.

It is but sober truth that we owe Hawthorne's one thoroughly achieved book and unique masterpiece "The Scarlet Letter" to his happy and harmonious union with Sophia Peabody. Not only do the profoundly sick and perverse images disappear from his "Note Books." He is at last able in those earlier years of his marriage really to project, truly to create, to send forth into the world a work separate from himself, living with a life of its own and therefore easing him of a portion of his inner burden. This book, alone among his books, moreover, deals with central things—with normal guilt, with genuine passion, with the operations of recognizable minds. It is for this reason that we accept the over-stressed symbolism of the scarlet letter not only upon Hester's bosom but upon that of Arthur Dimmesdale and even the more troublesome and unnecessary eeriness of little Pearl. The fable has high coherence: the unwise marriage of Hester to the aging and dusty Chillingworth, the lovely passion that flamed up between her and the young cleric, the terrible expiation conditioned in that place and age, and above all, Hester's rising to a vision of life which made that expiation less than an eternal necessity. "For years past she had looked from this estranged point of view at human institutions, and whatever priests or legislators had established; criticising all with hardly more reverence than the Indian would feel for the clerical band, the judicial robe, the pillory, the gallows, the fireside, or the church. The tendency of her fate and fortunes had been to set her free." It is Hester, too, who reminds Dimmesdale that what they did "had a consecration of its own," and that the true sinner in this coil of tragic circumstance was the revengeful old man whose sin it was to have "violated, in cold blood, the sanctity of a human heart." And so it is acceptable to the imagination, and the moral sensibility that Hester persuades Dimmesdale to flee with her and equally that their flight is frustrated only and again by that old man who had let malevolence so stain his soul that his power for good was, according to his own confession, withered and dead. "The Scarlet Letter," in brief, is a tragic tale. It is not the mere gloomy projection of an inner sense of guilt. Like all high literature it accepts life as tragic, but simultaneously represents the human spirit as triumphing at some point over the evil rooted in the hearts and embodied in the institutions of men. At its dark core glows a hope which reconciles the reader to a universe in which such things can be. It is this ultimate sense of reconciliation which tests the difference between the neurotic art-structure and the fully projected work of the poetic imagination. It is absent from the former; it is the final impression left by the latter. The poet speaking of himself has succeeded in speaking for mankind; he has universalized the concrete; experience has not become merely expression; it has become communication and therefore art. It is not without significance that the bearer of the spirit of liberation and reconciliation in Hawthorne's solitary masterpiece is a woman and that the tragic fable issues from such action as is fundamental to creatures of mortal flesh and blood.

Among the other three romances of Hawthorne, it is not difficult to agree with Howells in preferring "The Blithedale Romance." Less rich in mere texture than "The House of the Seven Gables" or "The Marble Faun," it is saved by a shrewdness of observation and a precision of speech which Hawthorne possessed but rarely permitted himself to use. He was, when not ridden by his guilt complex, one of the most sensible men of his age, capable of sound social criticism, healthy scepticism, a frankness of speech which his unemphatic manner has tended to obscure. I do not recall having seen any comment on his remarkable passage concerning the maidens of his period whom he supposes "to have become what we find them by the gradual refining away of the physical system." "Some philosophers," he adds, "choose to glorify this habit of body as spiritual . . . it is rather the effect of unwholesome food, lack of outdoor exercise, and neglect of bathing . . . all resulting in a kind of hereditary dyspepsia." The portraits of Hester Prynne and of Zenobia make it clear, of course, where Hawthorne's personal preferences lay. Defensively, too, he represents Miles Coverdale in "The Blithedale Romance" as in love with the feeble Priscilla. But the passage quoted indicates as well as any the healthy dealing with realities that make "The Blithedale Romance," despite its thinness and slightness, increasingly acceptable to a modern temper. The portrait of Hollingsworth, the sincere but professional reformer, is perhaps Hawthorne's soundest contribution to the study of human nature under the comfortable light of common day, and the portraiture of Zenobia with its half-unwilling admiration and its touch of normal human malice—"I recognized no severe culture in Zenobia; her mind was full of weeds"—is hardly less agreeable and refreshing. The book is full of such terse and precise observations as the one just quoted or as that concerning Hollingsworth's "terrible egotism which he mistook for an angel of God," or as that tenderer one concerning those "who were not yet so old nor had suffered so deeply, as to lose their faith in the better time to come." Thus "The Blithedale Romance" is not only a book that wears well in its more homespun way but one that makes the critic regret the submergence of the novelist in the mere romancer.

The trouble with "The House of the Seven Gables" and "The Marble Faun" is, of course, that they are all texture, all atmosphere, quite without bone or muscle, that is, acceptable intellectual or moral content. The Maule-Pyncheon curse is rather puerile machinery, not because the fathers' sins are not in truth visited upon the children, but because this process in the moral world does not take place in that fanciful void or with that melodramatic patness, but under the ironical sunlight in the rich surge of character and business. It is even truer, as Hawthorne magnificently remarks "that no great mistake, whether acted or endured in our mortal sphere, is ever really set right." But his creative energy was not equal to that of his conception and no heart has ever been deeply stirred by the terrible injustice that ruined Clifford's life[1] nor reconciled by the falling of the Pyncheon fortune either to him and Hepzibah or to "the descendant of the legendary wizard and the village-maiden, over whom he had thrown Love's web of sorcery." The phrasing of that last sentence aptly symbolizes the tawdriness to which Hawthorne descends in this book again and again. "The Marble Faun," finally, is not even informed by a moral idea just in itself, however fancifully embodied, but by a slight and unconvincing moral fiction. Rome is not Rome in the book any more than the myths of Greece remain themselves in his retelling of them. The veil of Salem hangs between—the minister's black veil. As an American, Hawthorne was the reverse of provincial; against the background of great historic phenomena he remains a Massachusetts villager.

Yet these two secondary romances, especially "The House

---

[1] Compare the same theme as treated by J. Wassermann in "The Maurizius Case."

of the Seven Gables," continue to exist as part of the furniture of our minds. Nor wholly of American minds alone. They are not the easiest reading today, especially for mature people. Nor has time deepened the originally faded colors of the tales and sketches. But the whole body of Hawthorne's work, grouped as it were, about "The Scarlet Letter," has today—eighty years after the publication of his single masterpiece—that quality which is loosely called classic. For what is a classic it may be asked once more? A writer who seems inevitable and irreplaceable within the landscape of the mind, whose absence from that landscape, when imagined, induces a definite feeling of impoverishment and loss. That mark of a classic Hawthorne undoubtedly possesses, at least for those who speak the English language. And what, it may be asked furthermore, gives a writer's work this classic, this necessary quality which the highest artists have in a degree so supreme that the world would seem intolerable in which Isaiah and Homer, Shakespeare and Goethe or Mozart and Beethoven had not lived and spoken or sung of and for and to us? The quality is derived from some deep element and experience in the writer's inner life which is, narrowly in a minor, broadly in a major classic, so integrated with an ever-recurrent instinct, need, experience or compensatory wish of other human souls, that the writer's work finds without seeking in each generation those who discover in it the embodiment of their inner needs. Nor will work which thus speaks permanently to men ever be without that beauty of form which is the precipitate of its spirit, which is indeed part of and insep-

185

arable from substance, which constitutes in the last analysis, the *act* of artistic communication.

VI

When Hawthorne and Melville, his junior by fifteen years, became neighbors at Lenox in 1850, Mrs. Hawthorne —vigilant in her adoration—is said to have uncomfortably suspected that a greater than her husband had entered their small circle. Hawthorne was recovering from the strain of the composition of "The Scarlet Letter"; Melville was trying to ease his stormy soul by writing "Moby Dick." By June, 1851, Hawthorne had finished "The House of the Seven Gables," which Melville generously welcomed, while he himself was still in torment over the white whale. "The tale is not yet cooked," he wrote to Hawthorne, "though the hell-fire in which the whole book is broiled might not unreasonably have cooked it ere this." From this glimpse of the two artists one could divine various qualities of both that are borne out by their works. Mrs. Hawthorne need have entertained no fear. At this period of his life at least her husband had the power of creative self-catharsis, of projecting finished works—forever separate from his psyche —into the world. That gift Melville never attained. He fumed and fretted over the demon in his soul; he fled from it literally to the farthest isles of the sea; he hurled at it brief thunderbolts of sheer but intermittent genius; he sought to bury it under mountains of words. Nothing availed him, poor man. Catharsis was impossible. He lapsed into a long silence, broken only by the voice of his querulousness, and lingered on to 1891.

The Gods approve
The depth, and not the tumult, of the soul.

The demon that pursued him has been revealed, a little hesitantly but clearly enough, by the researches of Professor R. M. Weaver. Left fatherless at thirteen Melville, with an overpowering fixation on his mother, expressed almost to the point of actual insight in "Pierre," found in that cold and handsome lady no response to his consciously, of course, filial ardor. He thought of himself as doubly orphaned and began to hate a world to him empty, cruel and loveless. He repressed his intolerably jealous hatred of his father and substituted for it a defensive idealization. This common device of neurotics broke down in later years and in "Pierre" the face that haunted him—"too familiar, yet inexplicable," that face "backward hinting of some irrevocable sin"—this face "compounded so of hell and heaven" "is the instrument by which the memory of Pierre's father is desecrated." From his adolescence on, then, the world was a homeless and an empty place and his soul cast out and orphaned. A "sort of Ishmael" he calls himself in "Redburn" and adds: "Talk not of the bitterness of middle-age . . . a boy can feel all that and much more, when upon his young soul the mildew has fallen. . . . And never again can such blights be made good . . . they strike in too deep." Ishmael he remained even to the ominous opening of "Moby Dick," questing forever after the mother-image, called Yillah from "the island of delight" in "Mardi," invoked in many moods in "Pierre": "*Who* art thou?" "Take thy thin fingers from me; I am affianced and not to thee!" The incest imagery haunts him even as it haunted Shelley. But he found release in neither art

187

nor life. At seventeen he fled from home and went to sea. Inevitably! "Such flight-like breaking of familial ties," an eminent psychologist writes, "is a typical reaction toward an overpowering fixation and almost always marks the beginning of an artistic career."[1] And Melville was destined to flee again and again, if not to Europe, if not always to the South Seas, then at least away from life, from reality and outward experience, from the world which had so early disappointed and blighted his soul.

What is the pertinence of this analysis of Melville, for the objective exactness of which all proofs from his own life and works, as well as from clinical material and from the revelations of other artists are in? It accounts for the fragmentary, chaotic, explosive and unguided character of all his work. The rounded work of art speaks of complete projection of the inner urgency, speaks of catharsis and control. More clearly than ever we perceive that the great artist is also the man of strong and valiant character, no Bohemian and eccentric and vagrant, and why Shakespeare retired with a comfortable fortune and built him a house and Milton and Goethe were servants of their states. The analysis has another purpose and use. It accounts for the atmosphere of all of Melville's books—that atmosphere of homelessness and emptiness, that desolateness of the heart which is present even in the Paradisal valleys of the Marquesas, which makes one shiver in "Redburn," which rises to a wild, despairing cry in "Moby Dick" and which is not absent even from the simpler and saner narrative of "Israel Potter." The final

[1] Dr. Otto Rank, to whose *Das Inzest Motiv in Dichtung und Sage: Grundzüge einer Psychologie des dichterischen Schaffens* (2nd ed. 1926) I am profoundly indebted, as all of literary criticism is bound increasingly to be.

image that arises from all of Melville's work is that of a big bearded violently excited man trying to shout down the whimpering, lonely child in his soul.

It will be seen at once that I consider the recent reëstimate of Melville to have somewhat overshot the mark. Great wits have praised him, but not, perhaps, those of most balanced judgment. He has his superb moments. But are those moments not rare and do they wholly repay the labor necessary to reach them? A younger generation, in search of that "usable" American past which Van Wyck Brooks so earnestly and sagaciously demanded long ago, has fastened its flag to his mast. Has not that generation been both deceived and self-deceived? Has it not substituted its desire and ideal for the reality? Melville was not a strong man defying the cruel order of the world; he was a weak man fleeing from his own soul and from life, a querulous man, a fretful man. It did not take reality—suffering, injustice, disease, poverty, public outrage or private wrong—to disillusion him. His life, as the lives of artists go, was not unfortunate. He was disillusioned from the beginning. He adopted all his life the regressive attitude of the neurotic—of the favorite child who wants the world to reconstitute for it the conditions of the nursery. Is that not evident even in "Moby Dick"? Much tried Prometheus does not defy the gods with that mad, sick violence, nor does he interrupt his defiance with babble about the brains of the sperm whale being accounted a fine dish.

The South Sea books, which first brought Melville into public notice, hold up remarkably well. There are enough pages of sober narrative and description in both "Typee" and "Omoo" to satisfy a strong natural curiosity concerning

189

the state of those islands before the so-called "civilizing" and also sentimentalizing process had gone too far. Melville saw the Marquesas now nearly an hundred years ago and that very fact, coupled with the undoubted vigor of his writing, tells in his favor. This holds good despite the fact that Melville himself had no scientific curiosity. The language of the islands is to him "unintelligible and stunning gibberish" that gives him "a headache for the rest of the day"; he really made no effort to understand the nature of taboo or to enter into the psychical processes of the islanders. They are mere "natives" to him; they annoy him; he is happy only when the valley is a substitute for life and a defense against it for him —a Paradise into which to flee. His attitude in "Omoo" is more objective and more manly. He brings his mind to bear on facts and conditions and abuses. His criticism of the missionaries is strong and sagacious and probably took courage in 1848. In no other book is Melville so tolerable a companion, so free of fretfulness and mere spleen. Yet both "Typee" and "Omoo" are somehow morose books—books, like all of Melville's, without charm, which is a mark of harmony, without sweetness, which is a mark of strength. Fayaway is not beautiful in the memory nor is the valley. The books, I repeat, are morose, not somber, hard, not severe. Yet that they are readable and are read today at all is a tribute which no critic dare underestimate.

It is not necessary to linger over the minor works. "Mardi" and "Pierre" are sheer phantasmagorias, clinical material rather than achieved literature. "Redburn" is the story of a boy who runs away to sea—the boy Melville, of course. It is strong where Melville is always strong: in the delineation of sordid and meaningless suffering, physical pain and humiliation. It is weak in characterization, in inner and outer form. It is distinctly inferior to R. H. Dana's contemporary "Two Years Before the Mast." Not without curious interest is the late "Israel Potter." But in this book Melville leaned heavily upon the actual memoirs of a soldier of the American Revolution and submitted a good deal to the corrective and discipline of historic fact. He nevertheless makes John Paul Jones an image of his own wild and weak rebelliousness. In the chapters on Benjamin Franklin in Paris, however, and in those that describe the battle between the "Bon Homme Richard" and the British frigate "Serapis" he achieves both his most human piece of characterization and his best-sustained and most attractive piece of descriptive writing.

There remains "Moby Dick," which is today acclaimed a masterpiece. But masterpieces, it has been pointed out, have invariably in them an ultimate spirit of reconciliation either, in former ages, to the universe or, in modern times, to the suffering but not overwhelmed spirit of man. This fact, capable of empiric proof by the examination of universally recognized masterpieces has very definite psychological and philosophical causes. Great works, furthermore, even great works of the second order like "The Scarlet Letter" or (still to stick to Melville's contemporaries) Emerson's "Essays," have a continuously or almost continuously high quality of execution, which carries one along even when the matter fails. The comparison has been made between "Moby Dick" and "Pantagruel," evidently by those unacquainted with Rabelais in the original. For Rabelais has a continuous beauty and liquid flow of speech that does not leave him even in his coarsest passages, such as that at the end of the fourth book. The Frenchman is always ripe and rich and self-contained, the American is raw and over-eager and ill at ease. The eloquence in "Moby Dick" is fierce and broken and sags every other minute into sheer jejune maundering or insufferable wordiness. The grandiose and the trivial are never far apart. There are things of a rich and memorable quaintness in "Moby Dick," such as the sermon in the Whaleman's chapel; there are passages that have the epic touch, such as that on the hunters of Nantucket; there are brief unforgettable images, such as that of "moody stricken Ahab with a crucifixion in his face in all the nameless regal overbearing dignity of some mighty woe"; there is occasionally a concentrated energy of speech as in those words of Ahab: "I see in him outrageous strength, with an inscrutable malice sinewing it"; there is, at least once, a noble pathos in the description of Queequeg's death: "An awe that cannot be named would steal over you as you sat by the side of this waning savage, and saw as strange things in his face, as any beheld who were bystanders when Zoroaster died"; there is, finally, toward the end a passage of no ignoble intensity through which Melville expresses with extreme concentration the pride of his peculiar woe. Yet it must be pointed out that in prose of the first order one can never, as here, pick out pentameters:

kindly diffused through feebler men's whole lives . . .
great hearts sometimes condense to one deep pang . . .
though summary in each one suffering. . . .

Such are the finest things in "Moby Dick." It were generous to admit that they constitute one-fourth of that long book; it is certainly indisputable that of the rest what is not sound and fury merely is inchoate and dull. What, in fact, has caught the imagination of a not unreasonably pessimistic age is that greatly conceived symbolism and allegory: Man under the name of Ahab scours the endless and overwhelming seas to hunt down that White Whale in which is concentrated all the blind malevolence of the desolate universe. He finds the Whale and the Whale destroys him and his men. The evil of the universe has triumphed. . . . Such, by the way, was not quite the ultimate conclusion of this Ishmael who was "not so much bound to any haven ahead as rushing from all havens astern." In the late verses of "Clarel," which often have a mellower and more human quality than his prose he speaks of real things, of the dangers of Democracy creating "an Anglo-Saxon China," of "the impieties of 'Progress,'" which is a great phrase, and so, facing realities and not only the demon within, he strikes at last the central human note:

This world clean fails me: *still I yearn* . . .

No, Melville is not even a minor master. His works constitute rather one of the important curiosities of literature. He will be chiefly remembered as the inventor of a somber legend concerning the evil that is under the sun. But to embody this legend in a permanently valid form he had only half the creative power and none of the creative discipline or serenity.

BOOK FIVE

Demos Speaks

I

Quietly and unobtrusively, as such things will happen, the predominance of the gentry in American letters was drawing to a close. What were Thoreau and Emerson, Hawthorne and even Poe but contributors to English letters from a province more remote in space than in atmosphere and temper? The analogy between them and Scotch or Irish writers of English is not inexact. Is not, in fact, Emerson more English than Burns and Poe not less so than his exact contemporary James Clarence Mangan? This, of course, is not a reproach but a definition. The New England writers could not but express an imported culture; there was no other. The identity of speech, moreover, made the emergence both of a folk and of a folk culture difficult and doubtful in America at best. To this day our writers may easily be divided into those who are more or less European or more or less of the American folk. There is James Branch Cabell, whose strictly American quality one would be hard driven to define; there is Theodore Dreiser who, though the son of German immigrants, is unimaginable except upon this soil, nourished by this life, speaking this American speech. The currents cross; the threads are tangled. But one need be no noisy nativist to feel a lift and stir when at last an American folk is formed and arises and produces men of a unique flavor, speech and vision: Lincoln, Whitman, Mark Twain.

That definition and becoming of an American folk— *Volkwerden*—evidently took place in the Middle West. It took place there first; it has found renewal and intensification in the Mississippi Valley ever since. Exceptions occur, Whitman being the earliest and still the greatest. Yet the wise instinct of poets, from William Ellery Leonard, New England Brahmin, to Carl Sandburg, child of Swedes, has recognized that folk-becoming in the Middle West in the symbolical figure, in both the fact and the myth of Abraham Lincoln:

"Folk-hero of the last among the races."

And the folk's selection of this figure as its hero illustrates its complete disregard of the Federalist temper of the gentry, North or South, and its preservation of that fundamental tradition by which America was to be a land of freedom and of mercy, of justice and of peace. I must add at once that that American spirit, though it seems, for the year and the decade to have been abandoned by the American folk, has lived on in the aims and activities of the best and most representative American writers. It informs our whole age of critical realism and lyric revolt. It lives in the verses of Leonard and Edna Millay, in the plays of Eugene O'Neill and

195

in the acute ironic documents of Sinclair Lewis. A still younger generation may feebly flirt with alien Fascist doctrine. The authentic American spirit born of the hope of fugitives and pioneers, disregarded by the provincial Eastern gentry of our first cultural period, reborn in Whitman, reintegrated by the people itself in the Lincoln myth, has never yet wholly perished from the land.

The historical Lincoln whose written words are accessible affords all the matter for the myth-making of the popular imagination. He was not the great stylist acclaimed by a scholarship more patriotic than discriminating. He was, in fact, far more important for American literature when, as in the short autobiographic sketch written to J. W. Fell in 1859, he was not, in any literary sense, trying to write at all. The vision that counts is that of the rude, untutored boy and youth in the solitariness of that pioneering scene, growing into the man somber and often self-distrustful, not given to any formal religiosity, relying without self-consciousness or emphatic gesture upon certain mystic monitions drawn, as it were, from the heart of mankind itself. "What I do say is that no man is good enough to govern another man without that other's consent." There is the quite homely, there the truly precious Lincoln, the same who slept better after signing a pardon—one of the very few Christians in the bloody history of Christendom. It is that homely Lincoln who had the highest sagacity: "Human action can be modified to some extent, but human nature cannot be changed." We need but place these sayings and not a few like them against the truculent raw glitter of Theodore Roosevelt, against the hollow and sepulchral elegance of Woodrow Wilson wherein the noblest formulations have an indefinably pinchbeck tone and savor—we need, I say, only place the sayings of Lincoln beside the sayings of those two others to feel the throb of that ultimately, beyond all swathing of fashion and event, authentic human spirit. His integrity was complete. "Labour is prior to and independent of capital. Capital is only the fruit of labour and could never have existed if labour had not first existed." . . . "This country, with its institutions, belongs to the people who inhabit it. Whenever they shall grow weary of the existing government, they can exercise their constitutional right of amending it, or their revolutionary right to dismember or overthrow it." But he is at his best when he speaks not of political theory or even of economic structure, but of mankind. In February, 1842, at Springfield, Illinois, he addressed the Washingtonian Temperance Society. The opening paragraphs of the address are a little jejune, a little "dated," as we say now. But soon he warmed to his subject and bade the temperance people to have charity and to use persuasion only, since in the world of moral values man would not endure force. "Assume to dictate to his judgment, or to command his action, or to mark him as one to be shunned and despised, and he will retreat within himself, close all the avenues to his head and heart; and though your cause be naked truth itself, transformed to the heaviest lance, harder than steel, and sharper than steel can be made, and though you throw it with more than Herculean force and precision, you shall no more be able to pierce him than to penetrate the hard shell of a tortoise with a rye straw. Such is man, and so must he be understood by those who would lead him." Even as mere

writing that is stronger and more fundamental than the
slightly arranged eloquence of the address at Gettysburg. As
the wisdom of a great soul it illustrates well why Lincoln

has prospered in the hearts of men

especially in the hearts of poets and why in this day of brutal
and stupid violence when the mere enforcement of law, irrespective of the law's consonance with the conscience and will
and heart of men, is regarded as righteous and virtuous,
Abraham Lincoln is more than ever the symbolic figure that
integrated the American hope and ideal not only for his
own time but for times to come in which poet after poet,
even to the latest, has continued the tradition of Walt Whitman in praise of him as *the* great American:

For the sweetest, wisest soul of all my days and lands—and this
    for his dear sake,
Lilac and star and bird twined with the chant of my soul,
There in the fragrant pines and cedars dusk and dim.

II

Walt Whitman—most strange and difficult figure in all
our letters and perhaps the greatest, certainly the most far-
reaching, far-echoing poetic voice. Rightly did he ask in his
own day: "Do you call those genteel little creatures American poets?" And if our poets, taking the word in its widest
and proper sense of creative spirits, are no longer all "genteel
little creatures"—it is due not least to his powerful and permanently valid example. So much being obviously true, it is
time now in an instructed age to inquire why all or nearly all
commentary on Whitman is characterized by either a faint
sliminess or a furtive dullness or by such downright misinter-

198

pretations and little white extenuating lies as André Gide points out with bitter amusement in the amiable biography of the poet by the late Léon Bazalgette. This inquiry will, moreover, lead us beyond its original purpose. It will illustrate and account for many of the marks of Whitman's style; it will throw light upon the quality of his sociological theories; it will once and for all silence the recurrent and foolish question why Whitman, desirous above all else of being a folk poet, has never been accepted by the folk, but finds his prophets and proclaimers from decade to decade among the febrile and the effeminate.

The secret is, of course, an open secret. But open secrets are more corrupting than closed ones. They lead to whisperings and snickers and furtiveness and withdraw the personality or the subject in question from rational discussion and solid interpretation. I purpose, then, in regard to Walt Whitman, to sweep away once and for all the miasma that clouds and dims all discussion of him and his work. He was a homosexual of the most pronounced and aggressive type. Nor has there ever been any good reason to doubt it. Considering his place and time the "Calamus" poems are of an amazing outspokenness. Consciously or not he probably counted on the fact that none but those similarly constituted would dare to understand. In addition he created a legend of himself, including the myth of the New Orleans lady and his children by her, as an escape and defense. And this, too, was natural since social groups demand not only certain norms of behavior but of constitution. There were always those, however, like John Addington Symonds and Edward Carpenter who understood him thoroughly and since the publication of the letters to Peter Doyle in 1897 any doubt left by the poems were, of course, destroyed. But the poems, in truth, leave no doubt and I shall not even trouble my readers with references to the scientific monographs on Whitman's abnormal constitution that exist in several languages. He announces frankly that the "Calamus" poems proceed in "paths untrodden," that they represent an escape "from all the standards hitherto published" in being songs "of manly attachment." They are. They make the matter, despite half-hearted disclaimers here and there, sudden slight accesses of prudence as at the end of "Earth, my Likeness," as plain as words can make it without direct obscenity. The poems contain the homosexual's atavistic subconscious memories of the men's house in primitive societies projected upon the present social structure and his hopes for it, which are so profoundly mingled with much communistic sentiment: "I believe the main purport of these States is to found a superb friendship, exalté, previously unknown . . . waiting latent in all men"; they contain the usual appeal to Socrates and the common fancy about Christ; they contain the usual symbols and subterfuges but also idealistically tinged homoerotic carnalities unparalleled, so far as I know, in any modern language. To the slightly instructed in analytical psychology the one poem "Whoever You are Holding me now in Hand," with its curious "Lilliputian"[1] fantasy, which throws some doubt on Whitman's robust aggressiveness even as a homosexual, tells the whole story and reveals the man's nature and appetences. Nor did this thread of self-revelation ever thereafter disap-

[1] I borrow this term from Dr. S. Ferenczi's acute solution of the Swift "mystery" in his address before the New York Society for Clinical Psychiatry given Dec. 9, 1926.

pear from his work. However hidden or elusive, this expression of his special nature does not cease. He takes final leave of the world in "Old Age Echoes" with that central confession on his lips.

I look composedly upon nature, drink day and night the joys of
    life, and await death with perfect equanimity.
Because of my tender and boundless love for him I love and
    because of his boundless love for me.

III

We are now at once in a better position to understand the esoteric character of Whitman's reputation and the fact that the democratic masses whom he celebrated have passed him by. The instinct that bade them do so was no unhealthy one. It needs neither knowledge of morbid psychology nor analytical insight to receive fairly constantly from Whitman's work and from the records of his life a slightly repellent impression. One has to conquer this impression before his great qualities can be disengaged and enjoyed. One can take pleasure not even in his own or others' account of his services as a nurse and wound-dresser during the war. There is too much false festiveness and coyness and posturing and embracing. One is not at all surprised after that at the anecdotes concerning street-car conductors nor at Peter Doyle nor yet at the disorder and sordidness and sordid quarrels of those last years in the Mickle Street house in Camden, which extended beyond his death. No wonder that the guardians of Horace Traubel's adolescence warned him against "the lecherous old man." There spoke the voice of the people. It was, alas, quite correct in the perception if not in the precise definition which it expressed. Whitman must have been a very dreadful person indeed. And this was a real misfortune to American literature, since this dreadful person happened to be a man of authentic genius.

The second element that has kept Whitman from more general appreciation is his form. The Whitman coteries and fellowships and his direct imitators have expressed a surprise at this, which only reveals the perverse ignorance of the sophisticated. Wherever the folk sings, whether in Negro spiritual or in Cowboy ballad or in sailor chantey or in Old World folk-song, it sings *in time*. Note the scientific precision of common speech! It sings in time and its pleasure is derived from the heightened consciousness of time which can be gained only by dividing time, beating time or, in other words, by creating rhythm. The stamping of feet and the clapping of hands, the systole and diastole of breath and in all likelihood physiological processes obscurer and more vital served to accompany that primitive singing voice or chorus which inevitably arranged its words, too, in time, in rhythm-groups, in meter. Thus it is evident that the most elaborate patterns made of regular or recurrent rhythm-groups such as the feet of classical prosody, are more primitive and more natural than those "numbers freed of law" which, quite mistakenly by the way, the ultra-sophisticated Horace attributed to Pindar. Prose, as every schoolboy used to know, is a very late art compared to verse. All primitive poetry is in fixed verse. A form that is neither verse nor prose is a late and learned invention. As a poet of democracy, then, Whitman presented himself as a person of peculiar and perverse moral atmosphere using as his means of expression a form as remote as possible from all tradition and normal instinct. Had that first edition of the "Leaves of Grass" been published in 1855, as of course it was not, with all the trumpeting of a modern best-seller, readers would still have preferred the romantic anthropology and jejune style of "Hiawatha" published in the same year. And in a profoundly human, if not in a literary sense, they would have been in that year quite within their rights.

I shall not enter upon any strict inquiry into the origin or sources of Whitman's form. Ossian, the supposed lawlessness of classical Hebrew poetry as translation exhibits it, blank verse, perhaps the experiments of Southey and Shelley—all these or any of them would have sufficed to justify Whitman in his impatience of the discipline of verse and in his historically false but otherwise rather gallant notion that a true American poetry ought to break with all traditions of form as well as of substance. He, in fact, had occasional hankerings after rhythms and measures that hummed in his ears. Thus he begins "A Boston Ballad":

To get betimes in Boston town I rose this morning early,

and "Song of the Broad-Axe" thus:

Weapon shapely, naked, wan,
Head from the mother's bowels drawn,

and "Song of the Universal" in this stately fashion:

Come, said the Muse,
Sing me a song no poet yet has chanted,
Sing me the universal.

But he lacked both patience and desire and perhaps the ability to continue with the indicated rhythms. Yet it is not a little curious to observe how many of his lines, and these not the least beautiful, have the habit of falling into metrical structures of which he was probably not wholly conscious. Among these lines may be found the galliambic meter:

As a father to his father going takes his children along with him,

and dactylic measures:

Now we have met, we have looked, we are safe,

and trochaic ones:

Here the frailest leaves of me and yet my strongest lasting,

and hexameters:

We found our own, O my soul, in the calm and cool of the daybreak,

and shapelier pentameters:

Shooting in pulses of fire ceaseless to vivify all.

Iambic rhythms necessarily abound, as in

Night of south winds—night of the large few stars,
Still nodding night—mad naked summer night,

or as in

Thou who hast slept all night upon the storm,
Waking renew'd on thy prodigious pinions.

And there are beautifully wrought alexandrines, such as

Singing with open mouths their strong melodious songs,

and

Or the brown land and the blue sea for maps and charts.

I am seeking in no wise to depreciate the form that Whitman

invented as his medium of expression. It is a genuine form; it is in his hands, if not in the hands of his disciples, a frequently great and noble form. I am seeking to point out that it was of all conceivable forms the least calculated "to teach the average man the glory of his daily walk and trade," because it could not in the very nature of things reach that average man's ear and that even Whitman, its inventor and only great practitioner, slipped back constantly despite himself into those rhythmic melodies that are so profoundly rooted in the nature of literature and of mankind itself.

No, Whitman's audience was restricted from the beginning and is not likely ever to be a very large one. Nor has he been hitherto well served by his critics and interpreters. Sullen contemptuousness about him has alternated with rapture. And the rapture has been worst of all since, as in the case of Oscar Wilde, it proceeded far too often from a special and a morbid interest. Lately, literary scholarship has turned its attention to Whitman. The results have not been happy. The facts about his life have been discovered and not frankly communicated; the appreciation of his work has been dull and formal. Thus at this late date a well-balanced word remains to be spoken.

He was at least from this point of view worthy of celebrating the life and death of Lincoln that, at his most lucid, he had a magnificent insight into the true meaning, into the genuine hopes and inevitable dangers of the democratic experiment. How archaic that sounds today! But the wave of black reaction that, following the World War, engulfed first Europe and then gradually rolled its evil waters westward may recede, even as that other wave of tyranny and terror following a great and disastrous war receded first in the year 1830, next in the year 1848, and the words of Whitman which to too many ears will seem mere literature today will again assume their true character as life and practical wisdom. He desired them to have that character, for he shared with Emerson the exact knowledge of the creative spirit in the modern world: "The priest departs, the divine literatus comes." But his ideas which form the background of his work and correct the impression left by his more undisciplined dithyrambs are to be found in the unjustly neglected prose of the "Democratic Vistas." Here he defines the purpose of democracy as helping man ultimately to "become a law, and series of laws unto himself"; and of government "to train communities . . . beginning with individuals and ending there again, to rule themselves." Here, too, he makes it evident that he has no romantic notion of the natural goodness of the masses of mankind and no very high opinion of the naturalness of their rights but, "leaving the rest to sentimentalists," takes his stand for freedom and flexibility, variety of character and experience, despite the "appalling dangers of universal suffrage" as the only ultimately safe and possible way of life. He is not blind to the fact that "society in these states is cankered, crude, superstitious and rotten." He likened the lust for material success to "the magician's serpent in the fable which ate up all the other serpents." He asked the crucial question: "Is there a great moral and religious civilization—the only justification of a great material one?" But his remedy for the evils he saw was more democracy, not less, an extension not a restriction of freedom, a full and happy chance for that democratic experiment from which he hoped well-being, moral and intellectual liberties and last creative spirits of another wealth and stature and character from "those genteel little creatures" who called themselves American poets in his day.

The "Democratic Vistas" should be read before the poems as both ideological background, I may repeat, and as corrective. For, wholly devoid as Whitman was of sureness of taste —witness his painfully shoddy use of French words—he let himself go in the poems with an unheard-of looseness of speech and of ideational logic. He is in the same poem noble and trivial, sagacious and foolish, capable of high concentration of speech and of the loosest babble. Moreover, the "Democratic Vistas" have shadow and the chief fault of the poems is their continuous glare. So much optimism calls forth the sharpest reaction, so much *fortissimo* makes one long for silence, so much indefiniteness of speech drives the reader to the extreme of demanding dry precision. That is the trouble with the poems, that they have no depth of color, no density except at rare moments; their mercilessly luminous expanse wears out the strongest eye. Not till the shadow of the tragic falls across a page, do we have severity or depth of tone. "Leaves of Grass" must be read in fragments and exists as literature only in fragments. A continuous reading of the book is one of the most enervating of literary experiences. The endless and repetitious pageant passes by, and though one admits the motive and reason of it to be one of the finest and most humane in all literature, a weariness sets in that after a while breeds rebellion and disgust. The parts, certain parts of Whitman's work are not less than great; the whole is unendurable.

But how great the fragments, in truth, are and how one is tempted, regarding them again, to retract the quite necessary negative view of his work as a whole. In almost the same breath he writes:

> All truths wait in all things

and

> Logic and sermons never convince,
> The damp of the night drives deeper into my soul,

and

> I am the man, I suffer'd, I was there,

which is one of the great lines of all poetry, and

> Agonies are one of my changes of garments,
> I do not ask the wounded person how he feels, I myself become
>   the wounded person,
> My hurts turn livid upon me as I lean on a cane and observe.

Out of these four quotations could be developed the exact nature of the messianic character and also of the creative spirit in literature and of the modern necessary ultimate identity of the two. Equally deep and quite literally inspiring are the highest expressions of his individualism and of his desire to have all men share that heroic selfhood:

> None but are accepted, none but shall be dear to me.

But the self that men are asked to assume is indeed heroic, for

> My call is the call of battle, I nourish active rebellion,
> He going with me must go well-arm'd,
> He going with me goes often with spare diet, poverty, angry
>   enemies, desertions.

And this tonic note recurs again and again and finds another perfect expression many years later in "Autumn Rivulets":

For I am the sworn poet of every dauntless rebel the world over
And he going with me leaves peace and routine behind him
And stakes his life to be lost at any moment.

In apparent contradiction to this theme is Whitman's theme of universal acceptance which is almost Russian in its chaotic leveling impulse. But this type of communistic passion is, as I have suggested before, often due to an abnormal channeling of erotic impulses. It is evidently so in Whitman. There is something coldly orgiastic about his long list of those who shall be equal to him and to any and to the best. But it is never long before he returns to his tonic note of individualism, of a democracy composed of freely consenting and varied personalities.

Produce great Persons, the rest follows. . . .
Piety and conformity to them that like,
Peace, obesity, allegiance to them that like,
I am he who tauntingly compels men, women, nations,
Crying: Leap from your seats and contend for your lives!

And once more:

I swear nothing is good to me now that ignores individuals,
The American compact is altogether with individuals,
The only government is that which makes minute of individuals,
The whole theory of the universe is directed unerringly to one
    single individual—namely to You.

How fine and generous and tonic that strain is, how necessary and noble this call to individualism and yet how futile and how insufficient it has proved itself to be in the years that have passed since Whitman's chief utterances! For from one point of view this singling out of the individual, any individual, and making of him the center of things, is but the traditional Protestant doctrine of the preciousness of the salvation of each soul and of the responsibility of each soul to God. From another point of view—and this is by far the more potent and visible—Whitman's call to unshackled freedom has been accepted by groups of each younger generation since himself who have liberated themselves from "piety and conformity" merely for the sake of liberation, but have never found other and newer objects to which to attach their love and loyalty. For Whitman and with him many others have failed to make the Nietzschean distinction between freedom *from* and freedom *for*! To detach oneself from a galling yoke is of supreme importance, if the light of a new ideal is already above the horizon. Otherwise the end is apt to be mere chaos. All thinking is a choosing among thoughts; all action is a selecting of a certain action among all possible ones. Every choice involves exclusion and hence the affirmation of a principle of choice. Life when sane in the higher sense is always guided. But Whitman proposes no new principle of guidance. And that is still another reason why he has failed as a poet by the very test which he so magnanimously proposed:

The proof of a poet shall be sternly deferr'd till his country absorbs him as affectionately as he has absorbed it.

He had, as a matter of fact, deeper and serener moments than the doctrinal and declamatory ones even at their finest

—moments of purely creative insight. In such moments he wrote:

And I will show that whatever happens to any body it may be turned to beautiful results,

and

Do not call the tortoise unworthy because she is not something else

and

Whoever degrades another degrades me

and

There is to me something profoundly affecting in large masses of men following the lead of those who do not believe in men

and the well-known hymnic dithyrambs of which the finest as well as the most perfectly sustained are probably "Out of the Cradle Endlessly Rocking" and "When Lilacs Last in the Dooryard Bloom'd." Nor are there lacking simpler and more precisely wrought passages, such as the lovely idyll of his mother and the Indian woman which forms the sixth section of "The Sleepers." There would be more of these to be singled out if Whitman, granting him of course, his style and manner, had had within them any certainty of touch. But he was not only essentially unlettered but strangely insensitive and uncritical. He can write as only Emerson had written in "Days"—in a pure, eternal fashion:

Amid a transparent clear belt of ether yet left in the east,
Ascends large and calm the lord-star Jupiter,
And nigh at hand, only a very little above,
Swim the delicate sisters the Pleiades.

And he can write:

> Eclaircisse the myths Asiatic, the primitive fables,

which brings the blush of vicarious shame to the reader's cheek, or

> Yet O my soul supreme!
> Knowst thou the joy of pensive thoughts? etc., etc.

which is close to mere drivel. America, in brief, has had to pay a heavy price for her most highly endowed poet being an unlettered man as well as a man of hopelessly eccentric personality. Nor has this common man's voice, for reasons sufficiently clear, been able to reach the common people whom he loved, nor do those more recent monitions concerning the uses of freedom which beat upon our hearts and consciences, permit the thoughtful and the responsible to give him that adherence which in the early years of this century seemed to be so completely his. Yet unforgettable when all deductions have been made, especially in view of what our literature was up to his time, and unforgettable together with Lincoln in view of the evil authoritarian sophistries of recent years, must be not only the chanter of those great hymnic passages, but the man who profoundly and truly never despaired of liberty, who believed with all his morbid heart that "whoever walks a furlong without sympathy walks to his own funeral drest in his shroud," and who was dedicated without wavering or falseness to "the good old cause, the great idea, the progress and freedom of the race."

IV

It was not the eccentric Long Islander of genius who first succeeded in speaking for the American folk. It was a younger man from the Mississippi Valley, a normal, busy, humorous, kind-hearted American, a newspaper man, prospector, pioneer, publisher, gainer and loser of fortunes, perfect husband, devoted father, pal of millionaires and clergymen and right-thinking men of letters, of lords and dukes and sovereigns too, later on—it was Samuel Clemens, eternal adolescent and hence creator of the finest picaresque novel composed for centuries—it was him whom the American people chose as their great spokesman and literary hero. And why should they not have done so? The sentiments and virtues that he represented are, rightly looked upon, necessary and eternal. The sentiments can be entertained after a more philosophical fashion, the virtues practiced with both more discrimination and more stringency. But I, at least, range myself morally— if not æsthetically and philosophically—with those who out of a sound and necessary instinct, the instinct after all of life and its continuance, rejected the barren homosexual and his new-fangled manner of neither speech nor song and acclaimed and still acclaim Mark Twain. Nor have the people been troubled by what Mark Twain considered the portentous free-thinking and cynicism of his later moods and posthumously published writings. He got not very much farther, as we shall see, than the village agnostic and admirer of Bob Ingersoll and managed to combine with his liberation from dogma such quaint popular superstitions as a faith in osteopathy and a disbelief in Shakespeare's authorship of his works. He was, moreover, a lover of liberty and tolerance, of liquor—in strict moderation—and tobacco, of his country but also of the world. Viewing him from too high a level one could make him out to have been puerile and absurd. But the American people was not ready—what people is?—to accept as its spokesman a Shelley or a Thomas Mann. I am seeking to justify its selection of and its continued allegiance to Mark Twain as sound, as neither unlovely nor ignoble.

He started out, of course, with a very great advantage. Writers of high importance have rarely been innovators of style and form of expression but have heightened and made their own an existent tradition. They are almost never of an inventive or ingenious turn and are contented, as Euripides and Shakespeare and Goethe were, to put to their highly personal uses forms, modes and even subject-matter already present in the consciousness of their people. This is exactly what, in his humbler way, Mark Twain did. He used an already developed and popular method of indigenous ironic humor; he used forms: the journalistic letter of travel, the sketch or tale, the rambling picaresque novel, which involved his audience in no initial difficulty of approach. To these he remained faithful to the end of his career.

The indigenous strain of more or less ironic humor came to him from that school of popular American humorists that may be sufficiently represented for our present purposes by Mark Twain's immediate predecessor and early friend, Artemus Ward. To Ward and to his fellows this strain must have come from the American folk itself, from anecdote and jest spontaneously arising and passing from mouth to mouth and told wherever men foregathered, drunk or sober. The inner spirit and quality of this humor is admirable and quite such as one would expect in the folk-humor of democratic masses. It is directed against pretentiousness and falseness, against all "putting on" of "airs"; its fairly constant intention is the discomfiture of the pretentious and false. It "takes them down a peg"; it exposes them to the laughter of their fellows. A less admirable aspect of this popular humor is its employment of the device of the practical joke. This device, too, Mark Twain took over. His sketches and stories are all written about a practical joke of some kind. But he is careful, unlike his predecessors, to be sure that the objects of the practical joke have justly lost the reader's moral sympathy. "The Man That Corrupted Hadleyburg" is an excellent illustration of this method.

This American folk-humor took perfectly definite forms, of which the chief were outrageous anti-climax, extreme understatement or exaggeration and the juxtaposition of moral or psychological contradictories. Even in Artemus Ward these forms had become rather hard and conventionalized. Mark Twain made them his own and drenched them in the continuous freshness of his spirit. It cannot be said that he introduced any important variations. They may be usefully illustrated from the works of Ward. Of anti-climax a good example is his description of his youthful leave-taking from his father: "I thought I saw tears tricklin down his venerable chin, but it might hav been tobacker jooce. He chaw'd." Still faintly remembered, too, is his quip: "I've been lingerin by the Tomb of the lamentid Shakespeare. It is a success." Exaggeration and understatement dot Ward's pages. A typical example of these is the following: "You can get half a mackril at Delmonico's for six dollars, and biled pertaters throw'd in." Here, of course, he uses both exaggeration and anti-climax. The various devices tend naturally to be used at the same time. The juxtaposition of contradictories is best

illustrated by Artemus Ward's most famous and still remembered saying: "I tell you, feller-citizens, it would have
bin ten dollars in Jeff Davis's pocket if he'd never bin born!"
The mingling of the several forms is well exhibited in his
"Thrilling Scenes in Dixie": "We careered madly to a steep
bank when I got the upper hands of my antaggernist and
threw him into the raveen. He fell about forty feet, striking
a grindstone pretty hard. I understand he was injured. I
haven't heard from the grindstone."

One opens the early sketches of Mark Twain and finds
the identical devices. "I brained him on the spot and had
him buried at my own expense." . . . "Words of such majesty that each was in itself a straggling procession of syl-
lables that might be fifteen minutes passing a given point."
. . . "You never saw a frog so modest and straightfor'ard
as he was, for all he was so gifted." But one also sees at once
that he abandoned, except in dialogue, the silly device of
grotesque spelling and, in addition, one observes as one reads
on that the man has both a more seeing eye and more poetic
soul than the Josh Billings and the Artemus Wards who
were, despite flashes of insight and brilliantly good sense,
hard, sordid, gaunt of style and spirit with a slight reek as
of stale whiskey and plug-tobacco. Soon, too, there are indi-
cations in Mark Twain's sketches of a freer use of the
imagination both in its reconstructive use as in "A Mediæval
Romance" and in its realistic function of creating character
as in "A True Story." The fact remains nevertheless that he
owed everything in regard to method and form to the newspaper humor of his early days and in regard to substance to
observation and folk-life. To letters or tradition he owed

little or nothing. His taste was even cruder than Whitman's; his diatribes against Jane Austen have a curiously tell-tale quality; revelatory in a quite final sense is the following passage of a letter to Mrs. Clemens written in his forty-fifth year: "I heard four speeches which I can never forget. . . . One by that splendid old soul, Col. Bob Ingersoll, oh, it was just the supremest combination of English words that was ever put together since the world began. My soul, how handsome he looked, as he stood on that table, in the midst of those five-hundred shouting men, and poured the molten silver from his lips! Lord what an organ is human speech when it is played by a master!" I have not troubled to inquire which oration of Ingersoll's this was. But, in truth, they are all alike, with their useful but shallow rationalism, their withered flowers of speech, their gesticulatory and often spuriously metrical rhythms. The writer of the letter, at all events, was not in any ordinary sense a middle-aged man of letters. He was the average adolescent-minded American—rooter at baseball games, political banquets, exhibitions of pseudo-heroic claptrap. He was that man plus genius. He was Huck Finn grown up.

But it is precisely this fact that makes Mark Twain unique and uniquely precious. He is our one American example of the bardic type of artist and sayer—our balladist, teller of folk-tales, one whom the common people can understand because he is theirs, because he is of their very blood; he has their morals and their manners, their spirit and their speech, all of which have changed surprisingly little since the days of his youth. Subtle and learned critics in their metropolitan isolation have projected upon Mark Twain their problems and aspirations. I gravely doubt whether he underwent any ordeal; if at moments he dramatized himself in this sense, his drama was a sentimental comedy of the good old American tradition in which there is a compensatory smile for every tear. Nor do I believe that he was frustrated by the influences in his life that he loved and honored most deeply. It is quite true that he chafed at moments under the literary and moral supervision of Mrs. Clemens; it has been related to me by a close friend of the family that he would at times write far more ribaldly and blasphemously than he himself approved of in order to be sure that Mrs. Clemens' inevitable strictures should not wholly emasculate his text. But he yielded to her point of view and to Howells' with an intimate and perfect inner consent. Olivia would not have been to him the woman that he desired not only to love, but in the old-fashioned and still widespread American folk-sense to revere and to set morally and spiritually above himself, had she freely shared his masculine tendency to blasphemous and ribald criticism of man, religion and society. He wanted her to share these propensities as little as he wanted her to drink and smoke. He wanted her to be all sweetness and purity and holiness, even as he described her in those atrocious yet touching verses that he wrote in the early days of his grief and his bereavement, comparing her to a spirit in a temple which shed its light softly for all who were near, but mostly for the ministrants within—himself and his daughters:

All loved that light and held it dear
That had this partial grace;
But the adoring priests alone who lived
By day and night submerged in its immortal glow

Knew all its power and depth, and could appraise the loss
If it should fade and fail and come no more.

He had, in brief, the traditional American folk-attitude of
the frontier—the literal idolizing of womankind as the
keeper, among rude and lawless males, of the flame not only
of the hearth but of beauty and purity and faith and sweetness and hope. And this deep-seated American instinct in him
led him in his dealings with "Joan of Arc"—neither ignoble
nor unimpressive as literature at moments—to drop all his
hard-won rationalism, all his healthy sense of reality, to go
in for sheer miracle-mongering and mystic claptrap and to
declare with unrivaled preposterousness that she was "easily
and by far the most extraordinary person the human race
has ever produced." It was the husband of Olivia Langdon
who wrote that. And how American that is and—in a sense
often unduly subject to this age's jeers—how touching and
how wholesome. Nor must it be forgotten that Mrs. Clemens
belonged to a higher social and cultural American level than
her husband and that her influence upon his manners and
worldly behavior was doubtless wholly salutary. Of course,
he grumbled. "When Livy is well I smoke only those two
hours on Sunday. I'm 'boss' of the habit now. . . . But
somehow it seems a pity that *you* quit, for Mrs. T. didn't
mind if I remember rightly." Is that remark and its tone to
his friend Twichell conceivable in any man of thirty-five
but an American? Yet it was wholly sincere, as was its implication that, though women might be unreasonable in detail,
their clearly established moral superiority entitled them to
that as well as to their husband's obedience. Thus Huck Finn
grumbled too when the widow told him not to smoke. "She

219

said it was a mean practice and wasn't clean, and I must try not to do it any more. That is just the way with some people. They get down on a thing when they don't know nothing about it." But Huck Finn, luckily, remains the eternal boy, unregenerate, not grown up, without "a lovely wife, a lovely house, bewitchingly furnished, a lovely carriage, and a coachman whose style and dignity are simply awe-inspiring . . ." Yet if Huck Finn or, rather perhaps that other half of Mark Twain's boyhood, Tom Sawyer, had come to enjoy these worldly blessings, it is in precisely such terms that he would have reported concerning them to a friend.

No, it must never be forgotten that Mark Twain was in very truth that double personality. Both aspects of it grew up with him; the Tom Sawyer aspect of it wrote books and became a great person and Mrs. Clemens and Howells and the Rev. Mr. Twichell and Edmund Clarence Stedman saw to it that the saltier Huck Finn in Mark did not run away with the imaginative but essentially respectable Tom Sawyer. But he was happily always that Hannibal, Missouri boy—that inimitably genuine child of the American folk of the Middle West. Scenes and turns of speech occur all through the records of his life that have, to those who know it, the authentic and enduring American tang. But the men of our age of critical realism, goaded by mass-stupidity and mass-tyranny, have protested against the common people of America to the point of losing all direct knowledge and vision of it. . . . And perhaps—strange that it should be left for me to make this observation—they have not affected their folk more profoundly because they have not loved it enough. . . . When Sam Clemens, aged eighteen, left Hannibal, Missouri, to go out into the world, his mother held up a little Testament and said: "I want you to take hold of the end of this, Sam, and make me a promise. I want you to repeat after me these words: 'I do solemnly swear that I will not throw a card, or drink a drop of liquor while I am gone.'" He kept the promise at least reasonably and for a reasonable period. But "Ma" was always in his confidence. He asks his brother Henry to be discreet: "Now, between you and I and the fence . . ." Brother Orion was not to be told. But "Ma knows my determination." One must know the American people to savor these phrases and moral attitudes. Mark Twain was American in the sense in which Burns was Scotch. He "learned the river," prodigious but wholly unliterary feat; the years pass. He is now twenty-three and hastening to Memphis where his brother Henry was killed in the explosion of such a Mississippi River steamer as he was piloting. He writes to Orion's wife "dear Sister Mollie." "Hardened, hopeless—aye, lost—lost—lost and ruined sinner that I am—*I*, even *I*, have humbled myself to the ground and prayed as never man prayed before, that the great God might let this cup pass from me. . . ." Poor Henry died. "But may God bless Memphis, the noblest city on the face of the earth. . . ." Was ever an eminent writer so *undifferentiated* at twenty-three and four and five? It is in that latter year that we first hear of literature, of reading and we find, aptly enough, perhaps, that Goldsmith's "Citizen of the World" and "Don Quixote" are his "*beau ideals* of fine writing." But this is by the way. He was making money and "dissipating on a ten-dollar dinner at a French restaurant—breathe it not unto Ma!" at New Orleans, and next we hear of mines and "claims" and possible fortunes and that "Ma says it looks like a man can't hold public office and be honest," and of journalism as his true field and of the meeting with Artemus Ward and still, at the age of twenty-nine we find him capable of writing seriously: "I address a lady in every sense of the term. . . ." But within the next two years, not without suggestions and hints difficult to estimate from Bret Harte, he made his mark and awoke to find himself famous one day and amazed, too, that "those New York people should single out a villainous backwoods sketch to compliment me on— Jim Smiley and His Jumping Frog." Fortune followed fame. First came the Hawaiian trip with its well-paid travel letters and his immediate success as a humorous lecturer; next came the famous Quaker City Mediterranean excursion which gave him the material for "Innocents Abroad," that immediately and permanently most successful of American books which told the rude democracy precisely what it wanted to know about the Old World and at the same time triumphantly confirmed that democracy in its own self-esteem. Now Mark carried all before him. He became betrothed to Olivia Langdon, the "little body," who "hasn't her peer in Christendom" and married her early in 1870 and established that lavish and splendid and, on a high plane, inimitably Micawberish mode of life that continued to the end. The hilarious description of the life, character and adventures of his brother Orion which he sent in a letter to Howells from Munich in 1879 reads, deeply considered, like a caricature of himself. As he was essentially not divided from the folk for which he wrote, so he was not divided from his own kith and kin by any difference of *vision*, only by genius—like the tribal bards of old.

What we seem, according to the published documents to be following, is in truth hardly the life of a man of letters. Not because Mark Twain wrote simply and sincerely, "I don't know anything about books," but because the record of composition, that is, of urgent expression, is so sporadic and haphazard. The chief preoccupations are with worldly affairs: with book-publishing, with that unfortunate type-setting machine on which he lost a fortune, with sudden, almost Orion-like schemes and speculations up to investments as late as 1901 in Plasmon, an English proprietary remedy, which was supposed to be a panacea for all the human ills that osteopathy could not reach. Largely, in other words, he lived the turbulent get-rich-quick life of the Gilded Age —the life of large earning, losing, spending, building and abandoning elaborate houses, a life uncritical, essentially unguided, a life, once again, wholly undifferentiated from the average life of his people and his time. A deeper and a finer note was introduced by his long stretches of residence abroad, especially by the brilliant and protracted stay in Austria. With the spontaneous sympathy of the unspoiled American for the Germanic civilizations, he acquired a remarkable knowledge of German and drew from the deep rich life of Vienna, from folk and art and landscape insights and monitions that were half joyful and half somber and had not a little to do with that gradual deepening of spiritual tone that comes gradually over his later years. But even here he was uncritical, being overwhelmed by a performance, beautiful in itself, no doubt, of Adolf Willbrandt's tepid neo-classic

"Meister von Palmyra" and ruefully comparing it to the theatrical fare—vulgar, noisy, trivial—offered by the New York theater on a given day. And one cannot regard without a gentle irony the author of "A Yankee at King Arthur's Court" being thrilled to his finger tips by social contacts with Archdukes and Archduchesses and making a tragic and solemn world-disaster of the pathetic but historically and politically unimportant taking off of the poor Empress Elizabeth. In this respect, too, he was the average American of his time who twisted the tale of the British lion and dreamed of being rich enough to have his wife and daughters presented at court. Nor was this all. Having barely recovered from the financial disaster due to the investment in the Paige typesetting machine, he promptly discovered in Vienna a Czechisch inventor named Schezepanic whose marvelous carpet-making machine was, according to Mark Twain's bubbling letter to Henry H. Rogers, to save the industries involved $75,000,000 a year. Thus he took his America with him to Austria. It was at Kaltenleutgeben near Vienna, too, that news of the Spanish-American war was brought him. Whereupon, like every other average good-hearted uncritical and thoroughly befooled citizen he wrote to the Rev. J. H. Twichell: "This is the worthiest war that was ever fought, so far as my knowledge goes."

There is needed, to round out any account of Mark Twain's character an analysis, however brief, of the disillusions and darker thoughts of his later years. This analysis may properly begin with the year 1889 and "A Connecticut Yankee at King Arthur's Court." For he felt that he had not spoken all his mind in that book nor spoken it vehemently enough. He raged at himself over "so many things left out. They burn in me." . . . And these things would, moreover, have needed for their expression "a pen warmed up in hell." It may well be doubted, however, whether Mark Twain left unsaid anything different in kind from what he succeeded in expressing: his hatred of cruelty and oppression and dirt and his perfectly sound American protest against a false romanticizing of these evils. Essentially, of course, the book is a valiantly optimistic one. It was during the succeeding years, marked by financial disaster, by maturer contacts with older civilizations, by the death, above all, of his daughter Susan of whom, gifted and charming as she may have been, he had formed an idolatrous and extravagant estimate, that he began to lose his American frontier optimism, that he became aware of the dark and desperate human problems, knowledge of which is, as it were, born with the children of older cultural soils, but which the American of Clemens' generation had failed to face. He had no philosophy, no values, no stoicism with which to face them. By tradition and character he was intellectually happy-go-lucky. He became profoundly depressed; he became impatient and almost petulant. He had nothing within wherewith to resist the late perception of human life as tragic. Nor did he seek in books or converse any knowledge of the thoughts whereby men in the past have sought to wring from the stubborn universe a triumph for the spirit of man. He knew neither Plato nor Spinoza nor Kant; there is no evidence that he had ever read Emerson. He sat down to develop out of his own head, like an adolescent, like a child, a theory to fit the facts as he seemed to see them, and the only influence discernible in his theory is that of Robert Ingersoll! Thus were written in the last year or two of the nineteenth century that allegory "The Mysterious Stranger" and that treatise in dialogues "What Is Man?" which seemed to Mark Twain so revolutionary and portentous, which filled poor Olivia with loathing and terror and which were not published till after his death. The gist of both is found in the letters. "Man is not to me the respect-worthy person he was before, and so I have lost my pride in him." And again: "What a shabby poor ridiculous thing man is, and how mistaken he is in his estimate of his character and powers and qualities and his place among the animals."

When finally we turn to these documents of his "Private Philosophy"—"which Livy won't allow me to publish, because it would destroy me"—we find the crudest and most shallow treatment of the most intricate matters; we find, quite literally, the ideas of a village agnostic. It is true, for instance, that nameless and numberless cruelties have been practiced by man against his fellows in the name of the "Moral sense." But merely to assert that is to assert nothing of significance. Mark Twain had no suspicion, apparently, of the existence of either anthropology or psychology, or any knowledge of the growth and function of *mores* and their connection with the totality of human development. He sought to solve problems which he did not know enough even to state. It is extraordinary how he escaped a knowl-edge even of Herbert Spencer. It is evident that he did. In "What is Man?" he seeks by the crudest and falsest analogi-cal reasoning to prove that man is a machine because he has no innate ideas—an extremely debatable position on its own ground—that there is no difference between selfish and un-

226

selfish action because the latter is accompanied by a feeling of self-approbation, and so on and so on. The whole thing was puerile when it was written in 1899-1900 and very properly aroused no more than a mild astonishment when it was given to the world in the second decade of this century. But all this, be it emphatically noted, does not count against Mark Twain; it counts for him. He was beautifully of a piece. He was Tom Sawyer and Huck Finn and the Connecticut Yankee and when youth and romance and boundless optimism went out of his life, he reacted very much as they would have done, as thousands of simple-hearted Americans in agnostic and atheist societies and clubs do all over the land and consider themselves bold thinkers and fine fellows and are so in very truth compared to their Fundamentalist neighbors, but only as compared to these and not in the great central world of the traditions of human thought and knowledge. And of their company was Mark Twain, the inimitable American, flesh and bone of the flesh and bone of his folk—infinite in kindness and generosity of heart, adolescent in intellect, liberating himself from one superstition only to fall straightway under the sway of others, loving liberty without any rational idea of its character or mode of attainment, proud of his land and people, yet easily made doubtful and put out of countenance by other civilizations and compensating for that depression by a harmless and even amiable truculence, strong only when wholly optimistic and collapsing easily under the onslaught of the sterner accidents of mortality, honest and within his narrow range of spiritual possibility truly aspiring and building, we will hope, better far better than he knows.

V

I have so far delineated a man rather than a writer. But the two are, of course, one and, if my delineation of the man is correct, it should be perfectly clear why he is the most popular—in a deep and not ignoble sense—of American writers and why, at the same time, it is unnecessary for the critic of letters to lash himself into an admiration *sub specie æternitatis* of nine-tenths of his works. Mark Twain would have been the first to absolve the critic from that effort and that task. Of that fact we have the irrefutable evidence in that memorable letter of protest and explanation which he addressed to Andrew Lang in 1889. The theory of letters propounded in that document is, like most truths, but a half-truth. Yet that half-truth or over-emphasized aspect of truth does complete justice to Mark Twain. His adequate and dignified expression of it illustrates the insight to which, at his most luminous moments, he could rise. "The critic assumes every time," he wrote, "that if a book doesn't meet the culti-vated-class standard, it isn't valuable. Let us apply his law all around: for if it is sound in the case of novels, narratives, pictures, and such things, it is certainly sound and applicable to all the steps which lead up to culture and make culture possible. It condemns the spelling-book, for a spelling-book is of no use to a person of culture; it condemns all school-books and all schools which lie between the child's primer and Greek, and between the infant school and the university; it condemns all the rounds of art which lie between the cheap terra-cotta groups and the Venus de' Medici, and between the chromo and the Transfiguration; it requires Whitcomb

228

Riley to sing no more till he can sing like Shakespeare, and it forbids all amateur music and will grant its sanction to nothing below the classic." I need hardly stop to say that in his defense of folk-art Mark Twain chose unhappy examples. The common people are corrupted, not sustained in what is best in them, by the soggy and shoddy dilutions of cultural art on which they are fed. But as a defense of folk-art and so of his own Mark Twain's argument is profound and pertinent. The folk-song is immortally good; the menace is Irving Berlin. Finally and happily in the same letter he applies it to himself: "Indeed I have been misjudged from the very first. I have never tried in even one single instance to help cultivate the cultivated classes. I was not equipped for it either by native gifts or training. And I never had any ambition in that direction, but always hunted for bigger game—the masses. I have seldom deliberately tried to instruct them, but have done my best to entertain them. To simply amuse them would have satisfied my dearest ambition at any time; for they could get instruction elsewhere, and I had two chances to help to the teacher's one: for amusement is a good preparation for study and a good healer of fatigue after it. My audience is dumb, it has no voice in print, and so I cannot know whether I have won its approbation or only got its censure. Yes, you see, I have always catered for the Belly and the Members, but have been served like the others—criticized from the culture-standard—to my sorrow and pain; because, honestly, I never cared what became of the cultured classes; they could go to the theater and the opera; they had no use for me and the melodeon." This theory of himself undoubtedly came to Mark Twain after the fact. He was one of the common people of America and spoke from and for and to that people from the beginning. But his rationalization of his practice is correct. He is our one folk-artist, both as a person and as a writer, comparable in office and function, in inspiration and accomplishment to the chroniclers and jesters and balladists of earlier ages. Regarding his voluminous works from this point of view one can with no great effort identify oneself with a type of mind and taste, no despicable one either, to which no sketch or jest or tale or essay has lost an element of freshness, wonder, liberation and delight. And one is happy that this is so and continues to be so. For Mark Twain is American in the older and permanently noble sense: no tyrant or moral meddler but sturdily and whole-heartedly for freedom and democracy, no cultivator of false and sinister reactionary subtleties but as in "A Yankee at King Arthur's Court" and "The Prince and the Pauper" and in an hundred other passages a strong defender of the better and freer life of the plain people, yet never flattering the people either, but valiantly and sharply castigating their hypocritic gestures, their moral delusions, their self-imposed limitations of heart and mind. Certain of their errors and follies he shares, for his spirit and theirs are essentially one. But this endears him to them and renders him accessible and makes him both guide and spokesman of their better possibilities.

He was too modest, however, in believing—if he did indeed harbor that belief steadily—that he could not be measured by what he called in his simple-hearted way the "culture-standard," that is, by the norm of permanent qualities and enduring values. Wherever he writes as a man his work is perishable and will become more and more what it already is, sub-literature; wherever he writes out of the memories of his boyhood and adolescence without excess of correction, straight from the experience of the folk, there he is precious and once or twice immortal. What he lacks wholly in any higher sense is form—form that is the fruit of suffering, of both personal and creative agony. His texture has no density and his shaping spirit no severity or aloofness. Even when his satire is bitter in intent, it lacks edge and point by the crinkled looseness and laxness of its vestiture. He cannot help being merely funny and merely "folksy." Or else he becomes in the popular and Ingersollian sense eloquent, and that is still worse. And he will be, at the same time, horribly senti-mental—slack, unstrung, deliquescent like the melody of "Home, Sweet Home." But all these faults are the defects of his qualities as a folk-artist. For it as such that he has no aloofness, that there is never a great distance between himself and his subjects, that he never stands above the world of illusion which he delineates nor indeed knows it as such. His triumph is the triumph of the balladist, the writer of the folk-tale that corresponds to the epic on a higher level, that necessarily becomes, in certain times and under certain civiliz-ations, the picaresque romance. "Huckleberry Finn" is then his triumph—a masterpiece despite the breakdown of form in the last fourth. But about "Huckleberry Finn" there are to be grouped certain other writings which form with it that Mississippi legend which is Mark Twain's contribution to the great and unique things in literature: "Tom Sawyer," cer-tain portions of "Roughing It" and larger portions of "Life on the Mississippi," the two stories "The Man that Corrupted Hadleyburg" and "The $30,000 Bequest" and sundry scenes and sketches carefully selected from his works. All these pages will be pages about Hannibal, Missouri, and the great river and the dusty villages and strange men and folk-beliefs of an irrecoverable epoch, of a curious and primitive and inimitably American civilization which Mark Twain not only recorded as in its living character it was, but which he raised, by the heightening and isolation of art, into a permanent realm of the human imagination. So in his small and homespun way Mark Twain, once more like the balladists of Europe, is related to Homer himself who, also, raised into the immortal realm of the imagination the life and conflicts of obscure villages among the otherwise forgotten Ionians of the isles and the Asian shore. A poor relation, a late descendant, but of the authentic lineage and blood.

BOOK SIX

The Rise of the Novel

I

Suddenly and belatedly, in the decade following the Civil War, the modern temper begins to assert itself in American letters. Romance passes and the novel assumes its dominant place. A thousand voluntary delusions and repressions still afflict literature. But the crucial transition from mere revery and fantasy to observation of the self and the world, to a serious awareness of man and society, has been made. It was first made prophetically as early as 1855 by Harriet Beecher Stowe. Her case presents the highest interest; it throws light upon the character and power of the novel as a form. "Uncle Tom's Cabin" is still on one whole side within the conventions of its time—a kind of sentimental Byzantinism in the delineation of character. Little Eva is own sister of Ellen Montgomery who wept her way through the pages of "The Wide, Wide World"; St. Clair, despite his Southern languor is not unrelated to the Rochester-St. Elmo tribe. But Mrs. Stowe's passion for the truth she desired to convey

233

made her regard with the power of that passion the realities which embodied her truth and use her imagination not in order to flee from reality but in order to embrace it to the point of pain. It was an imagination both sentimental and coarse. Yet because it sought deliberately to penetrate, to interpret and to heighten actual data of human experience, it achieved a density of vital substance that was strictly speaking a new thing in American letters. Vachel Lindsay has used the figure of Simon Legree in a poem as both man and myth. The poet's instinct was sound. Mrs. Stowe struck fire because she had both the steel of passion and the flint of life. Late as the romances of Mrs. E. D. E. N. Southworth and Mary J. Holmes and Augusta Evans Wilson lingered in remote corners of the country and obscure social levels under the blue-paper covers of the old Seaside Library and over the imprint of the house of George Munro of Vandewater Street, the sentimental romance was passing. A novel had stirred the nation to its depths.

The writers who, after the close of the Civil War, turned from the romance to the novel, had nothing of Mrs. Stowe's energy. For the great social passion of the age had been appeased and the Puritan tradition admitted neither the treatment nor the use of any other. But the awareness of life as it is more or less lived and of society in both its political and economic aspects was not again lost. The united nation, no longer so grossly and obviously split into two antagonistic societies, became conscious of itself as a nation with its own manners and speech and character and destiny and it was these that American writers now proposed to themselves to delineate. From this impulse sprang the sectional or regional

234

novelists to be treated hereafter who by cultivating their special state or section or even city, sought like the German cultivators of *Heimatskunst* or the French delineators of the life of the provinces from the Normandy of Maupassant to the Provence of Daudet, to contribute to the creative picture of the nation as a whole. An immediate neo-romanticism crept back with Bret Harte. But even this romanticism of the West had to feign to reproduce the color and sensation of reality, while it has not been sufficiently noted what a fresh breath of reality began to enter the lives of American children with the publication of "Little Women" in 1868 and how Jo and Amy and Laurie and Professor Bhaer replaced the snuffling imbeciles of the stories which Mark Twain never tired of deriding. Everywhere began a genuine if partial and inhibited examination of life. Literature attained its first measure of creative freedom and sincerity. The spirit of criticism remained extremely feeble; moral conventions did duty for facts, but the Meredithian conviction that life is worthy of the Muse was definitely embraced and never thereafter wholly lost again.

Poetry receded into a dim background; the drama was unborn; the essay lost in breadth of appeal. The nation became, as it has remained since, a nation of novel-readers. In that fact lay all hope and all progress both for taste and action, both for man and society. For of all the forms of expression invented by man the modern novel—the novel that began with Henry Fielding and culminates for this year and decade with Thomas Mann—is the most various and the most powerful, capable at once of the noblest breadth and the deepest intimacy, apt at the expression of all moods and impulses and ideas, of all conflicts whether between man and man or between the individual and society, more purging than the briefer shock of tragedy, more illuminating to average men and women than the difficult treatises of philosophers, enlarging experience, cleansing vision, bringing home to the obdurate bosom characters and fates differing from its own and thus serving the cause of understanding and tolerance and peace among men. If the history of the later literature of America is so largely the history of its novelists and novels it is because everywhere and not least among us the novel has absorbed into itself the functions of the other and older kinds and is to the majority of men drama and poetry, epic and treatise.

Among the many writers who after the Civil War turned to the novel and the novel's cultivation of reality, two surpassed all the rest in talent, intelligence and creative pertinacity. In 1871 and in 1874 it was not suspected, of course, that the publication of "Their Wedding Journey" by William Dean Howells and of "Madame de Mauves" by Henry James, Jr., were memorable events. Today, despite changes in taste and despite not only the blur of time but the large deductions that must be made, it is clear that these two publications announced the appearance of two men of letters, such as America had not hitherto produced. Hawthorne and Poe had been acutely conscious literary artists too. But both belonged to an older and an other order of things. Poets and romancers had always existed. The modern novelist, surveying man and society as these actually are in his age and land, was the new and characteristic literary type of the age of industrialism and democracy. Howells and James were the first Americans to represent that type with eminent seriousness and high success. Like their Russian and French colleagues to whom they were more indebted than to the English novelists of their own tongue, they added a concern for form to the scrupulousness of their observation; they regarded observation as a valid and immensely important kind of experience; they sought to reduce form, eschewing all adornment and vain beauty, to its one inherent function of rendering the all-important substance. To compare this theory of theirs and their extremely honorable practice of it with both the theory and the practice of even their more enlightened American contemporaries, is to gain at once a solid respect for them as both men and artists. Bravely and deliberately they swept aside all outer provincial and merely conventional limitations. There remained, alas, the limitations of their own natures which, as so often in America, were paralyzing. But that was not their fault. I am aware of the fact that Howells is almost unread today and that even Henry James has but a small circle of readers among the elderly and determinedly refined. But I am persuaded that the revolutions of time and taste will, in their strangely cyclic course, restore both to an honorable place in the history of American civilization and that small and rigid selections from their works will come to constitute a permanent element of the American mind.

II

It is almost forgotten that Howells was a country boy from Ohio, a printer and journalist even in his teens, and a self-educated man. One may well question the wisdom of that pilgrimage to Boston which he made at the age of twenty·

237

three. He became more of a Bostonian than the natives of that mildly glorious city; he managed to mingle queerly the niceties of Brahmin deportment and even the social prejudices of Back Bay society with his cultivation of the humble truth of life and his sincere and noble passion for the economic amelioration of society. It is futile, however, to regret either the pilgrimage or the identification with gentility which Howells achieved. We seek what we want and find what we need.

I hasten to recall the fact that the age of Howells and James, the years roughly from 1870 to the turn of the century, was the age of gentility. Both novelists had, more or less, to render the society in which they lived. And that society was the most ill-mannered that has probably ever existed. It was so disgustingly "pure" because it was so violently sex-conscious. It was so afraid of vulgarity because it was so immitigably vulgar. I may adduce, without delay, two characteristic and amusing instances. The new house that Howells' Silas Lapham was building on the Back Bay had not progressed much beyond the shell. Lapham and his daughters climb about the new structure on ladders. Young Tom Corey comes to join them and Lapham expounds the rising structure. "This is my girls' room," he said. "It seemed terribly intimate"; Howells adds, "Irene blushed deeply and turned her head away." These people evidently couldn't even think of a young woman's future room without an immediate image of sexual activity. The taboo was so strong because the thing tabooed filled their inner vision. The crimes most cruelly punished by a given society are those which its members are most eager to commit. This sex-consciousness rises to frantic heights, as when in James' "A London Life" a young woman implores a man, who does not love her, to marry her and save her reputation, merely because the two have been left alone in a box at the opera. The same repressed consciousness of sex fills the huge canvas of James' "The Awkward Age."

Of the quality of this situation and of the blight thrown by it upon manners and society, upon life and letters Howells seems to have been wholly unaware. James, as we shall see, was not. But Howells yielded without so much as an inner protest to Boston and this pusillanimity of his is the worm that may hollow out the otherwise extraordinarily fine structure of his best work. There is in his treatment of the major human emotions a shocking and contemptible moderation; there is in his attitude to marriage, above all, an unbearable stuffiness and creeping prose which, being so obviously characteristic of his age, makes one wonder that the Feminist revolt in America was not even more violent and acute. The superstition prevails among the unthinking that Howells and the genteel age took a high view of marriage. The contrary is true. The view taken of marriage was revolting to every generous instinct; it relegated married people, however young, to a situation that smelled of ill-aired clothes-presses and kitchen soap; it assumed as impossible and improper any poetry or passion in the relation of man and wife after the honeymoon at Niagara Falls; it consented drily to the elimination between people once safely married of gallantry, delight, even of courtesy and delicacy; it shoved them into the limbo of nothing but cooking-stoves and diapers with a quiet but relentless sadism. In so early a work as "A Chance Acquaintance" Howells writes: "Of his wife's wardrobe he had the ignorance of a good husband, who, as soon as the pang of paying for her dresses is past, forgets whatever she has." In this unsmiling sentence is the genteel age's view of the most important of human relations. It threw, to be sure, a sop to the sex it still called fair. "If my wife," says the young journalist in "The Rise of Silas Lapham," "wasn't good enough to keep both of us straight, I don't know what would become of me." This moral influence of women was a sincere part of the period's creed; on the same page of "Silas Lapham" Howells observes that "of the vast majority of married Americans, a few underrate their wives, but the rest think them supernal in intelligence and capability." There is no mention of charm or of any amenity. Wives, poor things, had to be contented with capability. The result was that they, as a natural compensation, drove their capability hard and the total image of married life to be derived from the delineations of Howells is that of men grossly henpecked by women who were stripped on principle of any of the attractions that alone can make female tyranny endurable. A rational man may happily endure the exactions of a delightful woman. But the women of the genteel age stood in evil odor if they did not cease being delightful—the exclusive right of the *jeune fille*—the moment they left the minister's house. We find, then, that with but one or two exceptions the married people of Howells are elderly in attitude if not in fact, and that this elderliness is accepted as the characteristic virtue of the married state. Thus bride and groom in "A

Modern Instance" are described as briefly parting "with an embrace that would have fortified older married people for a year's separation" and in so late a work as "The Kentons" Mr. Kenton is described as in that state of "subjection to his wife's judgment which befalls and doubtless becomes a man after many years of marriage." But this was not all. Even of those superlatively innocent relations which in his stories lead to marriage Howells' opinion was low. "The whole business of love and love-making and marrying is painted by the novelists in a monstrous disproportion to the other relations of life. Love is very sweet, very pretty. . . ." Thus speaks the otherwise neither foolish nor unmanly clergyman in "The Rise of Silas Lapham." And this view Howells shared or honestly thought he shared, declaring in "Criticism and Fiction" that grief, avarice, pity, ambition, hate, envy, devotion, friendship have all a greater part in life "than the passion of love." On his principle that the sovereign virtue of art was truth to reality, he was forced of course, in view of the inhibitions of his time and his personal practice, to take precisely this attitude. It is needless to insist on the crushing handicap imposed upon himself at the outset by a creative artist who regards as trivial the instinct which, as psychology has demonstrated and the great artists have always known, is implicated not only with our biological functioning but in infinite ramifications with our higher nerve-centers and is thus a central element of every human activity from the humblest to the most exalted. That Howells, with this handicap, comes off upon the whole as respectably as he does, is a very high tribute to his native gifts.

Both his critical theory and his artistic practice, even aside from the latter's permanent results, mark an epoch in the expression of American culture. It was no timid thinker who announced in 1892 that "what is unpretentious and what is true is always beautiful and good, and nothing else is so." What, alas, reconciled his contemporaries to Howells and reduced the weightiness of his achievement was that he assumed the limitations of his experience and his observation to be the limitations of truth itself. Nor was that quite the worst. He proposed the most magnificent of tests for the value of a work of fiction: "Is it true?—true to the motives, the impulses, the principles that shape the life of actual men and women?" He did not, I suspect, apply his own test with entire honesty and candor. He took refuge in the famous and amusing announcement that "the more smiling aspects of life are the more American ones" and attributed that supposed fact to the general prosperity and uncomplicatedness of American life. He admitted sadly that "all this is changing for the worse" and yet asserted with a rather mouse-like gesture of triumph that everything but "chaste love and honest passion" was "the exceptional thing in American life." It all depends, of course, on the interpretation of the words "chaste" and "honest." His own was such as to eliminate as by a fiat all but the practice of the feeblest and most inhibited of the species. Not content with declaring all American humanity to conform to a certain type of anæmic Bostonianism, he carried this standard into the past with an amazing effrontery for so mild a man and declared three-fifths of the literature commonly called classic to be "trash and often very filthy trash" and added his conviction that "nobody really enjoys it." In other words, quite like Poe's, Howells' critical theory is a rationalization of his practice which, in turn, was the inevitable expression of his nature. So that this critical theory has no critical, no objective value at all. But of this his contemporaries could not possibly be aware, so that his insistence upon the beauty and significance of the humble truth of life and his enthusiastic appreciation of the "great Scandinavian and Slavic and Latin artists" had its definitely beneficent effects. Among these artists he selected, of course, the milder ones and despite his fair acquaintance with German and his early devotion to Heine, permitted himself the absurd judgment on Goethe, which is symptomatic of the repressed and unconsciously sex-envious. It constitutes from Wordsworth on almost a test case.[1]

Careful of the structure of his rationalization Howells wrote of the kind of novels that he disapproved: "They hurt because they are not true." Nothing could be more exact than this statement. But his elaboration of it once more gives him away. "If a novel flatters the passions and exalts them above the principles, it is poisonous." To assent to that one would have to demand a definition of the flattering of the passions and an even more rigid definition of the principles to which the passions are to be subjected. "Unmoral romances," he assures us, are those "which imagine a world

[1] A psychological treatise could be written on this theme. The Wordsworth-Howells attitude assumes, of course, a legendary pagan-Don Juan Goethe, forgetting that he possessed none of the women he most loved but renounced them from Fredericke Brion to Ulrike von Levetzow "Entsagen sollst Du, sollst entsagen. . . ."

243

where the sins of sense are unvisited by the penalties." And that, once more, is profoundly true. Only, alas, one knows that Howells does not mean the immanent sins to which the activity of the senses, like all human activities, is prone, but the sins of sense as defined by parochial laws and perishing conventions.

In brief, Howells, like his age, was acutely and negatively sex-conscious. We have no need to be always protesting against that which does not trouble us. But he was so perturbed by the great normal dealings with love of the fundamental classics that he must needs call them "filthy trash" and must scold at Goethe, and in forty works of fiction delineated but one wholly tragic marriage and never permitted himself the description of any relation between a man and a woman not strictly legal. Yet it was he who denounced the "foolish old superstition that literature and art are anything but the expression of life" and admirably declared that in human life the novelist "finds nothing insignificant; all tells for destiny and character." Tradition and authentic personal report have it that as he grew older he grew ever sourer and more intolerant on this subject, rejecting in any American work what he would have permitted in a Russian or French one, falling into a kind of negative frenzy at the slightest suggestion of man's mammalian nature and hence as obsessed by sex as a fighting prohibitionist is by alcohol. This process of ambivalence, of simultaneous attraction and repulsion, of desire and fear, must be understood by anyone who wishes to penetrate to the true character of men and their ways. Lest the innocent imagine that I attribute to Howells and his age alien preoccupations, I shall permit myself to translate a passage from Sigmund Freud's great treatise "Totem and Taboo." "The peoples have an ambivalent attitude toward their taboos; unconsciously they would like nothing better than to transgress these prohibitions, but they are also afraid to do so; they are afraid precisely on account of the greatness of their desire and their fear is stronger than their desire. . . . The foundation of a taboo is a forbidden action toward which there is a powerful inclination in the unconscious. . . . For what no one desires to do would not need to be forbidden and that, surely, which is most emphatically forbidden must be the object of desire."

It is superficially amusing to find Henry James writing to Howells in 1904: "You are much more passionate than I." It was the simple truth. Howells' avoidance of human passion in his works is clamorous in its significant and sultry silence. Nor is tradition wholly ignorant of the aging novelist's uneasy and unconsciously guilty methods of sublimation. But these cannot yet be discussed with propriety. What one is not surprised to find is that at the core of his long and in all outward circumstances happy and fortunate career, there is a note of guilt and gloom, of preoccupation with death and with the disasters of the social order. This intimate note is the note of his unduly neglected poems published in 1895. In them we find not the usually blithe and kindly novelist who dwells on the more smiling aspects of life, but a soul deeply touched, considering the utter blamelessness of his life, by a sense of guilt and inadequacy, a "bewildered guest" at the table of life whose moral certainties, proclaimed in fifty volumes published over as many years, brought him so little of either comfort or tranquillity.

245

IV

It is impossible and would be futile to discuss in detail even a large proportion of the forty novels of William Dean Howells. They all have the same virtues, but these virtues would be more accessible had he written less. They would also be more resplendent, had they been distributed with a hand less sure. It may seem strange to blame a writer for the inveterate excellence of his workmanship. But if that excellence never blazes, there is evidently a tiresomeness in a flame which, being so mild, burns so steadily and so long. One would rather be either scorched or frozen. Nevertheless, his virtues cannot be made light of; the more one reads him the surer one is that in the fine sense of Jules Lemaître, he exists—he and his works, and can never wholly fade from the cultural landscape in America. There is no story of his that does not contain several characters seen and delineated with insight and precision, nor any without its smooth periphery and its unobtrusive structural felicity. He is capable of sudden solecisms of style, but writes generally with a by no means old-fashioned, that is to say with a permanently agreeable happiness and justness of expression. His works are full of thousands of keen observations, felicitous intuitions in the perception of character, valid and generous criticism of institutions. But except in one or two books the cumulative effect of all these many excellencies is a final tameness, not because Howells was so afraid to overstep the modesty of nature but because, according to him nature—including love and death and aspiration—was modest not with the modesty of the "alma Venus" of Lucretius, *"hominum divumque voluptas,"* but with the missish and vulgar modesty of a damsel in a hoopskirt.

He began with his principles firmly fixed but with his art, which was so much better than his principles, still tentative in method and a little wavering in aim. He had written pleasant but now quite negligible books of travel—"Venetian Life" and "Italian Journeys"—and approached the novel by a fresh use of the sketch of travel in "Their Wedding Journey." This gave him the opportunity of delineating the surface of American life, its scene and its people, with a sober exactness unknown before. He succeeds in doing that admirably at once. His touch as a painter of mere manners was already sure. He fails lamentably of course, granting him his very people, in the treatment of any relationship, however correct and conventional, between the sexes. For even Basil and Isabel March, of whom he was fond and to whom he returned in his second novel as well as in "A Hazard of New Fortunes" and "Their Silver Wedding Journey," could not have been so wholly unconscious in the very first weeks of their union of the purpose and function without which there would evidently be neither marrying nor giving in marriage. So that at once, in his first novel, that "poor Real life," which he professed so to love is made poorer than, at its humblest, it is. But he had his excuse, his rationalization ready: "As in literature the true artist will shun the use even of real events if they are of an improbable character, so the sincere observer of man will not desire to look upon his heroic or occasional phases, but will seek him in his habitual moods of vacancy and tiresomeness." I need not point out what phases of human character Howells, like Emerson,

247

classed if not among the heroic, then assuredly among the occasional ones.

Within two years Howells had taught himself how to build a story and published "A Chance Acquaintance." Here we have the first of those many plots, dear both to him and James and almost unheard of in any other literature, which hinge upon slight annoyances and subtle misunderstandings which the characters have not the energy to break through or to clarify. But here also we have the firm and often memorable if rarely quite profound enough delineation of character not only of the foreground personages: the Ellisons and Kitty and Arbuton, but of the episodic people, such as the English-speaking *habitant* of Ha-Ha Bay. And in this fact resides one of Howells' immense virtues. If his tameness did not make the reading of many of his books a duty and a burden, the hundreds of firmly delineated minor characters in his stories alone would make him the incomparable historian of the manners if never of the passions and ideas, of his age.

Within nine years after the publication of "A Chance Acquaintance" Howells had not only made himself master of his craft and method but reached his highest point of power. The intervening novels, especially "The Undiscovered Country," which deals sanely and finely with spiritualism and "Dr. Breen's Practice," a spirited defense, within his limitations of course, of the professional woman, have in an increasing degree both his virtues and his graces as a novelist. But his golden time was the early eighteen-hundred-and-eighties during which period he published "A Modern Instance," "The Rise of Silas Lapham" and "Indian Summer."

248

These are his best novels and by these, with the possible addition of "A Hazard of New Fortunes" and several later tales such as "The Kentons" and the rather amazing "Miss Bellard's Inspiration," he must stand or fall.

For reasons probably obscure even to himself Howells struck a deeper and more impassioned note in "A Modern Instance" than in any work before or after. The book is a rebellious book in which the rebellion is rigidly corrected first by the inner censor, next by the manners and publicly held morals of the author. This curbed rebellion is evident in the superb delineation of the character of Marcia Gaylord and in the inhuman priggishness of the conclusion which alone prevents the novel from being a great one. Marcia Gaylord is spoken of as a woman eminent for womanly virtues; she is the object of compassion throughout the book, of her admirable father's unwavering solicitude, of the pseudo-noble Ben Halleck's tragic affection. She is, in fact, a predatory and possessive female of a peculiarly dangerous and noxious kind, drawn with the most vivid energy and impassioned skill—an energy and skill that could spring from nothing less than an experience, personal or intimately vicarious, of the type. Marcia throws herself upon the man she wants and he is lost—to friendship, to society, to his calling; he must become her thing and the instrument of her biological functioning. She smothers him with her love and torments him with her retroactive jealousy and humiliates herself after each of her possessive bouts in order to leave him not even the poor consolation of a case against her. Howells' unadmitted knowledge of her true character is smothered and swathed with infinite and yet insufficient

249

dexterity. The author's and the reader's attention was to be withdrawn from Marcia's real quality by the superlative rascality of her husband. But of that rascality, at least in degree, Howells wholly fails to convince us and gives numerous evidences of having failed to convince himself. For poor Bartley Hubbard, coolly looked upon, is to be sure merely the *moyen homme sensuel*, but with his own decencies and abstentions. He has been something of a flirt before marriage, quite a mild and unbiological kind of flirt in a New England village. He doesn't really love Marcia. But when she throws herself at his head he immediately marries her and remains faithful to her. She leads him a wretched life and bedevils him generally and finally crushes him on a delicate point of honor. After a violent scene he runs away. But he would have come back—Howells leaves us in no doubt of that—had not a series of small disasters, including the theft of his purse, forced him to turn a highly ambivalent impulse into the raw fact of desertion. Poor Hubbard's essential honesty of purpose in the crucial situation quite gives Howells away. He wanted Marcia deserted and had his unconscious sympathy with Hubbard. He makes a great pother about the deterioration of Hubbard's character but shows him insensitive only on subtle points of honor and innocent of any gross breach of even the morals of the age. He wants us to believe him a monster because he uses an illiterate friend's conversation as "copy" and drinks a little more beer than is good for his figure. Yet he has drawn him, too, with such brilliant truth and vigor that we are indifferent both to the author's hints and to the goings-on of the choral prigs and rejoice with Howells' unrealized self at Hubbard's unwilling liberation. Marcia, true to form, has a gorgeous time being a martyr, emphasizing her martyrdom and innocence and importance in every way in which that sort of woman does emphasize them in order to hold, as she had always done, the moral center of the stage. And now, Hubbard being gone and Marcia ensconced in her noble suffering, the book—magnificent up to this point—breaks down. Not in workmanship, of course. But in the power to convince which, until that episode, it possessed in a richer measure than any American novel written before "Sister Carrie." For now Howells had to undo the moral damage or, as the modern reader would say, the moral veracity committed by his creative passion. Hubbard has to be brought to grief and Marcia to be rewarded. The trick is done with a high degree of external verisimilitude. Hubbard is quite damned by his innocent enough desire for a divorce. Marcia's father pleads at the bar of justice against that divorce and, for this caddish possessiveness, gets his private aureole. The refined Bostonians Ben Halleck and the Athertons indulge in antics and reflections unparalleled for silliness in any civilized age or literature. Howells had covered his tracks. But not sufficiently for cognitions he could not anticipate. Out of a passion of his own consciousness, however submerged, he had created for once characters, a fable and even a setting that are not tame, that are instinct with the ardor of irresistible expression—an ardor that lends power even to the delineation of the village of Equity and raciness to the minor characters, the Morrisons, father and daughter, Kinney, the newspaper men, above all to Squire Gaylord and his oppressed and patient wife. "A Modern Instance" is not only the best of Howells' novels. It stands alone. Here, hard as he tried to veil it, the man spoke out, and creative speaking out *is* art.

"The Rise of Silas Lapham," lacking the unconscious urges of "A Modern Instance," is the typical Howells novel at its best. That best, it must by now be clear, is far from negligible. The novel of manners as a *genre* has disappeared from serious literature, for the sufficient reason that we no longer regard either manners or moral conventions as ultimate and fixed phenomena. Knowing their origin and instability we seek either to go to their sources or treat them with an ironic vision of the people who labor under the delusion that they are, in fact, final and durable. Such Howells, of course, believed both the manners and the morals of his time and country to be. He writes from within this belief— a method confined today to sub-literature. But it is not to be forgotten that he shares this almost total consent to the *mores* of his age with both Thackeray and Trollope. Nor is it at all impossible that societies may again arise within which the creative mind takes a consenting and not as at present a revolutionary attitude and deals seriously with the values accepted by its contemporaries.

The moment we grant Howells his point of view, we see "The Rise of Silas Lapham" as very nearly a masterpiece of its kind. If the Barchester novels of Trollope can enjoy a return to enlightened favor, so can Howells' best novels of manners. The characters in "Silas Lapham" are better than well-drawn. The book was published in 1884 and its people are still admirably alive. Of how many of the acuter and apparently profounder and more brilliant books of today will a just criticism be able to make the same assertion in the year 1979? The Laphams and the Coreys are completely there and are differentiated with a delicacy and justness no less exact for being unemphatic. One is irritated again by the appallingly bad manners of the age, by the disgustingly low view taken of the marriage relation and by the twittering self-consciousness and unwholesomely repressed sexuality of the younger people. The scenes between Irene and Penelope Lapham are most offensive in this respect. But such, one is convinced, these people were, and one's irritation is caused merely by Howells' failure to see their quality. Yet he was, for his time, by no means supine and declared the indiscriminate self-sacrifice commended in sentimental romances to be "foolish and cruel and revolting." The action of the book, no small or trivial one, is built up with unobtrusive vigor and felicity; and certain culminating scenes, such as the Corey dinner at which unwittingly and innocently Lapham gets drunk, are models of the novelist's art. In the details of Lapham's downfall there are one or two unnecessarily arbitrary incidents: the burning down of the unfinished house, the expiration of the insurance on the day before. Some of the scruples entertained by the characters have a slight air of being entertained formally, rather than from the heart. But Howells would no doubt have said that they had better be so entertained, seeing how sinful the human heart is. There is again in the book that virtue which, after all, belongs only to the true creative spirit: the memorable reality of the minor and background characters. Such in "Silas Lapham" are Rogers, his one-time partner, Tom Corey's sister, the clerk in Lapham's counting-house and

Zerilla Dewey, her disreputable mother and her sailor husband. It has been correctly observed that Howells' picture of society in Silas Lapham dealt not at all with the larger American life of his day which was turbulent, passionate and raw, in which gigantic forces struggled and created. It is this aspect of the America of the 'seventies and 'eighties that Theodore Dreiser has rendered with such somber and massive power in "The Financier" and "The Titan." But the same criticism of choosing a limited field and leaving out the larger and more elemental forces of society could be brought against Jane Austen. Howells saw what he was capable of seeing and rendered that with both felicity and impressiveness.

There is no need to dwell for long upon his other works. His quality is, as I have said, singularly even. But in "Indian Summer," his own favorite among his works, he chose a subject for which he was hopelessly ill-equipped, of the realities of which he stood in mortal terror and which therefore he treated, by a defensive gesture, as comedy placed under a foreign sky. Not far below "The Rise of Silas Lapham" is "A Hazard of New Fortunes." But precisely because in this novel of New York he sought to come to grips with those larger and more tumultuous social forces which he could neither grasp nor master the book, despite an hundred excellencies, is less adequate and artistically satisfactory than either "A Modern Instance" or "The Rise of Silas Lapham." But those excellencies are in it and, in truth, did not fail Howells even in his old age. "The Kentons," published in 1902, is as felicitous as possible as a novel of the people and the manners that Howells knew and as late as 1905 in "Miss

Bellard's Inspiration" there is the character of Mrs. Mevison, who is Marcia Gaylord older, subtler and on a higher social level and now frankly acknowledged and rendered for what she is, and the delineation of the Mevisons' dreadful marriage. And the hand that drew this character and analyzed this relation was the hand of a master. I do not predict a Howells revival. That is not my function. But as this interpretation of the literature of America approaches our own age and deals with figures concerning whom time has not yet done its work of either silence or of consecration, it is my duty to exercise a judgment free of contemporary prejudices, including my own, and free of such perhaps wholly accidental things as the neglect of a given year or even decade. And that is what in regard to Howells I have sought to do.

v

It is authentically reported that Howells called Henry James the greatest novelist that ever lived. He was of course not that. But if Howells despite his limitations comes off worthily, it can be said that Henry James, suffering from limitations even more intimate and crippling, sustained as a man and an artist at the cost of such vast exclusions, comes off incomparably and magnificently. He does not touch our hearts and very lives as a few contemporary novelists and poets do. He is as stylist, master of form, creator of a body of memorable work, however many excrescences and failures we lop off the final canon, probably the most eminent man of letters America has yet to show.

All art, says Thomas Mann, comes into being "in spite of something," be it inadequacy merely or some over-acuteness

255

of the sensibilities or some abnormality or actual disease of the soul. Thus the artist's conflict and victory are more heroic than men can know. He fights with hands bound, with soul and body exposed, with lack of all weapons and defenses that belong to the blessed average from the beginning. Milton blind and Beethoven deaf are only symbols, but eternal and universal ones. Thus it is hardly needful to dwell upon an artist's lacks and insufficiency and cruel exposedness to the shafts of life unless and until an artist, like Henry James, presents the picture of limitations and lacks peculiarly devastating and yet triumphs not over them—they were too deep for that—but despite of them.

It was in the middle 'nineties that Henry James published in rapid succession those two volumes of novelettes, of which each is a masterpiece, called "Terminations" and "Embarrassments." Several of these novelettes deal with the life of letters. To these, Henry James wrote many years later in one of the prefaces to the New York Edition of his works, the author's relation has a peculiar closeness. "The states represented . . . can be fathered but on his own intimate experiences." Of these stories of the literary life "The Death of the Lion," quite like the somewhat earlier and exquisite "Lesson of the Master," is a wise and protective devaluation of things he could himself never attain; "The Next Time" is a just and dignified statement of the predicament of himself and those of his fellow-artists who, doomed to high and subtle quality, can never hope for either contemporary fame or its reward and yet in their human lives and characters naturally hunger for the justification that both can give. But there is another story, the first of the group called originally "Embarrassments," "The Figure in the Carpet," the interpretation of which is not so clear and plain. An enthusiastic young reviewer, the sort of foreground observer and relater of the story such as James loved for the sake of perspective, meets the distinguished novelist Hugh Vereker at one of those week-end parties in a great country-house equally dear to the novelist. The young reviewer has written an article on Vereker's new book which the latter, ignorant of its author's presence, characterizes offhand: "Oh, it's all right—it's the usual twaddle!" Warned of the situation and filled with the compunction of a kindly nature, the novelist invites the young critic to his room and tells him that he is not unique in not seeing Vereker's creative intention. Nobody sees. All "miss his little point." Yet there is something present in all his work, which is its central aim, "the very passion of his passion"; "it governs every line, it chooses every word . . . the very string my pearls are strung on." Vereker refuses to give away his secret; to discover it is, of course, the critic's business. The novelist has come to be amused at the universal blindness to that which he most wanted to convey and goes on weaving the web which many admire but of which none sees the pattern. It is needless to follow in detail the further action of the story. An acuter critic than the young reviewer finally discovers the secret of Hugh Vereker but it dies with him as well as with the one person, except the novelist, to whom he revealed the nature of his discovery. But the thing—and this is important—was no mystification. He lived long enough to see Hugh Vereker and to receive the novelist's confirmation and blessing.

I do not raise the question: what was the figure in Hugh

Vereker's carpet? The story is a story, a work of art, therefore concrete, and symbol and guide only in so far as the universal is to be found embodied in the particular. What Henry James conveyed is his perception that in the carpet of every weaver there is a figure and that this figure is no obvious and intellectual intention or motive, no such plea or argument or attitude as even the dullness of reviewers cannot miss and such as must shift and change slightly from work to work, but an intention that controls every word, a force that shapes the whole and dictates his character. And that force is, of course, the artist's psyche—its innermost quality and inexpugnable trend. The story, in a word, is both confession and, on a high plane, mystification. It is doubtful whether James was wholly aware of the figure in his own carpet; he knew that it existed; he knew that it was the deepest thing in his work, that it dictated subject-choice and treatment, substance and form and that it was the constitution of his self.

What was that self like? All that has been written on him is nonsense; it makes no sense. Or, like the behavioristic psychology, it flies impudently in the face of two-thirds of the ascertainable facts of human nature in order to be the mere bought servant of the cheap meliorism of an over-industrialized society. Among the chief, if not indeed the chief new cognitions of our age is this: that in the psychical order as in the physical one cause precedes effect and effect follows cause. The succession is often hard to disentangle and the nexus obscure. The fact remains. Why did Carlyle suddenly, after "The Life of Schiller," turn from his honest not inelegant eighteenth-centuryish prose and write undeviating "Carlylese" for fifty years? There was here a phenomenon of unconscious disguise, of fear lest the figure in the carpet become too clear. . . . And Henry James, starting out with the simplest and most pellucid of styles, hid himself ever more and more in the folds and swathings and integuments of a hieratic manner and a billowing cloud of words. The perspectives of his structural technique, which served to keep the ultimate actualities of his stories and his immediate reactions to them at a safe distance both from himself and from his readers, grew longer and longer until at last one saw his people and his story but at the end of corridors of phantasmagoric extension. For a procedure so extraordinary there must have been some cause. So must there have been for that early flight from his native country, for that long abandonment, for the infinite hesitation with which at the end of twenty years he consented to revisit the scenes of his youth. For Henry James had none of the ordinary causes for disliking those scenes. His lineage, station, circumstances as an American were such as to wed any man, especially one so capable of the feelings of a patriot, to his native land. Nor need we take seriously his implied and occasionally expressed opinion that the American scene offered few of the inducements or the circumstances that make for art. This plea, which has become commoner in much later years, turns out always to be the rationalization of either some defect or some weakness or inadequacy for the facing of both life and its expression in art upon comparatively normal terms.

Flight was the motive of Henry James' life and art, flight from his country, flight ever more elaborate and fearful from the rough surface of any reality down the dim length-ening perspectives of his structural technique, flight that grew ever more "artful" as he would have said and resembled in his later years nothing so much as the quaint scurrying and flitting of the animal to which he compared himself —"a still too susceptible and guileless old country mouse." Flight was his motive; frustration was his theme; flight and frustration intertwined were the figure in his carpet. But we know that men never flee *toward* but always *from*, and that the thing they flee from is not outer fate or circum-stance but the self that cannot be reconciled with fate and circumstance, that cannot meet them. The only thing a man ever runs away from is himself.

The accessible records of his life are significant rather for what they do not contain than for what they do. The early European experiences of Henry and William James with their parents made Henry's later flight the easier and more natural. We hear of uncertain health, of a faint-hearted attendance at the Harvard Law School; we know—and without this the whole career of Henry James is unimagi-nable—that the family was economically quite independent of toiling or spinning. In his early twenties he began con-tributing to the "Atlantic Monthly" and so began his more than fifty years' complete and exclusive preoccupation with the art of letters. The drifting for long periods to Europe was soon no longer followed by a drifting back, the earlier Paris and Italian days were exchanged for permanent resi-dence in England, a country for which he entertained so deep and indeed parochial a devotion as to rob his flight from America of the last vestige of conventional explanation. He was the reverse of international-minded or cosmopolitan and in his old age succumbed to the psychosis of war fever with strident abjectness. He warmly nourished indeed all the ordinary sentiments, being a kind friend, the most devoted of brothers, the fondest, as he would have said, of uncles. The one thing wholly omitted from his life was any relation, however conventional, to any member of the opposite sex or any flicker anywhere, during all the years, of a personal capacity for what is ordinarily known as love. He was evidently doomed to bachelorhood from the start, not apparently to the icy and rather proud bachelorhood of Thoreau, but to a sort of gentle and consenting old-bachelorhood which grew softer and more oldish as the years went on. The letters of his later years with their withered effeminacy and elderly archness, with their "many caresses all round" and their "copious embraces" and "I commend you all to felicity" and "fond chatter" and "I mustn't rattle on" and "I am compelled utterly to *drivel*" and "one's *too* dreadful," are not very agreeable reading and remind one of nothing so much as of a type of oldish bachelor, not unknown to university campuses and similar haunts, who, his mouth and chin well hidden by a beard, never sallies forth even on sunniest days without umbrella and galoshes and is credibly reported to spend his leisure hours behind closed doors in the confection, with needle busier than Penelope's distaff, of embroideries which in their exquisiteness and infinite elaboration may well be likened to the later prose of Henry James.

Let me at once repudiate any crude inferences from this account of Henry James. He was one of the most amiable and blameless figures in the long history of letters. On the basis of the ascertainable I describe the temper of his psyche, the climate of his soul in order to integrate expression with experience, art with life. To say that Henry James was a great artist is to say very little. To tabulate the devices of his technique or the verbal tricks of his style is an occupation fit for freshmen in a rhetoric class. He was an excessively peculiar kind of artist and it is this peculiarity, this special quality, which must be accounted for in the degree made possible by our present state of knowledge. He was a man, then, who found life and human experience hopelessly difficult of access. Hence he developed, in compensation, his faculty of observation to an unparalleled acuteness and sharpened his sympathetic sensibilities so that, the proper distance and perspective being given, he could seem to appreciate the normal passions and predicaments of normal people which he had never shared. From reading and social observation he wrung the last drop. He knew all that can be learned by vigilance and sympathy. But knowing, whether consciously or not, that nothing can ultimately take the place of participation, he developed that technique by what he "held most dear, a precious effect of *perspective*" and by elaborately beautiful indirection, which enabled him to describe passion without showing its sting, poverty without its direct pain and humiliation, self-murder without the agonies that must precede it, hopes turned distastrous without the heartbreak that attends them and all the actions and passions of mankind but as in their curbed outer gestures they affected an observer as acute and sympathetic but as cool and as remote from life as he himself.

He differed from Howells and from the regional novelists of America not only by the richness and steady effulgence of his art; he differed from them by sheer power of mind. His limitations were all temperamental, not intellectual. He consented ultimately to neither the bad manners nor the hypocritic moral gestures of his period. In the volume of short stories "The Better Sort" published in 1903 in which his style begins to show the too high elaboration, corresponding to no necessary artistic function, of his last period, there is a tale called "The Story in It" wherein dramatically and indirectly, of course, the whole case against the age is stated: "Yes, when I read a novel, I mostly read a French one, for I seem with it to get hold of more of the real thing—to get more life for my money. . . . The novel of British and American manufacture seems really to show our sense of life as the sense of puppies and kittens. . . . When it comes to any account of a relation, say, between a man and a woman—I mean an intimate or a curious or a suggestive one—where are we compared to them? They don't exhaust the subject, no doubt, but we don't touch it, don't even skim it." Such was more or less Henry James' opinion from the beginning. And though he himself treated but rarely and with infinite indirection the special subject of which he speaks but from any immediate knowledge of which he was excluded, he was determined throughout his long career to show life at its significant tragic crises and never, like Howells, avoided "rough subjects" as having no fitness for an American artist of the Victorian age. So eager was

263

he to treat life at crucial and tragic points that, incapable of the delineation of high passion, he was occasionally tempted to melodrama, as in "The Princess Casamassima" and in the earlier "Roderick Hudson" and was tempted again and again by predicaments arising from greed and by the spiritual sordidness arising out of material considerations as in "The Pension Beaurepas," "The Pupil," "The Spoils of Poynton," "The Wings of the Dove." He could never be accused of shirking desperate issues or twisting life for the sake of a happy ending. In "Mademoiselle de Mauves" the French rake tries to push his wife into adultery; in "Washington Square" the tragedy of Catherine Sloper's life is in her incapacity for tragedy and truly high passion as it was to be so many years later of the protagonist of "The Beast in the Jungle"; in "The Aspern Papers" a great love from the past sheds its all but spent rays upon a sere, autumnal scene; in "The Patagonia" suicide ends the frustrate life of the heroine; in "Mrs. Temperley" a suave, managing woman crushes young lives into a tragic futility; in that extraordinary story "Glasses" the destructiveness of vanity is illustrated by a supremely poignant disaster; in "The Turn of the Screw" the disastrousness of moral evil rises, a ghostly vapor, from the depths of the universe; in "What Maisie Knew" we witness, indirectly of course, all the major corruptions of life; the huge fabric of "The Golden Bowl" is woven about an adultery of long standing and malevolent stealth gradually and shockingly brought home to the consciousness of its victims. And just as Henry James did not avoid "rough subjects" so he did not avoid but rather woo and rejoice in those commoner elements of the art of fiction known as story interest and suspense. That "love of a story as a story which had from far back beset and beguiled" him was never far from his mind and this fact contributed to the ever-increasing disappointment, culminating with the total financial failure of the New York edition in 1908 of his novels, with which he viewed the public's hopeless indifference to his work. And many of his stories are in fact excellent stories as such and to the properly attuned reader the element of suspense is often quite steadily and quite movingly there.

What Henry James could, of course, never permit himself to know, since the admission would have broken down the huge defense mechanism by which the artist in him sought to disguise and compensate the lacks of the man, was this: that neither bold and tragic subject-matter nor his wanting in all sincerity to tell a story could make up to ordinary readers for that distance of his own from human experience which he was forced to externalize through the indirectness of his narrative technique and the ever thicker swathings of his style. Except within a limited field of social predicament and experiences of the literary life, he was forced to report rather than, in one of his favorite expressions, to render, because when it came to real passion and true crisis, he had never, so to speak, been on the spot. He had never been within experience. Hence he tells about it at second, sometimes at third hand, and it is not by accident that so many of his observer-narrators are either critics or painters by profession, since all he could report of the major experiences of life was their symptoms and gestures and never the things themselves. As he himself put it in one of those many hundreds of perfect sentences scattered up and down his works: "Where there is a perpetual fast there are very few crumbs on the floor." This reporting rather than rendering of his substance is, of course, familiar to all his readers; what has not been sufficiently noted is that slightly from the first and overwhelmingly after about 1900 his characters converse even upon the humblest occasions in a manner not only verbally but, what is more significant, syntactically so elaborate that the expression of life even on its aural side fades at last to a continuous unemphasized and undifferentiated whisper within the monotonous vaults of those cathedrals of frosted glass—"The Wings of the Dove," "The Ambassadors," "The Golden Bowl."

I have now sought to define the character of Henry James and of his art and to establish, in some measure, the psychical identity of the man and the artist. His limitations and their results should be clear. In spite of these he left a body of work which, when the largest necessary deductions have been made, is permanent in beauty, in subtle wisdom, in a quiet poignancy that never fails to reach the disciplined and tranquil heart. I know of no more unhappy symptom of the spiritual confusion of our immediate day than the noise, as of cracked trumpets, that surrounds the name of Herman Melville, and the silence which has fallen about that of Henry James. Let us sacrifice at once all of his work that is certain to lose rather than to gain and so, except for a few of the curious and the obdurate, to drift into forgetfulness. This perishable part will be seen, alas, to include practically all of his long novels in which there is in detail so much wisdom, so much genius and so much of the ardent patience of the artist. But by the very constitution of the man he could not fill an epic frame, for that needs epic substance and epic substance needs great passions shown in action and great conflicts and great developments. He began as a kind of American Jane Austen and achieved a perfect fiction in "Washington Square." But soon he strove after a deeper tone and a stronger rhythm and for these he had not the accompanying matter. One has but to state the themes of his long novels from "The Portrait of a Lady" to "The Golden Bowl" and to compare these with the thematic material of great fictions from "Tom Jones" to "Anna Karenina" and from "Wilhelm Meister" to "Buddenbrooks" and from "David Copperfield" to "Sister Carrie" or, to go into James' favorite field, from "Le Rouge et le Noir" to "La Terre" to realize that he had not the substance of life needed for the purpose of the great novel. Hence except in "Washington Square" he failed as a novelist and his occasional refuge in melodrama, as in the French sub-plot of "The American," exhibits his uneasy consciousness of a lack of material. His strength lay in another field. What he could do incomparably was to distill from certain recurrent predicaments and frustrations of life a quiet poignancy, an elegiac note of supreme loveliness. For this the shorter forms of fiction were his proper vehicle: the short-story and, above all, the novelette. He was in a sense aware of this and made himself, in truth, the indisputable master of the novelette in English. He thoroughly understood this form, though his unhappy prejudices confined him to the study of French examples and robbed him of acquaintance with the many masterpieces in this kind from Goethe's "Novelle" to the works of Gottfried Keller and Conrad Ferdinand Meyer. Master of the short-story form though he was, able in his own way to give it at times even the final click demanded by editors, he rebelled against its "rude prescription of brevity at any cost" and was never happier as an artist than when Henry Harland founded the "Yellow Book" and bade him pursue "our ideal, the beautiful and blest *nouvelle*."

It is significant that he began by writing novelettes, realizing from the first the fitness of this "shapely" form for the expression of his genius. His earliest narratives are all of this length and form as was his first and almost indeed his only popular success, the now rather wilted and withered "Daisy Miller." From his experiments in longer forms he returned, not without reason, very constantly to the novelette, following up at last even "The Golden Bowl" with a volume of narratives in his favorite form: "The Finer Grain." And this is the more significant since he very naturally suffered cruelly though quietly enough from his failure to reach any considerable public and since the novelette is a form with which, in the English-speaking world, neither editors nor publishers seem ever to know what to do, trying to palm it off now as a short story and now as a novel. Yet James never tired in his devotion to its fine qualities: isolation of material and depth of tone, restraint upon over-elaboration and yet the final effect of brimming fullness, the sustaining of narrative key and stylistic rhythm to complete satisfaction but never to satiety.

If we regard one or two of his shorter and more successful novels, above all "Washington Square," as novelettes, we are now in a position to isolate and name that body of beautiful and accomplished work by virtue of which Henry James' fame will be finally assured. Other lovers of his work may not agree to my specific selections. But the choice is large and the principle of choice the same. What we have then is: "Madame de Mauves," "Washington Square," "The Pension Beaurepas," "Lady Barberina," "The Aspern Papers," "The Author of Beltraffio," "The Patagonia," "The Liar," "Mrs. Temperley," "The Lesson of the Master," "The Pupil," "Brooksmith," "The Death of the Lion," "The Coxon Fund," "The Middle Years," "The Altar of the Dead," "The Figure in the Carpet," "Glasses," "The Next Time," "The Turn of the Screw," "The Great Good Place," "Broken Wings," "The Beast in the Jungle," "The Birthplace," "The Velvet Glove." I name these tales thus deliberately—an uncommon critical procedure—in the hope that they will be re-read and even republished thus and establish beyond cavil the place and influence of one of our very few American masters.

Of the marks of a master, a minor one if one likes, this selection of Henry James' work possesses all. These narratives have, first of all, the mark of perfection. The theme of each is completely embodied in structure and tone, in character and action, in the seamless interpenetration of all these elements. Whoever loves the art of fiction as, all other things aside, a fine art, one of the finest and most arduous of the arts, will return to these tales again and again and find them, whatever years and experiences and changes of mood and method may have intervened, as instructive in their fullness and flawlessness, in the felicity with which the intention of each is carried out, as he did when their first flush of beauty met his youthful eyes. How salutary for America and for American writers that, amid so much that is rude and fragmentary, powerful without form or pleasing without depth, we have one writer of whom this precious observation can be made. "It is really, at bottom, only difficulty that interests me," James wrote toward the end of his life. In each of these novelettes he met and vanquished a special difficulty. But only thoughtful research will in each case reveal the precise character of the difficulty. For it was indeed vanquished. He left no dust in his workshop. Each tale, however great the initial difficulty, has the high tranquillity of tone that belongs to the completely achieved work of art, whatever it may deal with of human dismay or woe; each is embodied in that crystalline style, warmed sparingly but sufficiently by colors as of an afterglow; each has to a degree rare among writers of the Anglo-Saxon tradition an inner musicality of its own like the musicality inherent in and interpretative of the narratives of Arthur Schnitzler.

It must not be supposed, however, that these stories of Henry James lack the ordinary attractions of fiction. Their characters are not less memorable for being unemphatically drawn. "Washington Square" is richest in this respect. Catherine Sloper, Morris Townsend and especially Lavinia Penniman are unforgettable creations. But so, though more briefly delineated, are the Rucks and the Churches, especially poor Ruck devoured by his women, in "The Pension Beaurepas," and Porterfield who never appears at all in "The Patagonia" and Colonel Capadose in "The Liar" and the softly destructive Mrs. Temperley and the inimitable

Meegans and the exquisite Morgan in "The Pupil" and the lustrous feeble Saltram-Coleridge in "The Coxon Fund" and the dead, unseen, faintly burnished and sinister Acton Hague in "The Altar of the Dead" and poor Flora Saunt in "Glasses" and the successful lady novelist in "The Next Time" and the noble lady novelist in "The Velvet Glove." Nor are these all. For by a few hints and innuendoes Henry James will sketch subsidiary characters and project the whole histories of authentic though in their nature faint and frustrate lives.

Of action no less than of character these tales have their rich and sufficient share. Crucial things happen and tragic things. The technique is, of course, his favorite one of indirection and by perspective. But this reporting as by the messengers in the Greek tragedies, which becomes intolerable in narratives of novel length, is fine and fitting in the novelette with its quiet initial assumption that all cannot be shown nor every subject exhausted, that glimpses and fragmentary reports which the imagination can weave on more largely must suffice. Here, in these novelettes in truth James' adherence to the Horatian *"ne coram publico"* gives the texture an added richness as of infinite implications, of vast wealth in reserve, and adds to the significance of what is said a constant beautiful sense of peripheral presage and implicit dream.

I must not pretend that Henry James, even at his best, always attains the vision that is necessary for the highest art. Too many of the predicaments he dealt with are those belonging to mere social conditions and conventions and therefore have no permanent meaning. He regarded British

271

aristocrats with a blank and painful awe and the story of Lady Barberina, for instance, is not, as he thought, the story of a creature of a special fineness of strain but of one of an impenetrable stupidity rendered the more offensive by not having at least the humility of her limitations. The stories of the life of letters fortunately escape this reproach almost wholly, as do a number of others in which frustration and tragedy spring from the inherent and permanent qualities of mankind. Such are "The Pension Beaurepas," "The Liar," "The Pupil," "The Coxon Fund," the incomparable "Altar of the Dead," "Glasses," "The Turn of the Screw" and "The Beast in the Jungle." These stories and certain others that deal with the life of the artist in a rude and careless world are his finest. In them he is a master more pure and perfect than any other American, a giver of high and lasting delight and an example of peculiar preciousness.

BOOK SEVEN

The Soil and the Transition

I

Chronology is deceptive; records become creative and therefore humanly true when the chronicler yields to the historian.
Time and space, now known to be relative to our position
in the universe, are dependent within human culture on
still other relations—above all, upon the inner relation of
men to their world. The Reverend Mr. Voliva of Zion City,
Illinois, returning from a voyage around the earth declared
that he had been sailing in a circle and that the earth is flat.
He can hardly be called a contemporary of Professor Ed-
dington. There are relativities of cultural time less spectac-
ular but quite as real. Thus when Professor Irving Babbitt,
whose emotional repudiation of an apparent spiritual chaos
I respect, speaks of standards, of decorum, of the inner
check, he shows only a shocking ignorance of the vast wealth
of knowledge which anthropologists and psychologists have
contributed to our understanding of cultural processes. Mr.
Babbitt does not know enough even to state his problem,

a very real one, in contemporary terms. He is like a primitive man still busily scratching the earth with a pointed stick long after the invention of the iron plowshare; he drags his burdens laboriously over the earth oblivious of the invention of the wheel. But nearly all critics and students of literature, coming to their task from the sterile traditions of either philology, in its conventional sense, or rhetoric, are in the same case. It is for this precise reason that I must explain and justify my procedure.

In American literature between the Civil War and the war with Spain there co-existed many cultural universes: there were the polite writers, whom I have already discussed, cultivators of a decorative art with a minimum of vital contact or content; there was the small group of eminent personalities treated in the last two Books, each of whom, except Walt Whitman, made his special compromise with his time, though each was tempted, after the fashion of the modern individualistic artist, to resist and transcend it, to become, as Whitman alone dared to be, both rebel and prophet. Side by side with these there lived and wrote in this period in America a large group of quite able men and women whose task was twofold: first to become conscious as men and as artists of the existence of a nation, that is, of a collective culture peculiar to America, next to assume to this collective culture of their time and country—the writer's necessary material—an attitude of either consent or refusal, of identification or revolt. For the moment it were well not to attach a judgment of value to either of these attitudes. Both are legitimate, both have produced great works in the past. It is indeed quite open to question whether the greatest works of the human imagination have not been produced when the artist identified himself largely with the collective culture and tradition of his folk. But in the period of American literature under discussion it is evident that those writers were truly of or beyond their time and pointed forward to that period of national expression at last achieved within our immediate days, who almost simultaneously with their becoming conscious of a collective American culture began, for both personal and pedagogic purposes, to resist it and to seek to remold it into something nearer to their ideal of a civilized and creative society.

The American writer's use of his necessary material presented a real problem in that period. Both literary and social forces strove against him. New England provincialism alone had had, especially since the appearance of Lowell's "Biglow Papers," a certain standing. The cultivated people of the Eastern seaboard were apt to regard all other American provincialisms as not only rude but disgusting, an attitude that, under various disguises, lingered to this very century and dictated much of the earlier criticism of Theodore Dreiser. In an amusing passage of her novel "Anne," Constance Fenimore Woolson in 1882 depicts a lady of Knickerbocker lineage amazed at anyone's making comparisons "between different parts of this raw land of ours, as though they had especial characteristics of their own." It will be said that Bret Harte and Mark Twain and Howells were broadly accepted. But Harte romanticized his substance into a fairy-tale and Mark was a humorist and Howells stuck pretty close to New England itself or to the New England tradition shifted in space but unchanged in temper.

It took genuine courage, genuine independence of mind to give literary treatment to the rude peasantry that peopled the Mississippi Valley. And it is from the treatment of this peasantry that our modern literature takes it rise. A quaint provincial aristocracy could be depicted by so conventional-minded a man as George W. Cable; Mrs. Stowe's "Old Town Folks" are of and for New England in the strictest sense; the "Hans Breitmann Ballads" of Charles G. Leland are, once more, humorous and the "Pike County Ballads" of John Hay sentimental and feebly romantic. The germs of our period of national expression are to be found in those few writers like Edward Eggleston and E. W. Howe who, whether consenting to it or resisting it, made the collective life of the American people the substance of serious literature.

From this necessary process there were still constant escapes. And the two chief methods of escape can be admirably illustrated by two writers of verse, both wholly without permanent value: Joaquin Miller and James Whitcomb Riley. Miller denied the new national substance by soaking it in the dregs of pseudo-romanticism, Riley by sentimentalizing it according to a preëxistent mood that had no direct relation to it. How little art is determined by outer circumstance and how definitively by the artist's inner structure is proven once more by the fact that Miller was actually born in a covered wagon and saw the pioneer life of the North West with the eyes of his body. But what he was born, alas, to see was himself pseudo-Byronically strutting about the mountains. He never saw the Sierras; he saw himself in a slouch-hat celebrating them. "The Nation" was quite right in attributing to him a "will in excess of understanding and the understanding ill-informed." His moment of success in certain literary coteries in London completely addled his feeble understanding and cut the last thread between him and his native scene. Thenceforth he took wholly to posturing and patronized exotic scenes in bad imitations of Swinburne.

Riley was fundamentally a far more respectable figure. His very employment of the Hoosier dialect was in his favor. In respect of nature he was capable of keeping his eye occasionally on the object, as in "You can hear the black-birds jawin as they foller up the plow" . . . or in the whole poem "When the frost is on the punkin." Once or twice, though only once or twice, as in "Little orphant Annie," he became almost a folk-poet. But he could never for long stick seriously to either life or nature; his general dealing with the collective folk-substance is false and shoddy. He cultivated flight into facile and conventional emotion which struck, of course, the answering chords in the bosoms of the insincere and self-deceived everywhere. He established a whole tradition of sentimental drivel well symbolized by the habitual title of his latest and, one hopes, last inheritor: "A Smile a Day." Riley, at all events, used his American material with hardly more sincerity, though with more of the gesture of that quality, than Miller himself. From both examples it is at least clear that the honest use of the native life in letters required at a certain moment in American history a high measure of both character and brains.

Three books broke the ground; three books pointed to the future and displayed in their yet feeble fashion the marks that were to belong to the period of national expres-

277

sion: "The Hoosier Schoolmaster" by Edward Eggleston, 1871, the novel "Democracy" which Henry Adams published anonymously in 1880 and E. W. Howe's "The Story of a Country Town," which appeared in 1883. None of them is a masterpiece; all are document rather than literature today. But they were germinal. Eggleston, moreover, the feeblest of the three as a writer, grasped clearly enough the creative problems that confronted the nation. He complained in his original preface of the disproportionate place taken by New England life in American books and correctly defined the movement of "provincial realism" some years later as an expression of the fact that "the Federal nation has at length manifested a consciousness of the continental diversity of its forms of life." He correctly asserted his own priority in taking up life "in this regional way" and described correctly "the broader provincial movement in our literature" which had grown up in the twenty years since the original publication of his book. That book is in itself a rude enough idyll of Indiana village life, which he exhibits in a good deal of its ugliness and barrenness but which he accepts wholly and uncritically by finally both sentimentalizing and melodramatizing it. The Cinderella motif of myth and legend has certainly never had a quainter or cruder embodiment than he gave it, nor did he know that by using it he was allying his Indiana village story to a fundamental dream fulfillment which has belonged for many ages to the collective group-mind. This fact accounts, too, for the popularity of "The Hoosier Schoolmaster" which was shared neither by "Democracy" nor by "The Story of a Country Town."

When Adams brought the MS. of his novel to the late Henry Holt he was forty-one and had already achieved distinction as a historian and diplomatist. That he was, as we shall see again in a later Book, a creative spirit whose misery sprang not least from his inability to reach the point of creative projection, is excellently proved by "Democracy." He had the makings of a novelist. The full-length figure of Senator Ratcliffe is done with power and precision; the Balkan corruption used as a foil to the corruption of democratic government is embodied in the figure of Baron Jacobi with a distinction and detachment which no other American of that generation approached; the scene of the President's reception as it passes through the sensitive mind of Mrs. Lightfoot Lee leaves a peculiar impression of spiritual horror created with fine economy. But since Adams did not continue novelist the importance of "Democracy" lies in its critical-mindedness. He rejects the life of the American collectivity at its densest and most representative place and point; he despairs of the Republic; he leaves the reader with not a shred of illusion concerning the national government and its method. There was, of course, in this resistance to the collective life the superficiality of the merely political student and observer. A nation has more vital and richer forces in its life than those that succeed in getting themselves embodied in the machinery of government. But Adams' novel, by virtue of its detached criticism of American life, was prophetic of that later period in which, in his old age, he was destined again to play an important part.

Of capital importance for the future was E. W. Howe's "The Story of a Country Town." For in it we have the first strong note of that long and bitter revolt from the American village, wholly stripped of its pseudo-pastoral and sentimental trimmings, which was to culminate many years later in the works of Edgar Lee Masters and Sherwood Anderson and many minors and which had its definite sociological background in the actual flight from the land and the huge increase in urban populations. In substance Howe left little for his successors to glean. But his book is not only bitter but weary; it cannot even summon the passion of its own defeat and despair. The man who wrote it had almost been subdued by the life about him to its own level. But all the dullness and depression, the lightlessness and joylessness of the neo-Puritan village of the plains are in it, all the concentrated ugliness of that type of manners and religion and human relationship from which the reaction in both American life and American letters has been so violent as to swing, as we shall see later, to opposite extremes: to the denial of all values, not merely of these; to the very curbing and fear of creative forces; to a sterility of the essential will in both the practical and the creative life.

What these three books as well as many others to be noted presently introduced to America, and did so whether they consented to the collective culture or were in revolt against it, was realism, was observation, was the method by which the writer utters and expresses himself through the medium of the outer world as it seems to him actually to exist. And this method, as the briefest reflection will show, is bound sooner or later to introduce the critical spirit. For the writer will necessarily describe what in the outer world has hurt him, since what has hurt him is most salient, and will thus be impelled to introduce measures and values which, though first drawn from his own hurt, he will rationalize quite properly and normally into an ideology which is critical in temper but may easily become creative in fact. Thus is to be explained the incomparable importance of that discipline of realism and naturalism which all modern literatures have undergone and which was inevitably contemporary with the scientific criticism addressed by the nineteenth century to the received notions in religion, economics and morals.

It must not be supposed that any very large public was aware of the change that was slowly coming over both American literature and life. The sales of even the novels of W. D. Howells were absurdly small; Eggleston was proud of his book's having sold as many copies in twenty years as a contemporary publisher's success sells in a single season; "Democracy" and "The Story of a Country Town" made no impression at all. The masses had their own bards: the romances of Southworth and Holmes and Augusta Evans were succeeded by those of the Reverend E. P. Roe; the book that swept the country was Lew Wallace's "Ben-Hur"; parents and children were moved and flattered by Mrs. Burnett's "Little Lord Fauntleroy"; the polite and cultured read the romances of Francis Marion Crawford, the pseudo-idealistic Edward Bellamy's "Looking Backward"; it was considered evidence of a discriminating taste to relish the humor of Frank R. Stockton's "Rudder Grange" and its sequels and his ingenuity as displayed in "The Lady or the Tiger." He was a writer not devoid of merit, though in such novelettes as "The Stories of Three Burglars" he drove his humor hard; neither was Frances Hodgson Burnett who in "That Lass o' Lowrie's," for instance, achieved a measure of intensity and strength. But none of these writers produced any work that has either permanent vitality or any share in the development of American culture. The minority that carries on a national culture is small. In my childhood in the 'nineties of the past century the books I found next to the Bible and Shakespeare in a not illiterate house in an American village were: "Uncle Tom's Cabin," "Ben-Hur," "St. Elmo," "Looking Backward," "Ten Nights in a Bar-Room" and a luridly illustrated exposure of the sexual wickedness of the Mormons. . . .

II

Of the sectionalists to gain a broad reputation the earliest was, of course, Bret Harte. He had the initial advantage of a section already romanticized in every American's heart by its natural splendor and by that release from the dictates of moral order which had accompanied the gold-rush to the West coast and was, with similar literary results, to accompany the later gold-rush to the Klondike. All the elements were given out of which the ingenious talent of Bret Harte wove the pattern of the typical American short story, the story of O. Henry and of the popular magazines, the story with the happy ending which editors are still seeking and still buying. The ignorant and the superficial have attempted to define the American short story as a special art form and have indiscriminately grouped Hawthorne and Poe, Henry James and the later New England practitioners with Bret Harte and his progeny. That is nonsense. The normal brief narrative among us has differed from the European narrative of the same kind in no such manner as idle criticasters suppose. In "Law Lane" Sarah Orne Jewett tells of a New England countryside precisely the same tale that Gottfried Keller told in "Romeo und Julia auf dem Dorfe"; if the lovers in her story are luckier than those of the Swiss master, it is for the good reason that in New England social forms were not so hopelessly frozen nor hatreds so profoundly rooted. And both Miss Jewett and Keller told the story because they found it in human nature. Now this type of story, of which the briefness is dictated by artistic and not artificial reasons, by an idea of rhythm and plasticity that rises in the artist's mind, is not *as a form* peculiar to any nation, but will express the impulse of a French, a German, a Russian or an American artist. And in this normal or classical type of short story, in the short story as expressing one of the eternal moods of literature, America, quite contrary to current babble, is poor. The meretricious short-story has pushed out the short story; periodicals will not buy the latter nor publishers risk collections of it in book form. American writers have again and again, usually leaning on not the best French models, attempted the short story as a form of both art and bread-winning and have failed. Henry Harland, although the stories in "Grey Roses" are a little sweetish with the sweetishness of Daudet, was given no encouragement to maturer efforts; the late Harris Merton Lyon, the De Maupassant, Jr., of Dreiser's "Twelve Men," found no market for his tales; the collection of them called "Sardonics" fell still-born from an obscure and bankrupt press; the man died early and embittered. Such, as will be

283

seen again later, is the commoner fate of the short story in America.

It is otherwise with the short-story. (The distinction expressed by the hyphen was made by the late Brander Matthews.) This type has had an unparalleled success; its confection is taught by experts; its sales rival those of other national trade-goods. Its formula was completely worked out by Bret Harte and is somewhat closer in character to the structure of a neurosis than to that of a work of art. For the groundwork of every neurosis is an inability to face the realities of either the self or the world. The patient wants essentially to be not himself in a world that does not exist. He is dissatisfied; he wants to be otherwise and otherwhere: a hero released from pressure in a world of revery. A writer who could be privy to the habitual reveries of his average fellow-countrymen would produce stories sure to sell by the million. But since few or none ever reveal the content of their reveries and wishes and daydreams, the successful writer in the broadest sense is he whose reveries, which he has the talent formally to externalize, to project, are more or less identical with those of his average fellow-beings. In a word, the immediately successful writer, the inventor, like Bret Harte, of a formula that unerringly hits the popular taste, is a man who differs in no spiritual or intellectual respect from the readers who accept him and is distinguished from them only by the gift of expression. He regresses sociologically to the bardic level—see the Introduction—he becomes once more mere choragus or mouthpiece of the tribe. By the same token the efficient editor of a periodical of so-called national circulation must be in the strictest sense an average man. Else he would buy stories that affront the revery wishes of his readers and his circulation would soon decline from the nation of the average to the parish of the distinguished of mind.

The formula invented by Bret Harte and since repeated with a thousand variations of content introduces the reader to a world of romance in which the ordinary restraints are loosened. Vicariously the reader can now rove and gamble and shoot and lynch and consort with outcasts and prostitutes. But the reader has not only this lawless individual self; he has another, a social self, a self that is crammed with terror and that answers to every liberation with a feeling of guilt. Hence it must be clear to this reader from the start —otherwise his reaction would not be one of pleasure but one of moral indignation, that is to say, of inner guilt projected on others—that he will be able to pay for his vicarious release by being present, at the end of the story, at the triumph of virtue and goodness and the moral order, the conversion of the recalcitrant and the noble death of gambler and harlot, the repentance of the erring and the reward of virtue. He must know, in other words, that his social self will be able to pay and overpay the debt incurred by the vicarious libertinage of his revery self. It is for this reason that "the work of regeneration began in Roaring Camp," that the gambler of Poker Flat dies a sacrificial death, that the glasses are charged for "Miggles, God bless her!" that Tennessee and his "pardner" meet in heaven and that the harlot hands over her son to the school-teacher with the words: "Help him to—to—to forget his mother!" It would be futile to continue with other of the famous stories or to show how the anecdotical poems of Bret Harte, which still linger in anthologies, follow the same pattern from the pseudo-release of pent-up impulse to the happy ending. It may be as well to add here, in connection with the origin of the American short-story, that the notorious happy ending is bad not because it is happy, but precisely because it is not. A happy ending to a human story profoundly rooted in both character and fate, were it attainable in such a world as the present, would be of an inestimable preciousness. The meretricious happy ending of the conventional short-story from Bret Harte to the present has no relation to such an one. It is, rather, a feebly propitiatory gesture; an *absit omen*; it is a sop to the slightly neurotic and wholly muddle-headed who ask of art as of life not reality but feigning, not catharsis but confirmation in immaturity, not cure but drug. And this phenomenon of the happy ending is, of course, closely allied to that entire psychology of optimism at any price which is so characteristic of the mass-life of modern America. This optimism, too, is symptomatic of a slight group-neurosis: of a profound and troubling distrust of both one's civilization and, above all, of one's self which must be extruded from the field of consciousness in order that the music of the real need not be faced. Need I add that other national groups are afflicted by other and often not dissimilar maladies of the soul and that America is neither more nor less ill-balanced than other nations? The extremes of arrogance and self-deprecation between which Americans, as such, often waver is, as we know from the analysis of the neuroses, but another common symptom of those who fear the effort of an adaptation to themselves as they really are in such a world as exists. Thus we come, from the point of view of the history of American literature, of American expression, to two important conclusions: the happy ending of the short-story, the entire Pollyanna-ish strain in American writing, the "smile a day" and "keep smiling" slogans, the structure of the fables of the Zane Greys and Harold Bell Wrights, are all phenomena strictly analogous for groups of readers to those devices of regression to the infantile or flight into either abasement or grandeur or escape into mere revery by which the neurotic type avoids the facing of the self and the world and the pain of adjustment to things as they are. The second conclusion is that realism and naturalism, that observation first and observation leading to revolt and pessimism later were a reaction in terms of self-cure and self-catharsis. The realists and naturalists sought to cure first themselves, then others, to face reality and next to make others face it, to cleanse themselves of childish delusions and then to communicate this process and its findings to their fellowmen. And the contemporary naturalists and satirists and critical realists have been rebels and extremists precisely because they found the process of self-catharsis so difficult and were themselves so closely allied to the American masses and group-neuroses which they fought to overcome. Of this much more must be said hereafter. At this point it is necessary merely to state the fact that, from the first feeble attempts at sectional realism to today, the history of American expression, articulateness, literature, is the history of a struggle toward adjustment to the realities of the self and the world, an attempt to restrain flight, to attain balance, to find a center and a solid bit of earth from which the creative imagination can truly begin to function. . . . All these considerations and conclusion I do not offer as "truth" but as "reality," as recognizable pictures of the so-ness of things seen by a mind itself necessarily implicated in the processes it seeks to clarify and describe. But this limitation the critic shares today not only with the historian and the psychologist, but with the physicist himself.

III

The sectional realism with which the period of national expression faintly began was in truth very feeble. The creative values left by these writers are few. They all or nearly all share one fatal mark; they were incapable of development; their first books remained their best. Thus, for instance, "Old Creole Days" and "The Grandissimes" of George W. Cable are still readable; his later books are not. Even his slight deviation from illusion and his moderate dealings with reality evidently produced a violent reaction within him and he fled his native city to become a religious propagandist in Boston. His field and home, old New Orleans, was of the richest, and some of this wealth spills over despite himself into his first two books. But because the old New Orleans life was French, he adopted the dreadful manner of Victor Hugo's romances and swathes even powerful and strongly felt or observed characters and episodes in a shoddy, discontinuous and unreal rhetoric. A lusciousness, lack of restraint and impertinent verbosity that characterized all the writers of what was then known as the New South are first observable in him.

New England, which always seems to decline and yet is

288

never quite drained of creative energy, comes off better even in this period. It is fairly certain that all that will remain of it or be seen to have any but illustrative and disciplinary value will be a few pages by Sarah Orne Jewett and Mary Wilkins Freeman. These two cultivated the short story, not the short-story. Their field of observation was excessively limited; the society they had before them to depict was the least fruitful that human artists ever sought to treat. In these New England villages the old maid was the typical person; men, except the old and feeble or an occasional minister, were nuisances or intruders. A European would not credit the existence of such a society. He who truly knows America knows better. Upon the whole both Miss Jewett and Mrs. Freeman kept their eye on the object. They did not, to be sure, stand above or detachedly aside from the matter contemplated. Miss Jewett was capable of faintly ironic moments; Mrs. Freeman took a good deal for wool that had never seen a sheep's back. Yet both are scrupulous within the measure of their intelligence and the reach of their vision; their entire sincerity and formal simplicity make for a mildly classical quality, for a sobriety and completeness of delineation within the tiniest of frames. They are at least never pretentious and rarely tricky; neither of them, like Margaret Deland of Pennsylvania, sought to treat large and intricate problems with the intellectual equipment of an average villager nor did they, like their somewhat younger Southern colleagues, Mary N. Murfree and James Lane Allen, make romanticized scenery do for both character and action; they also avoided the melodrama of which Helen Hunt Jackson's once famous "Ramona" reeks and which even the quite gifted Constance Fenimore Woolson considered obligatory to the complications of the novel. Both Miss Jewett and Mrs. Freeman confined themselves largely to the short story. The thinness of their substance was such as to be palatable in highly concentrated portions; even the novelette, as witness, for instance, Mrs. Freeman's "The Jamesons," makes a demand they could not meet. I seem to be describing them in terms chiefly negative. But their virtue resides, in fact, in their avoidance of the vices of their period. What remains is thin but clear, narrow but unpretentious, infinitely restricted but sober and complete.

Miss Jewett's vein was the thinner, but the finer of the two. "Deephaven" is a little book that grows upon reflection in the memory. The decaying maritime village in Maine with its widows and spinsters and superannuated seafaring men, with its pride and its delicate aroma of the past lingers definitely in the imagination. If "Cranford" is a minor classic, so is "Deephaven." The tints are unbelievably pale, but they have not at least faded in the weather of time. A few of Miss Jewett's stories are quite as fine and more substantial. In the very best she wholly avoids "plot"; she is content to render character—"Miss Tempy's Watchers"—or the pathos of frustrate lives—"The Dulham Ladies"—or a quality of the spirit—"A White Heron"—or, at her fullest, a complete tragedy in miniature, as in "Marsh Rosemary." She will find the universal in her little chosen plot, as in "Law Lane," or as in "An Only Son." She has, too, an elegiac note in her prose, a sensitiveness to the spiritual overtone of rhythm, of form, that separates her from her cruder contemporaries: "There was nobody to speak to him and the house was like a tomb where all the years of his past were lying dead, and all the pleasantness of life existed only in remembrance." If ever there came into being a library of American literature devoted to creative expression and not to document, a slender volume would assuredly be dedicated to Sarah Orne Jewett.

Mrs. Freeman had more vigor, but less fineness. She stooped to moralize and any member of this generation who moralized was lost. She attempted to reason and that was quite as fatal. But she knew more in concrete form than she would permit herself to abstract and the justly famous and inimitable confession of Babbitt at the end of his story was anticipated a quarter of a century earlier by one of Mrs. Freeman's old maids: "I ain't never done anything my whole life that I ought not to do, but now I'm going to." The trouble with Mrs. Freeman was, of course, that she never permitted herself to examine the precise content of that "ought." She was also contaminated by the trickery of the short-story. Thus a story like "The Last Gift" would be a little masterpiece of the noble and essential tragedy of life, were it not for that contemptible half sentence in the last paragraph—"he did not know he was to find an asylum and a friend . . ." which robs it of its truth and dignity and memorableness. Once or twice nevertheless Mrs. Freeman rose to veracity and power, above all in "A New England Prophet," a thing not unworthy of Hardy or Hauptmann, and in "A New England Nun," and human character is more than ephemerally embodied in such stories as "The Butterfly" and "The Revolt of Mother." At present there is over the entire work of such a writer as Mrs. Freeman a pallor beside the blaze of the living hour. But the too high colors

291

of immediacy will fade in their turn and it is not unlikely that in the twenty-first century lovers of the national literature will turn back and take a genuine if moderate delight in fragments of work, of which the moral and intellectual ineffectiveness will have become merely quaint, of which the artistic and folk-lore elements will stand forth in their proper value. The anthologies of American literature of that day, or even of a more distant one, will include Miss Jewett's "The Dulham Ladies" and Mrs. Freeman's "A New England Prophet" and confectioners of doctoral dissertations, if they still flourish, will write studious monographs on the other works, long slumbering in libraries undisturbed, of these ladies of New England.

Of the other sectionalists there is not even so much to be said. They set a necessary example; they constituted a proper period of transition; the works of several, closely examined, will likewise yield pages for the anthologists of the future. The latter will probably choose a passage from the excellent Mackinac scenes of Constance Fenimore Woolson's "Anne," a few pages from Thomas Nelson Page's "In Old Virginia," a handful of fables from Joel Chandler Harris' amiable semi-folk lore; they may even find a passage from Alice Brown, more certainly a descriptive bit, offsetting character or action, from James Lane Allen, probably, too, a sketch from the "Old Chester Tales" or "Dr. Lavendar's People" of Mrs. Deland. And they will see, even as we do, only more clearly, since their interest will be purely abstract and they will not have seen foolish brains still further addled by such performances as "The Awakening of Helena Ritchie," that the sectionalists both awakened and clarified the nation's consciousness of itself and its culture by habituating it first to the reading of fiction and simultaneously to native scenes and themes. Thus the novel in its triumphant contemporary sense was introduced, nor has the triumph of the type of novel the sectionalists created yet ceased. It prepared the way for works of another tone and temper. In the successful works of several contemporary writers of a younger generation, such as Mrs. Dorothy Canfield Fisher, for instance, it still persists almost unchanged.

Two more observations must be made on the sectional novelists. They were all good craftsmen of letters and accustomed the public to smooth work at worst and to accomplished work at best. They thus helped to create a taste and an instinct for the novel as a form of expression that has stood their successors in good stead. Nor should it be forgotten that their vehicle was not only the book but the better type of illustrated magazine which with them and through them educated a huge public in the art of reading. It was the age of the illustration, too, both in line and in color. The Christmas and Easter numbers of "Harper's" and "Scribner's" and "The Century" blazed with gold and purple and scarlet; the "art" was even more conventional than the stories; it was pitilessly pretty. Nor have the magazines, brilliantly contemporary in social study and survey, ever recovered from the type of fiction that made them great in those days. The sectionalists and the illustrators created the modern American audience; they spread the taste for reading and educated the reader to demand reasonably finished work. They were able to do this—and this is the second observation that remains to be made on them—because they were, like Bret Harte, distinguished from their audience only by articulateness, not by freedom of thought. They were not philosophical conservatives, like Mr. Paul Elmer More; they were not reactionary aristocrats, like Mrs. Edith Wharton; they were villagers with the prejudices and moral terrors of villagers; they were empty of ideas and rich in indignation; they were not even austere, they were only frightened. Their consequent success, beneficent enough in the broader social sense as I have shown, very nearly silenced the true fore-runners of a later period and made the struggle of the free artistic spirit in America unnecessarily difficult and prolonged. Their spiritual successors, among whom can be found writers as gifted as Mr. Booth Tarkington, still darken council and blunt the higher functions of literature by accustoming large sections of the public to the intolerable notion that the artist can be an artist and remain upon the public's own spiritual and intellectual level, and that hence art need neither be striven for nor attained but can be tasted and assimilated by common appetites and untrained digestions.

Yet so tenacious was the American public of its terrors and defenses, so timid of facing reality that even the mild and tepid veraciousness to partial fact of the sectionalists could not withstand the violent pseudo-romantic reaction which set in toward the end of the nineteenth century. To attribute that reaction to outer influences, those of Stevenson or of Rider Haggard, is purely superficial. Such influences may furnish an occasion; they never constitute a cause. From one point of view such books as James Lane Allen's "The Choir

294

Invisible" or S. Weir Mitchell's "Hugh Wynne" or Mary Johnston's "To Have and to Hold" or Paul Leicester Ford's "Janice Meredith" may be conceived of as continuing to cultivate the national field retrospectively. But for such an interpretation the books were too little serious, too thorough in their acceptance of all glitter in American history, particularly of the Revolution, as that of purest gold, too sleek in execution, too full of mere costume and pseudo-heroic gesturing and innocent love and knightly enterprise. Profoundly this movement was another movement of flight from reality into a world of pleasant defensive illusion. Perhaps the American people, cradled in the abundance of nature, having for so long in the process of conquering a continent with gun and axe and spade and plow substituted the hardships of the body for those of the soul, is peculiarly prone to this form of flight from facing the facts of both man and of his world. It is at least certain that the development from sectional realism to a naturalism, more or less inspired by contemporary science, was halted for sundry years toward the end of the nineteenth century by a pseudo-romantic reaction and that this reaction made art and life brutally hard for the forerunners of the period of national expression who were living and working in obscurity and often in want during these very years. But with this flight into illusion, with this inability to face facts, we must constantly reckon in the history of American civilization. The famous contemporary device of living "wet" and voting "dry" is of the same character and an identical gesture of flight may be observed when a chief magistrate of the republic as technically learned as Mr. Hoover[1] insists on the necessity of obedience to law and has nothing to say concerning the relation of law to either custom or conscience or the danger, noted by all students of democracy, lest majorities become as unbearably tyrannical as oligarchs. In the moral life we have escaped the cast-iron "purity" of the later nineteenth century only to drift into the amiable and humane but both psychologically and physiologically untenable meliorism of Judge Ben Lindsey. At any cost we must be optimistic, at any cost unresigned to the changeless elements of man, of nature, and of human life. We must be optimists and we must be right. The pseudo-romantic reaction coincided at its crest with the equally shoddy excitement of the war with Spain, and the mild and easy satiric discourses of Mr. Dooley, disturbing no one, rousing no doubt, were sold by the tens of thousands over the same counters that were loaded with Charles Major's "When Knighthood Was in Flower," Thomas Nelson Page's "Red Rock" and Mary Johnston's "Prisoners of Hope." Everybody was thoroughly muddle-headed and spuriously happy and at ease. Both Miss Jewett and Mrs. Freeman turned aside from their sober chronicles to write swashbuckling romances. Only a few recalcitrant and inarticulate youths, only a few obscure outcasts knew that nevertheless creative expression in America was at the cross-roads and that a new period and a new world were imminent. For those few saw beyond its traditional form the true significance of William Vaughn Moody's "An Ode in Time of Hesitation" and in the very year of "Janice Meredith" were quietly reading Frank Norris' "McTeague."

[1] Editor and translator of a Sixteenth Century Latin treatise on engineering.

I have delineated the development of literature largely from the point of view of prose fiction. Until the later rise of a new movement in poetry, of the belated birth of an American drama, of a brief popularity of critical thinking, it is necessary—with rare exceptions to be presently noted—to do just that. A writer to be significant must either have in himself some element of greatness or he must contribute to the line of development of his country's culture. Now in the period under discussion there was no writer who had any element of greatness, of independent and self-contained permanence, and only or almost only the writers of fiction spoke not for themselves alone but for the nation in its varying moods. There was no powerful personality anywhere; the men and women of the period were extraordinarily small, as it were, in human format. Nor can I except from this statement the nature writers, John Burroughs and John Muir, though both, and especially Muir, could write eloquent and even shapely prose; they both brought too little to nature to render nature significant; their observations are in the last analysis neither strictly scientific nor philosophic; unlike Thoreau they drew little from nature because they did not bring enough. It is the sheep-like quality of critics that causes them to mention these and to neglect a far greater writer, perhaps the most powerful writer of the period, Josiah Royce. But until the days of Professor Dewey and his disciples and the reduction of philosophy to a tool in a world of go-getters, America has always been happy in the literary quality of her philosophers. Royce was an idealist of a rather exorbitant type, as he could hardly not have been in his period and with his particular background. But his idealism was no conventional or flatly moralistic one. By an arduous and noble effort of speculative thought, embodied in treatises which both for structural order and textual eloquence are far above any other prose of his time, he sought to establish man's union with and yet separateness from the Absolute; he cared little about the freedom of the will, for he was a good man not eager to assign guilt and mete out punishment; he sought to make the universe a less lonely place for such a being as man and his spirit and his prose have a validity beyond the arguments with which he sought to establish his vision of the sum of things and the nature of the universe. But Royce stood aloof and aside. Within a few years moreover he was overshadowed by William James, who opposed to Royce's austere idealistic Monism a doctrine far more conformable to the mental habits of America. Thus Royce not only stood alone but was robbed of the chance, however slow to develop and however indirect, to influence the national life.

Where, then, since the sectional realists were overwhelmed by the cloak and dagger reaction and the most eminent personality among the thinkers of the age was a cloistered philosopher, and since the true forerunners of the modern movement were young and quite obscure—where shall we look for the point and hour of transition and what, precisely, is the character of the transition that took place?

The cultural scene at the time of the war with Spain is worth recalling, for within a very few years, although the reigning pundits did not know it, all was to be changed. From the obscure house of B. W. Dodge and Company was to issue a brief decade later a book called "Sister Carrie" by Theodore Dreiser and America was to enter the definite cultural current of the modern world. But in 1898 we were singularly untouched, provincial or, if one prefers, pure. Troubling suspicions of the true character of this situation were hushed by sincere but fallacious arguments like that of Howells, that the more smiling aspects of life were the more American. Thus Mrs. Freeman makes a New England lady say of Ibsen and Maeterlinck—a then current but absurd juxtaposition, like the later Hauptmann and Sudermann: one might as well have said Shaw and Pinero!—: "I don't know as I think they are so much above as too far to one side. . . . Sometimes it's longitude and sometimes it's latitude that separates people. I don't know but we are just as far from Ibsen and Maeterlinck as they are from us." To this convention of thought, that Americans were exempt from the ills and doubts and troubles that with the changing ages were besetting the rest of mankind, everyone held or tried to hold fast. And not only were we supposed to be personally pure but—despite the both foul and lustrous epic of the Gilded Age—both economically and politically in a state of idyllic innocence and peace. These superstitions the eminent writers of the period, Howells and Mark Twain, supported actively or by silence. Mr. Hamilton Wright Mabie, editor of the "Outlook," was symbolical of the polite foreground of American culture. For not only was he in some sort an *arbiter elegantiarum* but it was his proudest boast that he had as a contributing editor Mr. Theodore Roosevelt. Hence the only relief from avuncular mildness was the vulgar reactionary clamor of Roosevelt, who taunted

McKinley with not declaring war sooner, even as some years later, as chief magistrate, he was to reproach Mr. Lincoln Steffens and the latter's colleagues for their attempt to sanitate our economic and political life by hurling at them the epithet of "muck-rakers." And this epithet itself, as has not been observed, shows the period's slackness of language and hence slothfulness of thought. For if there was muck, as the phrase admits, muck which means manure, dirt, disgusting refuse, then they who raked it and so cleansed the common wealth of it were evidently conscientious citizens. But fact in either speech or life was wholly alien to the spirit of the period. What marked it was defensive self-apotheosis, the ordinary citizen dreaming himself to be half David Harum and half Theodore Roosevelt and so at the same moment, kindly and patriotically, shrewd and belligerent, a creature at home in slippers and simultaneously slaying wild beasts of the jungle, comfortable and not easily roused, but in defense of his country's honor or of virtue or weakness downtrodden anywhere a lion with Rooseveltian bristling mane. Such feeble substitutions in revery for the facing of reality are not uncommon in any age or land. The trouble in the America of 1898 seemed to be that no one was less gullible than anyone else. It follows that McKinley had no difficulty in withholding from Congress the abject submission that Spain had made and which rendered war even more futile and foolish than usual. Nor was anyone privy to the thoughts of those who themselves never let the right lobe of their brain know what the left was thinking concerning the annexation of Porto Rico and of the Philippine Islands. We were pure as a nation, precisely as our families, homes and institutions were pure and Richard Hovey wrote "Unmanifest Destiny."

Our culture in all its manifestations was of a piece. Mr. George Edward Woodberry taught inspiringly at Columbia but the substance of his teaching had no relation to the fundamental realities of life and hence none to those of literature. Mr. William Winter, our chief dramatic critic, worshiped at Stratford in the summer and in the winter took seriously the plays of Messrs. Bronson Howard, Augustus Thomas and Clyde Fitch. Consciously to admit to himself the fact that there had been a Théâtre Libre and a Freie Bühne and that the drama was once more a great art-form would have been like admitting to himself that he was a mammal, a fact both unclean and un-American. . . . It is evident, is it not, that we have risen culturally in the world, as the world indeed has not been slow to admit, and that the golden age of American literature is, happily for us who live in it, the present age? . . .

I return to the question of the transition and of a prophetic hour that communicated itself even measurably to the consciousness of a public. We shall not find that transition declaring itself as a consequence of the publication of the major work of Emily Dickinson, for few or none listened in those days to that voice. Nor shall we find it in the fresh and handsome rhythms of Richard Hovey who illustrated admirably the Nietzschean saying that liberation from under a yoke avails little without a will toward an intelligible goal. Hovey conceived himself to be a great rebel against the polite writers and wrote till the very end of his short life like an extremely gifted sophomore. From the college-tavern frowned on by pedagogues he drifted into a pastiche of mediævalism and wilted romance. A few of his quieter lyrics will adorn the anthologies; he was not a bridge to any future. Eugene Field shot more arrows toward a farther shore. Not, indeed, in his amiable verses for children nor even in his Horatian parodies, for these though continued by contemporary wits go back to a tradition at least as old as the early eighteenth century, but rather in the "column" which he conducted first in the "Denver Tribune" and later for many years in the "Chicago Daily News." He created that modern American type of jester to whom, as to the king's fool, much is permitted in pungency of speech and freedom of criticism. Of his successors the most learned was the late Keith Preston; the most elegant in verbal quip and literary flavor is Franklin P. Adams, the most richly imaginative and humorous is Don Marquis; the only one of any genuine intellectual gallantry is Heywood Broun. Yet even he runs into the conventional mould of a political party and an economic doctrine. The "column" invented by Field should have produced a Karl Kraus, a Kurt Tucholsky, at least a Georges de la Fouchardière. It has not done so yet. Non-partisan freedom of thought and speech seems still to flourish more in Vienna and Berlin and Paris than in New York or Chicago. But it is clear that Eugene Field was one of those who in the eighteen-hundred and nineties set out upon a road that still continues.

But as the symbolical transition figure I select not him, nor George Santayana of whose "Sonnets and Poems" no one had heard, but the poet and dramatist William Vaughn Moody. For it was his virtue to hold spiritually in germ all or nearly all the chief ideas and creative motifs of modern literature and it was his good luck to be heard when neither Bierce nor Crane nor Norris nor Phillips was taken seriously enough to reach the youth of the land in whose hands lay the future of both life and letters. The reason for this good luck is obvious enough. Both as a man and as a writer Moody, superficially considered, seemed conventional and harmless. He was a gentleman and a university professor and the co-author of a manual of English literature. He was no newspaper writer grimy from the police courts and no acrid Zolaist dwelling on dirt and ugliness nor did he strive, like Upton Sinclair, to show up the economic structure of society. Both he and his work seemed inoffensive, though it is probable that the group which gathered about him and Robert Morss Lovett entertained private heresies and specific rebellions prophetic of that somewhat later literary Chicago of which we possess the vivid chronicle in Harry Hansen's "Midwest Portraits." Nevertheless Moody in his writings offended definitely neither by substance nor by form. He was perhaps himself not wholly aware of all the creative implications of his work, as he seems certainly not to have been aware of the problem which confronted any poetry in the English language at that time—the absolute necessity for verbal and rhythmic refreshment. He was not consciously aware of it: creatively he was, as is shown by his definite though immediately abandoned tentatives toward new orders of poetic speech. But the point is that he did indeed immediately abandon these to fall back more and more upon a style, close in the lyric to that of the Pre-Raphaelites and in blank verse to that of Keats' "Hyperion." The pen-

303

alty for this use of utterly used up poetic textures is that the very great majority of his lines have no resonance, no vibrancy, that they are like strings unstrung upon a stringed instrument. The majority; not all. It bears witness to a poetic impulse and power of a very high order that the "Ode in Time of Hesitation" has so much of visual freshness, so much of concrete music, so much that gave the reader both the surprise and the satisfaction of poetry. For its form, the pseudo-Pindaric ode of the English tradition, is of all forms the most outworn and defaced, a thing of open scorn in the hands of British laureates from the eighteenth century on, galvanized into a momentary semblance of life by Lowell in the "Commemoration Ode," but in reality not only dead but ludicrous. And Moody took this form, long justly a jest and an abomination, and wrote:

> Soon shall the Cape Ann children shout in glee,
> Spying the arbutus, spring's dear recluse;
> Hill lads at dawn shall hearken the wild goose
> Go honking northward over Tennessee.

And he wrote:

> Now limb doth mingle with dissolvèd limb
> In Nature's busy old democracy
> To flush the mountain laurel when she blows
> Sweet by the southern sea,
> And heart with crumbled heart climbs in the rose.

This, if one likes, is a conceit and should therefore commend itself to Mr. T. S. Eliot and our latest poets with their definite "metaphysical" strain. But even those who do not overvalue that sort of thing will grant the conceit to be in the high manner of Donne or Vaughan or Crashaw at their noblest, whence it is clear that Moody had, at his best, a power of justness, above all, of precision in the use of the narrowly poetic imagination which had not existed in America since Poe. But that is not all. This ode, of which the texture is nowhere greatly below that of the passages quoted, is strictly new and modern in that it is not a blind glorification, like all previous formal political poetry in America, of some group passion of its hour—even the anti-slavery poems were that—but an uncompromising and bitter protest against the Rooseveltian adventure in vulgar imperialism.

> Are we the eagle nation Milton saw
> Mewing its mighty youth?

Moody asked;

> Or have we but the talons and the maw,
> And for the abject likeness of our heart
> Shall some less lordly bird be set apart—
> Some gross-billed wader where the swamps are fat?
> Some gorger in the sun? Some prowler with the bat?

From that point on the ode becomes more rhetorical, though still in no mean sense; that is to say, it becomes more the gesture of passion than its immediate fire. But luckily this did not happen before the bolt had been shot and reached the mark. Moody not only continued his protest against the annexation of the Philippines in the well-known lines "On a Soldier Fallen," which are unfortunately loose-girdled and conventional with a sing-song rhythm dear to American versifiers, but in the compact and grave though a little thudding blank verse of "The Quarry" issued a protest against the dismemberment of China and thus set an example for the poetic breaking of another set of conventions.

305

From political heresy Moody passed on to the more dangerous heresy concerning economic injustice. This, too, was a new note in American poetry—new above all in its precise formulation, its ungilded characterization of the possessing classes, its expression of the profoundly troubled conscience of the poet:

> Who has given to me this sweet
> And given my brother dust to eat?
> And when will his wage come in?

Here again in "Gloucester Moors" there is that unhappy tripping of the meter that enfeebles poetic speech. But there is also an extraordinarily prophetic grasp of the position of the humanist, who alone can save the world, between the deep sea of proletarian chaos and the devil of oligarchic stupidity:

> Then I strove to go down and see;
> But they said: "Thou art not of us!"
> I turned to those on the deck with me
> And cried: "Give help!" But they said: "Let be:
> Our ship sails faster thus."

Out of the poet's tender social conscience arose naturally enough the notion of a narrative poetry dealing with the simple lives of simple people. And such a narrative, bare and moving and profoundly human in motivation, is "Until the Troubling of the Waters" which is far closer in method to the narratives of Robert Frost or Mark Van Doren than to the British examples—Wordsworth's "Michael," certain of Browning's simpler monologues—which Moody undoubtedly had in mind.

But I have not yet exhausted Moody's prophetic insight

306

into the processes of civilization and therefore into those of literature, though he himself, for various reasons, died on Nebo and never entered the promised land himself. In the poem "The Brute" he grappled over thirty years ago with the problem of the machine, seeing it already become the slayer and master of men but not, like his foolish successors, making an idol of it, insisting rather on its subjection to purposes human and humane. And finally there is that excellent poem "The Menagerie" in which Moody made the first essay to bend the American vernacular to high poetic use. A dozen objections can be urged against the poem in detail. Moody had not, of course, Ring Lardner's ear for our folk-speech. He mixes it with pseudo-British vulgarisms. Nor can we be impressed today by an acceptance of idealistically tinged Darwinism. But once again Moody made the experiment uniquely and alone in his age.

He did not stop there, short as was his life. Though still often too traditional in execution and neither an exact nor subtle reasoner, he had a powerful intuitive grasp of the necessary development of the national literature. Without any models in his own tongue, without a living theater to inspire or guide him, he was the first modern American to attempt the serious prose play. No doubt "The Great Divide" flares into melodrama and the far more finely conceived and executed "Faithhealer" is both feeble and cloudy. But only a genius of the first order could have succeeded in the America of 1900 where Moody failed. His attempt was an achievement in itself; Miss Anglin's success in "The Great Divide" reintroduced to America at the very least the possibility of such a thing as a modern drama of literary quality;

307

it was at least a rebuke to the insincere inanities that cluttered a dead and mechanical stage. William Vaughn Moody was at least a poet and a scholar. The very presence of his spirit in the American theater helped to put in their dreadful place the Bronson Howards and Steele MacKayes and Hernes and Gillettes and Clyde Fitches whom personally interested or merely foolish critics tried to palm off as playwrights on the American audience.

He took a final step. He went beyond the realistic narrative in verse and the use of the vernacular in verse, both of which were to be so conspicuous in the years to come; he went beyond the prose-play which, on that level, he was the first American to attempt; he intuitively skipped the generations and attempted a neo-classic mood and manner. America has not reached its neo-classicism or neo-idealism yet. Nor will that movement when it comes, as it is certain to do, have any obvious characteristics in common with Moody's unfinished trilogy "The Fire-Bringer," "The Masque of Judgement," the fragmentary "Death of Eve." We shall not use the model of Greek tragedy, nor probably verse at all. But we shall creatively and imaginatively somehow embody the affirmations, the few possible affirmations of our age, duly conscious of science, duly scrupulous, as the idealists of an older day were not, to discipline and use our minds. Except for his traditional form that is what Moody attempted for his time. He is conscious of science; he attempts his reconciliation of God and man, of the One and the many in a fashion not so unlike that of Josiah Royce. Influenced by a powerful mother-fixation—see "The Daguerreotype," "Good Friday Night" and "I Am the Woman"—to which he reacted creatively and not neurotically, he placed at the center of his imaginative universe *das Ewig-Weibliche* and held human love to be not only divider but reconciler of man to his universe. The trilogy has memorable lyric interludes, such as the lovely song of Pandora: "I stood within the heart of God," and passages both choral and dramatic that have vigor and a certain eloquence. But as a whole it suffers fatally from the use of that type of poetic speech in English which had been worn by too many generations of use. Moody struggled after a personal accent. In vain. Diction was destined to be reborn through an entire movement. An individual poet was helpless. Hence the trilogy is not the easiest reading today, not because it is difficult but because the style has neither light nor resonance. Yet it must be abundantly clear that Moody is justly to be regarded as the symbolical transition figure between the polite age and the modern period in American culture. He was, at it were, a mirror in which the youth of his day could discern definitely if dim in outline the shapes of the future.

BOOK EIGHT

Sowers and Pathfinders

I

The nineteenth century was the century of easy solutions and of eternal truths that lasted ten years. There is a deep human pathos in this circumstance. For one kind of intelligible universe men desired at once to substitute another equally intelligible and stable in order to have a rest, however bleak, for their souls. It is now clear, tragically clear, if one likes, that the nineteenth century succeeded solely in asking the pertinent and crucial questions. All its answers were absurdly premature; all its solutions are strewn like withered leaves on an autumnal road. The disillusion, be it remarked, is not with science as an organon; it is with a type of mind that jumped to conclusions suiting its inner climate and then sought to impose its special interpretation, its somber subjective poetry, upon the world as truth and fact. Taine's theory of literary history and Haeckel's monism are two examples. Both men strove to rebuild the universe in the image of their minds. Whatever enduring value their work has is due to its creative power. It is poetry; it represents the reality of their souls. With a solution of eternal problems it has little to do. These creative dreams of a mechanistic universe which the scientific mind will end by knowing as completely as an engineer knows a machine have degenerated into a superstition as empty and as rigid as any previous superstition that ever plagued the human mind. And this superstition of mechanistic dogmatism is still most hotly entertained today in two civilizations: in the Marxist chaos of Russia where they persecute people for knowing that there *are* spiritual values and in the United States where men are penned in "graphs" and where Dr. John B. Watson is authentically reported to have written these scarcely believable words: "A yearly increase in salary is an important factor in the progress of an individual . . . if the individual is a writer, we should want to draw a curve of the prices he gets for his stories year by year. If from our leading magazines he receives the same average price per word for his stories at thirty that he received when he was twenty-four, the chances are he is a hack writer and will never be anything but that." This grotesque drivel is the ultimate *reductio ad absurdum* of nineteenth-century mechanistic superstition. It will be observed that its chief mark, like the mark of every superstition, is its stubborn ignorance of human experience, of history and simple fact. Here the simple fact, demonstrable and inevitable, is of course that the greatest writers of every age have never even, to speak *more Watsonii*, "made" the "leading magazines," the organs of broadly popular or lowest denominator group-expression of their age, and that a steady increase of emolument from such sources means the gradual deterio-

311

ration of a writer, since it means the gradual identification of himself with ever larger numbers and hence with an ever lower level. It means the renunciation of leadership, the abstention from creative activity, the approach to the comic strip and the antics of the clown. Now a non-behavioristic, non-mechanistic psychology approaches profoundly suggestive explanations of this universal and forever recurrent human experience. Of both the experience and the explanation the mechanistic superstition is blithely unaware.

I raise these questions not idly or impertinently. I raise them in order to point out how little we know and are probably destined to know concerning the interaction between the individual and the collectivity, the man and his age, *Geist* and the *Zeitgeist*. Which produced which? What are the factors of change? Of environment the influence is so doubtful and confusing in all but superficial matters as to be negligible. Emily Dickinson and Ambrose Bierce and William James and Stephen Crane were broadly speaking subjected to the same environmental influences as the polite and merely conforming artificers and critics whose reign they were undermining; assuredly the environment of Frank Norris was the same as that of his brother Charles and his sister-in-law Kathleen; Robert Herrick was born in Cambridge and studied at Harvard, Upton Sinclair is a Baltimorean and studied at Columbia. These are some of the writers who definitely and finally broke the genteel tradition and in their various ways ushered in the period of national expression. Did the environment and the age produce them, or did they not rather, as autonomous personalities, unconsciously cooperating, produce a new cultural environment and a new age by creating gradually, in the wise old phrase of Wordsworth, the taste by which they were to be appreciated? And since the mind creates even its shifting pictures of the universe, of the sum of things, in its own image, since demonstrably the knower cannot know except in harmony with the instrument of knowledge that he has, it is not at least absurd to assume that personalities create cultural changes. Why they are born at certain times to do so is a mystery. That it is the will of God is, properly interpreted, not the least rational of answers to this as to other ultimate questions.

Race is more tangible and concrete. Weismann's germ-plasm is only a metaphysical fiction, like all the final explanations of the scientist. Yet spiritual color of no indefinite kind does belong to the broadest of those groups which we call racial and the Latin color of Mr. Santayana's mind is beyond all question; and so is the African tinge in both the eloquence and the pathos of the prose of Mr. W. E. B. Du Bois; it was the blended Irish and continental strains in his blood that predisposed James Huneker to music and to the expression of the maladies of the modern soul; Lafcadio Hearn infused into his writings all the exoticism of his birth. Nor should it be forgotten, as has been done out of foolish political partisanship, that the most conspicuous and influential American poet of several crucial years immediately before the period of national expression set in was the German George Sylvester Viereck and that the American stage if not, alas, the American drama is definitely indebted to David Belasco. I am deliberately mixing men of widely varying age and character in order to point out both the quality and the multiplicity of the forces that helped to shape our cultural life in that interim and preparatory period between 1890, when the first poems of Emily Dickinson appeared or the year 1891 when the first volume of Ambrose Bierce was printed in San Francisco and that crucial year of 1912 that saw the first issue of "Poetry: a Magazine of Verse," the first volumes of William Ellery Leonard, Vachel Lindsay and Amy Lowell and the anthology "The Lyric Year" which contained "Renascence" by Edna St. Vincent Millay. All through those two decades the shining façade of the genteel tradition seemed as brave as ever. Neither Mr. Henry Mills Alden nor Mr. Richard Watson Gilder nor even so enlightened and severe a spirit as William Peterfield Trent suspected that anything was in the wind. Into the club of the graduate students of English at Columbia stalked Hamlin Garland in sombrero and riding-boots; he seemed to them to have no special relation to the native literature; Frank Norris was wearing out the brief remainder of his life as copy-editor of a publishing-house on East Sixteenth Street; that, too, passed unnoticed; one can imagine the scorn with which Mr. Brander Matthews would have received the information that in 1905 the future of our letters was implicated with nothing that took place in his noble drawing-rooms on West End Avenue and with everything that had its faint but definite beginnings in certain editorial offices, not in the best repute, in the Knox Hat Building at Fifth Avenue and Fortieth Street.

These offices were heavily carpeted in red; footfalls were to be deadened; the stealthy atmosphere was dense with cigarette smoke and in and out stole society reporters with shifty eyes, correct clothes and heavy perfumes. In the innermost office sat a bulky old man with magnificent white hair and patriarchal beard, a pasha of the Gilded Age, who thunderously grudged the contributors to his periodicals their penny a word. These periodicals were two: "The Smart Set" and "Town Topics." "The Smart Set"—abominable name! —was edited by a then young man named Charles Hanson Towne, who loved Keats and wrote agreeable and sincere but conventional verse. His taste in fiction was more robust; it was influenced doubtless by that of his friend Theodore Dreiser who was an editor for Street and Smith and then for a year edited the "Broadway Magazine," before he became chief of the Butterick publications on MacDougal Street. Towne had read "Sister Carrie" in manuscript and held it to be the greatest of American novels. For his magazine he sought stories that had the power and edge of reality and moral sincerity and verse more strictly girdled in both form and thought than was to be met in more respectable places. He found both; he encouraged the youngest and most obscure writers to whom all the great doors of official literature were closed. A brilliant and amazing study of origins could be made from the files of "The Smart Set" extending from the beginning of the century to 1908 when Henry L. Mencken and George Jean Nathan joined the staff as literary and dramatic critic respectively and dusk blazed into dawn.

The literary tradition of "Town Topics" was far older than that of "The Smart Set." Its editor was a small, bald, long-nosed man with pale clever eyes named Charles Bohm. In the service of the cruel pasha he worked without moving such long hours and smoked so many cigarettes that he died suddenly of an acute intestinal stoppage. He had no prejudices of any kind. But he knew good writing. He wanted writing not to soothe but to pierce. He hired precisely the right men at his penny a word and was careful of their sensibilities, never letting Percival Pollard or James Huneker or their successors know what his society reporters were doing. In the columns of "Town Topics," then, Pollard showed the first American awareness of the great movements that were transforming continental literature and there, too, Huneker practiced his craft from 1897 to 1902 and poured out a stream of fresh ideas on music and on the drama. And until the end of the World War "Town Topics" continued a school of critics and short-story writers and its columns, too, should one day be sedulously analyzed for the brilliant light that would thus be thrown upon our cultural history during certain years. . . . Is this gossip and not history? Then so much the worse for the latter. What I have here recorded might easily have slipped into the limbo of the officially forgotten, which would have been a great absurdity and a grave injustice. . . . But I must turn back to somewhat earlier years.

II

The critics and philosophers and poets of this interim period were sturdier and luckier than the novelists. The latter were fugitives from themselves and wanderers or recluses or young men who compensated for some profound inner weakness or inadequacy or unhappy temptation by a cult of horror and brutality and blood. They made great beginnings and were then stricken with aridity and disease

316

and died in their thirties or forties. The life of Ambrose Bierce is like one of his own sinister tales; Stephen Crane and Frank Norris were quenched by tuberculosis, one at twenty-nine, the other at thirty-two; Harold Frederic and Jack London and David Graham Phillips died in their early forties and O. Henry, who began to write only in his late thirties was granted a bare decade of work. Those of this generation that survived lost force and fire and took to conventional story-telling, like Hamlin Garland and William Allen White or else they were from the beginning not strictly speaking creative personalities, like the shrewd George Ade or again they blundered once into freshness and sincerity, like the playwright Eugene Walter, and then disappeared from the creative scene. Three exceptions there are: Upton Sinclair, Robert Herrick and Edith Wharton. But by their survival not only as human beings but as creative forces they belong to the period of national expression and not to the preceding twilit years.

The fate of the works of the transition figures has been very various. Bierce's tales have become little more than a curiosity of literature; the books of Crane and Norris are more important in their vicarious manifestation as example and influence than in themselves; the novels of David Graham Phillips still lead or, at least, did lead until the other day a kind of underground life in cheap reprints; Jack London alone achieved, especially posthumously, an enormous world-popularity for reasons to be presently discussed. Who now reads O. Henry or George Ade? The quarter of a century that has passed since they blazed on the horizon was cleft in sunder by the Great War; we seem to have traversed infinite distances in time and experience; nothing is as it used to be. Yet some of the work of all these writers "exists"; one goes back to it and reads it and finds a thousand shortcomings and inadequacies and even puerilities; one finds downright meretriciousness and drivel and ends by agreeing with their contemporaries that there proceeded from it a light of energy, of creative honesty, of freshness of at least intention that was new and has not wholly faded yet.

Ambrose Bierce stands quite apart and alone. He was no naturalist, no dabbler in science or student of economic forces. He saw neither people nor things; his concern was with neither characters nor with the world; he was housed tight with the indefatigable inventiveness of his cruel and somber fancy. One cannot even surmise by what shocking early experience, by what unhealed wound of the soul he was compelled to evoke again and again eerie astonishment and stark horror. The undoubted influence of Poe accounts for little or nothing. No man can write sixty-eight tales concerned with dread and death and all the last indignities of mortality without an inner compulsion. His power cannot be denied. Again and again he strikes the reader with horror and a kind of ugly and gasping awe; the endings of the tales are often on the edge of the unbearable. Nothing written of the horrors of the World War in recent years surpasses in the sheer exposition of either the death of the body or the corruption of the soul the Civil War tales of Bierce. Only these tales are morally and therefore in the last analysis creatively sterile, because Bierce showed himself conscious of no implication and disengaged no idea. The naked horror

318

sufficed him. That is equally true of the civilian tales and of the later collection: "Can Such Things Be?" He had rare moments of introspective insight: "What mortal can cope with a creature of his dream? The imagination creating the enemy is already vanquished; the combat's result is the combat's cause." But these moments are indeed rare. "The Devil's Dictionary" shows a mind neither agile nor incisive; the satiric definitions are commonplace in substance and muddy in expression. Bierce fancied himself a great radical, but he could not think to the root of any matter. Neither was he an artist in prose. His manner just carries his substance; the dreariest *clichés* did not trouble him. His gift lay wholly in producing that appalling assault upon the nerves by a curt and ingenious presentation of the horrible. That a definite taste for this sort of thing persists is attested by the existence of the Grand Guignol theater in Paris. It is the taste of weary and jaded souls. It is genuine enough and though the writers who minister to it are as sterile as the readers who possess it, Ambrose Bierce must in simple justice be ranked high among the masters of cruelty and horror.

It is otherwise with Stephen Crane. Though febrile and arid in both substance and style through some fatal defect in human warmth he left his mark. He was nearer the center of the cultural process than Bierce and discovered for himself a method which, unknown to him, had first been tried some years previously in Germany and called "consistent naturalism." Crane, like Arno Holz, imitated neither the passion nor the pity of Zola but restricted himself to a cold and exact rendition of proletarian life and circumstance. He discovered the slum as literary material and the speech of the old Bowery and the device of "impassiveness," except for an occasional coldly ironic implication. "Maggie: A Girl of the Street" and several tales, of which the best is "An Experiment in Misery," complete Crane's work in this kind, which is far more important than the more famous and accessible "Red Badge of Courage" or such stories of mere physical accident as "The Open Boat." No such novel as "Maggie" had yet been written in America and though the book is far enough from being a masterpiece it introduced a new and for the time tonic mood and strain. It shocked Gilder but Howells was enthusiastic and—significant scene —having invited young Crane to dinner, read him from the recently published poems of Emily Dickinson. Nevertheless a reputable publisher was not found for "Maggie" and the book has led a kind of underground existence. Together with several tales in the same manner "Maggie" was, however, demonstrably read by the right people, as such things always are, and Dreiser uses to this day certain wretched little tricks of speech that Crane invented.

"The Red Badge of Courage" is less important than "Maggie." The latter studies the horrors of the slum, the former of the field of battle. Since Crane had never seen war, the imaginative effort involved is both powerful and, within the limits set, complete. Nor should one underestimate the courage and sincerity that Crane showed in representing the fatigue and fear rather than the false glamour of battle. But the writing, despite brilliant flecks, is hard and cold. An ultimate lifelessness, a paralysis of some function of the soul is troublingly evident in all he wrote. "Let

it be stated that the mistress of this boy's mind was fear,"
his biographer Thomas Beer writes with great perspicacity.
The primal fear of life which psychological analysis reveals
in every soul was intolerably heightened in Crane's and
probably contributed to his lack of physical vitality and so
to his early death. He was drawn to delineate the things
he feared—bleak sordidness and poverty and, above all, fear
itself. After the success of "The Red Badge of Courage"
his position, both critical and economic, was excellent; James
Huneker became his friend and his years in England were
enriched by association with a group of creative spirits that
included Joseph Conrad. Nothing availed. He died before
his thirtieth year was completed. He had said not long before: "I'm just a dry twig on the edge of the bonfire." How
poignant that is and how true! His work lacks the sap of
passion and the vibrancy of music. His one bit of luck was
in his early development, so that his two chief works appeared as early as 1892 and 1894. It remains only to speak
briefly of the verses which so curiously foreshadow the practice of the Imagists fifteen years later. But these, too, acquired an adventitious importance through their priority.
Their conciseness is more often apparent than real; their
pessimism is of the vitality and not of the mind; they rarely
have either lift or sting. Crane lost the manuscript of them
once on an elevated railroad train. And many of them are
indeed revelatory rather than achieved. The best and most
moving of them all may be used as both symbol and epitaph:

> In the desert
> I saw a creature, naked, bestial,
> Who, squatting upon the ground,

Held his heart in his hands,
And ate of it.
I said: "Is it good, friend?"
"It is bitter—bitter," he answered;
"But I like it
Because it is bitter
And because it is my heart."

It was Frank Norris who brought to America both the theory and the practice of French naturalism. He studied art in Paris for two years and soaked himself in Zola and probably in Octave Mirbeau. "McTeague," his first mature book and incomparably his best, is far more akin to the works of the author of "Le jardin des supplices" than it is to those of Zola. "McTeague," apparently and indeed technically a perfectly objective story, is a very personal book. Thence comes its power, a power of intensity and concentration of effect that is rare in American fiction but which never fails to render fiction memorable when it occurs. The dentist McTeague and his wretched little wife and the morbid relations they sustain to one another were as real to Norris as the pangs of a throbbing tooth or an aching heart. Something in these characters and in this fable expressed and therefore released an obscure inner appetence and conflict of his own. Therefore the book has what no other book of the period has, what very few American novels had yet had at all: concentration, density, impassioned exactness, depth of tone, even an approach to severity of contour.

"The Octopus" and "The Pit" are works of a quite different character. Norris in "The Octopus" lets his poet, despising mere "literature," brood over Homer and wonder how the epic of the great and heroic West could be written.

It is this epic that Norris proposed to himself to write, with economic forces as heroes and villains, with men and women as puppets and victims of these forces, with cruelty and terror in detail but with a large general cosmic optimism as ultimate trend. He employs, in a word, the Zolaist formula even in specific details: he uses the premonitory symbol, as when the engine in "The Octopus" kills the sheep; he seeks to establish a Nemesis of forces as in the scene in which S. Behrman struggles in the sliding mountains of wheat; he tries for effects of sweep and largeness, nor is he afraid of sheer melodrama in the details of human fortune. The total result is not happy. Doubtless Zolaism was bound to invade America at its proper time. One is not sorry that it had not many disciples nor that Norris' influence has not been greater. The method, especially when lacking Zola's personal fire and fury and mud, is very tiresome and pitifully shallow. All the imponderables are slighted, all that most matters in human life is neglected. In such a passage as that which closes the third chapter of "The Octopus" we have Zolaism and so nineteenth-century mechanism at its most depressing. Poor Vanamee, who had been robbed of his beloved years ago under circumstances of melodramatic horror, consoles himself at long last and is reconciled to the universe because the Wheat—carefully capitalized—persists. "The wheat called forth from out the darkness, etc., etc. rose triumphant into light and life. So Angèle, so life, etc., etc., etc. O Grave, where is thy victory?" Precisely, despite the bad, shrill rhetoric, where it was before. Only more immediately depressing. Despite their unquestionable ability and sincere zeal these long narratives of Norris no longer belong to living literature. They usefully shocked and aroused and, in a certain sense, instructed their immediate contemporaries. Of the man's work only "McTeague" remains.

Just as the general superstition concerning the sufficiency of economic causes was bound to enter American literature, so was that other nineteenth-century superstition concerning the sufficiency of narrowly biologic causes. The bringing of these notions to our shores had one advantage: we were no longer provincial in isolation; we shared the provincialism of the century; we entered the central current of human art and thought and could profit by it when that current turned in a happier direction. Jack London, who gave our literature its example of Darwinistic determinism, was a far more highly endowed man than Frank Norris. He was a better writer; he had far more creative power; he had a greater flexibility of mind and a more liberal heart. Of the two central motives of his work that of sympathy with the disinherited of the social order is by far richer and more humane than his falsely scientific catering to the aggressive instinct latent in civilized man. He wrote, as is generally recognized, far too much and his best-known books are by no means his best. Thus on the side of his humanitarian interests the sound, concrete, restrained and moving "People of the Abyss" is very much superior to the lurid phantasmagoria of "The Iron Heel"; his cultivation of combative instincts is much more happily and restrainedly expressed in "The Game" than in "The Call of the Wild." It is quite probable that he will be remembered in literature by the sincere, plain pathetic narrative of his struggles with what used to be called the demon Rum in "John Barleycorn." His subliterary vogue which is enormous in lands as remote as Russia and as civilized as Sweden is due, of course, to his cult of brutality, of raw bone and gristle, of the triumph of red-bloodedness, all as based upon a thoroughly discredited interpretation of the survival of the fittest theory. The absurd and absurdly motivated books which he produced in this strain, however, have all or nearly all, a measure of imaginative power and narrative sweep; they have a spurious sureness of touch in characterization calculated to convince the unwary and innocent of mind. Perhaps his ablest full-length novel is "The Sea-Wolf," which can be used briefly to explain both Jack London and his popularity. The average, ignorant reader, shorn by civilization of the full expression of his primitive instincts, both sexual and aggressive, identifies himself with sadistic joy with the pseudo-Nietzschean captain and through this identification satisfies his lust for ferocity and raw force. Nor is that all. The satanic captain's cruelty is directed against a boy belonging to the most sheltered section of capitalistic society. Thus there enters the further motive of satisfied envy, parading sincerely as a desire for leveling justice and there enters, in the case of many readers, a satisfaction (through the relations of the cruel captain and the delicate lad) of unconscious homo-erotic wishes. No wonder that Jack London is popular and continues so. "The Sea-Wolf" also contains, however, an unconscious confession: the formidable captain collapses in the end, paralyzed and impotent. Something had slowly hollowed out that gigantic frame and that will of steel. Brutality, in brief, is the mask of inner weakness and aggressive cruelty a confession of ultimate impotence. Thus too Jack London, a man of many charming and amiable qualities, not without heart, not without a flicker of genius in his soul, unable to find his center of spiritual gravity between tenderness for his fellowmen and the defensive cult of brutality, died in his forty-first year worn out with drink and with overwork for the sake of tawdry and fugitive goods.

The early years of this century saw the emergence of two other writers of fiction not perhaps as gifted as Crane or Norris or London, yet more significant culturally and more precisely on the road to the future than those others. The two were David Graham Phillips and Sydney Porter, generally known as O. Henry. The reason for their importance lies in their choice of subjects, which is no accidental thing but profoundly dictated by character and temperament. Phillips always and O. Henry at his best scrutinized closely the actual scene of life in its common manifestations. By penetrating these, they penetrated to the permanently significant. They wrote neither about terror on the battlefield, nor about the questionable play of large economic forces nor about wolves reflecting like schoolboys who had read a text-book on Darwinism. They wrote about businessmen and their wives and clerks and chorus-girls and doctors and policemen. O. Henry cultivated a vulgar and knowing kind of euphuism and the happy ending that clicks agreeably in the magazine editor's ear. He was steeped in Kipling at Kipling's worst and his exotic tales have little to redeem them. But he did write "The Four Million" and other stories of New York. Phillips was an awkward and muddy writer; he more or less told the same story over again in ever thicker and heavier volumes. Yet was he not in truth the first Amer-

326

ican who made an attempt, at least, to deal honestly with the concrete lives and unvarnished adventures of men and women? He is surely the first who gives us the tang and taste of life in America as we know it and have lived it and since life does not change greatly in its essentials but only in its accidents, his work, rude and commonplace in an hundred ways, does nevertheless retroactively discredit in a subtle manner even the more honest delineations of American life that preceded him. He saw what no previous American novelist had permitted himself to see; he spoke out; he had a rude but sufficient power of characterization; his works contain portraits of people, such as that of Sophie Murdock in "Old Wives for New," which for their time and place dared greatly and successfully, which convince and even move and terrify. He was through with the sentimental pretenses of even Norris. He swept clean. "The genuine tragedies of life are three—poverty, disease and bereavement. All others are simply vanities of bloated self-exaggeration." Of course that is a very partial truth. But it was the truth that so needed to be sounded and to be embodied in American fiction. And Phillips proceeded to embody it by stripping of their self-importance and self-deception and unclean parasitic pretense especially the married woman of the middle classes. He did not spare the men, either, especially the young snobs and wasters, like those in "The Second Generation," who had lost the practical virtues of their fathers and had developed none that were new. But mainly Phillips dealt with the women of his time and his dealings had intimate knowledge and a fierce frankness and sincerity. The novels are too long and too ill-written and too repetitious. And this is most true of the best-known and longest of all, "Susan Lenox." But none is without an exactness and honesty of characterization that were unheard of before. An excellent epitome of his work in more concentrated form exists luckily in the novelette called "Enid" in the volume "Degarmo's Wife." It states both explicitly and implicitly his notions of life; it has not only his usual rude power of characterization but moments of subtle insight; it, at least, as type and example of the work of a profoundly honest and not ungifted man, should survive to commemorate him.

O. Henry knew quite as much as David Graham Phillips. But he intoxicated himself on his own euphuistic trickery. He was immensely ingenious and hence prone to meretriciousness. He has moments when he tells the honest and even devastating truth. But in another moment he is off performing verbal handsprings: "Cæsar has his Brutus, the cotton has its boll-worm, the chorus-girl has her Pittsburger, the summer boarder has his poison-ivy, the hero has his Carnegie medal, art has its Morgan. . . ." The crackling of these thorns goes on and on. The fables crackle too to the explosion of the end. The influence of the O. Henry short-story on American writing has been abominable; cheap smartness, vulgar knowingness, the substitution of ingenuity for creation—all these qualities were made more palatable to the undiscerning by O. Henry. College professors quoted him as a model in their courses. Dr. Watson and Professor Pitkin are probably still treasuring a subconscious memory of him. Though he is but little read today, his terrible progeny is all about us and menaces the development of our literature, for the plain and practical reason that brief creative narrative can find no market in the periodicals corrupted by the O. Henry formula. Any imbecile can feel superior by identifying himself with the smart narrator of the O. Henry yarn; thence spring both the evil and the popularity of the kind. Creative writing demands passiveness and humility of its reader. But people, like the average American, who are terribly unsure of themselves are afraid of humility, which is the virtue of the strong and the serene. Thus the O. Henry story swept all before it. The man got prices unheard of until then; his imitators still command the market-place. . . . There is another aspect. It is this, that in his best book, "The Four Million," he saw and for the first time rendered New York. He rendered its trivial aspects and its flashy side. But he rendered these with a picturesque sort of truthfulness. In spite of his preposterous absurdities, he caught the tang of, let us say, Herald Square in 1907. A perished, amusing moment is somehow captured and held fast. And the image he drew of New York imprinted itself on young minds all over the country and had something to do with the migrations and rebellions which later led to Greenwich Village and the development of forms through the first free experimentation with life that America had ever witnessed. His influence on life was happier than his influence on letters. This is a thing that cannot be proven. But no one who was very young in 1907 will doubt it. O. Henry discovered the hall bedroom. And the hall bedroom and free-lunch barroom contributed to our recent spiritual history which has taken place largely within an urban civilization. Thus there has been properly, inevitably more said here of the egregious O. Henry's stories than of sounder and soberer work: the bitter, sincere early studies of farming-life of Hamlin Garland, William Allen White's excellent "In Our Town," Harold Frederic's still agreeable Methodist novel "The Damnation of Theron Ware." The seeds of our period of national expression were sown under the stones of cities, of New York, of Chicago; many who now justly bear the greatest names wandered in their lonely and rejected youth in the New York of O. Henry and read his stories with both amusement and disgust and saw George Ade's "The College Widow" performed in 1904 and despaired of Winthrop Ames' "New Theater," despite Sheldon's "The Nigger" of 1909 and in the same year took a little brief courage when Belasco produced Eugene Walter's "The Easiest Way." Such were the shabby and inconspicuous beginnings of a movement, both literary and dramatic, that was later to command the attention of the world.

III

The two decades from 1890 to 1910—these transition decades of our cultural history—produced a body of literature more permanent than the work of the novelists who have been discussed and more permanent, as we shall see, than the work of their poets, save only one. A body of non-fictional prose was produced which, taken in its totality, represents one of the most powerful literary efforts in America. This body of prose to which the most imperfect attention has yet been paid by criticism and of which, curiously enough, the feebler portion has been the more discussed, was produced by a group of personalities far more salient and powerful than those of any novelists or poets of the period; for that prose was the work of William James, Henry Adams, George Santayana, Lafcadio Hearn, James Huneker and W. E. Burghardt Du Bois.

Given his literary vividness and charm, I should discuss William James even though he had been a philosopher in a far stricter technical sense than, in fact, he was or pretended to be. For the general validity of philosophical doctrine and vision is less in their "truth," than in the breadth and reality of the human experience from which they spring and for which they seem authentically to speak. "If art," writes Georg Simmel, "is an image of the world seen through a temperament, then philosophy may be called a temperament seen through its image of the world." Now the image of the world which suited the mind of William James was not only described and propagated by him in a style at once warm and lively, correct and pungent, picturesque and eloquent, but it commended itself as a sympathetic and congenial image to so great a number of his countrymen and immediate contemporaries and seemed then as, through his disciples it seems still, to express the precise American sense of life so thoroughly and happily that no poet may be said ever to have spoken more directly for his age and people than did this philosophical essayist for the American business democracy of his time. He met with no opposition; surly criticism of him came from the academic and philosophical camp, not from the general reader or the average student or the pedagogue. His "Principles of Psychology," 1891, at once became the Bible of the teachers' colleges;

"The Will to Believe" thrilled hearts in farthest denominational universities; "Pragmatism" appeared in 1907 and the democracy took philosophy, once a bug-bear, an annoyance and a reproach, to its bosom. The heavenly maid had come to earth; teas were given in her honor; she bore meliorism in her right hand and liberal Christianity in her left; she could embrace everybody and remain virgin. The suspicion that in the best of all possible worlds we were running the best of all possible civilizations straight to a millennium of righteousness and increased profits—that gentle suspicion had now received the stamp of philosophic truth.

The source of every philosophic as of every poetic vision is in life, is in experience—in the life and the experience of him who sees the vision. The adolescence and the youth of William James were one long illness. We hear of a "delicacy of nervous constitution," of "dorsal symptoms," of vain visits to watering-places in search of health; of four years of practical invalidism in Cambridge aggravated if not caused by moral and religious crises, productive of hallucinations and attacks of religious melancholia definitely pathological in character. Next we hear of a "crisis in my life," of a definite conversion. "My first act of free will shall be to believe in free will. For the remainder of the year, I will abstain from the mere speculation and contemplative *Grübelei* in which my nature takes most delight, and voluntarily cultivate the feeling of moral freedom, by reading books favorable to it, as well as by acting." The auto-therapeutic effort succeeded. "Not in maxims, not in *Anschauungen*, but in accumulated *acts* of thought lies salvation." Within six months he was teaching efficiently at

Harvard. His acceptance and utilization in practice of a living option or choice had *worked*, had proved its value, created by that act of choice, in action, in life and the world. Pragmatism was born and vindicated. No more "speculation and contemplative *Grübelei*," no more attempt to satisfy the essential metaphysical hunger by either the inquiry as to the nature of knowledge or the nature of the universe which knowledge reveals. For these inquiries had been integrated with illness, feebleness, despair. The therapeutic act of faith had saved him. He had "willed" it so and the will had "worked." So this working of the will in life became to him "truth." No wonder that the entire substance of his philosophy is packed in the chapter on the will in the "Psychology." "Will you or won't you have it so?" We can create the truths we need as we go along. Nothing succeeds like success.

No, the apologetics of the personal disciples of William James who loved and honored him, as he in all truth deserved to be, cannot defend pragmatism from its practical consequence of devaluating the contemplative life and the spiritual discipline of waiting for truth, nor from its abandonment of all values and of the tranquil and profoundly guided search for values. "Who gains promotions, boons, appointments but the man in whose life they are seen to play the part of live hypotheses, who discounts them, sacrifices other things for their sake before they have come, and takes risks for them in advance." And the embracing of these live hypotheses, if and when they do bring home the bacon of "promotions, boons, appointments"—*that* is truth. No wonder that pork-packers and publicity agents agreed

that divine philosophy was indeed charming. "Faith . . .
in many ways brings forth its own verification." How true!
But until we know *whose* faith in *what*, we have merely
stated a psychological truism and are as far as ever from
gaining either any insight or any values that will help us to
shape character or bring it into relationship with an intelligible world of values. Nothing makes any difference "but
a possible difference in practice"; "meaning, other than
practical, there is for us none." Again it all depends on who
makes the experiment, finds the practical result and hails
that as the meaning of truth. James cites "the young Italian
pragmatist Papini." He did not live to see what sort of
"truth" Papini later found workable. "All the sanctions of
a law of truth lie in the very texture of experience."
Whose experience? His who "gets away" with brutality,
tyranny, injustice? His special faith saved William
James, because he was a man of enlightened intellect
and exquisite spiritual sensibility. But the faith of the
burners of heretics often "worked" for them and brought
them power and satisfaction and vindicated for them their
view of things. Profoundly William James in his own person appreciated this dreadful paradox of the moral life.
"Like dead men, dead causes tell no tales, and the ideals
that went under in the past, along with all the tribes that
represented them, find today no recorder, no explainer, no
defender." But that is not pragmatism, which is rather *Væ
victis*, since the "truth" of the conqueror has "worked," has
prevailed. This is that "truth that is great and shall prevail," above all in defeat, in sorrow, in crucifixion, and not
the "truth" that has made the "difference in practice." Sim-

334

ilarly William James in his letters excoriates "the callousness to abstract justice, *the* sinister feature . . . of our U. S. civilization," and "the moral flabbiness born of the exclusive worship of the bitch-goddess SUCCESS." But where, according to the pragmatic philosophy, is the place or possibility of "abstract justice," of some fixed value either realized or striven for and what shall men seek but success if truth is merely "a class name for all sorts of definite working values in experience."

Personally James meant by pragmatism something finer and more balanced and spoke of the harmony that must and should exist among the different kinds of working truths within the miniature cosmos of the soul. But he himself, alas, notoriously went ghost-mongering in his later years, a human and amiable weakness, but on the pragmatic principle no weakness at all but the grasping of a to him living choice in the hope that it would work and so become true. Pragmatism, in brief, abandons both the search for spiritual or intellectual values as well as the critical spirit. It damns disinterestedness and the love of any thing or thought for that thing's or thought's own sake. And by these marks and qualities it delineated and expressed immediately modern American industrial civilization as no philosophy has ever expressed the mood of its historic day or the facts of its contemporary practice. Therein lies its significance, therein the memorableness and uniqueness of the triumph of William James. For he handed the torch on to Dr. Dewey, heir of his immediate success, prophet of an increasingly desolate and arid period of the spirit. Without William James' charm and depth of personality and per-

335

suasive graces of style Dr. Dewey has become, in an even higher measure, the philosophical spokesman of the age. Apparently unrooted by temperament or kinship in any humanistic tradition, incapable of conceiving of disinterestedness as either a virtue or a source of happiness, Dewey has drawn baldly and boldly its last consequences from the pragmatic attitude. "Success and failure are the primary 'categories' of life; achieving of good and averting of ill are its supreme interests; hope and anxiety, which are not self-enclosed states of feeling, but active attitudes of welcome and wariness, are dominant qualities of experience." Now it is quite true that the achieving of good and averting of ill are supreme interests and that "for a living being to control its welfare and success" is an inevitable aim of man. But this philosophy interprets good and ill almost if not quite in the terms of what seemed good and ill to George Babbitt of Zenith or at least to Babbitt's more eminent and less chuckle-headed fellow-citizens. These gentlemen all desired "organic response to cast in its lot with present auspicious changes to strengthen them and thus to avert the consequences flowing from occurrences of ill-omen." They would all have been strong for abandoning "the epistemological universe of discourse" in their busy, handsome, empirical world and one can hear them chant in unison at boosters' banquets the blessed words of the national philosophy: "Faith in the power of intelligence to imagine a future which is the projection of the desirable in the present, and to invent the instrumentalities of its realization, is our salvation." Philosophy was at last on the job and getting ready for team-work toward . . . toward what? Ah,

336

the triumph of this philosophy consists in its failure to define the "good" and "ill" and "desirable in the present" of which it speaks and letting it be understood that its good and ill and desirable were identical with the good and ill and desirable of a prosperous and hustling citizenry increasing output, boosting dividends, whirring toward a millennium (now rudely interrupted) of a car, a wireless set and open plumbing in every American home.

The disciples of Dr. Dewey have made it clear that philosophy has nothing to do with ultimate questions or the soul's comfort in loneliness or the confrontation of last issues. It has to do with the job. Quality, value, disinterestedness, the eternal and eternally true paradox of the moral order that a man *must* lose his life in order to gain it—with such things this dominant philosophy will have no traffic. No wonder that we have had an age of gin and moral confusion. The amiable Horace M. Kallen having allied himself by some strange inner contortion with this philosophy nevertheless lets the cat out of the bag, to speak *more Americano* and gives the show away: "It is a program to execute rather than a metaphysic to rest in." But man is a metaphysical animal even more profoundly than he is a political one. The dominant national philosophy tried to give the lie to the reality of spiritual values. And this had two results: the stronger novelists and poets of our contemporary period are more philosophical than the philosophers for the reason, so admirably put by Simmel, that he who reaches the depth of his own soul is at the core of the world. But the less robust and resisting spirits in our letters, finding themselves in a world hopelessly discrete, without inner re-

337

lations, without value, form or good, have wandered from one eccentricity of helplessness to another, from confusion to worse confusion in a chaotic multiverse and have finally abandoned meaning and hence communication as a conscious or unconscious act of metaphysical despair. For meaning and communication are impossible without certain agreements and the dominant philosophy and dominant vital forces of America had conspired to break down the eternal spiritual and moral agreements of mankind.

I have dwelt at some length on William James, the pragmatic philosophy and its results which, going even beyond Dr. Dewey and his disciples meet us again in the intellectual and moral quality of Dr. Watson and Professor Pitkin, because the period of national expression in America which we are approaching cannot be understood without that unique background in which big business, the roaring denial of metaphysical and moral values and finally the alliance of these with popular neo-Puritanism as expressed in the Eighteenth Amendment, formed a trinity of which the like had not been seen in all the long annals of mankind. I do not say that worse things had not been seen; that worse things do not exist—worse, darker, more cruel. But the cultural situation within which our period of national expression has taken place is *sui generis*, is, in the strictest sense, unique.

No strong forces arose to counteract pragmatism or its results. A tiny minority heard faintly another voice that came from the philosophical faculty at Harvard—a suave, muffled, exquisite but always alien voice, the voice of George Santayana. Nor has his audience increased greatly with his increasing fame. For he stood from the beginning wholly outside of America and not only outside of America but outside of the larger cultural world and climate within which America has its being. Had he disdained only the winds of ugly and foolish doctrine within America, he might gradually have become a leader of our letters and our thought. For no man more highly and exquisitely gifted for literature had ever made his appearance on the American scene or written with his feet on the American soil. But Mr. Santayana disdains the whole of Germanic civilization. The foolish folk in a state of war-psychosis who were pleased with his "Egotism in German Philosophy" did not know that that dagger had never left his hand and had always been aimed at their own hearts. For that prying into the nature of knowledge, that "malicious psychology" disintegrating "the idea of substance" arose, as Mr. Santayana took no pains to conceal, in England; Locke and Berkeley plowed the field which Kant planted. But this is only one, though a very central phase of the northern mind—"morose and barbarous at its inmost core"—that he disdains. For Protestantism and German idealism and romanticism and individualism whether in Goethe or Emerson, in Shelley or Whitman, in Ibsen or Nietzsche are all threads of the same web, figures of the same cultural and spiritual pattern; all belong to that world of *Streben*, of spiritual striving, of the re-valuation of values, of free and continuous creative activity, of the denial of frozen forms and fixed, changeless, authoritative wisdom which is to Mr. Santayana the world of heathenism, turbulent, chaotic and damned because it has refused to pour itself into that mold of Rome and of

Latin Christianity which he adores with a passion so poetic and in which alone he can conceive of man as living with decorum, discipline and beauty. He rejects not only the lower and self-defeating meliorism of his American contemporaries; he rejects all aspiration toward an other, nobler better society or way of life. He accepts the empiric world as grasped by "animal sense," by common sense, more unhesitatingly than William James himself. Within this chaos man has built a complete spiritual universe adapted to his needs and possibilities within which to live. To accept that universe in which ideals can have true power and beauty exist and morals are agreed upon—that is the life of reason. But since Mr. Santayana's picture of that finished, of that forever achieved spiritual universe is merely the picture of Latin civilization as that civilization is felt, even in the Latin countries, by only a minority of beautifully tempered souls, it is clear why his influence on American civilization was destined from the beginning to be negligible. As a philosopher he does not count for us. One might as well preach nudism among Eskimos or export fur coats to the Congo. Relations exist or they simply do not.

His aloofness and spiritual alienation from the sources and nature of our culture has been a pity and a grievous loss. For he is a great writer and within his self-appointed limitations a great sage. That, like the Nietzsche whom he ignorantly and petulantly disdains, he is more poet than technical philosopher is all in his favor. For dialectic is only the rationalization of vision and of all systems of thought it is the proof that perishes and the vision that remains. And Mr. Santayana has expressed his vision creatively in and through one of the few first-rate prose styles of our age, which is poor in highly organized and noble prose since such prose is the expression of highly organized and noble substance. The quality of a man's vision is embodied in his very syntax; it is not by accident that George Moore's sentences are faint as moonlight in outline or that Bernard Shaw's have hard, sharp clanging contours. Of American prose-writers of his own generation or the next there is none who is comparable to Mr. Santayana. To match him one has to go to the greatest of living stylists: to Thomas Mann, who far surpasses him, of course, in creative richness and variety, to Paul Valéry to whom he is equal in precision and superior in mass and sensuous loveliness and depth of tone. Mr. Santayana's style has, naturally, the defects of its hieratic and remote magnificence. It misses the emphasis of fullest life and the sharper accent of reality. It goes a little too steadily in purple and fine linen; when it says a plain thing plainly and heartily, it too obviously condescends. It is muffled and velvety and after reading many pages one longs for a sharper and a manlier tone. Yet its qualities are greater than its defects and if Mr. Santayana has remained an alien in America, he has offered America a precious and supremely useful illustration of the fact that even this forlorn age may produce a great style, if only a personality be found sufficiently deep, disciplined and self-contained. That illustration and that example remain. Nor should it be forgotten that if the totality of Mr. Santayana's vision will grow more alien and merely curious as time goes on, his high sagacity has strewn his not few volumes with sentences that ally him to the great French writers of maxims. The man who wrote: "Ethical absolutism, being a mental grimace of passion, refutes what it says by what it is," or "To call war the soil of courage and virtue is like calling debauchery the soil of love," and literally a thousand other maxims as perfect in form and as final in wisdom—such a man transcends ultimately all limitations and is bound to remain a classic, however isolated and rarely visited, of the language and the literature to which he has chosen to contribute.

IV

I turn from the philosophers to one far more philosophical-minded than they, to one who intuitively grasped the fundamental problems of his age and stated its real dilemmas. Henry Adams was sixty-six when he completed "Mont Saint-Michel-and-Chartres"; he was sixty-nine when he caused the manuscript of the "Education" to be privately printed. Yet when the autobiography was given to the public in 1918 it was at once profoundly felt to be, despite its archaic background, a book if not for all time, then certainly for this immediate age. For Henry Adams, with everything or nearly everything against him, had penetrated to the central dilemma—that word must be used again—by which the Americans and not only the Americans of his period and our own are faced. It took him very, very many years to disengage and meet that dilemma, many years of second-rate living and second-rate people and second-rate society. He never uses that word but he describes the thing. Ancestral pressure, excessively high in his case, the custom of conformity, that New England "poise which almost amounted to defeat" all held him back. The man was both poet and philosopher and dared till his old age to be neither. That was his tragedy. By a sort of ancestral convention he went on assuming that politicians were important and drifted back again and again to Washington despite the spirited and, significantly enough, anonymous protest of his novel "Democracy." He took seriously a good deal of pompous and foolish English society and it is at once pathetic and grotesque to see a mind of the quality of his permitting itself to be shocked by the self-deceptions and half-conscious shiftinesses of a Gladstone. In his youth, half out of snobbishness, half out of the first revulsion of the patient against the needed cure he missed the experience that German philosophy and poetry might have been to him. He came near grasping Beethoven one day and scurried back to where no one would cleave asunder the seemly Adams soul. The presence of genius in the form of Swinburne did once shake his depth, but he sadly went back to that America of the spirit where, as he ruefully admits, "passion and poetry were eccentricities." An Adams had no business to be eccentric or to handle "all sides of every question"; from Darwin he passes to politicians and journalists and even of the Civil War he gives, except in his acute delineation of a Southern mentality, an account on only the lowest political plane. No wonder that his education was retarded.

The sudden and cruel death of his sister first brought the confrontation of real issues. In no civilization but that older American one would a man of so high a type have wasted so much of himself on shabby inutilities. The years of teaching at Harvard completed weariness and disillusion. The most brilliant of American groups was rigid, inhibited, morose. "Society was a faculty-meeting without business." Then comes the twenty years' break in this extraordinary record. He is at last out in the open. He will face the music of totality. "As he saw the world, it was no longer simple and could not express itself simply. It should express what it was; and this was something that neither Adams nor La Farge understood." From now on he sought more definitely and consciously "what the world was," some coherence within it or law of coherence applied to it by the mind which would make man's relation to it intelligible and human life harmonious and tolerable. He found no such law. But his seeking it upon terms so clear-sighted was a great example, and memorable, too, is the delineation of the break-down within Henry Adams of that older world of coherence and apparent intelligibility into which he was born. And so he comes to the justly famous chapter on "The Dynamo and the Virgin" in which, though the date of it is 1900, he states the case of man and metaphysics in the twentieth century and the case of American man and art and is not at least unaware of the fact that these two cases are, in the very last analysis the same case: that, namely, of creative expression in any and all of its forms having nothing left to express but the narrowly individual, unrooted in any collective faith, binding, form, culture. To begin with, the old universe, even that of the Positivists, was gone. "Physics stark mad in metaphysics!" In Langley and Roentgen he perceived the universe that Einstein was to reveal. So nothing was left but *force*. There was the force of religion, symbolized by the Virgin of Lourdes—a force that came from great ultimate deeps of instinct, and there was the force disengaged by the new science and put to work. And what was man to live by? A good deal of modern spiritual life has wavered between the horns of the dilemma first clearly described by Adams. Men have worshiped the machine and becoming heart-sick and disillusioned have gone back to the Virgin. They have swung from the worship of one force to the worship of another and have found no rest for their souls. But as an American Henry Adams was troubled by still another matter. Behind the Virgin stood primordially and, however swathed, eternally the generative Venus of the ancient world, the eternal Woman. "When she was a true force, she was ignorant of fig-leaves, but the monthly-magazine-made American female had not a feature that would have been recognized by Adam. . . . Sex was sin. In any previous age sex was strength." Here was Henry Adams' great act of intuition: that America had largely cut itself off from access to the eternal forces that might be opposed to the force of materialism and the machine by relegating to the realm of sin the creative Venus, begetter of gods and men, of art and poetry and religion. "Adams began to ponder, asking himself whether he knew of any American artist who had ever insisted on the power of sex, as every classic had always done. . . . American art, like the American language and American education, was as far as possible sexless. Saint-Gaudens' art was starved from birth, and Adams' instinct was blighted from babyhood. Each had but half a nature. . . . All the steam in the world could not, like the Virgin, build Chartres."

I have said that Adams' act was an act of intuition. He

was not able to disentangle the various skeins of thought in which, by that high act of intuition, he became enmeshed; one wonders what readers have really made of these extraordinarily rich and subtle, but fundamentally not wholly coherent pages. Later knowledge has brought clearer insight and later experience has completed that of Henry Adams'. By the light of that knowledge and that experience his intuitive grasping of the crucial problems of American culture is seen to be but the more remarkable. For the strange aridity felt by Adams was felt by many of his younger contemporaries and by nearly all the American artists and thinkers who have come after him. But misled partly by the machine and partly, as Adams also foresaw, by the American woman's tragic error of "trying to find her way by imitating" man, a whole new literature though, as hostile critics have said to satiety, sex-obsessed, has brought us scarcely nearer to sex as a creative and unifying force. For sex as a creative force from which spring myth and ritual and religion and social bindings may be priapic, but it must not be cheapened; it may be orgiastic, but it cannot be bawdiness induced by gin. It is to be found neither in the rationalistic cheapening of Bertrand Russell nor in the cold debauchery of Ernest Hemingway's earlier tales. What Henry Adams prophetically saw was that, the world being at least for this moment in eternity without coherence to us, without such unity as the thirteenth century had, a satisfactory *modus vivendi* might be found *within* human experience as permanently given; it might be found by descending once more to the core and center of vital forces, by beginning over again. As things now were "the poet groped blindly for an emotion," and "woman had nothing to rebel against except her own maternity," and Henry Adams quotes the great exordium of Lucretius concerning that Venus who alone governs this frame of mortal things and is the giver of all happy and lovely gifts. He proceeds to outline his dynamic theory of history and his law of acceleration toward the prophecy that "a new social mind" would be needed to grasp the growing multiplicity of the world. But his profound and prophetic word has been spoken, the word by which he, arch-Puritan and New Englander *par excellence*, had shattered the mold of the world built up by his forbears and had declared the bankruptcy of the civilization that they had made. It could produce machines and politicians; it had failed to nurture love or poetry or religion or unity. Henry Adams is the symbol of the American tradition hurling itself into the flame of the altar to be consumed so that another tradition and another life might come to be born. Thus the "Education" is not only a great but a crucial book, a classic of both American literature and American life.

v

Lafcadio Hearn was born twelve years later than Henry Adams and superficially there can be no more violent contrast than between the Massachusetts aristocrat and the poor dwarf-like child of an Irish wanderer and a Greek girl, early abandoned in the world, starving half-blinded in American provincial cities, fleeing from one exoticism of either dream or fact to another and wholly submerging himself at last in the far and ultimate culture of Japan. Yet closely looked upon, the two men rebelled against a similar chaos, a meaningless multiplicity in Western civilization and Hearn was happier than Adams in this, that his quest for unity was or seemed to be ended and to have found its goal. In that quest and in the finding of that goal the whole literary activity of Hearn is both defined and exhausted. A profound intuition seemed to point his way. For his first quite characteristic work, "Some Chinese Ghosts," was written in New Orleans four years before he first saw the Far East and is based largely upon French sources. But even in this book he treats not only the world of Oriental legend but the ethical universe revealed in that world with a consenting tenderness that marks it as his appointed refuge from what seemed to him the sordid chaos of the West.

In 1890 he arrived in Japan and, as is well known, became after a time a Japanese subject and, having married a Japanese lady, embraced Buddhism. He curiously foreshadowed thus a post-war tendency, more noticeable in Europe than in America, to find some compensation for the disillusion with the Germanic and Latin cultures in those of the East. It is not fantastic to suppose that very personal elements played their part: his diminutive stature, nearer the Mongolian than the Caucasian, his peculiar countenance, the compensatory dignity that all Orientals accord to the scholar and the scribe. In Japan he was from the beginning no more a dwarf nor an outcast. He was distinguished, not peculiar. From the productive point of view it is important to remember that he came to Japan with a style already formed—formed upon the rather enameled medium of Gautier and the dense workmanship of Flaubert and yet quite unlike either, but rather characterized by a Celtic fluidity and murmurous absence of emphasis in its rhythms. This style, moreover, was as limpid as spring water; both its diction and its syntax were of the utmost simplicity; thus it was marvelously fitted to render the faint perfume and long subtle atmospheric vibrations of Japanese poetry, as well as certain effects of naked horror, like that in the anecdote called "Ingwa-banshi" in the volume "In Ghostly Japan," or other effects of brooding impersonal tenderness, as in the sketch in the volume "Kottō," called "Pathological" or, finally, the effect of a simple but perfect moral loveliness as in the exquisite epilogue to "A Woman's Diary" in the same volume. Such motifs he handled again and again. The most important was the last. For what, above all, he found or seemed to himself to have found in Japan was a beautifully natural and simple practice of certain ancient virtues that are worth more to a contented and dignified human life than all the machinery and culture and conflicts of the West. He never made this point in so many words; he was the least controversial of writers. But this point is in fact his whole point and it is this philosophical implication that tends to uphold the rather frail and fragmentary body of his work. What he was interested in was, as he makes clear in his introduction to "Japanese Buddhist Proverbs," "that general quality of moral experience which . . . must always possess a special psychological interest for thinkers." What he found admirable, what he wanted to convey to the West, to America, in all his best work was the quality of the moral experience of the Japanese people. It was from this point of view that he rendered poem and proverb, retold legends, described landscape and festival. His attempts to

349

blend the Spencerian philosophy with Buddhist mysticism are less sound and less important. He was another in that long list of romantic fugitives, beginning perhaps with Chateaubriand, who fled from the wounds inflicted upon them by their own civilization into a Utopia fancied or real and then described and recounted that Utopia as criticism, corrective, ideal for their countrymen. The close relation of Japanese life to Hearn's delineation of it may be gravely doubted. But the Japan that he conveyed was an exquisite and touching vision and that vision has, both artistically and philosophically, an enduring charm and value.

I come to a far more conspicuous and effective figure. Hearn's vision of Japan might have faintly influenced a quiet romantic soul here and there; his versions of Japanese poetry undoubtedly had their slight share in that reconstruction of poetic form which set in soon after 1912. But the entire modern period of American culture is scarcely thinkable without the long energetic and fruitful activity of James Huneker. He, too, was a fugitive. From the Philadelphia of his youth he fled to Germany and to Joseffy and to Chopin, master of the piano and of that ecstasy that he sought. But from his flight he returned, like the young Longfellow, bearing wealth and virtue to his countrymen. He fled again and again and always returned magnificently laden, drenched and soaked with impressions which he poured out over the arid cultural soil of his country in endless streams. A more powerful, critical and resisting mind might, at that particular period and for that particular function, have been far less fructifying. But no one in America was ready to exercise a critical reaction toward Stendhal or Nietzsche, toward Rodin or Degas, toward Brahms or Richard Strauss, toward Strindberg or Hauptmann. It was necessary first to know, to have a report, to gather impressions; some one had first, for a few people at least, to create an atmosphere within which these forces could make themselves felt. Now this is precisely what Huneker did. He did it not only, not perhaps primarily through his volumes of finished essays, of which the sales were always very limited; he did it through being an ill-paid "slave"—the word is his own—year in and year out to weekly and monthly periodicals and to newspapers. He slaved for "Town Topics" and for "Puck" and for "Scribner's" and at various times for the "Herald," the "Sun," the "Times" and the "Evening Mail." His means were always of the narrowest. Toward the height of his career he begs in terms that distress one both for him and for his employers for an advance of five hundred dollars. He died a poor man and before his time. "A critic—especially an American," he wrote to George Sylvester Viereck in 1909, "is of no particular importance in the scheme of things." Thus his own service and function were clouded to him, for if by 1909 there had come to exist an American minority that was aware of the direction of human culture, that group was largely the creation of James Huneker.

He started out as a musician and a musician he remained. That must never be forgotten. It shows in his method and in his style. He had little equipment but his sensibility; he sought in art little but ecstasy. He was the pure impressionist. But that is what America needed. For nearly all critics but himself cut themselves off from the majority of artistic impacts by anterior principles worthy of the W. C. T. U. But his sensibility was first rate in quality, for it embraced all the arts and it was united to a taste that was almost unerring. He had necessarily his weak and even his petulant moments. He could occasionally sink to the level of his environment and call tragedy depressing; he could miss the quality of so consummate a master in his special field as Hugo Wolf. But these moments of weakness were in very truth rare. Generally his taste had a quality of shrewdness; it could not be deceived, for instance, by the general meretriciousness of Oscar Wilde; from the level mediocrity of modern German painting he easily disengaged the greatness of Max Liebermann. He overestimated the French decadents and his stories are rather sorry imitations of the minors among them; but this is to be set down to the glamour of early student days in Paris. His very earliest enthusiasms were luckily for masters: for Wagner and for Nietzsche, who haunted him through all his thousand pages and who, intensest and most piercing of creative persons, set that standard of sheer ecstasy which he was to continue to seek all his life. Not that Huneker had not, when he chose, an intellectual relation to his idols. "Nietzsche, it should be remembered, was a great psychologist, perhaps greater as such than as a formulator of a philosophic system." But Huneker did not choose very often to use his mind. Driven constantly to write for bread, it was easier to be gossipy, allusive, splenetic, to make anecdote and enthusiasm do for substance.

His method was rhapsodical, as every music critic's must

largely be. For what can one render of music except an impression made by one medium in terms of the utterly alien medium of speech? The music critic's tendency will then be to drain speech of its conceptual element and to wrench it into describing the verbally indescribable. "After Chopin, Brahms? He gives us a cooling deep draught in exchange for the sugared wormwood, the sweet exasperated poison of the Polish charmer." A good deal of that "exasperated poison" tastes not a little like *eau sucré* today. But at the moment when Huneker wrote the phrases were marvelously felicitous. Perhaps Brahms and Huneker's dealing with Brahms have helped to rob that poison of its sting. The rhapsody of his method was tempered, not too happily, by an inveterate allusiveness. Everything reminded him of everything else. Cézanne's lack of sex appeal reminds him of George Moore's dwelling on it and that reminds him of an anecdote concerning the Empress Eugénie and presently we reach "the rancid note of an oboe in a score by Stravinsky." He quotes Hazlitt on Scott in connection with Henry James, which reminds him of remarks of both Huysmans and Landor and that of an observation of James on D'Annunzio and *that* of a phrase of Renan. Names and quotations are thus scattered up and down his pages like greenish capers in a gray sauce. Gossip and anecdotes abound. All the arts and all of artistic life are ransacked and rifled in order to render the multiform impressions of the peripatetic critic.

Such a method is evidently not made for permanence. It has no structure to uphold it. It is all flesh and no bones. Thus one is tempted to write of Huneker in his own figurative and staccato manner. Near the end of his life, wretchedly

353

hard up as always, he writes to W. C. Brownell: "Oddly enough 'The Iconoclasts' remains the best seller in my little collection of clotted nonsenses." The description is absurdly severe. But like every genuine artist Huneker strikes at his weakness more directly than any hostile critic. His style is, in fact, "clotted." Little is clearly or cleanlily worked out or defined. Sentences and paragraphs cohere not through inner logic but by virtue of a viscous quality. There is continuity but little growth, progression or direction. Impression is glued to impression, allusion to allusion, anecdote to anecdote. And yet, when all these deductions and negative definitions have been made, there remains of Huneker a body of work primarily of impressionistic criticism but including, at least, the amusing musical novel "Painted Veils" from among his attempts at fiction, that has especially in its totality an impressiveness which it is not likely soon to lose. For the man was immensely genuine and sincere and his range of appreciation was extraordinary. I have not the knowledge to follow him in the field of painting. But his dealings with music and literature were always profoundly vital, that is, they had the quality of life and living experience and that quality in a critic is always infectious and enriching. There were first the books on Liszt and Chopin which were perhaps restricted in their appeal. But he brought to America authentic news of Baudelaire and Stirner, of Shaw and Hauptmann and Wedekind, of Brahms and Richard Strauss and Arnold Schönberg and whenever he spoke of Flaubert or Wagner or Nietzsche, his style and method took on edge and fire. Through his tireless writing and also in the latter years of his life through personal influence on the younger critics he helped more than anyone else to change the cultural climate of America. The element of humorous grossness in him, symbolized largely by an ingratiating love of Pilsner, stamps him but the more as the necessary man of his land and age. An austerer and more scrupulous spirit would not so successfully have carried the war of modernity into all the rotting citadels of genteel criticism and Anti-Saloon League taste in letters. Since even Mr. Beard forgot him, I am glad to record how well Jim Huneker deserved for the Republic. . . .

Still other forces molded anew the country's temper in the transition years before 1912 and prepared the way for the period of national expression. Prophetic of later conflicts that were to render both somberer and richer the texture of American life and American expression, the Negro race lifted for the first time its voice. It was another voice from the mild croon of Paul Laurence Dunbar and the modest narrator's tone of Charles W. Chesnutt. The late Booker T. Washington was a moderate and, from the point of view of hostile whites, a conservative man. But the very part he played in the national life and his articulateness, all the more impressive for its homespun quality, were more significant than he knew. His generation, like that of propitiatory assimilationists among the Jewish people, was soon superseded by others who used a fierier tone and had a message of woe and of rebellion. The year 1903 which saw the publication of "The Souls of Black Folk" by Dr. W. E. Burghardt Du Bois may be marked as the year of the birth of modern Negro expression. I doubt whether Dr. Du Bois ever wrote again as memorably as he did in that crucial volume. His strength lies in impassioned narrative. He is strong and elo-

355

quent when he remains the prophetic historian of his people. There is a good deal that is declamatory and exorbitant in his later work. In "Darkwater" he calls wildly upon God and stops at no radicalism, however destructive. The result is a strain of hysteria. But literary criticism is an impertinence in the face of the sufferings and the injustice, the abysmal woes and apparently hopeless conflicts that he delineates and that the eyes of all decent and just men can see not otherwise than he sees them. He is, of course, quite like those extreme Jewish radicals of Eastern and Central Europe who might in a world of democratic and Christian practice not have been radicals at all, but who have nothing left them but the desire to bring crashing down the pillars of a social structure so rotten with hypocrisy and cruelty, so sodden with the blood of the weak and the guiltless. Thus Dr. Du Bois is more than a mere writer. As such an hundred faults can properly be found in him. He is the preparer and proclaimer of that Negro renaissance which has contributed richly, especially in poetry, to the latest phase of American literature. He is more. He is the prophet and representative of cultural conflicts which are destined to contribute more and more to the problem and character of creative expression in America.

VI

The poets of the period were mild, hushed souls, compared to the philosophers, the critics, the social prophets. The chief of them, moreover, came into the period as a voice from the dead. Yet it was this voice, the voice of Emily Dickinson, that was more and more clearly heard by those who were to be the poets and the lovers of poets in the years to come. Howells, as we have seen, read from the verses of Emily Dickinson to the young Stephen Crane. Of such occasions, the records of them inevitably lost, there must have been very many. For the ear was so weary of the pseudo-Tennysonian boom and of the loud mouthing of platitudes and even Moody's style sought to be more of a "grand style" than he had any means of making it. Most poetry had sunk to mere rhetoric and whatever the faults of Emily Dickinson, they were not faults of rhetoric. She never tried to write better than she could; on the contrary she often wrote worse than she might have done. But her very shortcomings, being so different from the shortcomings of the official poets, were felt to be endearing and almost virtues. Out of that initial feeling there has grown a cult and a tradition, against which there will be a sharp reaction unless a word of reason is heeded.

It has not been sufficiently noted that Emily Dickinson was an extremely fertile lyrist. The "Complete Poems" of 1924 contains five hundred and ninety-three pieces; the "Further Poems" of 1929 contains two hundred more. Now to be sure Goethe wrote over two thousand poems and I can think of none that is not perfectly executed and memorable. But that case is unique. Below that supreme level the poet of eight hundred poems is entitled to a high proportion of imperfect work and it is time, for the sake of her just and enduring fame, to grant Emily Dickinson her due quantity of lyrical attempts that did not soar but dropped. It is time, above all, for anthologists to disengage her clear and lovely successes and not perversely to display her as, perhaps, a powerful psychologist—she was often that—but as a writer of slovenly and grating verse. This criticism is addressed rather to the contemporary celebrators of Emily than to the poet herself. Her strength and her weakness were indissolubly one. Neither could have existed without the other. For the true glory of Emily is this, that none of her work is *"littéra-ture"* in the contemptuous sense of Verlaine. She had not only "wrung the neck of eloquence"; she seemed unconscious of it, unconscious in fact of any public hearer who might require completion of thought or finish of workmanship. In this entire unconcern with any possible auditor is both Emily's mystery and her triumph. Its consequence is that a note for a poem served her as well as a poem and that when either the rhyme that marked artistic completion did not come to her or the lyrical logic refused to unfold itself harmoniously, she was quite or almost as happy as in the contrary case. In a word, the very numerous notes and fragments among her poems, many having their special poetical or psychological interest, are to be regarded as notes and fragments. Doubtless during the eighteen hundred and nineties the very discords in her work were refreshing and the very fragmentariness of many verses exercised a slightly provocative charm. Those days are over. It is time to see clear. Here is a typical stanza:

> To lose one's faith surpasses
> The loss of an estate,
> Because estates can be
> Replenished—faith cannot.

Here the lyrical impulse, characteristic in both imaginative color and expression, failed completely after lines one and two. Perhaps a tradesman rang the bell or a headache came on or a chain of inner association took an untoward direction. At all events, Emily added a note as to how the poem should proceed: "Because estates can be replenished—faith cannot." But the poem had, in sober fact, not proceeded. It had stopped dead; it is a mere cultivation of singularity to pretend otherwise. The one example, typical of an hundred, will suffice. The poet is quite rich enough to bear inevitable deduction; her very great lyrical qualities of spiritual integrity, of cosmic quaintness and of moon-struck charm would but shine forth more triumphantly if ill-advised admirers did not too often leave obscure her successes and display her failures.

Her successes are many and varied and extraordinarily high. She can be of a compactness of expression and fullness of meaning not less than Goethean in Goethe's epigrammatic mood:

> On the bleakness of my lot
>   Bloom I strove to raise.
> Late my acre of a rock
>   Yielded grape and maize.
>
> Soil of flint if steadfast tilled
>   Will reward the hand;
> Seed of palm by Lybian sun
>   Fructified in sand.

She can add a new and heroic note to the eternal litany of love:

> Of all the souls that stand create
>   I have elected one.
> When sense from spirit files away,
>   And subterfuge is done;

When that which is and that which was
　　Apart, intrinsic stand,
And this brief tragedy of flesh
　　Is shifted like a sand;

When figures show their royal front
　　And mists are carved away,
Behold the atom I preferred
　　To all the lists of clay.

She can soar like the intense mystical poets of the seventeenth century:

Thou stirrest earthquake in the South
　　And maelstrom in the sea;
Say, Jesus Christ of Nazareth,
　　Hast thou no arm for me?

And she can blend sobriety with vision and exactness with lyric lilt:

They say that "time assuages,"
　　Time never did assuage;
An actual suffering strengthens
　　As sinews do, with age.

And she can mock as Heine mocked and display the seamy side of the universe as seen by the optimist:

Papa above!
　　　　Regard a mouse
O'erpowered by the Cat;
Reserve within thy Kingdom
A mansion for the Rat!

Snug in seraphic cupboards
To nibble all the day,
While unsuspecting cycles
Wheel pompously away.

She was, in addition, of her age in that she applied the scalpel of observation to passion and to pain and watched, even as she suffered, the phenomena of the interior life:

> After great pain a formal feeling comes—
> The nerves sit ceremonious like tombs;
> The stiff Heart questions—was it Me that bore?
> And yesterday—or centuries before?

And this process so fused intensity of feeling and of insight that in certain poems of this character she does, indeed, transcend the ordinary harmonies of form which often in lighter and brighter moods she simply failed to reach:

> I got so I could hear his name
> Without—
> Tremendous gain!
> That stop-sensation in my soul
> And thunder in the room. . . .
>
> I got so I could stir the box
> In which
> His letters grew,
> Without that forcing in my breath
> As staples driven through.

Once or twice, finally, she wrung out of that great central pain and renunciation of her womanhood mystical visions of wish-fulfillments in which, despite lapses, the style takes on a sudden note of ecstatic elevation:

> A wife at daybreak I shall be,
> Sunrise, hast thou a flag for me?
> At midnight I am yet a maid—
> How short it takes to make a bride!
> Then, Midnight, I have passed from thee
> Unto the East and Victory.

Midnight. "Good night,"
I hear them call.
The angels bustle in the hall,
Softly my future climbs the stairs,
I fumble at my childhood's prayer—
So soon to be a child no more!
Eternity, I'm coming, Sir,—
Master, I've seen that face before.

It will be observed that I have quoted none of Emily Dickinson's quite clarified and transparent and therefore justly most famous lyrics, neither "Our share of night to bear," nor "My life closed twice before its close," nor "Alter? When the hills do," nor "Heart, we will forget him," nor "I never saw a moor," nor "I died for beauty," nor "This quiet Dust was Gentlemen and Ladies." In a word, she was so wealthy a poet that she has no need of her failures and notes and fragments except for the student of her work and character. These were unique not in kind but in degree. The creative temper at its truest is always the temper that can make a great deal out of a very little. Poets and novelists who, especially in their mature years, are still avid after new experiences are likely to be substituting life for art because obscurely their essential artistic impotence is known to them. A voyage into exotic lands or a new bedfellow, both desired ostensibly for the sake of art, serve actually to put off the evil day of artistic failure. Thus Emily runs true to the form of the higher creative spirits whose power is measured by intensity and not by wealth or multiplicity of experience. The wonder is not that she was a great poet amid the poverty and narrowness of her experience; the wonder is that there was born in that Amherst house so great a poet that she needed only that house and the seasons and a few books and one supreme and unfulfilled passion to make her one of the very few great woman poets of all literature. And that wonder, the wonder of the occurrence of genius, is among the ultimate mysteries left as a source of human aspiration and awe.

To pass to the other poets of the transition period is difficult, for these other poets wrought within their time and did not, like Emily Dickinson, breathe into it from the cool chambers of eternity. Nor are there many to be noted of whom either a few strains survive or who definitely helped to usher in the period of national expression. Perhaps the most striking save one of the latter kind is Mr. Edwin Markham whose nobly benevolent white head seen in the Poetry society of later days seemed to give assurance that the spirit of Whitman was not dead. His best-known poem "The Man with the Hoe" set hearts and minds on fire in 1899. It is in simple truth not a very good poem; its eloquence is not profound; its end-stopped lines thud. But poet and poem were immediately taken up and mythologized by a considerable part of the American collectivity, and that fact in itself points to a high psychological and sociological achievement. For they who made the poet and the poem their own were the young, the free of mind, the generous of heart. Mr. Markham has written poems happier in poetic character. "The Man with the Hoe" is his contribution to the civilization of his country.

An undue neglect has been the portion of an interesting, fruitful and remarkably early attempt to draw poetry from the actual folk-life of America. This attempt was made by

William Aspenwall Bradley in "Old Christmas," a volume of verse-narratives dealing with the life of the Kentucky mountaineers. These tales in verse have both sobriety and power; occasionally, as in "The Strange Woman" they attain tragic dignity without sacrificing simplicity of texture; in the folk-lyric, too, as in the lines "Mother Goose on Goose Creek," Bradley struck a very fresh and felicitous note. How rich this vein, had it been worked, might have become is well illustrated by the superiority of "The Son" to all else that Frederic Ridgely Torrence ever wrote. But it was apparently too early for such work. Bradley fell silent; Torrence never repeated that single triumph.

A quiet and dignified persistence in the cultivation of simple beauty, an absence of trickery and rhetoric made slowly to stand out from among innumerable versifiers the three volumes which Lizette Woodworth Reese published between 1891 and 1909. She began to disengage herself from her contemporaries before the new poetry movement which began in 1912; she has survived it. The same is true in a higher degree of the early poems, especially the sonnets, of George Santayana. These were known in their time to only a few. But these few were germinal or prophetic minds. And in these sonnets they heard once more the true voice of the great English tradition in poetry, not the mouthings of the genteel rhetoricians and professional optimists and Beauty-mongers, but the iron monition of their day in minor but unmistakably authentic strains:

> Now ponder we the ruins of the years,
> And groan beneath the weight of boasted gain;
> No unsung bacchanal can charm our ears

Nor lead our dances to the woodland fane,
No hope of heaven sweeten our few tears
And hush the importunity of pain.

It remains only to speak of George Sylvester Viereck. His name and reputation have been repressed by critics and anthologists, because these were very properly ashamed of the actions and attitudes toward Mr. Viereck into which they were carried by their attacks of war psychosis. Today no one is likely seriously to deny that Viereck was the most conspicuous American poet between 1907 and 1914 and that there were few dissenters from the chorus of praise, almost of adulation, that greeted his successive volumes. Even the staid Richard Watson Gilder was dazzled; William Marion Reedy, Clayton Hamilton, William Aspenwall Bradley, William Ellery Leonard, Frank Harris, Richard Le Gallienne, above all, James Huneker were sure that the spirit of modern poetry had now first reached our shores. Nor was this all. Viereck's volumes of verse sold; they made money. They bore witness, in other words, to the utter weariness of men of the conventional mouthings of the genteel versifiers and to the perennial need of the poet. Unluckily the poetic school and manner which Viereck represented in America, that, namely, of the French and English late Victorian decadents, was even then on the point of extinction and may be said, in fact, to have enjoyed its last flicker of life in America and in him. Nothing seems more old-fashioned today than this loud sonorousness of execution and this public exaggeration of private sin and unnecessary repentance. Nevertheless Mr. Viereck's goings-on both as a man and as an artist had a definitely liberating influence on American life and letters at their particular moment; from their influence an astute prophet might have foretold the imminence of many of the revolutions which did, in fact, take place almost immediately. He wrote, moreover, better and better as the years went on and it is only his public clamorousness, compensating no doubt some private inadequacy or fear, that still keeps from their just place in the poetry of the period such fine sonnets as "The Poet" and "Finale" as well as a few among the subtler and quieter of his earlier poems. The always honorable experience of espousing an unpopular cause, which made poets of Abolitionists, also made a better poet of Viereck. By two things, at least, he has his definite share in the history of American expression: by anonymously planning and inspiring the anthology "The Lyric Year" which ushered in modern American literature in 1912 and by the lines addressed to his wife on Armistice Day, in which a recurrent human experience finds its simple but permanently adequate embodiment:

> Never on the winning side,
>   Always on the right—
> Vanquished, this shall be our pride
>   In the world's despite.
>
> Bravely drain, then fling away,
>   Break the cup of sorrow!
> Courage! He who lost the day
>   May have won the morrow.

BOOK NINE

The Development of Forms

I

A date and a year are symbols of one kind and forms are symbols of another. Forms that arise and break through in a given year record antecedent conflicts; they record the strain of experience and the travail of the soul. Council has been darkened by the academic study of influences, which has assumed that change comes from without. It comes from within; it comes from the soul that in its need goes forth seeking and, if the quest is great enough in power and in persistence, finds its appointed nourishment. I, too, shall take refuge in certain dates and outer events and discuss certain influences. But fiction could render far more precisely and powerfully than criticism what took place in America, what happened to the souls of Americans in the period awkwardly symbolized by the dates of 1912 and 1914 and 1918.

In sordid clamorous cities and especially on the green, dull campuses of colleges and universities young men and young women were suddenly aware that neither newspapers nor

367

books nor the droning of politician or preacher or professor any longer told them what they wanted or needed to know or had any relation to their experience of the life of moral practice or of beauty. They felt all things, but especially love and justice, after a fashion of which their elders knew nothing or, what came to the same thing, dared to know nothing. And the division between all public speech, whether by word of mouth or on the printed page, and all vital experience was so enormous and unbridgeable that the younger generation repudiated all form because it repudiated all meaning, correctly told by instinct that form and meaning are one. The term younger generation must, of course, be taken in a very circumscribed sense. Numerically these youths were excessively few. But they were somehow set apart here and there by the slight conspicuousness of their emphases which were indeed exaggerated now and then by the envy that is often at the core of condemnation. This situation was rendered somewhat acuter by the year 1914. For especially in the great mid-Western centers of population the immediate high-pressure partisanship of official America and of the press was received with both scepticism and irritation and many a youth who had until then slid quietly down the grooves of use and wont was stung into criticism and protest. The majority of these youths were later swept, as by a hurricane, into the great crime and disaster. But they had had their moment of criticism and protest and to the mood of that moment many thereafter returned. Thus it is true that all the seeds of our modern period were well in the earth before the war; it is equally true that the war immensely hastened germination and growth.

Nor was this all. We must not forget that pressure accentuates revolt. And it was the war which brought to a sudden crystallization that neo-nationalism which had in fact little to do with the carnage in Europe, but was the instinctive passion of fear aroused in the lower as well as in the higher strata of the Anglo-American population by the gradual articulateness of the later immigrant strains: the German, the Jewish, the Latin and the Slav. The gibe against Mr. Stuart Sherman that he was practicing Ku-Klux Klan criticism was essentially correct. The war did not create but brought into confrontation cultural and racial groups with their antagonisms of instinct and custom. The Anglo-American group made gesture after gesture of moral superiority, galling in the extreme to the other and temporarily helpless groups. Thus we had with apparent suddenness sharp cultural surfaces and friction among these surfaces. We had the just terror of those who saw the danger of a rickety polyglot polity, like the Austrian, and we had the equally just terror of those who feared a blank British Provincialism in which all but Smith and Jones would be helots by anterior decree. The Anglo-American group, having in its hands all the instrumentalities of power, was able to express itself most definitely and, in truth, devastatingly. Its fateful expressions were two: participation in the World War and the enactment of the Eighteenth Amendment which, more profoundly than is generally perceived, was the answer of the Anglo-American masses to the Germano-Celto-Semitic and Latin feeling and folk-ways. The peculiar situation of the Negro in the war, as delineated by W. B. Du Bois, the Negro revolt and migration, the acute heightening of the sexual ambivalence toward the Negro felt and more diffused now in all sections of the country—these were further elements in the civilizatory situation not, indeed, created, but brought to a sharp and sudden climax by the war and its immediate consequences.

From the point of view of creative expression the significant and upon the whole inevitable fact was that the youths who were on the point of open revolt against their cultural environment protested against the precise *mores* and repressions which the Anglo-Saxon masses now intensified in instinctive self-defense. And thus it came about that not only the sons of Germanic immigrants, like Theodore Dreiser and Carl Sandburg, but men and women of undivided American and Puritan descent found themselves culturally on the side of the minorities of other races and produced a literature given over almost wholly to critical protest against the morals and institutions of their ancestors. The creative life of America allied itself definitely against the older American folk and its ways. The sons and daughters of the Puritans set out to destroy and transform Puritanism. Hence all or nearly all that was being written or had recently been written in America out of that older civilization now fiercely on the defensive, lost all vitality as communication and hence as form. Neither Ezra Pound nor Edgar Lee Masters, nor Floyd Dell nor Max Eastman nor John Reed, nor Sherwood Anderson nor later Sinclair Lewis nor many others of similar name and descent could make anything of the meanings or the forms created by their fathers. They ranged themselves with the "new men," the strangers, the recusants and went for needed influence and example not to England but to the ancestral cultures of those others whom their own people were bedeviling and repudiating as fellow-citizens and fellow-creators of an American civilization. Against the background of these contrasts and conflicts and not otherwise can the development of forms, the great critical debate and the creative experience of modern America be understood. A trivial but psychologically significant and memorable anecdote has it that, in the lobby of the Garrick Theater, then the early and only home of the Theater Guild, one Anglo-American gentleman, sufficiently touched by culture, as his presence there showed, to have his doubts and his misgivings, said to another gentleman of the same type, in a tone of rueful fatalism: "But did the 'Nation' have to give its poetry-prize to a poem *against* the war, *about* a Nigger and *by* a Jew?" The poem in question was, in honest fact, not a very good poem. But it had been sincerely selected for the prize by an editorial committee representing the older and more aristocratic American strains. The children of the folk who indulged in the creative life were in open and fiery revolt against the folk. They are so still. . . .

II

The revolt antedated the war. One may select facts of various kinds for illustration. As early as 1908 a group of young men produced a magazine called "Moods," which drew its spirit and its sustenance from the protest inherent in continental sources. Here assembled James Oppenheim and Waldo Frank and Louis Untermeyer, who were to be found again editing the short-lived "Seven Arts" in 1916, and here emerged Philip Moeller. Here this group, later

371

scattered, began its honorable but somewhat melancholy assimilatory Jewish function of breaking ground, stirring minds, mediating between culture and culture, itself destined to no creative future. "Moods" was not the first "little magazine" in America; there had been, many years before "The Chapbook"; there had been "East and West" founded by William Aspenwall Bradley; there had been "The Pathfinder" at the University of the South and "The Morningside" at Columbia and in the two last at least had appeared names of later light and power. But "Moods" alone, though still feebly enough, contained the vision of the cultural development that was at the gate.

Or one may select such other facts as these, that between 1908 and 1912 appeared the first five volumes of verse of Ezra Pound and that they all appeared in Europe. Thus there had set in so early the movement of protest by expatriation, not unknown, of course, in an older America, but now prompted by other motives and leading gradually as the years went on to a fairly definite eddy within the current of our letters. Of higher ultimate import was the fact that, as early as 1906, William Ellery Leonard caused a slim volume of "Sonnets and Poems" to be privately printed. That he could find no publisher characterizes as closely as anything the atmosphere of the period, for his poems were cast in the strict mold of the great English tradition, but they were informed by a great spirit, too. Expression in America had, however, become so alienated from experience that editors and publishers took fright at the accent of living experience even when it was the experience of an elevated mind and character. They listened contentedly to the chirpings of the Madison

Caweins; they were deaf to the authentic speech of the spirit they feigned to themselves to be invoking. And thus America discredited in its actual practice classical form even when its younger poets did not dream of a revolution of forms. Leonard, by a felicitous translation of a poem by Arno Holz showed himself aware of the only imagist movement that had preceded the Anglo-American one in any literature. Personally he found the old forms, remolded in his own image, sufficient. And so did Edna St. Vincent Millay, whose "Renascence," appearing in "The Lyric Year" simultaneously with Leonard's first regularly published volume "The Vaunt of Man," uses the same traditional and long-consecrated form as Leonard's "Urbs Triumphans." Both poets infuse their spirit and their personal rhythm into their octosyllabic verses. But they followed in the footsteps of Milton and of Blake. The air however was so thick with verse that went through the gestures of "Renascence" and "Urbs Triumphans," while wholly uninformed by the spirit of those poems, that Leonard was simply not heard by his contemporaries until many years later and Miss Millay would not have been heard had she not, metaphorically at least, moved to Greenwich Village and made herself, most exquisitely and felicitously, the voice of a revolt in life if not in letters. In brief, the old forms could either no more be used for a communication that was to stir or sting or else when they were so used by younger poets their sting was blunted and their stirring went unfelt because hearers and lovers of poetry had quite correctly come to identify traditional forms with meanings that were utterly outworn and forever dead.

Thus we come to "The Lyric Year" in which appeared not

only Miss Millay, but William Rose Benét and Witter Bynner and Nicholas Vachel Lindsay with a very curious poem on O. Henry and James Oppenheim and Louis Untermeyer with vigorous and even plangent plaints for the disinherited and Miss Sara Teasdale with one of her most admirable lyrics. But about these few poems hovered the cloud of versifiers with words as of wool and rhythms that were wooden, pompously uttering nothing. They had no meaning left to communicate and so their forms were stillborn. From this circumstance arises the importance of the free-verse and imagist movement which is now half-forgotten and which, as we shall see, produced no poet of high rank or permanent import. But that movement had the value of a necessary discipline. It insisted upon precision, and the conventional versifiers no longer used their eyes; its rhythms or rhythmlessness was, at least, the individual act, however feeble, of a personal moment in the writer's life, while the writers of fixed verse turned on manufactured cylinders like those in a hurdy-gurdy. The considerations offered in respect of Whitman are not to be forgotten: rhythm, that is to say, meter and metrical feet, is no artifice; regular rhythm is profoundly rooted in human nature; fixed verse is implicated with the coming and going of the breath, the dance-gesture of human limbs, the rise and fall of the act of reproduction. Prose is a late art and unrhythmed poetry an ultimate and fugitive sophistication. It has not lasted or established itself in any literature. The school of Arno Holz is an historical curiosity today, even though Holz' "Phantasus" is probably still the finest volume of imagist work in the world. Accordingly Amy Lowell herself returned more and more to the classic

374

forms in her latest volumes; writers like Maxwell Bodenheim and Alfred Kreymborg have returned wholly to them; the flood of free verse has ebbed, leaving Ezra Pound and Carl Sandburg almost alone. It is but natural, then, that all the arguments for it, especially as urged by Amy Lowell, were quite specious. Even the fructifying influences were misinterpreted. Arthur Waley, for instance, is a writer of exquisite English prose; but authorities seem to agree that Chinese poetry is even more elaborately and intricately "fixed" than Occidental poetry. The French *vers-libristes* had, of course, nothing to do with the case at all; they rebelled against the last remnants of the rules of Boileau and wrote "free verse" in no other sense than Shelley did because he rejected the closed couplet of Pope and the Pindaric forms of Dryden.

The real justification of the free verse and imagist movement, in other words, was a psychological and creative justification. Drained meanings were being droned in dead unpersonal measures. It needed a complete break. Whatever the future was to bring, it needed first of all insurgency, destruction, the recovery by any and all means of the possibilities of personal expression. These needs were felt in England, too, though less acutely than in America. And so the earliest anthology of the new movement, "Des Imagistes," was originally published in England in 1914. It opens with the extraordinarily lovely Hellenizing poems of Richard Aldington which, though treading on light feet, are no more prose than the irregular unrhymed measures of Goethe or Matthew Arnold. H. D., the first American of the group, slighting her ictus more, clings, as she has done since, to the Greek tradition and inspiration, which of itself tends even in the deliberately laxest writing to an unconscious tightness and contour of form. There follows a single poem by Amy Lowell, "In a Garden," lovely enough to lead to the wish *o si sic omnia*, and lovely because to the brilliant distinctness of image there is added a soft but sufficient element of song. The American contribution is completed by several pieces of Ezra Pound. Of these the best and still best remembered is "Δώρια". And I shall take the liberty of quoting this poem according to its natural and inherent rhythm in order to illustrate further the regard for inner form with which the best of the free-verse writers began:

> Be in me as the eternal moods of the bleak wind,
> and not as transient things are, gaiety of flowers.
> Have me in the strong loneliness of sunless cliffs
> and of grey waters. Let the gods speak softly
> of us hereafter. The shadowy flowers of Orcus
> remember Thee.

A flood of free verse inundated the land. Alfred Kreymborg, a gifted poet and a man learned in both literature and music, organized the group that called itself Others. But his own determinedly naïve and engaging rhythms, from which he has since proceeded to classical measures of great imaginative freshness, are all that is left of the movement and the group. I add the name of Maxwell Bodenheim, pretentious and falsely sophisticated, but with an undeniable streak of acrid talent, who has also since written not negligibly in the traditional forms. With these the record may end. For Edgar Lee Masters and Carl Sandburg are not to be classed among the innovators. They used forms ready to their hand for a creative activity which shall be described in its proper place.

The innovators, Ezra Pound, Amy Lowell and Hilda Doolittle, have to their credit not only their own work but the release they offered for expression to hundreds, nay, to thousands at a crucial moment in American civilization. The free verse of innumerable poetasters is forgotten; it never contained any vital principle. But the poetasters and their friends and hearers were led in their own lives and so permanently in the exercise of their taste to reintegrate experience with expression. That there is today more freedom and flexibility in American life and a small audience on whom the serious creative artist may count is due in no negligible measure to the effect upon those who were young enough to be impressionable between 1914 and 1918 of the innovators of poetic form.

Of the permanent value of the work of these innovators no very high hope will be entertained by anyone who knows the history of creative expression. We do not know who invented the dactylic hexameter; we know that Homer and Hesiod found it ready to their hand; poets in all the Latin dialects of a large and then homogeneous region had prepared elaborate measures before Dante used one of these; it was not Shakespeare who invented either dramatic blank verse or the loose form of the Elizabethan play nor the euphuistic rhetoric nor the sonnet form; Goethe was contented with German folk-song and folk-play on the one hand and with the models of antiquity on the other; Ibsen and Shaw took the dramatic structure built up by a dozen Frenchmen in the course of the nineteenth century and put it to their personal uses and Hauptmann started with a variety of the same form invented by Arno Holz. Examples could be indefinitely multiplied. Fielding imitated Homer and Thackeray Fielding; Smollett used the old picaresque form which came through Dickens and many others as far as Mark Twain, himself, as I have shown, the heritor of a tradition and an existent form. The innovator is never a master. For the master has an overwhelming urgency of meaning, even though the meaning be only the meaning of himself. He is too pregnant with message, if that word be rightly understood, to play with form. He takes forms invented by ingenious but less creative predecessors or contemporaries and pours himself into them. The single contradictory example is only apparently so. Wordsworth made no fundamental innovation of form and the use of a diction simpler than the thick *clichés* of the earlier eighteenth century was everywhere in the air of literary England at the time of the "Lyrical Ballads." The masters transform existent forms by the might of their spirit; they never invent or innovate. It is of vital importance to insist upon this fact, which has its profound philosophical and psychological reasons, in the America and not only in the America of our period. Experimentation with form may forerun high creative activity; it is not and can never be the thing itself. It may be that a master will arise to use what is usable in the experiments of Dorothy Richardson and Waldo Frank and James Joyce; he has not arisen yet; the youngsters who play with imitations of the current experimentations in a controversial spirit illustrate nothing but their fundamental uncreativeness.

It is quite conceivable, on the other hand, that these experiments in language itself and in prose and in the narrative forms may remain interesting curiosities of literature to which, after a time, only the learned will return and of which the chief use will be seen to have been, as it was of the American free verse movement, to liberate forces in life rather than to contribute toward creation in letters. Such, at all events, has been the fate of that movement. Few people today read the verse of Amy Lowell and H. D. If Mr. Ezra Pound is still read or, rather, more discussed than read, it is due more to his picturesque and engaging character and fate than to his actual productivity. Since he, though still young, was earliest in the field, I may begin with him. An innovator and protestant, Mr. Pound is at the same time the most learned of poets or, rather, almost a poet of learning. He is translating and quoting, especially from the Latin and the minor Romance dialects as often as he is composing and his form is the form of an ingenious prose-translation of his favorite sources, strongly tinctured by the Greeks, by the English Bible and cut into lengths which often have a real or apparent congruence of either rhetorical or slightly rhythmic pattern. The influence of Whitman is noticeable, too, as in "Further Instructions," but it is not strong and has tended to fade from Pound's work. His great beginning gesture, by which he has founded almost a tradition and a school, was his repudiation of America:

> O helpless few in my country,
> O remnant enslaved!
>
> Artists broken against her,
> Astray, lost in the villages,
> Mistrusted, spoken against— . . .

That has its own sincerity and its own beauty. And so, despite the Whitmanesque flavor, has this other passage:

> How many will come after me
> Singing as well as I sing, none better;
> Telling the heart of their truth
> As I have taught them to tell it.

How brave a beginning! But the heart of Ezra Pound's truth has amounted to pitifully little: to *pastiches* of Provençal poetry, to echoes of the Greek Anthology and to scabrous Catullian pleasantries in either biblical or ultra-colloquial language.

> This government official
> Whose wife is several years his senior,
> Has such a caressing air with young ladies.

Was it for this that Ezra Pound became an exile, a torch and a legend? The "Envoi" dated 1919 is the most beautiful poem he has ever written; it is one of the most beautiful of American poems. But he could safely have written that lovely elaboration of the seventeenth century poet's "Go, lovely Rose," in any city, on any college campus of America. For its loveliness is learned and academic and has a touch of bookish dust.

> Tell her that goes
> With song upon her lips
> But sings not out the song, nor knows
> The maker of it, some other mouth
> May be as fair as hers,
> Might, in new ages, gain her worshippers,
> When our two dusts with Waller's shall be laid,
> Siftings on siftings in oblivion,
> Till change hath broken down
> All things save Beauty alone.

380

But, in truth, Pound's work smells, to use a sound old phrase, ferociously of the lamp. This self-appointed rebel and expatriate writes in a musty library; he ransacks the scrolls of the ancients and the mediævals and writes macaronic free verse, displaying a curious erudition and a plentiful lack of anything to say. This method or mannerism or chain of mannerisms culminates in the "Twenty-seven Cantos," published in Paris and London in two folio volumes of extraordinary sumptuousness and limited respectively to ninety and to one hundred and one copies. No other poet has ever had his work put forth with such stealthy splendor. But in these cantos Mr. Pound is almost wholly the antiquarian. Amid a farrago of reference and quotation, of document and allusion there are long echoes of Homer, not devoid of a mild grace or charm and longer echoes of Dante, as in the imitation of certain passages of the "Inferno" in Cantos XIV—XVI. But Mr. Pound has neither severity nor indignation, only an adolescent delight in excretory imagery. In all or nearly all the cantos there are brief moments of accomplished writing:

> With the first pale-clear of the heaven
> And the cities set in their hills,
> And the goddess of the fair knees
> Moving there, with the oak-wood behind her,
> The green slope, the white hounds
> > leaping about her . . .

But by far the greater part of the texture of the cantos is woven—the word is deliberate—after this fashion:

> The whole fortune of
> MacNarpen and Company is founded
> Upon Palgrave's Golden Treasury. Nel paradiso terrestre

And all the material was used up, Jesu Christo,
And everything in its place, and nothing left over
To make una compagna d'Adamo.

Why do I linger over this strange curiosity of literature?
Because the cultural history of America's modern period cannot be clarified for us nor recorded for the future nor yet, if
I dare to say so, diagnosed for a cure of its ills, which are
allied to the ills of all the world, without a constant insistence upon the phenomenon of the rebel who has nothing but
his rebellion, no stock in trade but his resistance and contempt, a just resistance doubtless and a contempt for things
contemptible, but who, his liberation accomplished, his irritation projected, has neither meaning nor message nor shaping power, nor new gods nor other altars. He reiterates his
hatreds in middle-age as in youth and flees to ever stranger
scenes and ever more violent contortions of language in order
to hide from himself and others the emptiness in his own
breast. And the tragic circumstance is that he does so hide
it, from those especially who desire it to be hidden, since
they are, alas, in the same case. And thus it comes about that
Mr. Allen Tate, one of the youngest of American poets,
salutes in "The Nation" the publication of the seventeen
cantos in phrases that illustrate his generation's paralysis of
thought and metaphysical despair and its disheartening consent to both. The cantos, Mr. Tate writes, "are not about
anything. But they are distinguished poetry." He assures us
that Mr. Pound "is a typically modern, rootless and interna-
tionalized intelligence" but is also—a few lines further—
"a traditionalist at bottom" and "a powerful reactionary,"
and that the cantos, like the "Golden Ass of Apuleius," are

a "production of worlds without conviction." It is evident, then, as some have long suspected, that it needs convictions —principles upon which the universe somehow coheres for the mind—for any kind of coherent expression, for articulate communication on any plane and that the absence of conviction in this sense reduces men, as it has reduced both Mr. Pound and his disciple, to the proliferation of meaningless verbiage. Thought, in brief, cannot exist without some principle of thought nor feeling without selected objects, nor life and its expression without that minimum of inner organization according to immanent law which alone can produce both meaning and form. . . . A hell of emptiness has been added to the other hells of man's experience and imagination. . . .

III

No wonder that one returns with wistful and affectionate gaze to 1912 when no one dreamed that the little renaissance of life and poetry would so soon wither upon its stricken tree. Miss Harriet Monroe founded "Poetry: A Magazine of Verse" and soon come "The Masses" and two years later "The Little Review" and "The Seven Arts" and the founding of the Washington Square Players and the Provincetown Playhouse and the Neighborhood Playhouse, of which much more presently, and despite the war and the Mooney case and a world gone raving mad, there was a wind of spring in the air in Greenwich Village and in other places. There were things to rebel against creatively; there were big and little martyrdoms to suffer. The dust of earth was edged with radiance. There could even be humor:

> They draw nude women for the Masses
> Thick fat ungainly lasses—
> How does that help the working classes?

So intense and indeed beautiful—let them remember!—was the life of the recusants that even free verse seemed to glow and that sober and historical minded spirits watched patiently the critical antics of Miss Amy Lowell. Remote in Brookline, trapped by lineage and station in all the popular orthodoxies in politics and culture she projected into literature her fierce revolt against her nature and her personal fate. Thus by her warfare for the liberation of form she seemed allied to the recusants' rebellion and liberation of morals and became something of a banner and a bugler to a generation whose deeper mood she did not share. Nor are her vigor and versatility and talent for the sheer technique of letters to be denied. She was somewhat hampered by the excessively high estimate she had of herself, with which she came out flatly in the "Critical Fable"—

> I'll hazard a guess
> She'll be rated by time as more rather than less—

and which is implicit in the extraordinarily interesting if quite Browningesque poem "The Sisters." But here as often she displayed that vigor of mind which definitely raised her above the rank and file of her poetical contemporaries. They would all have echoed her

> Confound Victoria, and the slimy inhibitions
> She loosed on all us Anglo-Saxon creatures.

384

Few had the ability to see that this protest and this cleansing were not enough. Amy Lowell, communing with the great women poets of the past, spoke toward the end of her life the final word:

> I cannot write like you, I cannot think
> In terms of Pagan or of Christian now.

Beyond the turbulence of controversy and the grandiose but empty creative gestures of her polyphonic narratives, she became gradually aware, as Ezra Pound, for instance, has never done, both of her own position, which she defined with great precision in the second of the sonnets to Eleonora Duse, and of certain mysteries of the creative life:

> Life's cruel plan compels
> The perfect sacrifice of one great soul
> To make a myriad others even a whit more whole.

More and more as the years went on she abandoned the exercises in free verse which nevertheless often had in her hands the hard but permanent glint and cool glow of jade or turquoise or lapis and wrote in the warmer measures closer and more native to the heart, as in those fine stanzas in her last posthumous volume on a book of Alice Meynell's poems given her by a friend now, too, dead like the author of the book:

> And you are dead these drifted years,
> How many I forget. And she
> Who wrote this book, her tragedy
> Long since dried up its scalding tears.
>
> I read of her death yesterday,
> Frail lady whom I never knew

And knew so well. Would I could strew
Her grave with pansies, blue and grey.

Would I could stand a little space
Under a blowing, brightening sky,
And watch the sad leaves fall and lie
Gently upon that lonely place.

So cried her heart, a feverish thing.
But clay is still, and clay is cold,
And I was young, and I am old,
And in December what birds sing!

Amy Lowell was, in fact, only fifty-one when she died. But the free verse springtime was over, Pagan and Christian ethos were as dust and her mind was too keen and scrupulous to suppose that the creative imagination could function in the void. So many of her contemporaries have thought that and have, instead of admitting that their December came upon the heels of May, substituted drivel and dirt for her honorable recognition of the necessity of new values and her significant despair.

A third poet, who will not be wholly forgotten arose from the free verse movement: Hilda Doolittle. Her work, which can now be studied in the "Collected Poems" of 1925, is quite homogeneous—frail, faint as sea-grasses, but having at its best a lapidary precision and spare grace of speech. The poet is interesting moreover in that she avoided the problem and the conflict which Pound will not face and which bravely faced, darkened the last years of Amy Lowell, by fleeing in good archaic romantic fashion into a Hellenic world derived from reading and from a melancholy homeless imagination. A very minor Hölderlin, she too has spent her years

das Land der Griechen mit der Seele suchend

and has thus avoided, with what half-conscious feeling of guilt and inadequacy may easily be conceived, the creative facing of her age. Yet even from that carefully guarded Greece of her imagination in which she has chosen to dwell and within which she has moved with so frugal but so quietly exquisite a grace the poet has not been able to keep the vicarious cry of her soul and her period:

> White, O white face—
> from disenchanted days
> wither alike dark rose
> and fiery bays:
> no gift within our hands,
> no strength to praise,
> only defeat and silence . . .
> Give back the glamour to our will
> the thought; give back the tool
> the chisel; once we wrought
> things not unworthy,
> sandal and steel-clasp;
> silver and steel, the coat
> with white leaf-pattern
> at the arm and throat . . .

That cry or rather murmur: "once we wrought things not unworthy" answers the December of Amy Lowell, answers the furtive contortions of Ezra Pound. In other words, that brief and lovely springtime of the American spirit which breathed and lived and touched all worthy foreheads with its winds from 1912 to 1920 led to no summer for the innovators in poetic form. Its happiest and loveliest record will be found in one of the most memorable of American books: "May Days, an Anthology" from "The Masses-Liberator," edited by Genevieve Taggard. Here are the poets of the age, all or very nearly all in their first freshness and hope and with the glamour bright upon their will, the poets who failed and the poets who have developed and grown strong and, in addition, many voices heard here only and not heard since who by the fact that they had briefly then the gift of song bear witness to the reality of the magic and the music of those days, from which came, despite the failure of the mere innovators, all of modern American poetry, the poetry of life as well as the poetry of speech.

IV

Poetry and innovation of poetic form were the earliest but by no means the only preoccupations of those years. They saw the rise of the American theater which, in a few short years, came to rival the German theater; they saw the rise of the American drama. Until then there had been no drama in America. For myself and for this book I repudiate once more the antiquarian argument that we must concern ourselves with bad plays and poems and stories, work meaningless in itself and without fruitfulness for the future, because the age in which those bad plays and poems and stories were written, produced works even worse. And that is literally the whole content of the antiquarian argument. Of John Lyly you may say that he influenced Shakespeare and of the improvised farces of Italy that they helped to shape Molière. Very well. Here then are the happy hunting-grounds of the research student. But not even that questionable excuse can be offered for concerning oneself with the plays of Clyde Fitch. There had been no American theater either, except the German theater in that old playhouse on Irving Place. There had been, since the first decade of this century, isolated good productions of European plays. Such things do not constitute a theater. The American theater may be said to have originated with that group of players who, under the leadership of Maurice Browne and Ellen Van Volkenburg founded the Little Theater of Chicago and produced "The Trojan Women" of Euripides in February, 1913. This group of players had a will toward the theater in that they had a will toward a renewal of the forms of life through creative expression. Having no medium belonging to their age and land, they chose an ancient and still universally valid one— profoundly valid as the next dread year of 1914 was to prove for all of Western mankind. And this was the mark of the several subsequent groups who founded the American theater, that they were men and women who had a vision concerning both life and art and of the integration of the two, which they were impelled to express through the medium of the art of the theater. No such motives could ever be assigned to David Belasco nor later even to Arthur Hopkins. But from such motives alone can a creative national theater arise. Hence in the history of American civilization these facts will be permanently memorable: that the Washington Square Players, under the leadership of Edward Goodman and Philip Moeller, gave their first bill in the Bandbox Theater in February, 1915, that in the summer of the same year at the Wharf Theater in Provincetown, Massachusetts, there were performed two one-act plays: "Constancy" by Neith Boyce and "Suppressed Desires" by George Cram Cook and Susan Glaspell and that during the same season Alice and Irene Lewisohn started their original productions at the Neighborhood Playhouse on Grand Street. Nor should a date in November of 1916 be wholly forgotten on which Stuart Walker began his New York production of the plays of Lord Dunsany.

The external history of these various theaters, especially of the Theatre Guild which developed from the Washington Square Players, has been recorded in a number of books. Nor am I concerned with that external history, but rather with these theaters and with the plays that came out of them as signs and tokens of a renewal not only in American art but of American life. The years were the years of the war and it is worthy of record that all the directors and players of these theaters were men and women less herd-minded than their fellows, less affected by the growing mass-psychosis and desirous of expressing in the medium to which their talents led them the inner freedom that was theirs. No friend or fellow-worker of the Washington Square Players in the days of the Comedy Theater nor any of the Provincetown group in the now legendary playhouse on MacDougal Street can fail to recall nor, having the opportunity, fail to record that these theaters were more than theaters in the current Anglo-American sense. They became symbol and expressive gesture of all in the land who were young in spirit, who had kept their freedom of mind against the intolerable darkness and pressure of that hour in history, who hoped for a measure of freedom and flexibility not only in the political but in the moral life of their country, and there is hardly a vital contributor to the period of national expression in America who was not at some moment a friend, a comrade or at least an impassioned auditor of these two groups of players and directors and playwrights. Behind both groups, but especially behind the Provincetown group stood that first Latin or Bohemian quarter in American history known as Greenwich Village, where amid the normal amount of mere rebellion and mere unguidedness, there lived and breathed for the first time on this continent a group spirit of the creative life, of shaping endeavor in both art and morals. I trust that others will record that scene and those years more fully and more intimately than I have either the ability or the opportunity here to do. But let no one underestimate either the scene or the period. If America is no longer a despicable spiritual province in the eyes of the world, if American art and American speech can meet those of the old ripe cultures of Europe upon honorable terms, that fact is due not least to the life that was lived, to the works inspired by that life or conceived or written between 1914 and 1920 in the Ninth Ward of the City of New York.

The Washington Square Players and the Provincetown group differed one from the other in strict accordance with the character of their founders. The former were sons of the Jewish bourgeoisie, international minded, born mediators among various cultures, expressing themselves, then, quite naturally and clearly through the moods of continental art and desiring these moods to evoke analogous moods within that American civilization which they hoped very properly to influence and help to shape within the measure of their power. The Provincetown group, on the other hand, were the rebellious children of the Puritans, nobly aware, as Susan Glaspell was to show in "Inheritors," of the tradition of libertarianism which is the true tradition of America and of their folk—a tradition which seemed to be going down to disaster under their eyes. The two groups complemented each other in the happiest fashion; each was conscious of that complementary function; the reproach that the Washington Square Players were not hospitable to native talent was not very bitter and the coöperation of the two strains of American culture can be studied in the composition of the group that stood trial as editors of "The Masses." The difference between the two groups and the differentiation in function continued. The Provincetown group produced Susan Glaspell and Eugene O'Neill and disappeared. The Washington Square Players became the Theatre Guild, one of the two or three most distinguished theatrical institutions in the world. Never so hostile to native talent as it was once reputed to be—one has only to study its record from the beginning on—it took over Eugene O'Neill in the years of his maturity and gave their first opportunity to be heard to Arthur Richman, Elmer Rice and John Howard Lawson. But these three have proved, like Lewis Beach and Gilbert Emery and so many other promising talents in the American theater, incapable of creative development and "Ambush," "The Adding Machine" and, on a somewhat lower plane, "Processional" have remained isolated performances. Nor must I fail to emphasize again that the Guild and the Provincetown Playhouse and the Neighborhood Playhouse and such similar phenomena as the coming and working among us of that great actor and director Emanuel Reicher had other functions than the incalculable and unpredictable one of developing a native group of dramatic writers. American life was renewed, American sensibilities were sharpened; little theaters were opened all over the country and produced plays which shed a fresh and liberating influence upon ten thousand stagnant lives. Life began to imitate art; in remotest Calvinist corners a new humaneness brightened dark faces and eased sullen conflicts. The new theater would have been a memorable phenomenon in the history of our civilization even though it had produced no single playwright.

But it did produce playwrights. It produced Eugene O'Neill who, by virtue of his power of creative development has his place in the flowering period of national expression; it produced Susan Glaspell who definitely belongs to the period of the beginnings of the American theater, who sums up in her work all the qualities and trends of those early years. She is the Puritan struggling toward freedom, toward unaccustomed expression. The life in her one-act plays, with which the new theater began, is strong but never rich. In truth, it is a thin life. Only it is thin not like a wisp of straw but like a tongue of flame. She is morbidly frugal in expression, but nakedly candid in substance. Her form and, more specifically, her dialogue, have something of the helplessness and the numb pathos of "the twisted things that grow in unfavoring places" which employ her imagination. She is a dramatist a little afraid of speech. Her dialogue is so spare that it often becomes arid. The bleak farmsteads of Iowa, the stagnant villages of New England touched her work with penury and chill. She wants to speak out and to let her people speak out. But neither she nor they can conquer a sense that intimate or vigorous expression is a little shameless. To uncover one's soul seems, in these plays, almost like uncovering one's body. Behind Miss Glaspell's hardihood of thought hovered the fear and self-torment of the Puritan. She was never quite spontaneous and unconscious and free, never the unquestioning servant of her art. She brooded and tortured herself and weighed the issues of expression. Thus the fault of her early one-act tragedies was an insufficiency of actual speech. Somewhere in every drama words must ring out. One ached in her plays for something to release the dumbness, complete the crisis, and drive the tragic situation home. Yet these plays were, except for O'Neill's, the first American plays that belonged to dramatic literature and not to the false and tawdry artifice of the uncreative theater. Their importance remains great and greater still the importance of Miss Glaspell's three full-length plays: "Bernice," "Inheritors," "The Verge."

The surface of "Bernice," like that of the one-act tragedies, is delicate and hushed. But beneath that surface is the intense struggle of rending forces. Bernice is dead, but a drama sets in that grows from her last words to her old servant and it is a drama that moves and stirs and transforms. There is hardly the waving of a curtain in those quiet rooms. Yet the dying woman's words are seen to have been a creative and dramatic act. Through a bright hard window one watches people in a house of mourning. They stand or sit or talk haltingly as people do at such times. Nothing is done. Yet everything happens—death and life and a new birth. The second of the three plays "Inheritors" left the hushed privacies of life and stepped stirringly into the forum of the national life. It is a perfect play no more than Hauptmann's "Before Dawn." It is the first American play in which a strong intellect and a ripe artistic nature grasped and set forth in human terms the central tradition and most burning problem of the national life quite justly and scrupulously, equally without acrimony and compromise. The American drama had not shown then and has scarcely shown since anything comparable to the delineation of the three generations of authentic American libertarians in "Inheritors" nor anything comparable to Miss Glaspell's dramatic projection of the decadence of the great tradition of American idealism nor anything so stirring in permanent dramatic force and fire as the beautifully credible fact that once more in a mere girl, inheritor of the spirit of both the pioneer and the continental revolutionary of 1848, there flamed up an inner purity of soul that prompts her to resist the evil ways and days upon which her civilization has fallen and to go forth to certain martyrdom rather than consent to the moral disintegration of both her country and her kin. "Inheritors," moreover, was more than a stirring play; it was in its day and date, a deed of national import. While Broadway blazed and buzzed, both history and literature were being made on MacDougal Street.

In "The Verge" Miss Glaspell blended the mood of "Bernice" with the thematic material of "Inheritors" and wrote a play concerning the eternal ways and difficulties of the human spirit. Had her art been even less accomplished than it was, her play would have marked an epoch in the history of the American theater. For to that theater such themes and motives as she used would before her have seemed utterly inconceivable, would have seemed the babble of the mad. She allied our theater to that of Hebbel and Hauptmann. Her successors have not been many. She said in dramatic form things profound and prophetic. She told us that want and disease and such crimes as the law reaches are not the only sources of pain in the world. There are people whom tyranny wounds, and the unreason that rules the world and the stagnancy in the minds of men. And these things wound and bruise them not only at moments of voluntary withdrawal and reflection, but in every hour. In the simplest conversations in their own households they feel, like Susan Glaspell's Claire Archer, that they are being nailed upon a cross of words. Like her they fear, perhaps above all, the "betterness" of things. For in that "betterness" they see unerringly only the old qualities and unhopeful methods and gestures more glaringly revealed. They do indeed yearn so for "otherness" that at moments of supreme despair, standing upon that uttermost verge of perception where the substitution of words for things and of formulæ for qualities burns with a bitter brightness in their brain, they truly wonder whether in that beyond of insanity there may not be a cure for that mad thing which people call sanity. . . . There is nothing didactic or polemical about "The Verge." Had there been it would have seemed more penetrable to many when they first heard it. Claire meets the eternal cowardice, the eternal herd babble in her husband, her sister, her daughter. Whether they stay at home or go to the ends of the earth, whether they brood in towers or hurry in streets, they see, feel, experience nothing of their own, nothing that expresses a separate relation between themselves and the universe. Between them and it is a veil of false words and lying formularies. Thus not even the normal sanity of people is a sanity at first hand. At any beyond they shudder as at the edge of monstrous chasms. How then can Claire, who stands on the verge of such a beyond of experience, not be insane? They are sure of it. They summon an alienist. And since indeed her mind in its flight from their sanity knocks at so fatal a door and finds it open, they are, by a supreme irony, confirmed and justified. That catastrophe is profound and may be rendered still clearer by another figure. The adventurer into the beyond sees his road and his goal. His fellows descry him solitary upon the verge. The terror of change seizes upon them—the terror that becomes hatred. Their cries deafen him, the dust of their stampede blinds him, stones wound him. He no longer sees the road or the goal. He loses way and vision. He is confused and sick in soul and blunders into madness or excess. The tragic guilt is where it always is—with the herd, with pursuit, with force, with the ax, the dagger, the cord. It is never with him who has sought the bridge, nourished life, loosened bonds. . . .

I have dwelt upon these plays of Susan Glaspell not only because they were profoundly significant for their day. Their significance remains. Their psychological, their creative structure is a thing apart. A libertarian mysticism inspires them, a fresh and inimitably American quality, the very essence of that rebellion of the children of the Puritans against their forbears and their forbears' folk-ways, which is the most notable as well as the most hopeful mark of the entire period. They shot beyond all other isolated attempts of the period

397

to renew the delineation of American life through the medium of the drama; beyond the compassionate naturalism of Dreiser's "The Hand of the Potter" or the stripped imitation of nature of Lewis Beach's "The Square Peg," or the acrid ironies, never holding out quite to the end of Gilbert Emery's "The Hero" and "Tarnished" or the fancy not without charm of Stuart Walker's "Jonathan Makes a Wish" or the few once promising comedies of George Kaufman and Marc Connelly, or the humorous realism of Zona Gale's "Miss Lulu Bett." Nor have later years revealed more fruitful methods in spite of brilliant and pertinent plays, isolated plays once more, such as the "What Price Glory" of Maxwell Anderson and Laurence Stallings or the picturesque and moving "Green Pastures" of Marc Connelly. Susan Glaspell was followed by Eugene O'Neill. The rest was silence; the rest is silence still. The Provincetown Players dispersed.

The Theatre Guild, soundly and even brilliantly established, was impelled to share in the new art that seemed, briefly, but magnificently, to have followed the war—the new art of the unconditional human cry against an evil and for a better world, an art-form, brief of life, as has since been seen, which could not stop to describe but strove to fling upon the scene symbolic visions that were to sum up whole histories, cosmogonies, moralities. Expressionism was in the air. None could escape it, however ignorant of the German originals. Eugene O'Neill wrote "The Emperor Jones" and "The Hairy Ape" and John Howard Lawson experimented with the form in "Roger Bloomer." The Guild imported expressionism first in the popularized and slightly cheapened form of Molnar's "Liliom"; later the Guild produced authentic examples: Georg Kaiser's "From Morn till Midnight," Ernst Toller's "Masse Mensch," and later still the "Goat-Song" of Franz Werfel. One American playwright, known hitherto chiefly for the authorship of a clever melodrama, found his true medium in the form of expressionism. Elmer Rice wrote and the Guild produced "The Adding Machine." It may be that the one vital reproach to be addressed to the Guild is that it retarded the development of one of the most important of American dramatists by not producing Rice's succeeding plays "Life is Real" and "The Subway" and thus set him upon that easier way which culminated recently in the elegant New York City topicalness, essential insignificance and resounding success of "Street Scene."

In 1923 these things lay in the future; "The Adding Machine" was seen to be not only a brilliant achievement in itself; it, too, from another angle, summed up, as did the plays of Susan Glaspell, the revolt and despair and so, by implication, the idealism and the hope of those years. The play, moreover, had that rarest quality, coherence and completeness. There were no holes in its roof. It gave, then, and still gives on reading the pleasure of both poetry and science, the warm, desperate beauty of life, the icy delight of mathematics. What Mr. Rice had to say was not new; it was not a thing that an artist could keep repeating. But it was, within the framework of the development of forms and so the development of life and civilization in America, immensely pertinent and deeply stirring. This particular world of ours, Elmer Rice told us in the play, deliberately hides or chokes with dust and ashes the very sources of human life. It has made fetishes of ugliness and monotony and intolerance. It has given to these fetishes high-sounding names. It is wedded to denial and has made a pact with death. From the intolerable repressions of Mr. Zero's life flares one explosion of the nerves. But it is an explosion of the sickened nerves only. Slavery is in the man's soul. He is, in reality, doomed to add figures, doomed to chant in unison the pack-formulæ. He cannot stay in the Elysian Fields with Swift and Rabelais. He cannot hear the music which is the music of life. The place is not respectable. It is no place for him. He "beats it"—beats it back to an eternal adding machine, back finally to an earth where slavery is his eternal portion and hope an ironic delusion. But this very theme and its treatment, to which the themes and treatments of "Life is Real" and "The Subway" are very closely allied, marks a barrenness which has, alas, been Elmer Rice's portion. Complete moral nihilism, as we shall see again and again, is in its own character crippling and unproductive. If one thoroughly believes that the universe is the kind of universe projected in "The Adding Machine," one has evidently, there being in the sound old phrase neither God nor hope in the world, no possible inner faith on which to base a creative act or found a creative development; one can still manufacture supremely clever and elegant amusement for a world of fools; one cannot look into one's heart and write. For the heart is determined to be empty. The failure of the Guild to develop dramatic artists and the failure of John Howard Lawson and Arthur Richman and of Elmer Rice, the most gifted of the group,

to develop creatively is due in large part to that moral nihilism of assimilatory Jewry which, blending with the American moral nihilism of what may be drastically but not impertinently called the "gin age," has blighted so many talents
in the course of the years. In Dreiser's "The Hand of the
Potter" there is at least his immense human tenderness;
Miss Glaspell had enough metaphysical stamina and disdain of success to produce a small but coherent body of
dramatic work. The new stages and the new playwrights
plowed up the soil of art and of life and changed the spiritual scene of America. But of all their activity only fragments remain, brilliant but barren fragments, save for the
work, with all its shortcomings, of one man, of Eugene
O'Neill, the single member of that group who had not only
art and knowledge, but that long persistent patience of
Goethe's sovereign definition:

> Nicht Kunst und Wissenschaft allein,
> Geduld muss bei der Sache sein.

V

Formal revolt came last in the art of fiction. The novel
was, generally speaking, content to embody new experiences
and fresh perceptions in that eternal mood of narrative
which has not changed greatly since the stories of Esther
and of Ruth and the tale of the fate and adventures of
Odysseus. Nor have the innovators of form in fiction yet
produced any clearly memorable work. But definite talents
that cannot be neglected arose within the ranks of the innovators and these have been quite recently followed by
a group of still other talents, closely allied to those of the

early nineteen hundred and twenties and the movement in its entirety is a marked feature of the literary landscape of our time.

Of outer influences upon the innovations in the art of fiction, I am unwilling to make much. The *Zeitgeist* has a great habit of stirring simultaneously in many quarters. The spiritual rebellions that followed the war, the gradual dissemination of the chief concepts of Freud probably met simultaneously in many expressive minds. It is, nevertheless, worth remarking that by the end of 1919 Mr. A. A. Knopf had published four volumes of the work of Dorothy M. Richardson in America and that, in the course of 1922, copies of "Ulysses" by James Joyce were being rather furtively circulated. It is at least equally important to mark the fact that Evelyn Scott's "The Narrow House" and Ben Hecht's "Erik Dorn" both appeared in 1921 and Waldo Frank's "Rahab" in 1922. Mr. Hecht did not continue his experiments in disorderly and violent notations, and the innovation in novelistic form may be studied in the works of Evelyn Scott, a talent of a very high order, and of Waldo Frank, of whose earnestness and theoretic profundity, at least, there can be no doubt.

The marks of the new fiction were and still are quite definite: they proceed from a common cause—the abandoning of the belief in objectivity, which had hitherto been both the substance and the soul of narrative. Instead of rendering objects these novelists render the effect of objects upon consciousness alone. They forgot, I might as well add at once, that the characters whose sensory perceptions they chronicled still remained objective to *them* and that hence

402

they had still to stick to objectivity in fact while abandoning it in method and by theory. Granting them, however, their method, the criticism had then to be made and remains to be made of their successors that the impressions of objects as rendered by them were of a constant and incredible violence. "The slant of red mouths opened laughters," Mr. Hecht wrote. Mr. Frank wrote: "The gas-jet she lit stood on the whitewashed wall, made it orange, made shadow of bureau and chair stand stiff like marionettes . . . stiffly agile . . . upon the orange glare." Evelyn Scott has much more sobriety and hence much more truth. For the fact is that objects affect us thus only in moments of extreme spiritual perturbation and to represent such perceptions as habitual is to turn life into phantasmagoria. This constant effect of phantasmagoria and of turbulence without depth is, in fact, the final effect of all of Waldo Frank's fictions: "Rahab" and "City Block," "Holiday" and Chalk Face." Their lack of creative tranquillity—a tranquillity at the core of the delineations in literature of maddest violence and deadliest tragedy—and their lack of plasticity are nerve-racking. The shredded prose glints and glitters, leaps and slides, cries and vociferates. There remain confused and tortured images. The mind has not been nourished nor the heart touched. It helps one very little that one is in agreement with many of Mr. Frank's critical pronouncements nor that one is happy to acknowledge the fruitfulness of many of his ideas. His fiction has none of the effects of fiction which still today the mind craves. Concerning the future we are not informed. We do know that the effects demanded of literature have not changed in their *essence* from Isaiah and Euripides to, let us say, Dreiser and Shaw. . . .

The abandonment of objectivity went to greater lengths, to the length, as is universally known, of chronicling only the stream of consciousness as it flows or is supposed to flow. The reason assigned was a most excellent one. The stream of consciousness is all we know; into that stream fall images as into a mirror and of these images we build a world. But we do indeed build a world of these images. We build both empires and histories and religions and philosophies. And that is the truth which the innovators have neglected. They leave the images alone. Mankind does not and in not leaving them alone is our essential life. . . . The analogy which was present to many of the innovators was that of the analytical situation. It is a false analogy, since the analytical situation has to be induced by the therapeutist by persuading the patient to discontinue the habits of censorship and reflection, of spiritual and intellectual guidance which constitute the habitual and normal life of consciousness. Nor does any analyst dream of reducing his patients permanently to the idiocy of mere unguided association chains. This is a temporary device for tapping the subconscious; like every therapeutic device it is abnormal and is suspended so soon as the treatment ends. It is precisely the new psychology—the *Tiefenpsychologie*—that has revealed the power of primordial guilt-feeling, the rigidness of inner censorship, the inescapableness of the heritage of the moral life. . . . The innovators in fiction and their successors sought to eliminate all these fiery realities or to reduce them to a minimum. From the stream of consciousness they ex-

404

cluded and still largely exclude the activities of the mind, the sensibilities of the heart. This exclusion is, in their work, a convention far more rigid than the conventions they rebelled against; as a symbol their convention is falser than the symbolic conventions they sought to replace. For though it is true that the stream of consciousness is uninterrupted, it is also true that the stream of sensory perceptions has its ebb. There are moments, there are hours in which we measurably exclude the visible and tangible world and turn in upon ourselves for reflection and meditation upon that stream of consciousness which constitutes the interior life. We recollect ourselves and survey our fate and make for ourselves just such a synthesis of our personal adventure in mortality as the highest art seeks to make of the earthly adventure of the whole race. . . . In such hours and not in such hours alone the humblest use their minds. Not that the human mind is anything to brag of; it makes a continuous hash of civilization; to speak of the horse sense of most people in this world is to insult a noble and useful animal. But the human mind exists and functions; when it functions well it is the source of any hope we have. But it always functions somehow. Nothing is so common and widespread as the making of judgments. Men at their crudest are not without principles of action. Ah, if only they were! Because the principles of the majority of men are mean and superstitious and barbarous. But there is no endless stream of sensation and revery flowing through the consciousness of these gentlemen. They stop the stream. They put their foot down. They do what they call thinking. They pass moral judgments. They live, in their own conceit, in a rational and ordered

405

universe. They mean to keep it so, even if they have to go on lynching-bees.

The innovators in fiction missed both the terror and the pathos of this fact. Man is, after his queer fashion, a reflective and a moral being. He does not live in a mental void. His ideas are, as a rule, phantoms and fears and no true ideas at all. But he thinks they are ideas; he thinks he thinks and is convinced that he governs his life by that thinking. To exclude that consideration and that fact is to exclude half of life and the groundwork of life. . . . The other half of life the innovators also sought to exclude as their successors are still, in their new "hard-boiled" manner, excluding—the sensibilities and affections of the heart. There was a just rebellion in the new fiction against custom and its rancors. So its characters were delineated as living freely. But they did not, in fact, live in creative freedom; they lived with an aimless fluidity dictated only by their shifting moods; they were represented as having exchanged a prison-house of custom and dead morals for one of flesh and nerves. The affections were represented as played out, useless as stage-coaches. To be civilized was to live by one's passions and one's nerves alone. Such was then as it has not ceased to be the sterile delusion of certain among the young and the self-consciously sophisticated. With this result, that none of these writers have delineated the passions either strongly or justly, but tepidly and tamely. A mere drifting with impulse may produce a moment of external violence. The strength and glory and terror of passion come from its being implicated with the higher nerve-centers, the whole stream of ancestral memories, with pieties, agonies, exaltations old and forever new as the heart of man itself. No wonder that the fictions of Mr. Frank and even of Mrs. Scott missed fire. Having, on principle and by the new convention no fire within, how could they kindle it in others?

What was the ultimate reason for these innovations in form which have continued to flow in a thin but visible stream, banked for several years in the Parisian magazine *transition*? The reason, which must continue from now on to occur in this study like a Wagnerian *Leit-motif*, is like all ultimate reasons a metaphysical one. The World War left or seemed to leave all the historical values hopelessly discredited. But the generation that felt and feels this moral and metaphysical chaos most strongly has had no passion toward and no will toward new values and has collapsed in that void of nihilism which Nietzsche foretold and diagnosed long ago as involving a necessary paralysis of the creative will and function. We communicate by implying values precisely as we live the practical life by some inner guidance upon some principle however tentative of action. He who has no principle of action would wholly desist from action and die, like the ass in the fable, which starved to death because it could not decide between the bundle of hay at its right and that at its left. Liberty means a new principle of action; it does not mean none. Thus communication implies values, because meaning implies values. Let the values be as new, as revolutionary, even as mad and perverse as you like. The absence of values, the denial that there are values lead to silence or to gibberish. I come back to a phrase used before: the meaninglessness of the later verse of so gifted a poet as E. E. Cummings, whose "Tulips and

Chimneys" of 1923 had a neo-Keatsian wealth and charm, is not a literary phenomenon; it is a mark of metaphysical despair. This despair is a despair of the meaning of meaning, of any attainable meaning, of the significance of anything that can be said. Nihilism has no principle of life. I am not surprised at the absence of creative development in Elmer Rice or Waldo Frank; I am not surprised at T. S. Eliot's seeking a source of values and so of energy in Anglo-Catholicism; I am not surprised at the pitiful enough antics of the new Humanists. Creation no less than procreation is conditioned in a principle of life and the principle of life of creation is ultimately and rightly understood religion: values and human bindings in the name of values that must inspire and mold expression. . . . Waldo Frank saw this long ago in connection with criticism. "In periods of basic cultural transition the criticism that does not start out from metaphysics and a true understanding of religious experience is idle, irrelevant, impotent and anti-social." Neither he nor any of the innovators have carried this cognition over actively into the field of life and creative activity.

The first works of Evelyn Scott alone remain of the earlier revolt in fiction. By her cold acuteness of psychological observation, by her peering exactness of physical vision she succeeded in giving "The Narrow House" and "Narcissus" and, above all, the autobiographical "Escapade" a hardness of surface that seems to protect these three books from decay. The books are not beautiful nor rich nor really profound. But they have an intellectual lucidity and a very partial but within its limits powerful and bitter moral vision that keeps them fresh and memorable. This is especially true of "Escapade," which I believe to be the one piece of permanent literature produced by the movement and the group. It is the record of an heroic adventure unheroically told, of astonishing fortitude unmindful of itself, of a martyrdom that is full of disdain for the world and whose impressiveness must be inferred. This adventure, moreover, had for its scene not only Brazil, but the Brazil of the common people—a place of poisonous beasts, poisonous diseases, heat, stench, ordure. A place, too, of unbearably sharp colors. And since Evelyn Scott is immensely sensitive to color and the moods of color, the picture she gives of the scenes amid which her high adventure was lived has an iridescence like that of fiery death and glittering decay. The book, moreover, both by this extreme acuteness of vision, this intense cold literary skill and also by its convention of *morbidezza*, of the necessary imprisonment of a noble spirit in mere sophistication, is a completely adequate chronicle of moods and people and scenes of which the influence upon American culture is definite and still potent. "Escapade" is the minor classic of the post-war mood of American moral radicalism: just, acute, cold, uncompromising, sterile. . . . Greenwich Village culminated and perished thus. . . .

The new fiction in its varying moods touched seasoned practitioners here and there. First in its sound mood of realistic frankness and ironic humor it inspired Zona Gale to abandon "Friendship Village" and write "Miss Lulu Bett"; next came the mood of exaggerated perceptual notation and inner monologue and Miss Gale wrote "Faint Perfume." This was a good example of the withdrawal of a novelist into that land of psychological wraiths where people neither eat nor trade nor kiss but merely whet their insight upon the processes that have these names. In this land, as in no land of earth, all is sinuousness and indirectness, tinge is substituted for color and blur for form and perceptiveness for passion. Instead of breadth and richness there is glint and evanescent aroma. Miss Gale is a very tender spirit; she had none of Evelyn Scott's cold fierceness. The sudden change in her work—taking her as a useful example—completes the picture of innovation in the novel for this first period.

VI

The intellectual stir of the war and post-war years, marked first by hope and glow and next by coldness and despair but still immensely alive compared to the stagnancy in American culture which had preceded—this stir was felt by talents here and there, the very briefness of whose flowering made them more characteristic for this precise moment in our history than the richer creative natures who built up their work through the years. Nor was this all. Veterans were encouraged to expression in America, like the eminent Yiddish publicist Abraham Cahan, whose moving and largely wrought narrative, "The Rise of David Levinsky," will some day obtain the position given to less sober and more glittering books; the impulse toward the creative treatment of the American scene was felt by those in whom it had not before arisen and in whom it did not last and single books of true excellence were produced, like "Dust" by Mr. and Mrs. Haldeman-Julius, like "Zell" by Henry Aikman. New subjects treated with a new freedom gave a fresh note to the work of already mature personalities, such as one finds in "6 Jayne Street" by Mary Austin. Youth was most deeply stirred, of course, and autobiographical novels of youth's fires and rebellions abounded. One of the most interesting of these was "The Outbound Road" by Arnold Mulder and for an hour one hoped for a novelist of the Dutch in America; the most famous and justly so was "This Side of Paradise" by F. Scott Fitzgerald, which contained, among other excellencies, an admirable diagnosis of the then practice of conventional novelists in America, which contained both eloquence and poetry and that creative ebullition, still unchecked and undisciplined, which has always belonged to the high promise of youth. The book was quite without intellectual center. That, too, was a proper mark of youth. But the author's gifts seemed to have the right amplitude of high promise and much in his pages was truly brave and beautiful. Nothing, unluckily followed, despite much ability and effort—nothing that was not arid and artificial; nothing in Fitzgerald's work ever caught again even an echo of that early rapture. Nor did Mary Borden redeem the brilliant promise of "The Romantic Woman," nor did still others sustain the tentative of their first flights. A curious study will some day be written concerning first novels and first plays and first volumes of verse published in America between 1914 and 1923. It will be a study full of pathos but rich in significance. It will illustrate the background of experience and experimentation of the beginnings of the period of national expression. And I imagine that he who makes this study will be impelled to make an anthology of poems and of scenes from plays and scenes from novels and that this book, never rising to any great height, will yet be a quite beautiful book and an inimitably American book and that it will tell the competent reader more about America and the human soul in America than the tomes of historians. . . .

There remains one figure, sign and symbol of those brief, heroic pitiful years, the figure of Floyd Dell. He sums up and illustrates all that has here been said, all I have attempted to delineate of that "little renaissance"—the phrase is Carl Van Doren's—in life and letters which, little as it was, has changed the cultural aspect of America. It was in 1914 that Floyd Dell came from newspaper work in Chicago to New York and joined the staff of "The Masses" and took up his abode in Greenwich Village. He was already full-fledged radical, poet and stylist. He found the glory of love and the other glory of resisting not without danger the disastrous course of a mad world. And under the sway of these supreme experiences he wrote month after month poems in "The Masses," especially a group of sonnets, which strike home to the center of both poetry and thought and those incisive, scrupulous, tight-girdled essays which were both tonic and release to all the best spirits of the time. Conscious perhaps that his experiences were typical experiences of his age and country he proceeded to embody them in fictions which would be recognizably autobiographical even without the amiable confirmation in Harry Hansen's "Midwest Portraits." Thus Dell published "Moon Calf" in 1920 and "The Briery Bush" in 1921. And this record of a poet and a recusant during those crucial years has not only grace and insight and the true colors of things

412

and thoughts and passions but it is richly peopled with the characteristic souls of those striving, aspiring days, from which so many changes have come. It has both individual and representative value; it has beauty both in itself and as a symbol. Together with its author's poems and essays it constitutes a true possession both of American letters and of American life. Once more in 1923 Floyd Dell appeared with "Janet March," which again has not only artistic but historic significance in that it recorded authentically and well the highest point of the American feminist movement, which like all the movements of those years though generous and high, was too regardless of perdurable human qualities and needs not to change and become wholly transformed within a brief space of time. Perhaps even then there was no girl quite like Janet March—so wholly, so magnificently released from superstition, moralistic terror, ungenerous tenacity and social confusion. Perhaps there never was; perhaps there never—in view of certain fundamental biological and social needs—could or even should have been such an one as she. But it was Floyd Dell who summed up the hopes, brave if extravagant and the ideals, beautiful if a little ungrounded, of those years. . . . Meanwhile "The Masses" had been succeeded by "The Liberator"; the heroic days in which Floyd Dell and Art Young and Max Eastman and their friends were tried on the charge of "conspiracy to obstruct recruiting and enlistment" had sunk into the past; Greenwich Village was no more and the Provincetown Players had given Eugene O'Neill to Broadway. Reaction and peace and thick prosperity ruled the American world. Of these forces the "Liberator" died in 1924. Dawn was over. There came the dust and heat of noon. And the spirits who had lived and created only because they were of that dawn either fell silent or addressed themselves to the harmless but wholly different task of making a living by writing. To Floyd Dell, however, it had been given before that time not only to live but to leave a record of the life of those years, during which for the first time experience and expression were definitely and consciously integrated in America, years which therefore laid the foundations for a free and continuous creative activity. The artist in America was at last reasonably free to function and reasonably certain to gain a hearing as one impelled to creative expression rather than as a mere entertainer or a homilist.

BOOK TEN

The Great Critical Debate

I

In the history of American civilization there is no more important event than the rise of the critical spirit during that quarter of a century between the publication of the first volume of Paul Elmer More's Shelburne Essays in 1904 and that of Joseph Wood Krutch's "The Modern Temper" in 1929. These names and books and the associations they evoke in even the moderately literate suffice to prove how deep, how to the very core of man's life and thought, criticism cuts. In every critical reaction toward art or toward life, whether articulate or not, the whole man is involved. For that man is the necessary bearer within the varied strata of the self, first, of the experience of the race, next, of his folk and finally of his personality; in him are embodied immemorial traditions and instincts, religions and philosophies; his consciousness has been molded by age-long recollections and aspirations and comes thus weighted and freighted to meet his individual fate and date and world.

415

His most casual "I like" or "I do not like," "I approve" or "I detest," if properly traced to its ultimate sources, is intertwined with the very roots of human experience which is not, for such a being as man, naked and unrelated experience, as it seems to be in the animals, but experience reacted upon by spirit and issuing thus in love, religion, philosophy, in poetry and prose, in painting and music, in superstition and folk-ways, in social bindings and releases, in science and in ethics. These are the contents of human experience within which the raw facts are instantly transmuted into *values* by the inevitable action of the human spirit. Criticism is the disengaging and weighing of these values into which men transmute their experience and from which alone experience derives both its *meaning* and its *form*. Hence the contention between two first-rate critics is more significant than the struggle between armies with banners. For what they are contending about so soon as they rise above the merely philological level is nothing less than the structure of the universe, the nature of man, the meaning of life, the right goal of all thought and the proper aim of all endeavor. The so-called æsthete or defender of "pure" art or "pure" poetry does not differ in essence from his fellows. Only his reaction toward the totality of human experience and its inherent values is one of negation, feebleness and despair. He is like a sick or feeble-witted child which, cut off from both knowledge and intelligent recreation, pretends that the paper-dolls upon its counterpane are best, since no knowledge is worth acquiring and no game worth playing. . . .

From this indication of the nature of criticism it follows

at once that criticism can never be popular, since most men are unwilling to disengage and discuss the values by which they live but that, on the other hand, the rise of the critical spirit within a given civilization is a symptom of health and of maturity. Such it has undoubtedly been in contemporary America. For the critical spirit had hitherto been no force in American life. Except for Emerson's quite sovereign aphorisms scattered thickly in his essay on "The Poet," which no one evidently had understood, much less heeded, American criticism even in quite sensible pages by Howells and quite incisive ones by Henry James had always been remote in temper and hushed in tone. Nor, until quite recent times, had there been any organ of critical thought through which an important and homogeneous audience could be addressed. Such organs came into existence when "The New Republic" was founded in 1914, when Oswald Garrison Villard detached "The Nation" from the "Evening Post" in 1918, when Albert Nock and Francis Neilson started "The Freeman" on its too brief career in 1920, when toward the end of the period Henry Mencken founded "The American Mercury" in 1924. But these organs did not suffice for the expression of the critical spirit. The weeklies were limited by considerations of space and "The Mercury" more severely limited by Mencken's nihilistic dictatorship. And thus there appeared as a curious and characteristic American phenomenon volumes in which critical groups expressed their more or less fiery reaction to both life and letters, to folk-ways and politics, to religion and philosophy, to the humors and tragedies of the American scene. Such were "Civilization in the United States by

417

Thirty Americans," edited by Harold Stearns in 1922, "These United States," edited by Ernest Gruening in 1923, "Our Changing Morality," edited by Freda Kirchwey in 1924, such, finally, is "Humanism and America," edited by Norman Foerster in 1930. The contributions to these volumes vary immensely in seriousness and quality. They sink very low and rarely rise very high. What made all the volumes significant for, at least, their day and date, was the recognition of every contributor to every volume that criticism, whether of art, letters, morals, politics or thought is a criticism of values. Thus these volumes dealt, whether well or ill, at least with such fundamentals as an older America had generally refused to face and to discuss at all. America, in the phrase of Van Wyck Brooks, was coming of age.

II

It is security that eliminates or smothers the critical spirit. This was, at least, profoundly true of America where no one had spontaneously either the elegant intellectual curiosity of the French critic nor the truth-seeking ardor of the German *Geisteswissenschaftler*. There was no chance of our suddenly having either a Rémy de Gourmont or a Georg Simmel. The elder critics, of whom Randolph Bourne was soon to write with such quiet incisiveness in his "History of a Literary Radical," did not doubt that literature was a decorous illustration of a system of ethics, manners and economics fixed and frozen for all time somewhere in England, sometime in the nineteenth century. In that faith Hamilton Wright Mabie and Brander Matthews died; in that faith aged survivors of that period still live. But there were two critics in America who held their beliefs upon terms far less facile and rosy and holding them thus, they were the first to perceive a chill wind from a bleaker world blowing upon their comfortable certainties. Clayton Hamilton was at ease in Zion. Irving Babbitt and Paul Elmer More were not. They felt that the old order was changing; they issued warnings before warnings seemed of need or use to their duller colleagues. It is they who, contrary to the common notion, started the great critical debate in modern American literature. The first volume of More's Shelburne Essays appeared in 1904 and Irving Babbitt's "The New Laocoön" in 1910; from 1909 to 1914 Mr. More was editor of "The Nation"; in that capacity he warned a young reviewer not to be too "romantic" and when the young reviewer published his first novel strongly deprecated its realistic details, though approving its general tendency. . . .

But we may mark 1910 as the year in which the fundamental critical debate definitely arose. For in that year appeared not only "The New Laocoön" but Joel Elias Spingarn delivered at Columbia his famous lecture on "The New Criticism." Babbitt announced the fundamentals of both the fears and the credo of his school. "Society," he wrote, "is plainly suffering from a lack rather than a superabundance of discipline and restraint." And further: "Man grows in perfection . . . in almost direct ratio to his growth in restraint and self-control." To a foreign observer these statements might seem, though neither profound nor very discerning, yet truisms of a harmless sort. They could not appear so to America, above all, not to the youth of America. For that youth knew with a dreadful certainty that

Babbitt did not mean that limitation within a self-imposed law of being which, as Goethe told us long ago, alone reveals the master and alone can give us freedom. Babbitt, one knew, meant neither self-restraint nor self-control, but the uncritical subordination of the self under that neo-Calvinism in both art and morals which had made so cruel a thing of American life and had come near to striking a great nation with complete creative paralysis. So far the moralist. In his critical function Babbitt, despite his great learning and his reflective temper, permitted himself to talk nonsense. Of realism he said that it is "art without selection" which is a *contradictio in terminis* and illustrates at once the shocking inexactness of which the conservatives, despite their philosophic pretensions, have always been guilty. Babbitt meant that the realist chooses subjects and illustrates them by a selection of details, neither of which are to his liking. But since the Harvard professor was sworn to oppose impressionism and all its ways, he gave his purely personal opinion the outer form of a philosophic maxim. Similarly he complains that in modern literature "expression triumphs over form," another of these spurious philosophic formulæ, seeing that form is the body or embodiment of artistic expression. It is not clothes but flesh. So much the briefest self-examination should have taught even an academic critic who himself cannot imagine as the expression of his personality any opinions but those he has come to hold embodied in any but the prose form which he actually masters.

It was this utter remoteness of academic criticism from the plain facts of the creative process which caused the delight and the sense of liberation with which Joel Elias Spingarn's lecture was welcomed. What many had thought and known was now expressed. Nor was this all. The revolt came from within the academic ranks. Spingarn's accomplishment and learning could be denied by none. It cleared the murky air to have it announced that "every work of art is a spiritual creation governed by its own laws," and that poets "express themselves, and this expression is their only form." "All art is lyrical," Spingarn truly declared and "every poet reëxpresses the universe in his own way." It was particularly important to have it explained in America that style is not an embellishment but is, in fact, "the poet's individual vision of reality, 'the music of his whole manner of being.'" Here were the great truths found by Goethe and Emerson rephrased for contemporary use. Unfortunately Spingarn did not end there. He had studied under Benedetto Croce and he proceeded to undermine all that he had said by adding the theory of the Italian to the effect that, though art is expression, it is the expression of nothing in particular in a vacuum. It sounded extremely handsome and refreshing when Spingarn wrote: "It is not the function of poetry to further any moral or social cause, any more than it is the function of bridge-building to further the cause of Esperanto," and the form of the statement, which is thoroughly sophistical, made a flat denial impossible. It is not, indeed, the *function* of poetry to further any cause. But creative literature is the expression of the total personality; it is important and beautiful and great in proportion to the depth and richness and spiritual energy of the creative personality and hence to suggest that the work

421

of Euripides and Dante, of Milton and Goethe, even of Shelley and Whitman is not the expression of the poets' moral and metaphysical being, but only of an abstract æsthetic functioning—to suggest that was factually and intellectually quite on the level of Babbitt's "art without selection" or "expression triumphs over form." An empty æstheticism was opposed to an empty moralism.

The year, it must be remembered, was 1910; there was no open controversy between Babbitt and Spingarn; the whole critical debate in modern America has been rooted too profoundly in ultimate antagonisms to permit of direct debate or frank polemic. No one would, in 1910, have dreamed of attaching special significance to the fact that Babbitt, though of middle-Western birth, was a New Englander by long residence and profound attachment and that Spingarn was a New Yorker and a Jew. Both were pleading *pro domo* within the framework of America; the one was seeking to preserve the America of his fathers; the other was seeking to conquer America for his children. Had an actual debate been joined between the two, there is no doubt that, though the youth of America would have been largely on Spingarn's side, Babbitt would upon the whole have come off much better than his opponent. For Babbitt's program and philosophy, however feeble intellectually, had behind them the strength of his race and his cultural inheritance and were thus conformable to his deepest instincts, whereas Spingarn's program and philosophy were a tissue of international borrowings in which, by a psychical device as honest as it was unhappy, he caused that element to predominate which most thoroughly falsified the moral seriousness of his inheritance. . . . This debate concerning critical methods was, in other words, a debate between philosophies, cosmogonies, religions, races. It was a conflict over the future of American civilization. But few or none suspected this fact until crudely and rudely Stuart Sherman, badly attacked by war psychosis, flung it into the public's face in his volume "On Contemporary Literature" in 1917.

The fundamental debate continued during the succeeding years in such a manner as to seem no debate at all. For the two parties to it dwelt in worlds sundered from each other and remote. It is doubtful whether Henry Mencken, despite his pertinent though indiscriminate gibes at the "birchmen" in the academes, studied the "Shelburne Essays"; it is even more doubtful whether Paul Elmer More spent his leisure hours reading "The Smart Set." Each might, however, have studied the other during the pre-war years with great profit; More might have seen that a rationalization of Calvinism could not possibly meet the needs of a contemporary society; had Mencken read More's crucial volumes, "The Drift of Romanticism," 1913, and "Aristocracy and Justice," 1914, he might have perceived amid much that was perverse and a little that was repulsive, that there are elements of thought and experience against which the merriest and most brilliant nihilism forever hurls itself in vain. But neither the Calvinists nor the Nihilists—these nicknames are to be justified presently,—saw or heard each other nor, above all, knew themselves to be such. More, as he has recently complained, was thoroughly hated but little read; Mencken correctly seemed to the younger writers and thinkers of the period a liberator from foul repressions, from paralyzing restraints,

423

from tyranny and stupidity and the sheer drivel of the respectable. Nor are his services during those dark years ever to be forgotten or overlooked. His place as an intellectual liberator in American letters is secure.

Thus it is clear that in criticism, as in other departments of America's articulate life, all the major problems had arisen before the war. That catastrophe served merely to define the problems more clearly, to raise their visibility, to cause scrupulous minds consciously to examine the quality of American life and American art. Such a mind was that of Van Wyck Brooks whose "America's Coming of Age" in 1915 spoke a word of balanced and tranquil wisdom. Brooks used no very incisive phraseology; his influence has always been unhappily restricted by a want of stylistic power, but his analysis of the American cultural scene, his sensitive perception of the fact that even in the best American writing of the past one seeks in vain "a certain density, weight and richness, a certain poignancy," were used by him to clarify the central difficulty of a Calvinistic business civilization—its inability to integrate experience, which it despised, with creative expression; its failure therefore to humanize society and to provide atmosphere, bindings, relations within which either life or art could thrive or be productive. In 1918 Brooks followed up "America's Coming of Age" with "Letters and Leadership" in which more richly and soundly than before he pointed out the externality of our cultural situation, the unhappy American terror of experience, the unpracticality of the regnant critics of all schools. To American "deficiency of personal impulse, of creative will" he added the "moral absentee-mindedness" of the critics; he drew a pertinent and almost perfect picture of our plight. He was little heeded, even as later "The Freeman," whose literary editor he was, could never gain more than a few thousand readers for its combination of libertarianism and cultural insight. The extremists, Calvinists or Nihilists, foaming hundred-percenters like Sherman or blazing satirists like Mencken, filled the public scene. We shall see how this situation has continued to prevail in America to the very brink of spiritual and artistic catastrophe. Now as then angry polemics drown the voice of the purged and considerate mind.[1]

It was during the years of the war and during the years immediately succeeding it that the debate grew most furious. It was in 1918 that Irving Babbitt undertook directly to answer Spingarn's "New Criticism" of eight years before; in the same year Mencken published in "The Evening Mail" his "Criticism of Criticism of Criticism," which was reprinted the following year in the first volume of "Prejudices." Babbitt's "Rousseau and Romanticism" also appeared in 1919. Meanwhile the new weeklies, led by "The Nation," took up the battle on the side of liberalism and the temper of the country's intellectuals could be gauged by the fact that "The Weekly Review," founded to counteract the liberal weeklies, died of inanition after the briefest of careers. In the forum

[1] On this single occasion I must break the rule of not mentioning my own contributions to American letters. In this chapter, however, the picture would be falsified, were it not pointed out that I sought from 1915 on to provide a critical and philosophical *via media,* conformable both to permanent spiritual needs and the special requirements of the age in the following volumes: "The Modern Drama," 1915, "The Drama and the Stage," 1922, "The Creative Life," 1924, "Cities and Men," 1927. These volumes have met with not a little public favor; like the theoretical works of Van Wyck Brooks, they have pleased neither Calvinists nor Nihilists and have thus rarely been drawn into the critical debate.

425

of publicity the conservatives were represented chiefly by Stuart Sherman whose activity culminated in a paper called "The National Genius," which appeared in "The Atlantic Monthly" for January, 1921, and was reprinted in his "The Genius of America" in 1923. In 1920 and 1922 appeared the second and third volumes of Mencken's "Prejudices" and in 1923 Carl Van Doren's wise and well-tempered "The Roving Critic." And it is worthy of remark that all these volumes attained a popularity such as critical writing had never before attained in America nor very frequently elsewhere. It was profoundly if not always consciously understood that criticism cleaves deep and that the battle joined between, let us say Stuart Sherman and Henry Mencken was no squabble between rhetoricians, but a philosophical warfare over all that men hold dearest and over the future of our civilization itself. Hence criticism of the more narrowly literary kind was slighted, such as Brownell's feeble and wavering but not inelegant following of Sainte-Beuve or such as T. S. Eliot's remarkable and closely reasoned essays in "The Sacred Wood." There was a joy of battle in the air, for Mencken and the editors of "The Nation," among others more or less like-minded, were convinced, and quite rightly, that they were fighting against both governmental and mass repression and seeking to save for Americans those last vestiges of moral and intellectual liberty without which life is a blunder and a shame. . . . Thus and only thus can the temper of those years be rightly understood and their importance in the development of American culture estimated. But the dust of those battles has long gone with the wind; the central problems remain and beat upon the world's soul

426

with a quieter but deeper ache than ever. None can doubt that who is willing to look with an equally unprejudiced eye upon the Neo-humanists on the one hand, upon Joseph Wood Krutch's "The Modern Temper" and allied documents on the other. For as we have Norman Foerster and his group and Krutch and those younger poets who despair of all meaning in America, so have we Neo-Catholics and sur-réalistes in France, so have we National Socialists—by no means all mere rowdies and vulgarians—and a flight toward proletarian art and communist delusion in Germany. Reaction has bred reaction everywhere and extremes have begotten other extremes and liberty and reason, righteousness and tolerance have few or none to defend them. Hence I shall now examine as nearly as it is given me *sub specie æternitatis* the central conflicts of the great critical debate and the personalities, chiefly Paul Elmer More and Henry Mencken, who represent and embody them.

III

In the first volume of the new series of "Shelburne Essays," "The Demon of the Absolute," More recalls the loud controversial days during which he was "the least read and most hated author in America" and during which "the wolves" of criticism were all upon his track. He quotes a diatribe of Mencken against the conservatives in criticism. He, of course, was not omitted. "Ah no; *et tacitum vivit sub pectore vulnus.*" There is something engaging in that personal touch; there are those, however, among the wolves and there have always been, who were not unaware of the facts which, known to Paul Elmer More himself, of course, caused the wound of the injustice done him by Mencken and others, to burn so long, however quietly, in his breast. He is infinitely different from the caricature of a dull "birchman" so long imposed on large sections of the American public. He is, first of all, one of the soundest of American prose stylists. If he is heavy at times, it is with a grave and not unpleasing heaviness as of Johnson in his somber moods. But he is, despite his theoretical protestations, of his age in that, at its best, his prose has both romantic glow and romantic echo. Of Catullus, for instance he wrote as follows: "He who walked in the terrible company of Cæsar and Mamurra, of Clodius and his sister the *quadrantana*, may have dallied with the day; but under his fine linen might be felt the surface of steel, and in his hand he carried a dagger, and not a lily." Again, concerning the first great stanza of Francis Thompson's "The Hound of Heaven" he wrote this sentence: "Here, at least, thought and image, emotion and rhythm, are in liberated and mighty accord, and the result is a stanza which pulses in the memory like the sound of a bell swaying amidst a waste of obscure waters." The man who wrote these passages and very many not inferior to them is evidently a fine and sensitive artist in prose. He is, moreover, within very stringent limits, a continuously interesting and even powerful critic of letters. He is at his best in such essays as those on Wordsworth and Shelley in which he opposes measure and good sense to the too ungirdled extravagances of romantic appreciation or when, as in the essay on Tennyson, he defines the relation between Victorian prettiness and intellectual compromise. Up and down his many volumes, in addition, are numerous passages of critical appreciation which are likely long to keep both their interest of substance and their sober charm of manner. His limitation, strictly for the moment on his own ground and principles, is upon some reflection most patent in that he almost never attempts high and difficult subjects. A single paper on the theme of "Paradise Lost" and another on Shakespeare's sonnets stand quite alone. He is fond of dealing with second- and with third-rate talents. One would have expected of him a Sophocles, a Swift, a Montaigne; one is put off with Thomas Bailey Aldrich and Louisa Shore and, at best, Arthur Symons. The essay on Nietzsche in "The Drift of Romanticism" is an exception. But one needs, surely, to be no disciple of that stormy prophet to recognize that essay to be disgracefully ignorant and prejudiced, that is to say, hopelessly uncritical. But when these large deductions have been made the volumes of Paul Elmer More still remain an impressive body of literature. Few American prose-writers have upon the whole a quality so continuously high through-out several thousand pages. Less than that it were a prejudice as unbending as his own to accord him. Nor is this quite all. That icy scholasticism of temper which he affects is often broken by a cry as of the heart and by the echo of a mystical experience, from the quality of which no man can withhold his respect. It is in all sincerity that Paul Elmer More quotes as his own the old plangent cry: *"Quaerebam quid amarem, amans amare!"* It is out of the depth of a spiritual experience beyond the reach of his most conspicuous opponents that he asks: "How can one look into the mirror of one's own life, and not perceive that the sense of something immutable and unmoved exists in some way side by side with the sense of

429

everlasting flux, that there is within us some central peace subsisting at the heart of endless agitation?"

Quotations such as these could easily be multiplied from More's writings. And it is surely not the spirit that lives in them which made him the "most hated" of American writers and set the "wolves" of criticism upon his track. Yet in his late plaint there must be something of disingenuousness or a great capacity for self-deception. For he cannot have forgotten the essays that constitute "Aristocracy and Justice" and since it was clear to the dullest that his concrete opinions issued inevitably from his conscious philosophy, he should have been prepared for attacks more searching than Mencken's humorous invective; he should have known that he was outraging the deepest sensibilities, the most ardent convictions of all who nourished any hope for the world and for mankind. That Mencken was his chief opponent was, upon the whole, his good luck. For More and Mencken are divided by racial temperament and manners rather than by ultimate conviction. More hates democracy on account of the exceeding wickedness of men's hearts; Mencken hates it no less on account of the exceeding thickness of their wits; More's ideal is a theocracy with clerical aristocrats as the rulers of mankind, Mencken's is an oligarchy of *Junkers.* More wants the populace to be obedient and go to church on Sunday morning; Mencken is willing to let the enslaved "boobs" get drunk on Saturday night. Mencken, in brief, likes European folk-ways while More clings to those of Victorian New England. Both are angry and slightly sadistic reactionaries. More likes to fancy himself in a black robe and Mencken sees himself in shining armor. . . . That was the irony of the controversial years, that libertarians gathered about Mencken who, by ultimate principle was none at all and that therefore More, consistent Calvinistic reactionary, was never met on his own ground. There was another reason that made the battle in its outward aspects a sham battle. The adversaries had no concrete common ground when it came to the substance of letters and philosophy. More had not impartially read any book written later than 1890, Mencken had read hardly any book written before that date. Both men are at once monsters of ignorance and monsters of learning. Hence More suffered in an enforced truce; his adversary gave him no opening; Mencken, not suspecting the lack of a common philosophical level which alone can render true controversy possible, deplored More's apparently pacific temper and was convinced that he had annihilated him in the superb invective reprinted in the third volume of "Prejudices." He did annihilate the Stuart Sherman of those days when he described that critic's "fundamental theory—to wit, the theory that the test of an artist is whether he hated the Kaiser in 1917, and plays his honorable part in Christian Endeavor, and prefers Coca-Cola to Scharlachberger 1911, and has taken to heart the great lesson of sex-hygiene." But satire, even satire as pertinent and stinging as this, can touch only obvious folly and stubborn dullness. It leaves a sinister but coherent moral and philosophical system somehow anchored in a racial temper almost if not wholly untouched. The proof came years later when young men calling themselves Humanists gathered about the solitary but never captured banners of Babbitt and of More. Mencken had no metaphysic to oppose to More's; therefore he never touched him; the neo-humanists are Mencken's Nemesis. More quietly sowed dragon's teeth; Mencken had none to sow. . . .

Let us return to "Aristocracy and Justice" and to More's theory of life and letters and to the content of that mystical experience of his and let us remember that the ineffable disaster brought by Calvinistic Puritanism upon the world issues from its iron division of life into a realm of pure grace and a realm of irretrievable sin; between these there must be no commerce; the reply of the soul in the realm of grace to the natural man in the realm of sin, that is, to nine-tenths of human life must be an uncomprising No. It must be the negative fiat of the famous inner check. You must not humanize, nor reclaim, nor seek to cultivate or sanctify human life; you must not seek to interpenetrate *Natur* by *Geist*, nor must you seek to save from injustice or stripes or hunger or crucifixion your fellowmen. For by doing so you show "social sympathy," you are in danger of being a mere humanitarian and seeking to "throw the blame of evil on the laws and on society" and of thus weakening "the responsibility of the individual soul to its maker and inflexible judge." No, this is no caricature. I am quoting Paul Elmer More, not garbling his text. He returned to the charge in "The Drift of Romanticism" and had the strange courage to assert that there may be observed "a direct ratio between the spread of humanitarian schemes of reform and the increase of crime and suicide." But it was in "Aristocracy and Justice" that he laid down his fundamental principles and shrank from none of their infamous consequences. He defended the breaking of the Colorado coal strike of 1914 by armies of paid bullies and spies, a method at which even Federal judges have since blushed, and declared that "to the civilized man the rights of property are more important than the right to life"; he went farther: he berated Jane Addams for laying at the door of society the moral breakdown of a child between twelve and sixteen, who found the burden of supporting a whole family greater than he could bear; he objected to Miss Addams' investigation of the connection between working-girls' starvation wages and their morals. This, Paul Elmer More declared, was "not helping the tempted to resist"; the girls should starve and use the inner check and be virtuous; in regard to that lad whose story Miss Addams told, he asserted that "with the idea of an avenging Deity and a supernatural test there disappeared also the sense of deep personal responsibility." The theory coheres. There is the realm of grace in which functions the inner check; there is the realm of sin which must be left in outer darkness and confusion, in tears and blood and dirt. You say "No" to it with the inner check and obey your masters and take what wages Mr. Rockefeller chooses to give you and remain virtuous on four dollars a week. . . . Well, no wonder that More can find no words for disaster or irregularity in the moral world but "trull" and "sordid liaison." He would have explained to the woman taken in adultery of the Gospel about the "responsibility of the individual soul to its maker and inflexible judge"; in the place of the good Samaritan he would have asked by what carelessness and weakness and failure to exercise the inner check the man had fallen among thieves. Nothing natural is to be healed or saved or made beautiful or holy. There is an "exaggeration of sex in the clothing seen in the streets."

433

Exactly. Sex must not be charming. It belongs to the realm of sin and must be defiled. Thus dirty stories are well enough. Tennyson is known to have told them and Paul Elmer More "is not displeased at this evidence of earthly coarseness in the man." . . . Sexuality arrested at the psychical stage of adolescence is frequently a contributing factor in a Manichæan philosophy. . . . Freud deals with the "bestial," according to More. . . . Briefly: Iron negative laws, representing the inner check of the realm of grace, anterior to nature and independent of it in a stringently dualistic universe, are to be promulgated by Aristotle, Irving Babbitt, and Paul Elmer More. He who does not obey these laws in the world of art is a "romanticist" or a "naturalist" and is no better than he should be. In the secular life these laws are to be enforced by strike-breakers and the threat of hell-fire. . . . We are to return, in a word, to the New England theocracy with public penance and stripes for the sinner, to a society that must be uncreative since human experience being wholly sinful must not issue in expression.

We are back with Jonathan Edwards, with a society that can have no literature save homilies and elegies on defunct clerics. Neither Babbitt nor More would, of course, consent to this *reductio ad absurdum* of their theories. Yet that reduction is not a violently unjust one. It serves, at all events, to offer the strongest possible illustration of the ancestral trend of their theories; it proves that the humanists and neo-humanists represent the last reaction of pioneer Puritanism against the reintegration of experience with expression or, in the recent phrase of George Santayana, the "genteel tradition at bay." But were this all, its importance in the history

434

of American civilization would be comparatively slight. The melancholy fact is that the theories of More and Babbitt have shown a certain endurance and have gathered new disciples in the old age of their proponents, because nothing was opposed to them except a complete nihilism—except the robust and salutary but wholly unphilosophical negations of Mencken, except the shabby worldliness of George Jean Nathan and the dolorous "wise-crackers," except, on a far higher plane, the gray and almost pathological despair of Joseph Wood Krutch.

The humanists, it must be remembered, offer certain principles which are *formally* true. It is true, as Babbitt wrote in "Rousseau and Romanticism," that "man becomes human only in so far as he exercises moral choice" and there is no objection possible to his more recent definition of humanism as "the act of selection, in the final imposition on mere multiplicity, of a scale of values." That man is a valuing animal, that he can exist humanly only by selecting moral values to which to cling and by which to live is a truth embodied in human practice from the beginning and radiantly expounded in all the works of that Friedrich Nietzsche, whom the humanists affect to despise. Why is that? Because the humanists see the world as dualistic and as static. The values they mean are the values of the seventeenth century. By choice they mean not a continuous and creative choice, but the enforced choice of Calvinism. According to them all truth was long ago discovered and is now in a frozen state. Hence their bitter and unfair hostility to a new psychology or indeed to any research, whether in literature or in science, into the facts and forces that shape man and nature and human life. According to them authoritative wisdom exists in fixed and final form; the books of life are closed; they are like that Caliph Omar who caused the Alexandrian library to be burned on the ground that if the books contradicted the Koran they were blasphemous; if they agreed they were useless. No, this is no exaggeration. In his essay on "Genius and Taste" Babbitt wrote: "To repudiate the traditional Christian and classical checks and at the same time fail to work out some new and more vital control upon impulse and temperament is to be guilty of high treason to civilization." The utter folly and reactionary rage of this statement is concentrated in the apparently harmless words "at the same time." For humanity is engaged in precisely this process of working out a more vital set of moral and spiritual values, more conformable to its true nature and present development and knowledge. It has been engaged in this task for some centuries and the task is barely begun. And the beginning of that task was necessarily the profound initial conviction that the traditional values no longer sufficed. Such is always the beginning of the search for new knowledge, new values, another and a better life. The research is then developmental and its method is by trial and error. The fiat of the humanists that nothing shall be doubted or discarded until a new thing is ready to take the place of the old would throw mankind back to the cruel stagnancy of arrested primitive tribes who have forgotten the very reason for the practice of rite and observance of taboo and like the animals go through the same gestures from generation to generation. Thus it is clear how the humanists have perverted formally correct statements into absurdities. To the nihilists they have

436

answered correctly that without values, without guidance man cannot live. But in the content of their admonitions they have meant values that no rational man has been able to accept for more than a century and the guidance of Jonathan Edwards.

It would be instructive but needless to dwell at length on the quite private mystical experience of Paul Elmer More in which he discovered "the illusion of beholding the infinite within the stream of nature itself instead of apart from that stream," in which the extra-naturalness of the "infinite inner check" and the fact that "character is the will to refrain" were revealed to him. On the basis of these private intuitions he builds up a pseudo-philosophical structure, quite like that of the schoolmen, careless, as he says in another connection, whether the disposition of himself and his colleagues "is in harmony with the nature of things," but concerned only "with their self-consistency." His inner processes are, in fact, thoroughly romantic and both Babbitt and himself are subject fundamentally to the very kind of romantic muddle-headedness which they feign to abhor. More builds his whole philosophy on a subjective intuition; Babbitt's most recent announcement is that "the final appeal of the humanist is to intuition." Well, then, what is wrong with the fact that "the whole movement from Rousseau to Bergson is . . . filled with the glorification of instinct?" Intuition for intuition and instinct for instinct, I would prefer even those of Rousseau and Bergson, neither of whom is among my masters, to those of Professors Babbitt and More. The truth is, of course, that our humanists have, without applying either the inner check of reason or the outer check of knowledge and fact, elaborately rationalized their conscious and subconscious preferences. They have sought in the usual slightly sadistic fashion to make their limitations serve as truth, decency, decorum and to impose their inhibitions upon all mankind. Truth or, if one prefer, reality can proceed only from large and noble and free personalities. Repression begets intolerance and the weapon of the constricted soul is the whip. . . .

It is time to proceed to the theories of art promulgated by the humanists. These have made a great noise in the world. And they have done so once more on account of the theoretic feebleness of the liberal and radical critics. The absurdities of the latter were very great. They proclaimed either chaos or an abstract æstheticism; they declared the ultimate subjectivity of all judgment, a doctrine as difficult to refute as the total unfreedom of the human will and yet daily rectified by, at least, this profound consideration: that the subjective judgments that have by their acceptance become objective, which have, in other words, made their way in the world in the nobler sense, have been the judgments of those who, like Goethe, like Sainte-Beuve, have not emphasized their arbitrary and subjective freedom, but their scruples, their insight won through suffering and reflection, their wisdom gained sometimes in agony of soul, and from whose works and ways there arises a spirit of dedication to both truth and humanity. George Jean Nathan was right enough when he said that there were two irreconcilable first principles of criticism, his own: Whatever interests me is good, and that of the academicians: Whatever is good interests me. But here evidently there enters that question of personality, of spiritual quality. We should be far more inclined to be interested in what seems good to Nathan if we were convinced that he had found good that which has been found so *semper, ubique et ab omnibus*. But one is afraid that Nathan does not really find the "Odyssey" or "Paradise Lost" or the second part of "Faust" either interesting or good. And when Henry Mencken who is nevertheless, as we shall see, a great writer, returns to the mediæval view of poetry from which the early renaissance critics sought to defend it, namely, that it deals with beautiful lies or unrealities, we suspect that he no less than Nathan has never been able to submit his spirit to the action of the great and authentic masterpieces. When, in addition, we read Mencken on Beethoven and Brahms and find him not only sound but elevated and not only elevated but in subconscious agreement with the Goethean theory of criticism, we are not unresigned to the conclusion forced on us by the texts that in literature he usually talks nonsense. For literature is implicated with his favorite intellectual prejudices, which are transitory and local in character, and music represents to him his one contact with the world of imperishable beauty and significance.

In this clamorous confusion, reduced to sheer silliness by the last lees of the Croce-Spingarn theory in which art is stripped of its communicative function and so reduced to pathogenic babble, Paul Elmer More's saying that the critic's "task is a continual weighing of values" seemed properly enough the voice of order and of reason. When he wrote in "Definitions of Dualism": "Art is the attempt, by means of the subjective imagination, to establish the experience of the individual in tradition," one had, at least, the sensation

439

of criticism returning to that solid ground on which discussion was both intelligent and fruitful. And the bringing back of criticism to its own ground and sphere is, in fact, the one definite service performed by Babbitt and More and their disciples. The content of their own theories can be guessed by the glance we have given at their temperamental Calvinism, based on a mystical experience of the crudest dualism and rationalized by a dialectic from which all modern scientific knowledge of either the world or the soul was carefully excluded *ab initio*. Since they could not directly derive their critical laws from Jonathan Edwards and since they were men of very great learning, they went back to Aristotle, to the French seventeenth century with Babbitt, to the British mystics of the seventeenth century—not, be it emphasized to that John Milton who advocated divorce and liberty of speech and publishing—with Paul Elmer More and by carefully excluding with a gesture of moral and metaphysical disdain all that did not fall in with their preconceptions, by excluding as factual material most of modern and all of contemporary literature, they arrived at a theory of letters that sounded decorous and had, at the cost of these immense and absurd exclusions, a specious and superficial coherence. In their amusing arbitrariness they selected carefully even in their chosen moods and periods only the works that illustrated their tight Calvinistic notions. They never mention, as I have said, the prose of Milton; one looks in vain for a reference to the "Fables" of La Fontaine or to the works of Henry Fielding; where are "Le Roman comique," where even is La Bruyère? Babbitt leans more or less upon the bosom of Racine; except for Plato, it is not easy to discover whom

More reads with genuine approval. Had one, in truth, to confine one's reading to works commended without reservation by them, one's studies would be absurdly circumscribed and unbelievably drained of variety and the substance of life. Of Aristotle himself their selections are careful. They have all, even to More himself recently, taken to baiting Theodore Dreiser as a favorite sport. They have never offered Dreiser, to whom their entire discussion is Greek anyhow, the obvious passage in the fourth chapter of the "Poetics": "It is a matter of daily experience that of those things which in real life we view with displeasure, a plastic representation delights us, so it be executed with close verisimilitude, such as, for instance, representations of the lowest animals and of corpses." I do not myself consider this passage at all pertinent to a discussion of naturalism in modern literature; the failure of the humanists to deal with it and the pictures and passages of Homer that Aristotle seems to have had in mind is simply offered as proof of their disingenuousness on their own ground on which the critics who opposed them have been unable to contend with them.

For definitions of the humanistic theory of letters, of art, I may legitimately go to Irving Babbitt. Not, indeed, to that "Essay at Definition" in the symposium of 1930 in which the late apparent triumph of his cause seems to have caused in him a slight vertigo of power, so that he makes damaging admissions, such as that "the final appeal of the humanist is to intuition," and assumes the full panoply of the theocratic cleric: "One should not be moderate in dealing with error"; in which he ranges himself "unhesitatingly on the side of the supernaturalists," which even certain dis-

ciples have found a difficult saying and in which he emphasizes once more that "the higher will"—that, of course, which
good humanists derive from their intuition—"is a will to
refrain," and mainly, one is sure, a will to make others refrain from what the intuitive higher will of the humanistic
neo-Puritan disapproves. From such a theory the step to
witch-burning and night-riding and heretic-hunting is as
brief and logical as it was in Plymouth Bay. No, for tolerable definitions of the neo-Puritan theory of the arts it is
better to go to "Rousseau and Romanticism" and to the essay
on "Genius and Taste." "Now creative art, in distinct ratio
to its dignity, deals not with what may happen in isolated
cases but with what happens according to probability or
necessity." . . . "According to the older school, art aims
not at the expression of the individual, but at the universal
—the 'grandeur of generality.' " . . . The critic must "rate
creation with reference to some standard set both above his
own temperament and that of the creator." . . . "And if
this standard is to be purified of every taint of formalism, it
must not be merely traditional or rationalistic, but must rest
on an immediate perception of what is normal and human, a
perception that the critic, like the creator, can win in its fullness only with the aid of the ethical or generalizing imagination." Now these definitions are an inextricable coil, I shall
not say of truth and error but of reality and unreality. They
are, above all, unpsychological, that is, they do not take into
account the observable facts of the creative process; they
quite leave out the artist in action. They have all the marks
of definitions made by men who, uncreative themselves, have
no inner knowledge of the process by which experience be-

442

comes not only expression but, precisely as they would have it do, expression that has "the grandeur of generality." These are critics who desire, in the sharp but exact words of André Gide "a criterion that shall relieve them from the necessity of exercising their own taste and a prescription which shall permit them to write masterpieces without effort, suffering or genius." Not understanding the inner facts, they flee to outer rules. Thus it is perfectly true that great art deals with what happens according to probability or necessity. But that is because the great artist's consciousness and genius so includes humanity, as Emerson saw long ago, that in speaking of himself he speaks of and for all and by the expression of his private emotions expresses and heals not only himself but the souls of generations yet unborn. Thus is to be understood the fine and profound saying of Thomas Mann: "Psychologically love of the 'I' and love of the world cannot be differentiated at all. . . ." It is seen then, that to begin with the humanists had laid hold of a truth which in their voluntary isolation from knowledge and their involuntary ignorance of the creative process they simply did not themselves comprehend. Their appeal to an external and anterior standard, outside of both creator and critic, reveals its meaninglessness at once when Babbitt declares it to "rest on an immediate perception of what is normal and human." On intuition, then. And on whose intuition? On his who has "the ethical or generalizing imagination." Well, and how is anyone's possession of that imagination to be determined? And on what definition of it? In brief, every rigid standard implies a still higher and more rigid one and that a still higher and so on *ad infinitum*. Roman Christianity has met this difficulty by making the Church an eternally true and infallible interpreter of revealed wisdom; orthodox Judaism has partially met it by assuming that all truth promulgated by righteous men in any age was from all eternity implicit in the Torah. It is evident that without some such assumption external standards or criteria, standards anterior to practice and criteria independent of the continuous observation of empiric facts, are hopelessly unattainable by such a being as man in such a world as the present. The best mind among the humanists, that of T. S. Eliot, has of course faced this ultimate dilemma. "Humanism is in the end futile without religion," he writes. And as in his heart of hearts he must know, not only without religion, but without Rome. Thus, as I started out by implying, the humanist movement in America today is analogous—*mutatis mutandis*—to the Neo-Catholic reaction and to the mystical nationalist reaction in contemporary France and Germany.

It is evident, at all events, that the discussion of More and Babbitt and of their disciples has brought us into deep waters, has made us face ultimate issues. Hence it is not I who shall reproach the young, the generous and the aspiring for fleeing even to this philosophy in the dearth of all philosophy and to this metaphysic, feeble as it is and intellectually dreadful as is its goal, in the midst of either clamorous or despairing nihilism. Babbitt-baiting, as I wrote long ago in another place, cannot suffice. Henry Mencken's best satiric pieces are among the best in the world. They rank him, as we shall see, with Juvenal and Dryden. But let us see what, as a critic and a thinker and a metaphysician—for all criticism ultimately becomes that—he had to offer the youth of America after his strictly liberating function, a very great but temporary function, had been completely and sufficiently exercised. He began indeed soundly and even nobly: "Beauty as we know it in this world is by no means the apparition *in vacuo* that Dr. Spingarn seems to see. It has its social, its political, even its moral implications. The finale of Beethoven's C minor symphony is not only colossal as music; it is also colossal as revolt; it says something against something." Nothing could be better than that. Nor has there often been a more pertinent and brilliant and for its day more useful piece of writing than that survey of "The National Letters" with which the second volume of "Prejudices" opens. Not only are the characterizations true; they are superbly expressed. "A sort of timorous flaccidity, an amiable hollowness . . . a general irresolution, a pervasive superficiality" marked American letters. "In all that mass of suave and often highly diverting writing there is no visible movement toward a distinguished and singular excellence, a signal national quality, a ripe and stimulating flavor." This was indeed a Daniel come to judgment. And no American who truly knew his country and its folk could help rejoicing at the intrepid crack of that satiric whip: "In so foul a nest of imprisoned and fermenting sex as the United States, plain fornication becomes a mark of relative decency." But this brave and radiant structure was built on stubble. "You will spend a long while going through the works of such typical professors as More, Phelps, Boynton, Burton, Brownell and Babbitt before ever you encounter a purely æsthetic judgment." But he had very correctly told Spingarn that there is no such thing as a purely æsthetic judgment! And his unwillingness to meet the con-

445

servatives on their own philosophic ground, which is the only proper ground, he shows by lumping together an empty popularizer like William Lyon Phelps and a first-rate philosophic scholar, dangerous by virtue of that temperamental power which he throws into the scale of reaction, like Paul Elmer More. And at the end of the essay the cause for the mildness and timidity, the feeble and undistinguished character of so much of American writing is declared to be quite the same assigned in a different mood for slightly differently seen phenomena by Paul Elmer More himself: "the lack of a civilized aristocracy!" Confusion can go no farther. And that confusion has, alas, continued whenever Mencken has written of anything but music. Of that art he has written as no other American—with beauty, with fire, with a love that creates wisdom. But when he leaves music he is intellectually lost. Thus, according to him, the creative process is wholly dependent on metabolism, "religion and the arts are only second-rate means of achieving man's chief purpose in the world," which is "to escape some of the pains of reality by denying boldly that they exist," which is a tenth-truth stated with downright silliness and involving a dualism even more primitive than that of More. But he clings persistently to that notion of high literature: "For the business of poetry, remember, is to set up a sweet denial of the harsh facts that confront all of us." And again: "A man of fifty who still writes poetry is either an unfortunate who has never developed, intellectually, beyond his teens, or a conscious buffoon." No memories of "Paradise Lost" or the second part of "Faust" gave Mencken pause. In the last volume of "Prejudices" he returns to the charge. The purpose of poetry "is

446

not to establish facts, but to evade and deny them." In brief Henry Mencken has simply no organ for perceiving the character of great literature. He must have heard of Homer and the Attic dramatists; he has certainly read Shakespeare and even Hauptmann's "Der arme Heinrich"; he must have looked at "Faust," since German is his favorite literature. Yet he continues to talk about poetry in the terms of a village free-thinker of religion. Hence it is not surprising that his definition of the critic is one that would apply admirably to Tom Sawyer in the act of showing-off: "He is trying to arrest and challenge a sufficient body of readers, to make them pay attention to him, to impress them with the charm and novelty of his ideas." Yet in spite of that airy definition of the critic he can be as hidebound as the humanists in detail and issue fiats about the "chief purpose of prose fiction" and about who stays and fails to stay "within the legitimate bounds of the form." What has become here of the critical function, that "urbane and expansive" one, which is merely "to make the matter discussed seem charming"? Such muddle-headedness has, of course, deep roots. Mencken is wholly inaccessible to either metaphysical or moral ideas. Granting him, as one must and indeed desires to do, the American satirist's fine old privilege of exaggeration, it must still be remembered that he offers certain ideas permanently and persistently as his own. "Perhaps man is a local disease of the cosmos—a kind of pestiferous eczema or urethritis." All melioristic schemes are "current sentimentalities"; war is a fine thing if indulged in by Nordic gentlemen; democracy is a delusion; the "booboisie" should obey their betters, apparently, a modification of pseudo-Nietzschean oligarchs, chi-

447

meras, in brief, as empty as those pursued by village Fundamentalists—myths, simply, of another kind. Beyond this rather adolescent and defensive truculence of spirit Mencken is a sincere libertarian and as such has struck again and again the bravest and most effective blows against the gradual narrowing in and lopping off of liberties once held to be peculiarly American. But of the ultimate spirit of liberty he is as pathetically ignorant as he is of the character of high literature. "It does not surprise me that the majority murdered the minority; the majority, even today, does it whenever possible. What I can't understand is that the minority went voluntarily to the slaughter. Even in the worst persecutions known to history—say, for example, those of the Jews in Spain—it was always possible for a given member of the minority to save his hide by giving public assent to the religious notions of the majority. . . . Well, then, why did so many Jews refuse? Why did so many prefer to be robbed, exiled, and sometimes murdered? . . . Is it actually noble to cling to a religious idea so tenaciously? Certainly it doesn't seem so to me. After all, no human being really *knows* anything about the exalted matters with which religion deals." I have quoted at some length, but in truth the whole essay on "Martyrs" from the third volume of "Prejudices" deserved close study as a *locus classicus* of that nadir in American liberalism and libertarianism that gave the reactionaries their wholly legitimate opening. For it is clear from this essay that Mencken simply does not know what either religion or literature is. He mistakes the historical symbol for the spiritual fact; he does not see that the martyrs of the ages, Jewish or Christian, men of science or men of peace, embodied in

448

their recusancy a creative act of the highest metaphysical self-affirmation, that in this resistance even unto death of free personalities to the majority, the mass pressure, the Fundamentalist rage of their hour in history we owe the highest hope, the deepest assurance of the reality of spiritual values, the one sure pledge of the human dignity to which, in tensest crises, otherwise nameless and undistinguished men can in all ages rise. But those who took upon themselves the Cross of Christ and those who died and still die to sanctify the Name, and those who rot in prisons everywhere for the sake of peace and freedom are as strange to Henry Mencken as Goethe's

> Der nur verdient die Freiheit wie das Leben
> der täglich sie erobern muss,

or Milton's purpose, which is rightly interpreted that of every creative speaker, to

> assert Eternal Providence
> And justify the ways of God to men.

It is now not difficult to sum up the essence of that great critical debate in America which, arising a quarter of a century ago, still continues and by its plowing up of ultimate and final issues marks a distinct epoch in the history of our civilization. On the one hand were learned Calvinists promulgating a theory of life and letters which, following its emotional and racial line and leaning leads directly to belligerent nativism, to strike-breaking, the activity of vice squads, prohibition agents and night-riders, but which, following its intellectual pattern and scholastic trend, leads just as inevitably to Rome. On the other hand stood Henry Mencken and his

449

closest associates, endlessly repeating the materialistic short-cuts of the darkest nineteenth century and opposing to the cultivation of all deeper spiritual values a mentality and Nihilism patterned on those of Robert Ingersoll and Ernst Haeckel.

In spite of that it remains true that during certain crucial years the liberating influence of Mencken was of the first order of importance in the national life of America and that his eminence as a satirist is due not less to his limitations than to his talent. For he was confronted by conditions against which a scalpel would have snapped; it needed an ax, and of that weapon Mencken is a wielder of the first order. He had to deal with a society putrescent with gross and ugly and tyrannous delusions, with the tragic hypocrisy of the "war for democracy," with the rebirth of a nativism that sought to make helots of all Americans not of one special blood, with the apparent triumph of moral and intellectual repressions that degraded every man to a potential spy upon his neighbor and covered the land with a spawn of informers and defamers and lynchers of the body and of the mind. Our traditional liberties were being murdered and justice became a thing dishonored by the laws it had to enforce when it was not openly bought and sold. A subtler and more sensitive, a more spiritual minded man than Mencken might have been subdued and abashed and silenced. Not so Mencken. Free men and thinking men choked as in the miasma of a swamp. Mencken wrote: "Wilson: the self-bamboozled Presbyterian, the right-thinker, the great moral statesman, the perfect model of the Christian cad." Once more there was air to breathe. He wrote of the cultural sterility of the South: "One thinks of Asia Minor, resigned to Armenians, Greeks and wild swine, of Poland abandoned to the Poles." He wrote his brief papers on "The Dry Millennium": "It is the chase that heats up the great mob of Methodists, not the Word." He wrote his essay on "The Forward Looker" and his inimitable "Suite Américaine" and "People and Things" in which he invented a new and highly effective technique of satire; he had the courage in "The American Tradition" to carry the war into the heart of the enemy's country and in "Justice under Democracy" to show the inherent poltroonry of the Volstead Act. On politics, on religion, on morals and poetry and love he continued to talk shallow and bumptious nonsense. But as a satirist of the gross and common vices and delusions of his age and country he remained for years of an incomparable vigor and fertility, inventiveness and zest. His prose, deeply tinged in tone by Macaulay, but wholly his own, wholly the expression of his temperament, became more and more an ideal instrument of manly satire and severe invective and attained at his strongest moments a curbed fury and packed concentration that make for permanence. Such moments he reached in not a few longer and shorter passages, in the entire essays called "Totentanz" and "Metropolis" and in his very highest achievement, the superb and unforgettable "In Memoriam: William Jennings Bryan." By virtue of these passages and papers he belongs, as I have said, to the company of Juvenal and Dryden. And to them should be added, to show that this spiritually purblind wielder of the satiric ax owned both a heart and a soul, the lovely and not ignoble celebrations of Beethoven and of Brahms.

IV

I am unwilling to leave this record of the central critical debate in modern American literature a purely negative one, reducing to absurdity the ultimate notions of both the Calvinists and the Nihilists, paying due tribute to Paul Elmer More as a critic and stylist and to Henry Mencken as a satirist, but creating in the reader's mind the impression that there have not been nor are other tendencies in American critical thinking which are less extreme, less contentious, more hopeful. For such is, in fact, not the case. Only amid the clamorous pseudo-certainties of the extremists the voice of humanity and of reason has not been very clearly heard. And in a confused and brawling and spiritually mist-swept age few influences have fortified a serener criticism and its practitioners have been less pertinacious and loud than those in the divided and embattled camps. As early as 1923 Carl Van Doren proposed "vitality," the continuous bearing of the spirit of life from age to age, as the test of a work of art; in 1929 in an essay with the unhappy academic title "The Importance of Style," Henry Seidel Canby struck very near the root and source of the problem of creative speech, and in the same year in "American Estimates" equally near to the problem of the development of our literature beyond the period, once fertile but now quite sterile, of critical or ironic realism: "A hundred critics shouting 'Down with Babbitt' are not worth one poem, one novel, one play, which represents all that Babbitt is not, but may very possibly desire to be. A little less recrimination, please, and a little better example." But Van Doren has, for some reason, been unwilling to engage in the discussion of ultimate issues and the integration of his convictions as a thinker with his practice as a critic. Except for his admirable monograph on Swift he has, indeed, fallen silent. The books of Canby which one cannot open without finding evidences of sensitive perception and correct thinking miss fire through some want of stylistic authority and personal force.

There remains Joseph Wood Krutch, whom I have mentioned among the Nihilists and whose "The Modern Temper" summed up, in fact, the nihilistic despair of a definite moment in the history of that generation which follows immediately the middle generation in American letters. Both as symptom and as expression, both as history and as literature, then, that book has its place and its importance. But doubts of his own sweeping negations came to Krutch, if not during the actual composition of the volume, then not long thereafter. He wavered between a continuous and a discontinuous universe; he chose upon the whole, the latter alternative, as at least a truth of function if not of essence, when he spoke in his Conclusion of the "maladjustments which subsist, not between man and society, but between the human spirit and the natural universe." But this view at once opens vistas of both ideal and practical effort. For it is evidently one of the marks of human life not to cease from the attempt to mold nature nearer to the needs of the human spirit, to conquer and to shape that natural universe or, in the words of Thomas Mann, to bring *Natur* under the subjugation of *Geist*. "For nature and civilization," that great artist and thinker writes, "involve no contradiction; the second is only the ennobling, not the denial of the first." Such is, in fact,

453

the active view that Krutch has taken by the implication of his own activities: by his analytical solution of the problems of Poe's life and works, which involved, at least, faith in a scientific method and faith in the value of truth attained by its use, and equally by the constant warm assumption of the reality of values, in both history and letters, in both life and its expression, which informs his "Five Masters," perhaps the one American volume that ranks with the critical works in that French tradition of the free and "undulating" mind which stretches from Sainte-Beuve to André Gide. In that tradition there are no rigid principles or frozen systems; there is inquiry inspired by love—that spirit of love which Goethe denied to Platen, which Nietzsche had in mind when he counseled the critic and thinker to pass by that which he could not love and which irradiates the close of "Port-Royal" and all the greatest passages of Sainte-Beuve. That, too, is the spirit of Krutch's maturer work. It informs the beautiful ending of his fine study of Proust; it beats with a warm and sober pulse in that moving passage in the essay on Cervantes in which he speaks of the legendary consecration which has been the portion of the major figures of literature. "What many men have wept over is the sadder for their tears and what many men have laughed over is made not merrier, to be sure, but more precious by the echoes of that dead laughter. Thus the great figures of legend and literature grow more meaningful as they endure. When we touch them we touch not only them, but also and at the same time all those who have felt for them, making ourselves part of a great continuous tradition of human sensibility." The man who wrote that is evidently no "hard-boiled" nihilist at heart, but a humanist in the true sense—a student and a lover of mankind and its history. He approaches more and more by all the implications of his maturer work that *via media* of criticism which may well be called, for our purposes, the tradition derived from Goethe and transmitted to us by Emerson, and which, to clarify the errors and confusions of the conspicuous Calvinists and Nihilists, should now be positively set forth.

Art is expression; its motive is self-catharsis and communication. But it is the expression of the total man, a creature not only of a hunger for food and reproduction but of other hungers—for society, for knowledge and for God. And this total man, this artist who is impelled to publish himself to his fellows is impelled to do so because he belongs to them and they to him; he is part of the collectivity even as rebel and revolutionary; he is mouthpiece first of his clan and race and city, next of all mankind, because he is integral part of race and clan and kind. He is not abstract speaker, but man speaking. He seeks to justify himself to himself, to his fellowmen, to God. And because he is a man among men, flesh and bone of their flesh and bone, spirit of their spirit, his justification of himself justifies them; his interpretation of life justifies their lives. Therein lies the secret of the possibility of creative communication: it lies not in the sentiment but in the *fact* that men are brothers, made of one substance and creatures of an equal fate. It follows that the criteria of subjectivity and objectivity of *method* belong to the perishable realm of manners and fashion and that the most intimate autobiography may have a broader human significance than a work intentionally shaped toward

455

generality. All the world's lyric poetry proves that. Catullus still wrings the heart which Seneca cannot touch. It follows too that certain modern renunciations of communication are pathogenic; they belong to a morbid excess of every artist's normal resistance to the anguish and exposure involved in the act of creative communication; the sound or great artist justifies himself by speaking to and for his fellows; he utters his profoundest secrets so that others may be helped and purged by partaking of them. At the root of all creative communication is a motive that may coarsely but not falsely be called pedagogical. The secretest lyric cry is preserved and published by the poet in order that other human souls in equal case may partake of the poet's catharsis and liberation. Hence creative art—not artifice or journalism or writing for money or for the amusement of the mob—but creative art is moral in its own nature; it needs no defense; its moral value is inherent; within its scope the moral and æsthetic categories are one. And that is true, once more, because art is expression of the total man and the artist is a man among men. Hence his experience is, however heightened and intensified, an analogue of all human experience even as, in Goethe's words, "everything that exists is an analogue of all that exists and it is therefore that we always simultaneously perceive existence as both discrete and interwoven."

From these facts it follows that art is powerful and beautiful and moral in proportion to the depth and wealth of the concrete human experience which it can convey and so communicate that its full force is felt by other men. Even as the artist being a man, contains all humanity, thus his experience contains at least in germ or symbol all experience. Hence in art the concrete has the tendency to become abstract and the particular to become the general. Therefore, to cite Goethe once again: "This is the nature of poetry, that it utters the particular without thinking of the general or indicating it. But he who vividly grasps the particular receives the general as a gift, even though he knows it not or learns it late." This is the truth which Emerson perceived when he spoke of "the ravishment of the intellect by coming nearer to the fact," even as he perceived the further truth that, since the poet is a man among men, so his concreteness becomes universality, when he said: "The young man reveres men of genius because, to speak truly, they are more himself than he is." This, then, beyond all perishable shapes and fashions, is the nature of art: Genius— the generative or creative spirit, as the etymology of the word well bodies forth—projects as *form*, in order to satisfy its hunger for an immortality beyond the immortality of biological begetting—its experience both of the soul and of things, both of substance and values and by the necessity of that act of projection and communication declares its oneness with and its love of its kind.

Values moreover, to come to the point that is crucial for criticism, are inherent. Man can neither act nor create, neither live nor write, without choice, nor can he choose without a principle of choice. But this principle of choice in both life and art differs not only from age to age but from genius to genius within the same age and in this difference of principles of choice conformable to varied temperaments and mentalities lie the wealth and significance, the flexibility and hope of human culture. Thus liberty of life and art is absolute, but not abstract. For the only possible liberty is liberty of choice and of principle of choice, not liberty toward chaos, but toward a new cosmos; not liberty from law, but liberty toward a new law. This inherent necessity for law, for a principle of choice, however new and fresh and iconoclastic in action, was seen and explained very long ago by Kant. "Freedom of thought means the subjection of reason to no other laws than those which reason gives itself. The contrary notion is that of a lawless use of the reason, from which it naturally follows that if reason refuses to subject herself to self-imposed laws, she will be compelled to suffer the yoke of laws dictated from without. For without a law of some sort nothing, not even arrant nonsense, can function or exist." Hence genius functions under a self-imposed law and creates values as it goes along. In this creation of values through form lies its highest service; from it may be derived too, if one is willing to follow Kant thus far, a metaphysical defense of the validity of the values that genius creates and of the universality of its concrete experience and principle of choice. For genius, Kant declares, "is that endowment bestowed by nature which gives its law to art. And since this endowment, being the innate creative power of the artist, itself belongs to nature, one might sum up the matter as follows: Genius is that innate endowment through which nature gives art its law." It was a vision of this metaphysic that caused Shelley to place upon the lips of Apollo words deeper than he had conscious knowledge of:

458

I am the eye with which the Universe
Beholds itself and knows itself divine;
All harmony of instrument or verse,
All prophecy, all medicine are mine,
All light of art or nature.

But it is not necessary to embrace that belief in a continuous universe which underlies these quotations. The validity of the practice of genius can be much more firmly derived from its humanity, from that authentication of the fact of human brotherhood which the necessity for communication itself implies and proves. Art is social and moral and religious and metaphysical, not because it has to be made so, but because man is so and because the artist is a man. That was clearly perceived by Sainte-Beuve when he wrote: "Literature and literary production is not, to my mind, distinct and certainly not separable from the whole man and his organization. I can appreciate a work, but I can hardly judge it aside from a knowledge of the man himself, and I do not hesitate to say: By their fruits ye shall know them. The study of letters leads me directly to the study of morals."

From this whole argument, which has the support of the best psychological knowledge at our command, it follows that there are no external or fixed standards by which either genius may be known from without or creative activity guided from within. Yet are we not, as frightened conservatives feign, delivered up to the mere surges of a meaningless flux. "What is our purpose here," exclaimed Goethe, "save to render the perishable imperishable!" And that is indeed what true genius does and by the imperishableness of its vision embodied in form it is known. Not, be it noted,

459

by a cold and abstract continuance, but by its power to enlighten the mind and stir the heart of man from generation to generation, by its permanent expression, in a word, of experiences and values forever human. I am myself of the opinion that the great artists have in common one mark: the perfect balance in them of nature and mind, of passion and its spiritualization and that thus they illustrate the realization of an ideal profoundly summed up by Thomas Mann: "Effortless nature, that is mere crudity. Effortless mind, that is rootless and insubstantial. A high meeting of nature and mind upon their path of yearning in search of one another—that is Man." But other thinkers may see in the masters other marks. The chief proof of their being masters is that they are here, that they remain, that the concreteness of their experience and their values has the tendency to become more and more universal and not less and less as time goes on until, in a few supreme examples, they are identified with the human heart, with the spirit of mankind itself.

What guidance in this theory has the young artist? He has the example of the masters which he betrays at once by seeking to imitate them. No advice to youth is sounder than the advice to contemplate the classics. But it must not be given in the spirit of the rhetorician; it must not regard the classics *as norms of practice but as examples of the creative spirit in action.* The masters experienced life under the guidance of immanent laws and expressed it in forms inevitable to their natures and disciplined themselves to the achievement of self-appointed aims. That their experience and their laws, their forms and aims are human and universal is their felicity and their mark. The artists of each age must take the risks of art and of life, the risks which the old wisdom of the race knows to be very great. Many be called, few chosen. Or, better still, the saying of Plato: "For 'many' as they say in the mysteries 'are the thyrsus-bearers, but few are the mystics.'" A profound humility must accompany the highest effort and next to his skin the most ardent artist, however panoplied without, will always wear the ascetic's shirt of hair. . . . It is once more Sainte-Beuve who summed up the entire matter in an incomparable passage, as true and as pertinent in America today as when he wrote it more than eighty years ago. "And so my conclusion, when I speak of making one's election and choice, is by no means that we are to imitate even those who delight us most among our masters in the past. Let us be satisfied to feel their quality, pierce to their meaning, to admire them, but we, late-comers that we are, let us try at least to be ourselves. Let us choose among our own instincts; let us have the sincerity and naturalness of thinking our own thoughts and feeling our own sentiments—for we can always do that—and let us join to that the more difficult effort of elevation and of aiming, if that be at all possible, toward some lofty end. Speaking our own speech, submitting to the conditions of the ages in which we are placed and whence we draw our strength as well as our faults, let us from time to time, with foreheads lifted toward the hills and eyes fixed upon the groups of those mortals whom we revere—let us from time to time ask: 'What would they say of us?'"

461

BOOK ELEVEN

The Naturalists

I

Naturalism or realism is a permanent mood and method of human art. Its aim is, as we have seen, according to Aristotle, to produce pleasure by the delineation of such objects as in reality excite displeasure and even disgust. Within narrow limits this definition has a measure of truth. Again and again in the powerful pamphlet novels of Upton Sinclair things and circumstances are delineated which in reality would fill us with loathing. They fill us, on the contrary, as delineated, with indignation, with pity and with terror. But they do so precisely because the author has a purpose, because these hideous and these dreadful things are suffused by the writer's passion of indignation and of pity. Hence it is clear that the Aristotelian definition does not go far enough. The impulse toward naturalism seems rather to be the creation of the illusion of concrete reality in the service of a powerful passion. Homer delineates the disgusting beggar Iros, the "greedy-gut known far and wide: ever he filled his belly with food and drink, yet had neither power nor force," in order to heighten our sympathy for Odysseus, in order to foreshadow through the ridiculous combat between him and Iros the triumph of the disguised hero. This is an example of very primitive realism. Its inner spirit is better symbolized by the ironic method of Cervantes, desirous of sweeping from the minds of men the delusions of chivalric romance and by the fact that Henry Fielding wrote his first fiction in order to counteract the unmanly softness and unreality of Richardson's "Pamela" and proceeded thereafter to the creation of his masterpieces. And as we come nearer to modern times, in which all intellectual and artistic issues are more sharply defined, we see with increasing clearness that the mood of naturalism—in Ibsen, Strindberg, Hauptmann, in the French novelists who reacted against romanticism—is inspired by a resistance against delusion and vain sentimentality, against mere decorum and mean propriety, and that it is inspired, invariably inspired, by moral ardor. It has constantly the ardor for truth; it has almost as constantly the note of human compassion; its desire to enlarge the field and subject-matter of art is almost always guided, especially in the Germanic countries, by the belief in human brotherhood, by tenderness for the disinherited of the social order. It is as selective as any other mood or method. For art is selection. But it selects under a principle of choice which is consciously and emphatically moral. All sound art is, as I have attempted to show, moral in its inherent character. Naturalistic art is preëminently and burningly moral by the very character of its motive and inspiration. The bad critic is known by nothing so much

463

as by this, that he condemns as immoral in naturalistic works the selection of details that offend his effeminate decencies or threaten to penetrate his calloused conscience. Naturalistic art has, as we shall see, its rigid limitations. It alone cannot permanently suffice the human spirit. But it is an inevitable and inevitably recurrent phenomenon in the history of creative expression. It is always a beneficent and moral one.

It was such and is such in contemporary America. Nowhere else had art become so poverty-stricken by its exclusions; nowhere else as here under the dominance of the Calvinist distinction between the realm of grace and the untouchable realm of sin, had expression become so divorced from experience or the poet been so constantly forced, by the most brutal public and economic pressure, to remain silent or to adopt the trickeries of the mere artificer. Hence here the naturalistic revolt, so soon as it had the good luck to be embodied in powerful personalities, was bound to be extreme in method, as in Dreiser, or bitter in temper, as in Ring Lardner, or vociferous to the point of its own self-destruction as art, as in Upton Sinclair. For the passion of our resistance to anything is strong in proportion to the force of that thing either within ourselves or in our world. And all the artists of the period had to fight first the residuum of what they hated in themselves, Catholicism in Dreiser's case, Southern Episcopalian gentility and Puritanism in Upton Sinclair's, the itching to be a success and an immensely "regular fellow" in that of Sinclair Lewis. They fought upon two fronts: an inner and an outer one. And their having so long and bitterly to keep battalions of the spirit upon that inner front will be seen to account for their weaknesses and limitations. We have many powerful artists in America in this age; we have but few who are detached and severe and are not too involved psychically with what they both delineate and resist. But it were well to drive home the point at once that the American naturalists reconquered life for art, reintegrated experience with expression and were the liberators of our cultural life. I shall not plead—vain effort anyhow—for the permanence of the works of any one of them. Doubtless they seemed greater than they were in 1920 and equally doubtless, their work of liberation accomplished, they seemed smaller than their stature in 1930. But they accomplished that work of liberation—the greatest, most fruitful, most permanently effective in the history of American civilization. "Sister Carrie" and "The Spoon River Anthology" and "Babbitt" will probably not burden drawing-room tables in the year 2000. It is safe to assert that the historian of our civilization will be profoundly mindful of them and of what, for their time and therefore for the future, they wrought and accomplished.

II

On the threshold of the naturalistic movement in America we are met by a curious and difficult figure. It is the figure of Mrs. Edith Wharton. Her early stories, immensely intelligent in substance and of a blade-like elegance of execution, were avidly savored by the well-bred and slightly emancipated; "The House of Mirth" took the public by storm in 1905, largely, no doubt, as affording the bourgeoisie a glimpse into gorgeous and forbidden realms and a simul-

465

taneous chance to feel superior to these gilded idlers and wasters. The quality of the book was better than that of its public fortune. It remains to this day the most satisfactory of Mrs. Wharton's longer and more characteristic works. Neither "The Custom of the Country" nor "The Fruit of the Tree" equals it in rounded beauty or textual felicity. The later and latest works gradually renounce the special distinction of the earlier ones until in "Hudson River Bracketed," for instance, we have simply a competent but mediocre performance. Mrs. Wharton, in brief, has been far too much the professional novelist to sustain the qualities which first and very justly brought her fame. These were—I must use the word again—an unflagging distinction of manner and a very high and very penetrating wit. Nor was this all. Her people were very much alive and several of her earlier books at least had that virtue so immensely rare in our letters: architectonic beauty, beauty of inner structure. Yet her work is fading and crumbling and will probably be almost forgotten until a time so detached from the present arises that people can go back to a little of it as to something quaint and sweet and lavendered, wondering that at so late an age a woman as intelligent as Edith Wharton could have taken seriously the conventions of a small and unimportant social group, could have in ultimate judgment identified herself with these futile and fugitive notions and confronted the moral world with the standards of a silly and a cruel game. Yet that is what from first to last she has done. The tragedy of Lily Bart in "The House of Mirth" is not represented as that of a woman crushed by the trivial notions of trivial people; Lily is shown as one whose weakness, not whose strength it was, that she could not win upon the contemptible terms of their idiotic game; the nemesis upon Undine Spragg in "The Custom of the Country" is not the inherent nemesis of stupid and promiscuous ambition but her final failure to make her way into a given social group. Nor has Mrs. Wharton shifted her point of view. Wars and revolutions, cataclysms and catastrophes of man and nature leave her hopelessly a lady. In her last volume of stories called "Certain People" and published in 1930 there is a tale "After Holbein," in which we are invited to see the grim pathos of two old people not in the fact that having utterly wasted their lives in foolish and trivial things, they are left wholly empty and stranded in their ignoble age; we are asked to regard it as pathetic that these diners-out and givers of banquets can dine out and give banquets no more. There were moments, as in the novelette called "Sanctuary," in which Mrs. Wharton seemed to herself to have touched the fundamental integrities of life. But before she has quite reached them they are transformed into the code of a class and thus cheapened and emasculated. Except in "Ethan Frome," where she abandoned her unlucky class and kin, her art, despite its brilliant execution and occasionally penetrating wit, is an art without spiritual vitality. It is a hothouse, not a garden. There is neither breeze nor brook. Water trickles through a pipe of lead; the air is dead with stillness and the sky is dim through a correctly slanting roof of glass. . . . Creative art not only may but must portray the world of illusion. Art sinks to artifice, however, if the writer is himself enmeshed in the illusions he bodies forth. In primitive periods or in hours of revolutionary ardor the artist may identify himself wholly with group and clan at the risk, to be sure, of sinking to the bardic level. But such an identification with gross and obvious illusion on the part of a highly personalized artist of the modern age constitutes a flight from the fundamental necessities of both art and life. Its nemesis is first an increasing futility and next a gradual oblivion.

To pierce through the illusions of his particular world was the chief and honorable purpose of the many elaborate novels of Robert Herrick. In "The Common Lot," "Clark's Field," "The Memoirs of an American Citizen" and "Together" he set himself large and inclusive scenes, delineated many characters and sought by both breadth and scrupulousness of portraiture to exhibit and record, without argument or open propaganda but through the inherent processes of art itself, for the benefit of his countrymen, especially of those of the prosperous and ruling classes, the moral and material illusionism of their lives. He had seen increasing unhappiness and increasing confusion and attempted, by strictly creative methods—by showing not by preaching—to reveal in contemporary American society the lack of significant values and integrity of conduct which, beyond all accidents, seemed to him correctly to be the causes of the wretchedness and the confusion which met him everywhere. The result of his efforts is a series of social documents not without interest for the student of the future. But this fine scholar's novels remain in the last analysis the novels of a scholar. He knew exactly how a great novel should be written. The fusing fire was not in him, the touch of madness and genius; no angel ever troubled the waters of his soul. His very merits are tiresome and his books have everything except the principle of life itself.

The third of that strange enough trio which employed serious minds immediately before the appearance of Theodore Dreiser is Upton Sinclair. His neglect by critics and reviewers bears witness to nothing but the childish temper of our civilization. For it would have been so easy for trained minds to allow him his talent, his touch of genius, to pay a just tribute to the strength and unselfishness of his social passion and the essential nobility of his life and at the same time to invalidate his fundamental and central arguments. Among his robust and yet somehow fiery pamphlets, for instance, it would have been profitable to take to heart "The Brass Check," to take to heart with many grains of judicious salt those on education, but to display his hopeless inadequacy to the subjects of his thinking, by replying to "The Profits of Religion" as follows: All your facts are probably correct. But you leave Hamlet out of your play. Priests have been able to do what they have done because man is a metaphysical, is a religious animal and the doctrines and myths of religion are symbolic projections of universal inner processes. An equally complete reply could have been made to "Mammonart" and "Money Writes" by exposing the known processes of creative expression. But the truth is, of course, that what Sinclair calls "Big Business" is nearly as stupefied by a silly economic determinism as himself. Ultimately, in fact, he and Mr. Rockefeller are very much at one: both are strong advocates of Prohibition, that is to say, of sumptuary legislation imposed by an absolutely sovereign state. For liberty neither one has the slightest respect; we hear nothing about the limitations of state-sovereignty. It is undoubtedly true that Mr. Rockefeller and his compeers prefer Christian capitalistic patriotism to be taught in the institutions they support; nothing can persuade me that Upton Sinclair and his compeers, were they ever to take over the seats of learning, would permit anything to be taught that seriously conflicted with atheism, economic determinism and the angelic qualities of the proletarian class. Between two sets of fallacies so coarse and fatuous it would be difficult for a rational mind to choose. Nor is this all. Sinclair swallowed Wilson's war for Democracy whole and separated himself from the Socialist party and rivaled Sam Shipman's "Friendly Enemies" in "Jimmie Higgins." He has apologized since. But so have many "kept" professors in capitalistic universities. Pacifism between wars causes bosses and proletarians to lie down together. His public acts upholding the traditional American right of revolution have been dictated by the purest and most admirable motives; they have been robbed of all significance by his Russian fellow-communists, among whom one has heard nothing of liberty of speech or the press or of the right of the oppressed bourgoisie or intelligentsia or even the Socialist party to register an effective protest. Hence Upton Sinclair can be thought of as dangerous only by those as muddle-headed as himself. The melancholy delusion that a change in economic technique or the tyranny of one class rather than another will cure or even diminish the follies, the vices and the cruelties of mankind remains a delusion. Between capitalistic sadists and communistic masochists the voice of reason and goodness is scarcely heard today; it has not on that account lost its inherent and eternal authority.

His great quality is his passion of pity for his fellowmen. Only one creatively inspired by this passion could have written the story of Jurgis and Ona and their family in "The Jungle" and other portrayals of the life of the poor and the oppressed. At this point he touches Gerhart Hauptmann. But unlike the German dramatist he has not been content with an inherent message. His novels, except the close-packed and consistently well-wrought "100 Per Cent," snap in half like the plays of Brieux and hasten heatedly from creation to tirade. Sinclair is entirely right in declaring all art to be propaganda, things which the artist considers ought to be spread abroad or made known. But if he will examine great art, from the "Medea" to "The Weavers," he will find that the propaganda, the things to be made known, are found in the total intention and never in the texture of the work of art. If the intention is to be uttered in the texture, the utterance is one inevitably wrung from some character in action. But he has always been too impatient to let his books ripen into art. He has been too eager. Now great art is never eager and true power is never odd. Art will portray all the turbulence of life and all the sufferings of man and still keep a profound tranquillity and patience at its core. Not only has he raced through the individual book and so shattered it as art, but he has rushed from book to book, writing "Boston" hot on the heels of the tragedy that it portrayed and rather than wait upon a creative warmth within, publishing such tawdry imitations of himself as "Mountain City." But from what he himself has told us in "Love's

471

Pilgrimage" and has permitted Floyd Dell to add in elucidation, one suspects this eagerness to be a substitute for the breaking down of quite other barriers and inhibitions, precisely as his advocacy of sumptuary legislation is rooted in humiliations suffered in adolescence and as perhaps his entire revolutionary activity is ultimately dictated by contrasts between various members of his own family. I do not mean, of course, that experience should not lead to doctrine. But one has the impression in certain cases that suffering has been too uncritically accepted as the groundwork of doctrine, that its intellectual quality is too thin and its emotive force too turbid.

He remains, despite these considerations, despite the Fundamentalist structure of his psyche, an arresting figure. Like Zola or Brieux, he arrests by vigor, passion and fertility rather than by the quality of his work. But vigor, passion and fertility are in themselves notable qualities. Again and again throughout his many volumes there are passages and episodes that strike home to the heart and to the mind and page after page of both delineation and appeal that have the voices of bugles. I am wholly unimpressed by his vast popularity abroad. To the communist masses in Europe the horrors of American capitalism are just as truly wish-fulfillments, irrespective of fact or art, as the glories of strong manhood and pure womanhood are to the readers of Zane Grey and Harold Bell Wright. Nor do I think it pertinent that, since the death of Eugene Debs, Upton Sinclair is the chief of a faction, despite the fact that the "outs" have this advantage over the "ins": they are not corrupted by power and hence their tyrannous impulses are latent. But no literature, least of all that of America, can afford to neglect a figure as strong and as gifted as Upton Sinclair, works as various and, in a good and high sense, as exciting as his own: fragments, to be sure, except "100 Per Cent," and fragments of fragments, but many of them aglow with pity and with terror and with truth.

III

What was it that, from the first, set Theodore Dreiser apart from these contemporaries and fellows of his and made the definitive publication of "Sister Carrie" in 1907 one of the two or three important dates in the history of American civilization? The man himself served to answer the question and serves to answer it still: the powerful, rudely molded figure with those peering eyes, that mouth like an ill-healed wound, that slow indomitable tread. Here was no artist either dapper or Bohemian. He had an amusing passion for Bohemia, but was kept out of it by what he was. Here was no troubled scholar or over-eager propagandist. The man absorbed life, drew it in, glutted himself upon it and transmuted experience into expression without antecedent prejudice or interposing fears or proprieties or doctrines. His talk about "chemism," his shabby materialism, dotted by flights toward ouija-boards, is nonsense. But it is such sheer and obvious and childish nonsense that one simply passes it by. It is annoying but not disturbing. It is on the level of Victor Hugo's intimacy with God. It does not ripple, must less dam the steady stream of life through Dreiser's books. And that stream of life was what America needed—a stream brimming and strong enough to wash

473

away, to sweep away by power rather than turbulence, the mean and outworn and lying simulacra, the figures of straw and bran, the scarecrows and, at best, the painted mario-nettes that dotted and crowded the cultural landscape. It is no merely historical estimate to say that those who read and fully savored all the implications of "Sister Carrie" were those who were to liberate our culture and create our modern literature. That hour lives in this. It is, on the contrary, now becoming a question whether the hand of Dreiser does not lie too heavily on the literature of his country, whether it were not more hopeful to see the youngest novelists rebel against him rather than, with whatever eccentricities of mere technique, continue that inquiry into the so-ness of things which he began.

It is common knowledge that in those beginnings every man's hand was against his and that rancor and abuse, the spite of petty reviewers, the timidity of publishers and the legal prosecution of his books—leading to the eight-year-long withdrawal of "The 'Genius' "—followed him until some years after the World War. These things did not touch him, did not for an hour deflect him. Ignorant of the fact that autumn would bring him fruitage of both fame and comfort, he wrote his huge and laborious books—itself under the circumstances a moral effort of the first order—with steady and unswerving seriousness, relieving his feelings meanwhile by nothing but certain private jeers at the dulness and inherent "swinishness" of the supposedly literate classes. In such a career there is evidently a moral strength that gives it both coherence and dignity. It would be an error both grave and dangerous, however, to suppose that the long resistance to his art and the sheer stupidity of that resistance did him no harm. If ever an eminent writer needed to be at once sustained and constantly corrected by criticism both cordial and severe and by the atmosphere that criticism so practiced can create, Dreiser is that one. He started out by no means wholly insensitive to either beauty or justness of expression; he had a pathetic ambition for both taste and form. Abuse and dull resistance inevitably aroused a stubborn self-will in him, a pardonable contempt for criticism itself. He stamped on through the jungle. All aims but the central one for veracity of substance disappeared in the process. His style grew more and more slovenly, his solecisms more and more grating and monstrous. He broke through; he came out of the jungle into the open with all his finer literary sensibilities stone-dead. Now it was too late. Criticism had missed its hour. His last book, "Dawn," is the most vilely written of all his books. He is the worst writer of his eminence in the entire history of literature. He is matchless in badness. That he is so, is the gift to the culture of their country of the polite and conservative critics of the more or less Calvinistic persuasion.

He needed so sorely the corrective of a warmly humanistic culture and criticism on account of the bleakness of his origins. He has been called a peasant. He is not that. The peasant blood is rich in tradition and music. Peasants become poets, witness Burns, Keats, Hebbel. It is the landless proletarian in an industrial civilization who, whether he keeps a small shop or works in a factory, is cut off from all cultural inheritances and has nothing within him wherewith to resist adopting the ideals of the master class immediately in sight above his own—money, women, plush furniture, cut-glass chandeliers, paintings beyond his taste, bad writers, eccentric cults. Such is especially the fate of the American immigrant. He is cut off from his ancestral peasant cultures. Dreiser's family was German. But the language and its peasant tradition of lyrical culture are not his. The arid Middle-Western towns of his childhood and boyhood were all he knew. There life began. "Who would not dream upon a gilded chair?" That sentence from "Sister Carrie" is infinitely pathetic and significant at once. The whole of "The Financier" and "The Titan" are in it. For what has Frank Cowperwood at the end but gilded chairs? He does not even know how to seek other or inner satisfactions. And Eugene Witla in "The 'Genius' " who is, in many points at least, a confessed self-portrait, is not even he too long at the mercy of both gilded chairs and their possessors? This rootlessness of Dreiser, since it is shared by surging millions, is of course, a part of his great strength. It enabled him to write over and over again the one folk-legend of industrial America, that of the youth, male or female, who goes to the city and acquires the gilded chairs. Had he had no tale to tell but this and no style but that increasingly rude one of his, he might have become no more than a gigantic Horatio Alger. He had, luckily, two other motives: a vast and brooding pity for his fellowmen and sex, sex both carnal and mystic—sex in the large creative sense, seen as primordial force and energy, precisely as defined by Henry Adams for the future of his country.

In "Dawn" he has confirmed what both the early novels and "The 'Genius' " and "A Book about Myself" had led one strongly to suspect: that all his fables and all his motifs are deeply rooted in the experiences of his childhood and adolescence. His frankness is amazing and the case is complete. These revelations do not in the least detract from either his force or his eminence. For they contain a psychological situation quite normal in character, though unusual in accompanying circumstance. A strong mother fixation leads to its regular father hatred which disguises itself as a hatred of the father's faith and morals, as—in this case —a towering and unquenchable rage against Catholic Christianity. So far reason can support instinctive reaction. But the father's just objection to the life and conversation of the daughters of the family is identified by the sex-starved and pleasure-starved boy with mere superstition and he goes to irrational lengths in siding with mere looseness and crass dishonor. And it is this early reaction which, despite a touch in him of very German romanticism of feeling, causes him, in continuous defense against Catholic doctrine and morality, in continuous compensation for the guilt-feeling both toward his father and toward his father's morals, to insist in season and out on the "chemic" determinism of human action and the mechanistic structure of the universe. To these he must cling, otherwise the father was right and the sisters and he were wrong, and this conclusion he cannot endure. For the admission would release the guilt-feeling toward the father which, nevertheless, bursts out creatively again and again in the tender and masterly delineation of old men, from Gerhardt, the father himself, to such substitutes as old Berchansky in "The Hand of the Potter." But even this did not suffice. He must defend the sisters against the father: one in "Sister Carrie," the other in

477

"Jennie Gerhardt"; he proceeds next to build into creative structures the compensatory reveries of his poverty-stricken and humiliated boyhood and youth in "The Financier" and "The Titan" and finally in "The 'Genius'" justifies his own career, his break with his father's moral system, the dissolution of his marriage, the life of art as he has been impelled to live it. In "An American Tragedy" at last he chooses a theme outside of his immediate experience. But this subject-choice is dictated by the same old inner urgency. For Clyde Griffiths, who, too, has a wayward sister, is the child of poor but religious-minded people and through him and his story, the writer says creatively: there in such a civilization and universe as this—there, save for the miracle of genius and moral force, go I! And it would not have been my fault! Again the father is defeated and put in the wrong. To this creative passion for reporting his cause aright he adds direct confession in "A Book about Myself" and finally in "Dawn," which is announced as but the first volume of an autobiography on a scale of unparalleled hugeness.

Dreiser's works, in a word, like the works of other and greater writers, like Goethe's and Tolstoi's, are one long confession. But we know that this self-revelatory and self-justificatory urge is at the core of all powerful and important literature, irrespective of form and technique, and that the representative and so universal and so permanent value of a piece of literature is in proportion to the largeness, inclusiveness and rich humanity of the individual whose confession and self-justification it constitutes. A million Americans have known a fate not very unlike Dreiser's. To him the gods gave the power to report that fate, first for himself, next for those others. How many lads in obscure towns have not been "immeasurably depressed by encounters with poverty and misery"! How many could not say with him that these encounters were "the genesis of my awesome fear of winter and cold and want of good clothes and good food which, specter-wise, marched at my heels for years." How many have not nursed the strong compensatory daydreams of poverty and humiliation: "The mansions that should belong to me! The footmen, even slaves, who should bow and genuflect before me! The beauties who should note and receive me, eagerly and with passionate admiration and love!" And who that knows by direct observation provincial America does not recognize the adolescents' party with its kissing-game in "Dawn" and the account of sexual yearning and frustration in Chapter XLIX! In other words, the substance of Dreiser's creative confession is immeasurably rich in common human substance and it is this wealth in human substance, this immense authenticity that has caused him to triumph in spite of the mean and often ugly artistic texture of his works.

Nor is this all. As even Henry Adams saw and every un-clouded mind knows, the terribly sore spot in American life has been and still is in the sex life of the vast majority. The Calvinists will not acknowledge and cultivate what they hold to be the life of sin. It must be repressed; it must be denied out of existence. It must not be used and guided. It offends, according to the loathsome Pauline saying; it must be plucked out. Hence Dreiser's frank and sharp and profoundly serious dealing with sex as a primordial and pervasive and creative force was from the start and still is an epoch-making act of vicarious liberation. No wonder that the Calvinist critics resisted him to the utmost or that Stuart Sherman stigmatized the behavior of his characters as "animal behavior." One may differ very strongly with Dreiser in detail; one may smile over his romanticizing of a wretched little bawd like Carrie Meeber and suggest that advertising "art" was quite the proper occupation for such lazy unguided and ungirdled sensualism as that of Eugene Witla. It remains true that his eminence, his eminence above all within the framework of his country's literature and civilization, is due to his dealing with sex, to his constant assertion of the import and, in truth, the sacredness of that generative process and function which is at the very core of life. It is the Calvinists who cheapen sex and degrade it, not Dreiser. And it is but just, in view of the eccentricity of certain individual judgments and delineations of his own to quote the passage from the eleventh chapter of "Jennie Gerhardt," the most felicitously wrought of all his books, which is the key-passage of his life and work: "Certain processes of the all-mother . . . when viewed in the light of the established opinion . . . are considered very vile. We turn our faces away from the creation of life as if that were the last thing that man should dare to interest himself in openly. It is curious that a feeling of this sort should spring up in a world whose very essence is generative. . . . Although the whole earth, not we alone, is moved by passions hymeneal, and everything terrestrial has come into being by the one common road, yet there is that ridiculous tendency to close the eyes and turn away the head as if there were something unclean in nature itself.

480

. . . Surely there is something radically wrong in this attitude. . . . No process is vile, no condition is unnatural. The accidental variation from a given social practice does not necessarily entail sin." How moderate a statement, the enlightened European, especially of the Northern countries, would exclaim. Well, for America, particularly in its creative form, it was and it remains a statement of crucial and historic importance, for it is still fiercely denied and cruelly fought by law, by apparent custom, by the pressure of public opinion both sincere and hypocritical. And hence Dreiser's serious treatment of man's generative instinct remains his great creative act as an American. It makes up for the lack in his work of other values, for the tawdry ambitions of characters whom he admires, for the yearning for gilded chairs, for the involvement in the mere gear and machinery of life, for the inability to imagine ultimate satisfactions beyond the lower illusions of mortality. . . . It constitutes at once the inner significance and moral force of the whole body of his work.

It must not be supposed, of course, as has now and then been done, that the writings of a man of his stature can be without artistic virtue. Far from it. He possesses the central artistic virtues, though he lacks the peripheral ones. Unfortunately in art, as in life, the latter, though trivial without the former, are often decisive. Who would be enraptured by a woman of perfect bony structure and the measurements of a Venus, but with strawy hair and lackluster eye and coarse and broken skin? The illustration is exaggerated but not unjust. Dreiser has the root of the matter in him, which is detachment and transcendence during the creative process. He can keep his eye on the object, only and solely and entirely on the object, which so brilliant an executive prose-performer as Mrs. Wharton, for instance, can never do. He can take the clay and mold men; he can create the relations between them. He has given us Hurstwood and Hurstwood's story, perhaps his purest triumph, and the deep pathos of that truly good woman Jennie Gerhardt, and the incomparably rich and subtle delineation of that typically American marriage between Eugene Witla and Angela, and the parents of Clyde Griffiths and their world. And he has set upon their feet and projected into the world a host of minor characters: Drouet in "Sister Carrie" and old Gerhardt with his unforgettable word and gesture: "Gas, yet!" in "Jennie Gerhardt" and the old Irish politician, Aileen's father, in "The Financier" and still others in "The 'Genius' " and "The American Tragedy," down to the very bellhops. . . . It is a large work, broad, varied, peopled. What counts against him is, once more, the heavy amorphous verbiage, which will seem duller as time goes on, the unrestrained meticulousness in the delineation of the trivial, the increasing grittiness of his texture. But his power and truth are so great that they will long irradiate their muddy integuments. Nor will the future, whether he have few readers or many, be able to deny him either his liberating force or his predominance in the literature of his country during the first quarter of the twentieth century.

IV

The use by reviewers, especially during certain years, of such adjectives as "sex-obsessed" has in itself a part in the history of American civilization. It is symptom and judgment. For the bitterness of these reviewers, middle-class Americans in all parts of the country, bore witness to their own obsession and to the agonized cry of their souls: What I dare not do, you shall not do! For he who acts is not obsessed by the notion or image of that action. It is he who refrains from necessary action who is haunted by his deeds undone. The resistance of the reviewers was in itself a proof of the correctness of the delineations and arguments of the writers at whom they were so angry. Now Dreiser was, of course, never sex-obsessed. He merely reinstated the generative instinct in its proper place in the scheme of things and of art. But there was one writer concerning whom the reviewers, though in a sense so different from their conscious perception, were entirely right. Sherwood Anderson, though they did not know it, is their poet and sayer—the poet of the sex-obsessed American, who must be so because life, as he knows it and must live it, has shriveled and withered in him the possibilities of action, of liberation and of healing through action, and who is therefore obsessed or, more correctly, possessed by the image of the passionately desired and somehow unattainable. . . . This pattern of psychical structure meets us throughout the history of American folk-life, from Cotton Mather's execution sermons to the Anti-Saloon Leaguer, who is not at all concerned over a rational treatment of the problem of alcohol, but who mythologizes his fierce temptation to drunkenness as the Demon Rum and whose acrid clamor means simply: What I dare not do, you shall not do! . . . Sherwood Anderson unconsciously reveals this psychical pattern in his efforts as an artist to escape it. I do

483

not know whether happier ages will read his works as literature. To the student of human nature under the conditions of provincial neo-Puritanism there must always belong a high interest to these documents with their toneless murmur as of one who has exhausted eloquence and passion and found them of no avail, with their tortured sense of life as a thing immitigably ugly and mean, with their delineation of dull misery so ground into the bone that it no longer knows itself for what it is. Nowhere in all these many pages of Anderson will this student find a breath of freedom or of joy—never the record of an hour of either passion or serenity. Life is walled in; it is imprisoned from itself, from the sources without which it withers and dies. Who will knock down the walls? There is no one, least of all the writer himself. He tilts at the walls; he curses the walls. Like John Webster in "Many Marriages," he is driven to the verge of madness, to strange and obscene antics. He flees, but his flight, too, is futile. The walls, raised by the hands of innumerable ancestors, stand. For, in truth, the walls are within him, not without. The skilled reader will find the whole matter of Sherwood Anderson and of his relations to his folk summed up, half consciously, half unconsciously, in the prose-poems of "A New Testament." "I am one who has walked out of a tall building into the streets of a city and over plains into a forest that fringes a river. My notion is one of escape. I can no longer bear the life led in my father's house. I am a child and cannot escape out of my childhood. There is a door through which I cannot enter, a wall I cannot climb. The idea of escape long ago attacked the seat of my reason. . . . In the streets of a city, after I had walked out at the window of a tall building, a man came to walk with me. He held a small stick in his hand and twirled it over his finger. He said God would forgive my transgressions if I would go in at the door of God's house and cease walking up and down. . . . God lies on the ground in the forest. . . ." The imagery here is almost as uncontrolled by the conscious mind and hence as revelatory as the imagery of dream. And that is so throughout "A New Testament" which, published in 1927 and so in the decline of Anderson's mere vogue, was neglected. But the extraordinarily clear sexual symbolism of these pages sheds the strongest and clearest light upon the substance and character of his whole work.

He lived the ordinary life of the neo-Puritan populace until the threshold of middle age. He now sought gradually to cure the ills inflicted upon him by that life through art, through the self-catharsis of creative expression, through plastic objectifying of experience. But continuity of utterance was almost insurmountably difficult and the plastic projection of his inner world equally so. Something within fought against healing and against creative expression. For the two things upon his level, halfway between the neurotic and the artist type, are one. Thus except in the short-story or the sketch he cannot get ahead, he cannot get nearer the ultimate healing purpose of expression. He begins a fable of novelistic length and stops and begins again. At a certain point the inner censoring forces are too strong. So, too, he tells of his early years in "A Story-Teller's Story." But he has not succeeded in speaking the self-liberating word. So he tells the story of his boyhood over again in "Tar." But here, too, he wanders about the periphery; he cannot strike to the center. A year later he publishes "A New Testament" and here, at last, in the form of uncontrolled or almost uncontrolled revery he publishes his inmost self. I must not now, even though justified by the existence of the published word, quote further from "A New Testament" and so invade the privacy of a man so gifted and serious, a colleague and living contemporary. A seriously undertaken psychograph of Sherwood Anderson will some day add important elements to our knowledge of both art and life under neo-Puritanism.

It must be abundantly clear now why Sherwood Anderson's work is so fragmentary. "It was certain I had not," he tells us, "for many years of my life, known what I wanted." But it is the precise mark of the artist, as distinguished from the productive neurotic, that he knows what he wants, though strict formulation, except in the terms of creative result, may escape him. He is very single of aim and drives straight toward his work. Anderson wants to be deflected. By "drinking bouts to ease the confusion of my mind," by daydreaming and dramatizing himself into the rôle of a born teller of tales, an instinctive maker of narrative, the one thing in the world he is not, or at last and more sophisticatedly by fleeing from the very ends of expression and creation and self-catharsis in instinctive submission to the influence of Gertrude Stein. In her he found a writer driven to utter her secret yet constantly inhibited from doing so and feigning, as a defensive rationalization, that one could no more utter oneself through human speech until that speech was shattered into meaninglessness and the communication at once needed but neurotically inhibited could no longer take place. He did not, luckily, follow Miss Stein the whole way to sheer babbling.

But it is possible that her influence made for the writing of "A New Testament" and so afforded him a personal, if not a creative release.

His work is fragmentary in character and, as a whole, already fading. He could not speak clearly and plastically for the many tortured souls he represented because he could not speak out for himself. But he had his moments of expressiveness in both story and parable; he had his hours, and may yet have others, in which he achieved expression. He did so in the tales "I Want to Know Why" and "I'm a Fool" and "The Door of the Trap" and in the terrible and inimitably American parable concerning the foreman who stared at the girl in the office and murdered his wife in the story called "Brothers," and in many other passages in stories and novels. And into these pages he distilled the bitter, stale lightless and hopeless conditions of man's essential life amid the masses of the Middle West. He provides both confession and indictment, both delineation and judgment. His art is the half-articulate cry of tormented souls in a self-made inferno. It is not likely to lose its validity at its few moments of fusion and accomplishment. If any subsequent confirmation of its truth and its necessity at those moments were needed, that confirmation is furnished by the fact that the youngest of American neo-realists, submitting themselves to the influence of James Joyce rather than to that of Gertrude Stein, are still busy expressing a similar bitterness over conditions of human life almost too foul and dreadful for utterance. The best of Sherwood Anderson is thus justified by, for instance, the books of William Faulkner. This type of art can help us no more. We shall find a new idealism or our literature will perish. But its continued production bears witness to certain dreadful urgencies, hatreds and shames in American life which burst again and again into crippled but inevitable speech.

v

It was and still is in truth the revolt against the quality, emphatically, too, the moral quality of American life, which has tended to make of naturalism, whether in its revelatory or satiric moods, the first coherent and homogeneous movement in our letters. Is it not this spirit of moral revolt that allies Dreiser and Anderson with Lewis and Lardner and with the youngest neo-naturalists? Is it not this revolt that cries once more from a book so little memorable in itself but so symptomatic of its land and time as Dorothy Parker's "Laments for the Living"? The age of "gin" succeeded the "war for democracy"; in certain centers and circles there followed upon mere repression a vast amount of drunkenness and sexual looseness. But neither extreme can bring a shadow of that inner balance and true contentment which men, by all that is most rational and human in them, are impelled to seek. The revolt, whether through exact delineation or irony or a blending of the two, is itself a seeking. And it has been so intense and imperious among us that it drew poets away from their tradition of dealing affirmatively with the central and the permanent in human life, for it was just that which in America had become warped and defiled.

The first of these naturalistic poets was Edgar Lee Masters. For many years he had written conventionally noble verse and so mastered his instrument. There came, for the

488

first time, through the revolt of youth and the breaking up of poetic form, a breath of freedom and flexibility to the American scene. One could speak out and even, though one was a respectable citizen and active lawyer, publish. Thus, taking the free-verse innovation as he found it and allying it with one of the great traditions of literature through the "Greek Anthology," Masters composed and William Marion Reedy of St. Louis in his "Mirror" published, the pieces that constitute "The Spoon River Anthology." It should be added at once that the impression created by frivolous critics, who are themselves swayed by the mere vogues they set going, that "The New Spoon River" of 1924, is either inferior or a mere sequel to the first, is false. A new age, the war and post-war age had come with even deadlier follies and fiercer wrongs intensifying the old, and Edgar Masters, rising now more than ever "to something like prophetic strain," applied his matured mind and art to the new terrors which life had added to the old. In the first "Spoon River" Masters' purpose was descriptive and revelatory. He sought to tell what lay under "the false chronicles of the stones"—the furtive animalisms under the outer austerities, the foul small tyrannies that smothered life, the unexampled falseness of both thought and action. He desired, as he wrote later,

> to uphold the singers and tellers of stories
> Who keep the vision of a nation
> Upon the clear realities of life.

In the second "Anthology" he accuses. For what had been private hypocrisy in the nation had now become public law and to the pressure of mob opinion had been added the force of open cruelty and unendurable wrong. Now the veteran of the Civil War, the survivor of a ruder but more honest age, is made to raise a cry of direct accusation:

> You call this a Republic,
> Where happiness is hunted, delight is defeated,
> Thought is throttled, speech is choked;
> And where sickness, lying, thieving, hypocrisy
> Are encouraged and enforced by the Great Beast?
> And where Dullness, the eunuch, is enthroned
> Amusing himself by swatting flies
> With a scepter of lead!

The two anthologies, then, constitute a single work with a crescendo of intensity following the development of the poet's age. This work has several qualities that make it notable among American works, qualities that are preservative in their character. Edgar Masters is one of the few writers of his period who have style. I do not mean manner, which many writers have and which may be added to style or exist without it. Nor do I mean the effort to write gracefully. This effort can succeed and coexist with an almost total absence of style, as in the books of Joseph Hergesheimer. Style cannot be sought after, like correctness or surprise or a telling way of saying things. It proceeds from either severity or elevation of mind and character; it is allied, however far or faintly, with the spirit of either Swift or Milton. Now in a measure not high in itself, but high in relation to his age and land and its writers, Edgar Masters has that severity of mind and character that makes for style. This is proven by the fact not that he imitates the "Greek Anthology," but that he imitates it successfully, that he re-creates its method and its moods in an age indescribably different from any of the many centuries which find a voice in those Greek distichs. He can sometimes hold this note of style throughout a whole poem or epitaph, as in "Hare Drummer" or in that on Thomas Trevelyan with its admirable close;

> And all of us change to singers, although it be
> But once in our lives, or change, alas, to swallows,
> To twitter amid cold winds and falling leaves,

or in that notably fine rebuke of the pioneering ancestress of an American line:

> What is this I hear of sorrow and weariness,
> Anger, discontent and drooping hopes?
> Degenerate sons and daughters,
> Life is too strong for you!
> It takes life to love Life.

Sometimes this wavering and uncertain but genuine gift for style will light up a poem not otherwise among the best, as in those descriptive lines from the second "Anthology":

> Brisk as a dwarf, glittering with victorious malice,
> Notched and elfin as a frosted oak-leaf,
> Bitter with nut gall—

But again and again a poem or even two successive poems will be quite irradiated by it, as those on Lionel Grierson and Arielle Grierson, and there are moments, rare but recurrent, in which the fire will be so intense as to fuse the poet's manner with the more classical moods of poetic speech.

> Imprison the eagle with the crows
> Who know not what the eagle knows,
> He will croak a little when crowded,
> Or whistle when his soul is clouded.
> But free him back to be with the eagles,

How he flaps his wings and shrieks,
When the lightning the heaven streaks,
And all the peaks call to the peaks.

Now this gift for style which Edgar Masters has argues for severity of character and that, in its turn, for brains. And I do not in fact know any American book in which there is more fundamental brainwork, more sharp and accurate thinking about life, than in the "Spoon River" anthologies. When Dreiser tries to think he writes like a child; Sinclair Lewis lives intellectually from hand to mouth. Masters has revealed the structure and quality of the moral life of America in the neo-Puritan machine age with an unerring and incorruptible intelligence. He has revealed that life creatively in the strictest sense. His method is always dramatic and concrete. There is character and fable of an hundred novels indicated in the epitaphs and each illustrates the American moral scene with vividness and power. Nor are the books without a central and controlling theme and that theme is inevitably the theme of sex:

What is *that*, that it should produce
Shame, terror, crime, ruin and crucifixion
All over America?

But Masters—and here he shows his brains again—is no utopian dreamer who believes that a decenter code of public morals will heal all human ills. What his vision sees in the anthologies as well as in his unduly neglected novel "The Nuptial Flight," is love as an expression of the total human personality, no isolated instinct amid others that can thrive while it remains unsatisfied or warped. When man has satisfied hunger and sheltered his body from the winds, love remains—love that is not only procreation but creation, that is the source of contentment, beauty, aspiration, art. But love does not unhappily, like the satisfaction of hunger, come to all. A universal need, it is as rare in its harmonious and full fruition as beauty or genius. That is the pervasive tragedy of human life, inherent and unalterable. But in this age and land and polity stupid and unjust law and foul, intolerant custom sharpen this tragedy beyond all need and vex and corrupt a thousand souls who might recover and rebuild life and add light and fruitfulness to the corporate existence of which they are a part. About this central theme the rich and varied life of the "Spoon River" anthologies is built. The future may prune and abbreviate this work even as the "Greek Anthology" is not impoverished by judicious selection. A core will remain that may well resist the ravages of time.

Two other poets, extraordinarily different in temperament both from one another and from Edgar Masters belong properly to the movement of naturalistic revolt. These two are Carl Sandburg and Robert Frost. The one is, like Dreiser, an urban proletarian of recent immigrant stock; the other the descendant of eight generations of New England farmers. A treatise concerning the psychology of literature could be derived from these facts and from the work of the two poets. The proletarian nobly and richly inspired by the sufferings of his class chooses the most artificial and sophisticated of media under the delusion that classical forms have no relation to the folk who primarily begot them; the peasant, truly close to the land, the folk and hence to the forces that create fundamental tradition is unswerving from the first in his adherence to the eternal necessities of form, desirous only of cleansing form from accidental dross and temporary worthless accretions. So, too, in the matter of substance. Sandburg addresses himself, from motives that none can fail to honor, to the shifting accidents of the economic order, Frost to nature and to the heart of man. Sandburg began by writing:

> I wish the kids had never come
> And rent and coal and clothes to pay for
> And a grocery man calling for cash,
> Every day cash for beans and prunes.
> I wish to God I never saw you, Mag.
> I wish to God the kids had never come.

Who can fail to be touched by the stripped poignancy of these lines? But Frost began by writing:

> "Home is the place where, when you have to go there,
> They have to take you in." "I should have called it
> Something you somehow haven't to deserve."

From the periphery of life we are taken back to the center, from the poignancy of an hour to the eternal preoccupations and from forms to form.

Harry Hansen tells us that one of Carl Sandburg's favorite remarks is this: "Think what Shakespeare could have done with the emotion behind the sonnets if he had been free, not bound by any verse form." From this statement, in which there are almost as many fallacies as words, another treatise on life and literature and the errors of the unrooted in human culture could be derived. Shakespeare's emotion is not behind but in the sonnets; the emotion and the form are identical; thus and thus only could that emotion have been born; the antecedent emotion was not this but only its seed or, in another figure, its raw material. The creative process

494

had intervened and transmuted life into art and the temporary and accidental experience into an eternal and universal
one. Shakespeare was not bound from without; the verse
form did not come from without; it grew from within and
united the individual Shakespeare through the collective or
folk-stratum within his psyche to mankind—mankind which
itself created the music of essential form, derived in turn
from physio-psychological processes, from language as incantation, from verse as dance and gesture and worship, from
the unity, broken only within historic time and still observable in primitive art, the complete unity of incantation, religion and sex. Thus arose the ballad measures from which
was wrought the Greek hexameter, thus immemorial Latin
hymns and charms and lullabies:

> Lalla, lalla, lalla:
> i, aut dormi aut lacta;

thus the Germanic measures of lyric and ballad even to those
of the American folk poetry that Sandburg himself has collected; thus the trochaic rhythms of the Finnish folk-epic.
The folk sings; man does not speak until enormously late in
history; and then as the representative of a minority within
an historic culture. Shakespeare writing the sonnets asserted
the only kind of freedom that exists: the freedom of pouring himself into an enduring form of communication, the
freedom, in brief, of submitting to a law dictated from
within. . . . I dwell upon this matter in connection with
Sandburg, because the fallacy of failing to differentiate between the fundamental and the accidental in human tradition has become a common one especially among writers who

consider themselves, even as Whitman did, as belonging to the people. Under the delusion that they represent the people they abandon it. They write free verse instead of singing; in fiction they cut themselves off from the eternal folk-mood of narrative, common to Homer and your neighbor in a Pullman smoking-car, in order to indulge in antics imitative of the news reel, the headline of the newspaper or the loud-speaker. Hence they succeed only in speaking to the sophisticated about the people, not to or for the people. Homer told *about* spears and shields, not *with* them; the Arab tale-tellers do not form genii and palaces and houris of the desert sands in which they crouch. They chant and tell . . .

Sandburg's naturalistic revolt, then, is a very sophisticated one and his use of the American vernacular is primarily refreshing to those who are satiated with the too smooth formulæ of cultured speech. As such it coöperated with other forces in American life that made for the reintegration of experience with expression. Much of his work has already a doctrinaire and therefore wilting quality, like the fierce argumentative fictions of Upton Sinclair, and it is ironic but natural that his finest passages are those in which he speaks in terms of at least vestigial rhythm of things and thoughts that are common to the ages, as in "Cool Tombs" or "Grass" or "Flash Crimson." Life has quite gone out of the militancy of

> Omaha, the roughneck, feeds armies,
> Eats and swears from a dirty face.
> Omaha works to get the world a breakfast.

Luckily Sandburg has pondered the history of man which he once affected to despise and drawn from it that old lesson of humility which he restates not unimpressively in his own medium:

> And the wind shifts
> and the dust on a doorsill shifts
> and even the writing of the rat footprints
> tells us nothing, nothing at all
> about the greatest city, the greatest nation
> where the strong men listened
> and the women warbled: Nothing like us ever was.

Robert Frost's revolt against convention in both substance and form may be called the classical revolt, for it is the recurrently necessary return from artifice to expression, from accepted falsehoods to veracity, from fashions to nature. It is the revolt that wants not novelty; its aim is to recover the freshness of the permanent. The likeness between him and Wordsworth is, of course, obvious. The close comparison does not fail to bring out the virtues of the American poet. He never blazes with immortal fire as Wordsworth did on certain miraculous days. He is subtler and more constantly just; his blank-verse narratives and dialogues, though none approaches the naked grandeur of "Michael," are closer to the exact life of the folk for whom he speaks. He is more even in accomplishment. His trafficking with grandeur is rare, but his dealing with nature while it never flashes into Wordsworthian rapture, has a constant closeness and quiet magic.

He has never taken the trouble to explain his revolt or its method in set critical terms. But there is a sonnet in "Mountain Interval" called "The Oven Bird" which in quietly transparent fashion cannot but be interpreted as the poet's

497

deeper thought concerning himself. This bird is one who sings of nothing new or startling, but of the things that belong to eternal feelings and processes. And this bird

> would cease and be as other birds
> But that he knows in singing not to sing.
> The question that he frames in all but words
> Is what to make of a diminished thing

—of things, one may assume, diminished not *from* but *to* what actually and in fact they are, because

> We love the things we love for what they are.

In that line is summed up the naturalistic principle at its strongest and purest. Reality must suffice and we must find within life as given the values by which to live it. The poet has his moments of revulsion and desire for escape:

> I'd like to get away from earth awhile.

But those moments are brief:

> Earth's the right place for love:
> I don't know where it's likely to go better.

Our proper food will nourish us; if we try strange meats we shall be like Frost's "Cow in Apple Time," concerning whom he tells a modern fable so homely and so lofty at once. He desires, in brief, to get back to essentials; to strip speech as well as things of vain delusion, false heightening, inorganic adornment. He keeps his eye unfalteringly on the object; he accepts life as tragic but not as hopeless and the beauty he wrings from the world is an inherent one. Hence he has no need to argue or deride. Complicated social and moral phenomena are out of his line. Peasant-like he cleaves straight to permanent essentials in his delineations of both man and nature. Very greatly he admits the force of human passion in "Fire and Ice" and accepts ultimate and tragic consequences in such poems as "The Impulse." But though he is no conventional optimist, he is not hopeless either. Mankind has a way of striving; there is, at the least, a fundamental moral energy in human life; the "Tree Fallen Across the Road" cannot really halt us:

> obstruction is in vain:
> We will not be put off the final goal
> We have it hidden in us to attain,
> Not though we have to seize earth by the pole
> And, tired of aimless circling in one place,
> Steer straight off after something into space.

These are his two recurrent notes: the acceptance of life as tragic, for himself as in that remarkably fine sonnet, "Acquainted with the Night," for others in all the objective pieces and in the statement, rare but recurrent, of a frugal but gallant hope:

> Though all our blandishments would seem defied,
> We have ideas yet that we haven't tried.

He is not happy when he tries directly to reason, as in the title poem of "New Hampshire." He is at best when from phenomena in life and nature, seen with the highest sobriety and poeticalness at once, he wrings a meaning which is both personal and universal, concrete and therefore general. He does that again and again in the "Grace Notes" of the "New Hampshire" volume, in "Fragmentary Blue," in "The Runaway," "Stopping by Woods on a Snowy Evening," "Blue Butterfly Day," "Good-bye and Keep Cold," "A Brook in

the City," "Gathering Leaves," "The Kitchen Chimney,"
"The Lockless Door." These are extraordinarily satisfactory poems, profound and lucid. Lucidity and emotional
depth without crying and vain haste—"the depth and not
the tumult of the soul"—these are indeed Frost's great qualities. Upon the slightest of his best lyrics the memory can be
nourished and the heart can lean:

> The way a crow
> Shook down on me
> The dust of snow
> From a hemlock tree
>
> Has given my heart
> A change of mood
> And saved some part
> Of a day I had rued.

His tone deepens in the later poems. He has more commerce
with naked fate and, as in the superb "Canis Major," looks
oftener at the stars. He condenses a particular fate and a
universal problem into the few lines of a sonnet, as in "The
Investment"; he blends a sublime country shrewdness with
an extraordinarily just and significant statement of the urge
of a sane life after both inclusiveness and form in the twelve
lines of "The Armful"; in dealing with nature his music,
though not his speech, grows more elaborate and has a soft
mystical overtone; his moral temper, finally, grows more
somber and more stoical. He will not judge the age:

> at an unearthly height
> One luminary clock against the sky
> Proclaimed the time was neither wrong nor right.
> I have been one acquainted with the night.

In every age life may be well lived. "Acceptance" of fate is necessary; the moral affirmation of essential life as it is:

> Now let the night be dark for all of me.
> Let the night be too dark for me to see
> Into the future. Let what will be be.

Robert Frost is evidently no minor poet and the naturalistic revolt in American letters has produced nothing that savors more of the permanent than his best work. And this is so because he addressed himself to the permanent and sought life's meaning there. It may well be argued that he is therefore a less virtuous writer than those who could not withdraw themselves from the remediable wrongs and sufferings of their fellowmen in this polity and in this age; it is certain that for a poet this lack of active social virtue may constitute the highest felicity and even wisdom.

VI

The naturalistic revolt in America against the quality of our national life turned from its revelatory and accusing mood as in Dreiser and Masters to a mood of irony and satire. The new mood could not, of course, exist alone. To satirize life it had to be described. That which is to be derided must be simultaneously revealed. But the difference in tone and temper between Dreiser and Sinclair Lewis may be justly described as the difference between inquiry and satire. This difference in temper and aim leads to differences in method. The discouraging dullness of contemporary criticism is illustrated by the fact that the epithets "journalistic" and "photographic" have been applied to both novelists: to

Dreiser's patient attempt to see and record the reality of things and to Lewis's broadening, sharpening, even distorting of men and things at his best and strongest not to show them, but to show them up. Both are artists. Each selects and shapes his material under the necessary dominance of his temperament by which the method of his expression is determined.

I am conscious of the difficulty of a critical appraisal of the work of Sinclair Lewis. In approaching it at different times critics have been swayed, whether consciously or not, by very personal feelings engendered by the cultural life of America. His first works were welcomed with unparalleled acclaim because all were glad to see in brilliant and contemptuous satiric presentation, not unmingled with sadder and deeper notes, that which irked and wounded and harassed them too. The public followed the critics; a large minority was ready to laugh with Sinclair Lewis at the grosser foibles, the emptier gestures, the more clamorous spiritual stupidities of American life. Hence at an early age Lewis became extraordinarily famous. Perhaps no novels since "Uncle Tom's Cabin" had struck so deep over so wide a surface of the national life. The titles of both "Main Street" and "Babbitt" were unhesitatingly accepted into the American vernacular. They spread to all lands of English speech and a British cynic did not hesitate to name a book on America "The Babbitt Warren." To belittle these achievements, to fail to remember them, as is being widely done today, especially among the emphatically or professionally cultured, is the result of either malice or dullness. Let the books *sub specie æternitatis* look like what they may. But try, to translate a useful German idiom, try to *think* them *away* from the history of American civilization. It is evidently impossible. Then the indiscriminate belittling of Lewis which is the fashion today is wholly uncritical.

After "Babbitt" he wrote "Arrowsmith," in many ways a finer and a richer and deeper book than its predecessor. Then came "Elmer Gantry" and apart from a coarser execution, it was evident that Lewis was applying to another aspect of American life a formula derived from his own practice. Unhappily "Elmer Gantry" was followed by the highly amusing but obviously repetitious "The Man Who Knew Coolidge," by an injudicious pot-boiler, as if Sinclair Lewis's pot had to be kept boiling by any sacrifice of his intellectual or artistic integrity, and by the sincere and neither shallow nor inelegant but, according to the standard he had himself set, feeble and somewhat sapless "Dodsworth." And then, as the first American man of letters, he was given the Nobel Prize. Something very like a groan went up from America. There was in the situation much to confuse judgment. Lewis himself, according not to gossip but to open reports in the public press, did not bear the glory that had come to him with equanimity or ease. I would not record these matters did they not, as I hope to show, have a definite bearing upon both the psychology of the artist in America and upon the literary relations between Europe and America in this period.

We are very far indeed from the days when Sydney Smith asked: "Who reads an American book?" For the Continent of Europe today, if not for England, the answer must be: Everyone. Translations of the works of the more eminent American contemporaries abound in Germany, in France, in

503

Holland and the Scandinavian countries. Spanish and even Italian publishers are beginning to follow this example. But these books are rarely read by Europeans and more rarely criticized by them as works of art, comparable to European works of the creative imagination. They are regarded most often as documents which the European mind uses to fortify its waning sense of superiority by feeding upon American criticism of America, or else it uses them as a warning for Europe, in the sense of Georges Duhamel, against that Americanization, that standardization and mechanization of life which the cultivated European regards, whether rightly or wrongly, as due to the example and influence of the United States. Hence the more non-polemical an American work is, the smaller—except within restricted circles—is its European success likely to be. For Europe consciously or unconsciously regards America, upon the whole, as a young barbarian. To expect mature and disinterested art from such an one were evident folly. With one possible exception, then, contemporary American authors are esteemed in Europe in proportion as they are eccentric or, better still, in proportion as they can be esteemed to be violently anti-American. Not literary values are sought in their works, but that special quality, considered specifically American, which caters to the pre-judgments and hence to the comfort of the European mind. Of Dreiser, for instance, it is said that all he does has been done in Europe. He is not needed. If an American work imposes itself by a sheer literary power, its success is still rationalized by readers and reviewers as due to some inherent criticism of America and so to its usefulness in upholding European self-esteem. From this point of view it is clear that "Babbitt" is the ideal American book. And it may be asserted with great positiveness that it was Babbitt which the Swedish academy crowned and rewarded. How were the members of that academy to know that America was so weary of critical realism that it was, in reaction, tempted to be weary of Sinclair Lewis too and quite unjust to him, and that the spiritual life of America had entered another phase—a phase marked by a thirst for values, for beauty and idealism upon some terms, however new or stringent, for works that were to deal not with the perishable traits of a given civilization in a given age, but with the eternal life of mankind? Thus the awarding of the Nobel Prize to the author of "Babbitt" was felt in America to be a kind of anachronism, as though one were to burst in upon a company of cultivated Americans proud of being the bearer of the news that Henry Mencken of Baltimore had discovered that there are no gods. The force of anti-climax could go no farther!

These facts and considerations bring us to the crucial and strange tragedy of the creative artist in America—his almost if happily not quite universal inability to develop, to strike within himself new rocks whence might spring living waters, his apparent petrification at a certain point. Dreiser has never developed beyond "Sister Carrie," nor Masters beyond "Spoon River," nor Hergesheimer beyond "Linda Condon," nor Lewis beyond "Arrowsmith." On the threshold of middle age all these extraordinarily gifted men, gifted and powerful by the standards of any contemporary literature, stopped dead. The lyrists seem to be in better case. The novelists, alas, stick so closely to their last as to seem to have in them something of the cobbler. The age races by them and leaves them where they were. Hence they come to be anachronisms before they are old men; hence their works, however excellent, being not stages in their development, but fixed and final measures of them, tend to be undervalued while their authors are still in the flower and vigor of their years. And the resistance to them of a younger generation with its change in taste and ideal serves still further to inhibit and to enfeeble them. I shall not be understood as agreeing with those sterile youths of varying ages who haunt the cafés of Paris or Florence and declare, meanwhile producing nothing, that art cannot flourish in America. The contrary is true. The American artist is in many ways the luckiest in the world. He is sustained by a reading public of remarkable extent and flexibility of culture, which helps him easily to bear the ribald stupidities of most current criticism. He has the best chance of earning a livelihood for himself and his family by sound and uncompromising work—a supreme advantage which only the quite idiotic will even affect to despise. His sources of inspiration are the universal ones. Yet somewhere near middle age he stops; he is finished; he imitates himself. What were André Gide if he had gone on indefinitely rewriting the "Symphonie Pastorale" and not proceeded to the extraordinary experimentation of "Les Faux Monayeurs" and turned next to the stringent classicism of "L'École des Femmes," or Bernard Shaw if he had continued "Widowers' Houses" indefinitely and not become the intrepid visionary of Methuselah or the passionate historian of Saint Joan, or Thomas Mann if he had kept on writing realistic novels even so highly excellent as "Buddenbrooks" and not given us in "The Magic Mountain" the "Divine Comedy" of this age nor proceeded next, as he is now doing, to re-create the ancient Orient and to search for the ultimate beginnings of our spiritual culture? What were even Arthur Schnitzler if he had written eternal variations on "Liebelei" and not produced the philosophic novel "Der Weg ins Freie" or the broad epic drama "Der junge Medardus"? It is useless to say that these Europeans are more gifted than their American colleagues. Example after example could be given of other European artists clearly not so gifted as Sinclair Lewis, who nevertheless develop, strive forward, change with the changing years, exfoliate and ripen. I do not pretend to be able to offer any explanation of this tragic fact in the creative life of America. It is surely useful to point it out and to define what many must have felt and suspected. It serves, at all events, to explain the case of Sinclair Lewis. In his fortieth year he published "Arrowsmith"—a work within its own limits and judged by its own intentions, of the very highest excellence. With that method and in that direction no progress could be made. In that creative mood Lewis could no more surpass himself than Thomas Mann could have surpassed "Buddenbrooks." The great and significant difference is that Thomas Mann did not dream of trying; he knew, guided by profound artistic instinct—he knew, to use the strong vernacular phrase, exactly what o'clock it was. His ear heard from the beginning the gong of eternity, unapt at listening to the clamor of the day. . . . And Sinclair Lewis wrote "Elmer Gantry" and "The Man Who Knew Coolidge" and "Mantrap" and "Dodsworth." It is pitiful for him and tragic for American literature. No wonder that "Babbitt" and "Arrowsmith" are absurdly disesteemed today, as they

507

would not be were they the stages in the development of a great creative career, were they the masterpieces of their author's first manner and earlier years, were they the brilliant and varied and sagacious preludes to but one deeper, riper and more universal work. No wonder that his serious reputation has declined; no wonder that his receiving the Nobel Prize in 1930 was felt by the most thoughtful and sensitive of his countrymen to be an anachronism and a blunder.

But he who is not swayed by the special critical climate of either an earlier or a later year can afford to hold the balance level and esteem the best works of Lewis at their just value, which is high, according to their exact influence, which was great and beneficial. "You must not ask more of people than they have to give," says an old nun in one of Somerset Maugham's fine Chinese sketches, and thus unconsciously enunciates the sad and final principle of all practical criticism whether of people or of books. You must not ask of Sinclair Lewis a knowledge of beauty or of either the glories or the subtleties of the passions or any confrontation of eternity or any ideal richer than the intellectual integrity of the scientific mechanist who has made a religion of an exactness which does not exist. You must not ask for any magic in the texture of his works or for anything that has to do with poetry of perception or feeling. But that there are many mansions in the house of art is proven by the fact that you must not ask Molière for any of these things either and that for some of them you will also ask Dickens in vain. Nor are these names chosen at random. Molière and Dickens have this in common, that they depict manners, that they work from without inward, that they universalize the particular not so much by intensification as by broadening; they symbolize by inclusiveness rather than by disengaging essences. Thus they give us Jourdain and Tartuffe, Micawber and Pecksniff. This method of portraying human nature has fallen into some disrepute in this age, partly by comparison, to be sure, with nobler and higher methods, but largely, alas, under the sway of the cultivators of inner monologue and of others who substitute vain subtleties for plastic power. It is no accident that the bourgeois *gentilhomme* and Tartuffe and Micawber and Pecksniff have all become proverbial figures and that we say "a Tartuffe" and "Micawberish" and "Pecksniffian" precisely as we say "the Babbittry" or "a regular Babbitt." These inclusive and all-too-human grotesques are produced by the delineators of manners, who are usually not creative spirits of the deepest and richest kind. But the reason why at their strongest they produce their powerful and enduring effects is because manners symbolize moral constitution and moral constitution springs from a blending of society with the soul itself. And hence these rather dry-souled depictors of types and caricatures, from La Bruyère to Sinclair Lewis, who have so little to give us of passion or sensuous beauty and nothing of ultimate wisdom at all, rank high among the moral historians of mankind.

Let us take Sinclair Lewis, as every writer should be taken, at his best. Let us leave aside "Main Street," though it has almost become a folk-book, on the ground that, despite its many excellencies, Lewis had not established a sufficient distance between himself and the world of illusion he depicted and identified himself too far with the feeble and superficial yearnings of Carol Kennicott. And let us regard "Elmer Gantry" and "The Man Who Knew Coolidge" as we regard those rude, strong farces of Molière, which we value because we see in them the hand which wrought "Tartuffe" and "Le Misanthrope." And let us fix our attention on "Babbitt" and "Arrowsmith." In the light of what has been said it is seen at once, of course, that no reproach was ever more stupid than the reproach of flat realism brought against Lewis. No such person as George F. Babbitt of Zenith ever existed nor any such as the magnificent Dr. Almus Pickerbaugh and his eight Healthettes. These personages belong with the Micawbers and their twins, with the Kenwigses and their Morleena, with the Crummleses and their Infant Phenomenon. No booster or Rotarian ever made such a speech as the annual address delivered by George F. Babbitt before the Real Estate Board of the city of Zenith. But it is the speech that every booster and Rotarian may have made in his uncensored dreams. It is the essence of Rotarianism thrice purified by the vision of the ironic mind. It is Rotarianism made eternal and perfect for our delectation and the laughter of posterity. No health inspector ever sent out the gorgeous invitation which Dr. Pickerbaugh addressed to his "brother males and she-males" nor instituted a Three Cigars a Day Week or a Can the Cat and Doctor the Dog Week. These things and the poems of Frink and all the meetings and banquets in "Babbitt," especially the gathering of the alumni of the State University, and the activities of Cliff Clawson in "Arrowsmith" and of the two-fisted, progressive physicians with their Bindledorf Tonsillectomy Outfit—all these things are the reverse of flat realism; they are the products of a satiric imagination of a very high order. They are true, immensely true, much truer in fact than any reality. They are art and, within their strict limits and on their own level, astonishingly rich and varied and energetic art.

Nor is this all. Lewis belongs to a profounder and more tragic age than his more illustrious predecessors; the age works for and through him and lends him its deeper implications. Thus it was granted him to give us not only the visible image of Zenith with its noise and hustle and glare but to show us, deep buried beneath these, the helpless hush, the spiritual stagnancy, the dimness and confusion. Babbitt is a symbol and also a symbol of his city. His life is speed without aim, matter without form, activity without desire. With a forlorn cheerfulness he says at the end to his son: "Practically I've never done a single thing I've wanted to in my whole life." A mechanical civilization and a system of morals with which the will can no longer identify itself— these forces now move on on their own impetus. They are implicated with the economic structure and threaten the dissenter with exile and hunger. Thus life is lived in the shadow of a circumambient fear. Babbitt, for all his joviality and bluster, is a creature of fear. He fears his business associates, his friends, his political representatives, his wife. He fears for his business which gives him prosperity without wealth, for his home that gives him order without comfort, for domestic affections which keep out bleakness but do not warm his soul. He has never done what he wanted to do; he possesses nothing that he truly wants. His friend Paul Riesling, being not a symbol and type but a human being, is destroyed by the conflict. Fear at last drives Babbitt back from his timid wanderings to the celebration of things as, for him, they are. The thing is story and parable, moral history and its interpretation, no less pertinent and rich today than when it was written.

In "Arrowsmith" this civilization is depicted in a more leisurely and freer form. It has not been properly observed that "Babbitt" is a very rigidly built book, rising from that base of a single day in Babbitt's and his city's life toward a sharp spire of fable and meaning. The structure is almost too geometrical and, also, from Chapter XXXI on, the tip of the spire is blunted by excess of matter. Arrowsmith is more fluid. It is less apologue and more story. It is more various in scene and more richly peopled than its predecessor. It has far more of the rhythm and true rumor of life. It is less neat and tight and more largely creative. In it, moreover, this civilization meets an ideal—very nobly and adequately embodied in Dr. Gottlieb, again a great type rather than a great person, but very proper for his function within the framework of the novel. This ideal, the specific content of which may well be questioned, is a high and necessary one according to its form and intention, for it is that of uncompromising intellectual integrity. The choice of this ideal against which to depict American slackness and rant, dullness and confusion, is once more—*mutatis mutandis*—the ideal upheld by Molière in "Le Misanthrope." It is the highest ideal to which this type, to whom ultimate spiritual values are inaccessible, can rise. The playwright and the novelist of manners desire people to be sincere and honest and intelligent. Of love and aspiration he knows nothing. Twice Lewis had glimpses of a higher realm of both art and ideal: once in the character of Paul Riesling in "Babbitt," once in that of Leora in "Arrowsmith." But he seems himself not to be aware of the essential not accidental difference between these and all his other characters. Perhaps the reaction against him is part of a larger movement in American civilization, of a despair over the aridness of life so great that a depiction of it, however brilliant, no longer meets any serious mood, of so keen a hunger after values by which to live that the integrity of the laboratory scientist seems an ideal of straw and bran. . . . In so far as a reaction against Lewis is due to such causes it is, for its day and year, justified. It remains no less true and will be acknowledged in due time that he has added to American literature two works, two novels of manners, which ally him definitely and permanently with the masters in that kind.

VII

The impulse to depict American life critically, whether by patient exposition or by satiric presentation, to reveal, in other words, that which has wounded the artist's mind or his sensibilities—this impulse is evidently the strongest in modern American letters. Many, as will be seen, whom this impulse gradually left, were nevertheless first moved by it to expression. Such an one is Eugene O'Neill. Others, like Hergesheimer, in whom this impulse was secondary from the start, are nevertheless moved by it at certain moments in their career. The revolt of creative minds against the texture and moral quality of American life was almost universal. And to its moods of exposition and buoyant satire there was gradually added a third—a mood of bitter distaste and cruel tedium, a mood of contemptuousness so sharp as to be weary of itself, a mood beyond triumph and therefore beyond open satire. This mood, which is found once more in several of the youngest neo-naturalists was first and most powerfully exemplified by Ring Lardner. With many years as a sporting editor and writer behind him Lardner first gained the attention of Carl Van Doren and other sagacious critics by a series of literary caricatures of definite types of those whom the American vernacular has come to call "dumb-bells." His method of quiet relentlessness in the exposure of human folly was already perfected in these sketches. But their texture was thin; the characterization was almost that of the comic strip, although the handling of vernacular speech was already masterly. It was, as it has remained, of an unbelievable symbolic accuracy; it is heard and recorded with the exactness of an icy hatred and contempt. Next came the short stories with the three-dimensional characters and their far higher density of texture and it may safely be asserted that the best of these stories with their deadly sureness of aim and steely impassiveness of manner are among the most powerful of their kind in modern literature. Perhaps the cream of Lardner's ferocious jesting is this, that, on account of his very impassiveness and hard superficial *bonhomie* he has been able to sell his merciless tales to the periodicals that cater to the very fools and rogues whom he castigates. In these stories the reader is introduced to a kind of American hell—a hell of relentless dullness and cold cruelty in which the victims of that dreadful dullness are degraded by being utterly inured to it, in which both the perpetrators and the victims of cruelty deceive themselves and each other by using the vocabulary of American sporting-page optimism and Fundamentalist "folksiness" and Forty-second Street magniloquence. The most famous of the stories is "Haircut." It is also the best, since in it alone are two human beings not fiercely stupid and vulgar to the marrow. These two are victims, of course. But they exist. Never again does Lardner relent to his *bête humaine*. Dreadful creatures people "Alibi Ike" and "Champion," foul hypocrites "The Love Nest," poor clods in human shape "The Golden Honeymoon," pretentious fools of a ghastly emptiness "Travelogue" and "Some Like Them Cold." And the devastating thing about Lardner's work is that no American exists who has not a thousand times heard these accents, seen these faces, observed these gestures. These bitter and brutal stories belong not only to literature but to the history of civilization.

Not all the naturalists of secondary rank shared the acrid vision of Lardner. And much excellent work of such rank was done during the entire modern period. It is difficult to select either names or works. No critic can read everything nor read, however widely, with a level equanimity of mood and acuteness of perception. Nor will any be wholly unswayed by those subtle and imponderable elements that dictate preference. These things are inevitable. Hence I shall not apologize for not finding enough definite quality to justify treatment in the works of writers so well-known and so different from each other as Ellen Glasgow and Gertrude Atherton. Appreciation being much surer to be right in questionable cases than the lack of it, I do not hesitate to select among the minor naturalists George Frederic Hummel, Thyra Samter Winslow and Ruth Suckow. Hummel's work is very uneven, though never without insight or power. He has, so far, made his permanent mark with but a single volume: "Subsoil, The Chronicle of a Village." This book, however, has a sober classical quality, a measured strength, a fine sanity. More than any other book on the American village is it allied to such delineations of peasant life as those of Gottfried Keller. Hummel does not extenuate; he does not gild his village; there are folly, madness, crime. But his large and generous humanity gives him the kindliness of detachment and unimpeded strength. A comparable sobriety informs the excellent stories of Thyra Samter in both "Picture Frames" and "People Round the Corner." Here all is exact but the modesty of nature is duly observed. Extreme types are avoided or else all types are seen in an ultimate spirit of human love. There are stories in these volumes, such as "A Manhattan Cycle" or the tender "Her Own Room" or the forlornly pathetic "When We Get in with Nice People" that would grace, in their own kind, any literature. The critics of our press have, among other things, on their consciences the comparative neglect of such work as "Subsoil" and "People Round the Corner" amid the extravagant claims made for the ephemeral and the shoddy. Ruth Suckow has been luckier than her colleagues, perhaps because her strength lies in the novel rather than in the short-story. Of her novels "The Odyssey of a Nice Girl" remains the best. Here is that same sobriety and moderation and humanity that is likely to mark the better kind of naturalistic work. From the unpretentious delineation of these simple German-Americans of the Middle West there arises a deep sense of both the pathos and the value of human life and love. And it is by that communication of a certain eternal quality in human existence and in the monitions of the human heart that such books as "Subsoil," "Picture Frames" and "The Odyssey of a Nice Girl" are likely in their quiet way to survive works far more brilliant and immediately effective.

With Thyra Samter Winslow and Ruth Suckow we have reached a younger generation—a generation which often would not consent to its possession of the impulse and temper of the naturalist alone but, deeply and justly aware that a change in taste was imminent, strove to refresh and render vivid its chronicling of reality by the addition of devices that were supposed to symbolize the age of speed and of the machine. Such a writer is John Dos Passos. The notion, for instance, that the moving or talking picture has changed one whit the passions or the mental processes of humanity, though belied by the fables and emotions communicated by the pictures themselves, is an error so widespread as to have given the novels of Dos Passos with their devices borrowed from the headline, the news reel and the camera a reputation for originality which an examination of them does nothing to sustain. Not that they lack merit. The tales and episodes that make up "The Forty-Second Parallel," for instance, are powerful examples of a harsh and desperate naturalism. Their character is not in the least changed by the failure to narrate and the attempt, repugnant to the nature of literature, to show forth as with reproductive machinery, the passing of time and the change in historical background and atmosphere, nor is such a change effected by the use of the Joycian trick of writing two or three words as one. I shall be accused of resisting originality; I deprecate only its spurious imitation.

True originality, which is originality and personal freshness of vision and of style, was brought to the American novel by Ernest Hemingway. He began to write under the influence of Sherwood Anderson, an influence which he was soon to repudiate with something of unnecessary violence in "The Torrents of Spring." He developed meanwhile that manner of his which was later to ripen into a style. Even at its earlier stage of manner, this way of writing had in it something strong and sound and refreshing. For it stripped speech of the otiose and the equivocal and sought to limit expression to that of fact and sensation. As dialogue it had all the aspects of a trick. But even as such it was never meretricious. For in "The Sun Also Rises" it organically symbolized two facts born out by the whole creative structure of the book: the spiritual despair of those fools and wasters and its ultimate result in the abstention from all expression save the oath of irritation and the cry of enfeebled desire. In this book, moreover, there was present another quality always of good augury for a young writer: strong sensuous experience and the power of communicating it, so that one carried away from the story a memory of sensations—the hot sun on the sand of Spain, the coolness of sharp shadow, the sting of brandy in the throat. So far Hemingway was merely the most gifted of the new "hard-boiled" writers, that is to say, of those impelled to depict life in order to express their disgust for it and hence their own spiritual despair. This mood obviously forbids development of thought or art by what it is. From this mood Hemingway liberated himself and wrote

"A Farewell to Arms." And this book, the excellence of which was at once felt and acknowledged, proves once again the ultimate identity of the moral and the æsthetic. For Hemingway's manner became style and fragmentariness became structure and his bluntness won resonance and overtone because he was inspired by the affirmation and not the denial of passion—passion of indignation and passion of love. He transcended the moral nihilism of the school he had himself helped to form and wrote one of the few quite beautiful and satisfactory books in contemporary literature. The simply wrought fable has two culminations—the laconic and terrible one in which the activity of the battle police brings to an end the epically delineated retreat of the Italian army with its classically curbed rage and pity ("The questioners had that beautiful detachment and devotion to stern justice of men dealing in death without being in any danger of it") and that other and final culmination in Switzerland with its blending in so simple and moving a fashion of the eternal notes of love and death. The love story is of an extraordinary strength and tenderness, of an extraordinary faith, considering the age and the author's immediate cultural antecedents, in the value of the quite simple and permanent elements of our mortal lot. "Often a man wishes to be alone and a girl wishes to be alone too and if they love each other they are jealous of that in each other, but I can truly say we never felt that. We could feel alone when we were together, alone against the others. . . . We were never lonely and never afraid when we were together. I know that the night is not the same as the day: that all things are different, that the things of the night cannot be explained in the day, because they do not then exist, and the night can be a dreadful time for lonely people once their loneliness has started. But with Catherine there was almost no difference in the night except that it was an even better time. If people bring so much courage to this world the world has to kill them to break them, so of course it kills them. The world breaks everyone and afterward many are strong at the broken places. But those that will not break it kills. It kills the very good and the very gentle and the very brave impartially. If you are none of these you can be very sure it will kill you too but there will be no special hurry." The critic who has seen the development of so many highly gifted Americans arrested before even the normal noonday of their powers had been reached and has seen them search in vain within themselves for an enlargement of the sources of creation, may well watch with some anxiety the writer of this passage and this book. Since the emergence of the writers of the middle generation Ernest Hemingway alone has struck an important new note—a note at once human and, in the ultimate sense, philosophical in American literature.

The other neo-naturalists have wholly abandoned the melioristically inspired inquiry of Dreiser, the similarly motivated satire of Sinclair Lewis—all moral energy, all human hope. In the level tone of a disgust so deep as to be almost placid they tell us over and over again—Morley Callaghan, Nathan Asch, William Faulkner—that man is a vile animal crawling about on a heap of ordure. It may be so. But it is also true as a matter of unanswerable experience and fact that art so motivated will die of its own weariness and emptiness. For art means highest energy and energy must be fed from some source. In this desert there are no springs.

The most gifted of these young neo-naturalists is undoubtedly William Faulkner. He has preserved one active emotion, a very fruitful emotion for the naturalist: a fierce hatred for all that has given him pain. The dreadful Mississippians in his pages are set forth with ferocity and therefore with sharp vividness. Jason Compson in "The Sound and the Fury" is convincingly projected as a scoundrel of most loathsome nature; the father in "As I Lay Dying" is portrayed with an equal brutality. Laboriously one gathers these and other characterizations hardly below these from Faulkner's needlessly intricate and essentially confused books. For these tormented and tormenting devices of interior dialogue, this painfully conscientious abandoning of the mood and method of narrative, which is the natural and inherent method of the story, whether in heroic poem or folk ballad or romance or novel—all this was undoubtedly organically determined by the structure of the psyche and hence the method of expression of James Joyce. In him therefore, quite without going into the merits of the case, it was inevitable. I am yet to be convinced that what he could not but do is other than a sincere and laborious affectation in young American writers from Mississippi or Iowa or Hester Street. Is it not in fact a substitution for the meaning they can no longer find either in their own hearts or in life itself? Is it not allied to that metaphysical despair which has led, as we have seen and shall see again, to the abandoning of meaning, to the hopelessness of any meaning *in* meaning? And may not art, of which the source is in life, be enriched and strengthened rather by a transcendence of moral nihilism than by an indulgence in devices strictly analogous to those by which the regressive neurotic seeks to save himself from the affirmation of his true self within the given world of our mortal lot?

BOOK TWELVE

Beyond Naturalism

I

From the beginning of the modern movement in American literature there were artists whose need to speak creatively and to justify themselves was not implicated with the wounds and humiliations dealt them by the social and economic order. That order in itself had inflicted no pain on them; they had no motive for resisting or correcting it by delineation. Hence the symbols which they used were not, at least primarily, the symbols that create an illusion of strict reality; they used symbolism less concrete and more general by which to body forth their aspirations, their conflicts, their desire for justification and for permanence. Their way is more difficult than that of the naturalist because there are so few symbols left in this age within the texture of civilization which the artist can use to communicate himself. Everyone understands the symbol of reality in art and, whether in a mood of agreement or dissent, the mood of resisting or changing or satirizing things as they are. But with the enfeebling, except upon the lowest plane, of all the traditional symbols of religion and of patriotism, the non-naturalistic artist is hard put to it to find symbols of expression that will enable him to communicate himself to his fellows. Art other than naturalistic and so social operates in a void; it has no values and symbols agreed upon, no recognized coinage of the spirit in which to pay its self-contracted debts. In the name of what ideal shall the artist speak? Of a purely personal one? Then he jeopardizes his power of communication; for it is evident that men cannot comprehend anything that is not, at least, in germ present in their consciousness. It is the absence of common ideals and common values, of symbols agreed upon, that throws the idealistic artist in this age so helplessly upon his abstract self; it is this absence of a common language in the deeper sense that renders so many contemporary productions in all the arts inaccessible, tortured, obscure, uncommunicative. A painter of old painted a Crucifixion and the symbol with all its values was accessible to all men. Their hearts and minds were open. Hence they had little or no difficulty in distinguishing this Crucifixion from all other Crucifixions and thus of appreciating this individual painter's personal vision and passion and character. By using a symbol of known value the artist was enabled to communicate himself. He had a bridge between himself and his audience. Today a painter paints, as children say, out of his own head. It is hard to comprehend his personal idiom, because he has at his command no general symbol. Who and what are these scenes and creatures upon the canvas? They are feeble, necessarily feeble, because no individual has the power of building those strong and universal symbols which humanity through

long ages has caused to ripen in its womb. It is for this reason that the great poets of the past have invented little or
nothing. They took as subject-matter what was already in
the consciousness of their people in their age—history, myth,
legends of gods and men, tales that had flown for years from
mouth to mouth. Such were the subjects of the Greek poets
and of Shakespeare, of Goethe and even of Wagner. But
there are no new symbols like that, none so deeply imbedded
in the collective consciousness—none, that is, except that
symbol of the illusion of the real which the naturalists use.
The individual cannot invent new myths and legends. Hence
it is not by accident but by a strange inherent necessity that
so many non-naturalistic artists are nevertheless driven to use
the symbols of contemporary reality nor that, despairing of
new symbols and desiring to proceed beyond naturalism, they
seek once more to revivify the old symbols, like Willa Cather
in her flight to Catholicism or Edwin Arlington Robinson
in his to Arthurian legend, or that they swathe themselves in
mere decoration like Joseph Hergesheimer, or that they feign
to themselves, like T. S. Eliot or Paul Valéry that form is
all-significant, substance of no import, and that works live
by the amount of intelligence with which their outer and
visible technique was wrought. In a word, we have substitution for or escape from the iron fact that art issued from
religion and is forever allied thereto and must, in sober truth,
again become more and more religion as religion itself loses
its hold upon the minds of men. Thus is to be explained, to
take a trivial but significant instance, the vast popularity of
a book like Thornton Wilder's "The Bridge of San Luis
Rey." The puzzled question asked of fate in that tale is such

525

a question as all men, even the simplest, have asked in their meditative hours. The appeal of the book was a religious appeal. And for that appeal in a nobler and more powerful form mankind is waiting.

For at the core of modern life there is a fear of life. The old ideologies bore a great part of the burden of man's life for him. He prayed to his gods, fought for his country and begot his posterity within a framework that justified these things. Today he questions even when he still feigns to himself to believe. Guilt and fear are at the heart of all his fundamental acts and thoughts. His universe has been shattered into a multiverse; nothing binds him to it nor to his fellows. He lives and acts in a bleak void unguided by any principle that makes his actions and thoughts within an intelligible world either coherent or satisfactory. All the old paths are obliterated. In view is a "waste land." The Catholic and Anglo-Catholic and so-called humanist reactions all bear witness, despite themselves, to this fact. And from the entire situation can be rationally derived the continuance and continued appeal of naturalistic art; since a perception of the apparent so-ness of things and of the existence of crime and folly within our social and economic system are the only bindings or, if one likes, common intellectual denominators, left to the greater part of mankind. Yet it becomes more and more evident that naturalism, too, is gradually becoming enfeebled, because its activity could never transcend a critical stage. It helped men to flee from under a yoke, but had—and this is no reproach—no path nor goal to offer. We know what Dreiser hates. What does he love? Upton Sinclair offers a new synthesis to which a group of younger men the other day declared their at least theoretical adherence. It is, I am convinced, not to be thought of that any considerable portion of Western mankind will content itself with the religion, the binding principle, of mechanistic Communism. For in another arc of the horizon are other dawns: a vision of the physical universe that is the reverse of mechanistic, a psychology that repudiates root and branch a mechanistic account of man's inner processes, whether racial or individual, and subordinates even the reproductive instinct to the instinct for survival, a simultaneous breaking down in physics, psychology and metaphysics of the sufficiency of causality as ordinarily conceived. Yet for the day and year these new visions, imperfectly grasped and by but a handful, seem only to add to the vast confusions of the cosmos and man has no place where to lay his head.

From all these circumstances the emergence of a neo-idealistic literature may be confidently predicted; from them is also to be derived the almost simultaneous appearance of non-naturalistic or semi-naturalistic art with the work of the critical realists in the America of our time. It is the same urge toward wholeness and coherence and so toward new symbols that we find prophetically in the great nineteenth-century figures: in the passing of Ibsen from social realism to the mystic symbolism of "When We Dead Awaken," in the iron flight from earth in Shaw's "meta-biological penta-teuch," in Gerhart Hauptmann's transcendence of "coherent naturalism" and return to the mystic perceptions if not to the faith of his fathers. It is the urge and the cry incomparably formulated so long ago by Nietzsche, who knew that man cannot live by either nihilism or superstition: "I wander

527

among men as among fragments of a future: of that future which my eye beholds. . . . And this is the goal of my creative ardor that I create oneness and coherence of that which is fragment and riddle and cruel accident. . . . For how could I endure being Man, were not man creator and reder of riddles and the redeemer of accident unto order."

The poet that men are waiting for is the poet who will redeem accident unto order for them. And the attempt to redeem accident unto order has been, however feebly and unconsciously, the attempt of all these contemporary Americans who were, by temperament or on principle, not content with the method and the aims of naturalism. Among these American writers there is none who is great and I may seem to be breaking butterflies upon metaphysical wheels. Yet these writers acquire an importance beyond the value of their works by being seen in their true aspect as phenomena within a larger movement and by being so studied definite trends within their writings such as, to give a single example, Eugene O'Neill's increasing dependence on the discoveries of analytical psychology, will assume their proper import and meaning.

II

It will be expected that the study of those American writers who passed beyond naturalism be begun with the work of James Branch Cabell. It is not necessary to disappoint that expectation, despite the fact that Cabell did not pass beyond naturalism; he never reached it. He is, as perhaps became a Virginian aristocrat and genealogist, a belated romantic—one who shows all the symptoms of good, old-fashioned romanticism: an innocent disillusion with reality in any of its aspects, a sedulous cultivation of all the methods of flight into a prettily reconstructed mediævalism, a use of romantic irony as an expression of his disappointment and a mild scabrousness with tongue roguishly in cheek. "The idle singer of an empty day" like William Morris, though quite without that gifted poet's social preoccupations and creative coherence. Cabell, like his own Felix Kennaston determined "lovingly to deal with an epoch and a society, and even a geography, whose comeliness had escaped the wear and tear of ever actually existing," and he did so because he "believed this country to be the one possible setting for a really satisfactory novel." Now the artist who has passed beyond naturalism seeks not escape from reality into fairyland; he wrings from reality its permanent meaning and underlying principles of being and his hope is to produce a work far more real than any reality subject to time and chance. According to Cabell "books are an avenue to forgetfulness"—like cinema pictures or "glad" novels or plays for tired business men. But it is the function of art, above all things, not to make men forget but to remember and to heighten their consciousness of existence and of its meaning. No wonder, then, that Kennaston ends upon the pretty sentiment: "It is only by preserving faith in human dreams that we may, after all, perhaps some day make them come true." It all depends upon the meaning attached to the word dreams. If it is used by Kennaston as a synonym for rational aspirations, for active hopes both moral and social, one might be glad to take the sentence to heart. The whole tenor of Cabell's work is against any such interpretation. Kennaston meant the escape from life into revery and dreamy wish-fulfillment—revery and wish-fulfillment, moreover, of a distinctly adolescent cast, having to do with shimmering change of unearthly scene, with fighting minus danger and the romantically tinged pursuit of promiscuous amours. Such is the substance of "Jurgen," the chief work of the "Biography," which first had its hour of notoriety on account of the silly legal attack made upon it, and which has since sustained a limited popularity both because of its supposed salaciousness and on account of its falling in so well with the daydreams of those whose development has been arrested at the threshold of both action and passion. There being many such in America, the reputation of James Branch Cabell is high. But it is significant that people are divided into a group that "simply adores" the tales of Poictesme and Storisende and another group which finds it almost impossible to read three consecutive pages of them. And the latter group will be found invariably to be a group of rational and virile minds. The fields of earth are on fire under our feet and Cabell offers us the daydreams of a romantic adolescent; there is a famine and he goes about hawking expensive and soon cloying sweets. Kennaston, the symbol at least of Cabell, is represented as not wholly unaware of the character of his undertakings. "There is no escaping, at times, the gloomy suspicion that fiddling with pens and ink is, after all, no fit employment for a grown man." Kennaston's suspicion was correct. His use of pen and ink, despite its skill and grace and learning, was only "fiddling" and would, in fact, never have been undertaken by a man who was inwardly grown up. It is the eternal occupation of either the adolescent or the neurotic who will not face life in fear of defeat, in fear that it will not conform to his childish demands and cater to the exorbitant demands of his at once quivering and arrogant ego. It is the psychical mechanism of the morbidly sensitive child who will not play with other children but sits in a corner nursing daydreams in which he is always the cleverest and strongest, the handsomest and most triumphant. . . . The high repute of the works of Mr. Cabell has not been attacked by critics, partly out of a faint snobbishness; partly for the amusing reason that those who were fit to criticize him found him almost impossible to read, and lastly because scholarship and a love of good prose seemed too rare in America to be discredited on other grounds without a pang. His prose is, indeed, not only correct but constantly graceful in diction and liquid in rhythm. The trouble is that there is nothing in all these romances for the mind to grasp; one fumbles in a sunny mist; one hopes from page to page to come upon something either sharp or solid; that hope is soon abandoned and next it becomes clear that even the grace of this style is often falsely arch and knowing or effeminate and teasing. The style, in brief, is married to the matter and both are *articles de luxe,* like gorgeously enameled cigarette *étuis* diamond and ruby studded, or riding-crops with jeweled handles. . . . But art is like bread or wine or oil, sustenance without which the spirit cannot live. . . .

A sharp and instructive contrast is offered at once by the work of Joseph Hergesheimer. It is true that, in the saying of Faust, two souls have always lived within his breast, but it is also true that the stronger of these two has prevailed often enough, though never without a struggle, over the feebler. To a critic who had praised "Cytherea" Joseph Hergesheimer once wrote that a bit of chiffon at a woman's shoulder meant more to him than all the problems and agonies. It may be so. The fact remains that he has addressed himself again and again to problems and agonies and has thus and only thus, whatever comfort and profit his decorative cinema novels, "The Bright Shawl" and "Tampico" may have brought him, produced the few works by which his reputation stands or falls. From the beginning he sought the significant pattern of life in the past. But he was not quite clear about that aim in his own mind and smothered history under archæology. He emptied the East India museum at Salem into "Java Head"; even in "The Three Black Pennys" he loses his way again and again amid accessories. The gesture of beauty which he sought as that which gives life meaning he found too often in aspects not stern or enduring enough. It is true, as he says in an early story, that "apparent trifles often hold a steadfast loveliness more enduring than the greatest tragedies and successes"; but he has been too often tempted by this truth or half-truth and thus led away from beauty to prettiness and from working in marble or oak to fashioning in porcelain. The best of his early work is that in which the tone he seeks to render is somber in its own nature: as in that fine tale of mid-nineteenth-century New England, "The Dark Fleece"; as in the first third of "The Three Black Pennys," where the American forest so impressively surrounds the frills and furbelows of an artificial age. He has been less and less felicitous as he has yielded to the glare and gaudiness of tropical scenes and colors; their dazzling quality has obliterated the true tones that he so often found on his palette of pastels. But his ambition has always been a reconciling element in him. From the decorative and the exotic he has always sought to return to that early quest of significant beauty in the gestures of the past, as he did recently once more in "The Limestone Tree." For epic delineation his talent is too fragile and his effects too fragmentary and "The Limestone Tree" has no episodes so strong and memorable as "The Three Black Pennys." But the composition of "The Limestone Tree" links his later with his earlier years and renders easier a definition of his talent and its fruits.

He has sought, then, to disengage both in the past and in the present the beautiful gesture, the thing beautiful, above all, to the eye, in which he finds the meaning of life and of the world. One might, under this aspect, compare him to such a writer as Théophile Gautier or, rather, Théodore de Banville. For he has not Gautier's enameled surface nor his strength of casting, as it were, in bronze. Being, moreover, of necessity a novelist, he has had to diffuse his sense of visible beauty over too many pages and so, losing concentration, has too often fallen into mere decorativeness. Much of that large portion of his work is trivial; all of it is perishable. And that is so because in these books there was no inner principle of life to sustain the structure or to turn decoration into beauty. There was but one force that could, for an unreligious modern like Hergesheimer, turn decorativeness into beauty and render organic works conceived after the manner of his. That force was the force of human passion. It is demonstrable and clear that without religion or sex beauty is trivial: from those forces alone a beauty issues that can sting and burn and that will not, like silken shawls or embroidered fabrics, molder a little sooner or later into dust. It is no accident that the two books of Joseph Hergesheimer which today at least have the aspect of permanent additions to American literature are "Linda Condon" and "Cytherea."

It is significant enough that the scene of both of these books is laid in the present and in New York and Philadelphia, and that the framework of both is realistic enough. Yet both, especially "Linda Condon," have something of the legendary and even a touch of the allegorical by which Hergesheimer remained true to his constant desire to disengage beauty from the welter of the impermanent. Thus neither the immensely realistic portrait of Linda's mother, nor the dusty New York hotels in which the girl spent her childhood nor the vividness of other characters rob either the fable or the scenes of the symbolical guise under which Hergesheimer desired us to perceive them. The book, as a whole, is like Linda herself, "remote and perfect and faintly wistful"; it is enormously simplified in method despite its contacts with the roughness and the muffled tumult of life. And the reason for Hergesheimer's success in disengaging significant beauty here from the New York and Philadelphia of his age, is that he was inspired not by his taste for the decorative, but by a powerful and ancient and eternal idea that has to do with love, with sex, with creative begetting. On this idea Socrates discoursed to Agathon and his other friends that night they sent the dancers and the flute-players away; Dante dedicated to it his "Vita Nuova," and Shelley his "Epipsychidion." Linda Condon is more than a lovely person. She is that "image of some bright eternity" of which Shelley dreamed; she is one through whom the Platonic archetypal Idea of Beauty shines more clearly than it is wont to do; she is the end of all quests for the sculptor who, before he knew her, might again have said with Shelley,

> In many mortal forms I rashly sought
> The shadow of that idol of my thought,

but who, having found his "idol," burnt himself out with the spiritual ardency of his effort to transfer to clay or bronze that gleam of the eternal beauty which shone upon him from her who was not only a mortal woman, but also

> La figlia della sua mente, l'amorosa idea.

Such beauty, and here Hergesheimer's controlling thought symbolizes what is best in his talent—such beauty has little commerce with earthly things, but like great tragedy effects a catharsis in its lovers and worshipers, "a wringing out of all dross." To both her husband and her lover she remained essentially unapproachable to the end, but she guided both of them—to paraphrase Du Bellay's famous sonnet—to that high heaven where they could recognize face to face that Idea of Beauty which they had adored on earth. The story is an allegory of the search for beauty; it is, whether quite consciously or not, probably Hergesheimer's own search which has led him so often to mere decorativeness, sometimes almost to tawdriness, but which, being the strongest and the noblest part of him, served of itself to inspire a beautiful and shapely book.

But this legend, this apologue which dealt only with "the consecration and the poet's dream" did not suffice him. He proceeded, as has not been remarked, to tell over again this tale of beauty and of the search for beauty in other, wilder and more stirring terms. For the creative and the procreative instinct are one. The doll Cytherea is, like Linda herself, a symbol and she is a symbol of but another aspect of that force which Henry Adams chose to name the Virgin. No wonder that in the novel called "Cytherea" the lovely form achieved by Hergesheimer in Linda Condon breaks and shivers into dissonances. Pipes shrill and timbrels clash; there was also, in the end, the wild ecstasy of Keats' verse. But though it was sweet in the mouth, it was terribly bitter in the belly. And that is because for Lee Randon, the protagonist of the novel, there was in this age no wholeness of beauty and meaning and ecstasy after which to strive. From his wife's "convention of modesty . . . which amounted to the secret idea that the reality of love was disgusting," what did he flee to but the abnormal passion of Savina Grove? "When it was over, I didn't miss Savina, I couldn't even call her individually back to my mind; and the inhumanity of that, the sheer ingratitude, was contemptible." But that was because Savina was not the Aphrodite of the Greeks, nor was she called the Cytherean because she arose from the waves off the coast of Cythera but because Phœnicians, who were the island's earliest colonists, introduced the worship of the goddess there. And that Phœnician Astarte was not the bland and kindly deity of the Greeks. Like Savina Grove she was all Circe and not Penelope. There was neither beauty nor harmony where her shrines stood. Bitter torment alternated in her temples with wild orgies, even as it does, though the threshold of the orgiastic is never quite crossed, in

Hergesheimer's story. Here, as nearly everywhere else in American literature, we have the same tragic conflict and the same immedicable hurt. Fanny Randon dwells in that old Calvinistic realm of grace in which the senses are cheapened and, as Hergesheimer points out, lied about and outside of that there is only the wilderness of sin in which, because no one will reclaim it, Astarte-Savina has her sultry sensual abode. Prohibition or drunkenness, Puritan frigidity or debauchery. Naturally Lee Randon confesses in the end: "She was stronger than I; Savina was the goal and I was only the seeker . . . and in absorbing me she was content." But there is no beauty and no peace in the being consumed in so fierce a flame, nor is it tolerable to drag out the prim and false years of mere respectability. Where is that other road or truth? "The truth, I have always heard, will make you free; but for what?" That was the necessary ending of the tale, the necessary conclusion for Joseph Hergesheimer. He wanted life to be whole and intelligible through beauty, which is one of the great central aims of both art and thought. Fearing that in this age the beauty born of the generating Venus was lost, he sought to put himself off with accidents, with decorations, with lovely harmonies, too, like "that pattern of wild geese flying low" that begins and ends the story of "The Three Black Pennys." No longer content, at his strongest, with these evasions, he determined to face the realities of his quest and, representing the generative Venus or Virgin first under the aspect of the Platonic idea of beauty, he produced a charming and masterly book in "Linda Condon." But when he set out to seek beauty and delight and the wholeness that comes of both amid the aching reali-

537

ties of American life he found only Fanny Randon and Savina Grove, only the eternal woman at the distaff or her who turns men into brutes. He found "fragments and riddle and cruel accident" and found, too, that he could not be "the redeemer of accident unto order." Thus he plunged back into the decorative, now of a coarser and more flaring kind than in the days of "Java Head"; wearily he retold on a plane nearer the vulgar flat realities of daily life the tale of Cytherea in "The Party Dress" and finally essayed in "The Limestone Tree" the period novel. Will he ever return to grapple on serious terms with the redemption of life through beauty? . . .

It is no easy matter to write of Willa Cather. From about the middle of her career on claims have been made for her which are childishly extravagant. The blare and blaze deafen the ear to her well-wrought speech and blind the eye to her admirable powers of description. These phenomena tend to repeat themselves in the history of letters and to bring in their train the same revenges. It is more than likely that in the inevitable reaction against indiscriminate touting the work of Willa Cather will suffer from undue neglect. It will be a great pity, for her talent is a beautiful one and she has both a serenity and a tenderness that are rare. Her style is far surer than Hergesheimer's who will permit himself to commit solecisms like "clouds nebulous and bright"; it is not always an unself-conscious style; there are lapses of taste in her last book which surprise and shock. But at its best her style has moments in which beauty and wisdom are blended. "When kindness has left people, even for a few moments, we become afraid of them, as if their reason had left them.

538

When it has left a place where we have always found it, it is like shipwreck; we drop from security into something malevolent and bottomless." That, in spite of the two crowded *its*, is notable; and so is this: "We think we are so individual and so misunderstood when we are young; but the nature our strain of blood carries is inside there, waiting, like our skeleton." And best of all is this: "How the great poets do shine on! Into all the dark corners of the world. They have no night." These three quotations, it will be observed, are all from "My Mortal Enemy," which is Willa Cather's masterpiece and is likely to outlast her more elaborate works. But they can be paralleled if not quite matched on many pages of her other books.

She has been from the beginning concerned with the realities of the soul, which have been the essential realities to her and this is a great quality in her and in this age almost an heroic one. That she has conceived these realities in terms increasingly parochial—that is a matter perhaps beyond the province of the critic, at least in respect of a living author. But her present goal can be seen very early in her work. A discrete multiverse was unbearable to her from the beginning. The boy, lying in the grass in "My Antonia," is aware of a momentary oneness with nature: "I was entirely happy. Perhaps we feel like that when we die and become a part of something entire, whether it is sun and air, or goodness and knowledge. At any rate, that is happiness; to be dissolved into something complete and great. When it comes to one, it comes as naturally as sleep." That "becoming a part of something entire" is of course the Nietzschean redemption of accident unto order. Hergesheimer sought that redemption through beauty and beauty failed him; Willa Cather has not only sought but found it in the Holy Roman Catholic Church and in its "safe, lovingly arranged and ordered universe, not too vast, though nobly spacious, in this congenial universe" in which the Holy Family works miracles in the desert of the South West and immured recluses are visited by angels and missionaries to the Indians gain the holy joy of martyrdom. Her development toward those glorified devotional tracts "Death Comes for the Archbishop" and "Shadows on the Rock" has been quite unfaltering; it is part of that neo-Catholic flight from the too harsh realities of both the world and the universe in this age which one sees in other equally gifted writers, such as François Mauriac and Jean Cocteau and which in other countries is paralleled by flight to mystic nationalism—by merging one's being into a "something entire" which is conceived of as the nation, the people, whether German as among the Hitlerians or Italian among the Fascists, in its mystical eternal and abstract character. In Willa Cather this return to Catholic Christianity has been, as became her sex, less motivated by metaphysical hunger than by the needs of the heart, and in "Shadows on the Rock" there is an admirable passage, philosophical enough too, within its limitations, concerning the preciousness of human pieties expressed in terms of an ancestral faith: "*Inferretque deos Latio*. When an adventurer carries his gods with him into a remote and savage country, the colony he founds will, from the beginning, have graces, traditions, riches of the mind and spirit. Its history will shine with bright incidents, slight, perhaps, but precious, as in life itself, where the great matters are often as worthless as astronomical distances, and the trifles dear as the heart's blood." In brief, Willa Cather is the representative in American literature of that neo-Catholic movement, visible especially in France, which bears witness to a continuity of power in the Church which the most hopelessly alien outsider cannot but respectfully acknowledge. That outsider may, on the other hand, legitimately doubt whether Willa Cather's last two books, "Death Comes for the Archbishop" and "Shadows on the Rock," properly dear and precious to her coreligionists, will be seen to be contributions, except as exercises in style, to that American civilization of which American literature is the creative expression.

Her earlier books were closer to the tendencies of the national life: those fine clear pioneering tales, of which the best was "My Antonia," with their magnificent Western landscapes and those heroic and yet so warmly feminine women, Alexandra Bergson, Thea Kronberg, Antonia Shimerda who carry into whatever sphere a large and primitive maternal mood. Next came in 1922 "One of Ours," a book in which Willa Cather allied herself very closely with the dominant revolt against the moral and spiritual quality of American life. For Claude Wheeler had "the conviction that there was something splendid about life, if he could but find it," and almost echoed Babbitt: "I've never yet done anything that gave me any satisfaction. . . . I wonder whether my life has been happening to me or to somebody else." Here was, then, her opportunity to write her epic of God-seeking. Instead she let catastrophe dispose. The World War is her *deus ex machina*. The story stopped; it had no ending. There is much rich and sustained writing in the book. The account of the pestilence-stricken troop-ship stands high among examples of modern American prose. The snapping in the middle of the fable and therefore of the meaning of the book destroys it as both art and thought. But Willa Cather has never been happy in the longer forms until, as in her last two books, she began to substitute legend for the pattern that proceeds from character and the clash of characters and the struggle of man with the universe. By eliminating conflict she has achieved a static form like that of the Italian and German primitives in painting and this form she can go on applying changelessly to legend after legend. Unwilling to consent to any other meaning but having not yet reached her later manner, she wrote "The Professor's House" which again, like "One of Ours," snapped at a given point and avoided a conclusion. American criticism has not been sufficiently aware of the influence of *Weltanschauung* on the conduct of a fable. Of this influence Willa Cather's work, both the earlier and the later, offers a striking example.

It follows that, leaving "Death Comes for the Archbishop" and "Shadows on the Rock" aside in a special category, Willa Cather's most notable and certainly most perfect works are the two novelettes, "A Lost Lady" and "My Mortal Enemy." The beautiful form of the novelette, celebrated by Henry James, sufficed her for these two portraits of women, of Marian Forrester and of Myra Driscoll, both seen with that ultimate intensity of creative vision which leaves character both enigmatic and transparent, both indefinable and yet wholly plastic. None quite knew to the end the secret of Marian's ardor or whether she was really lost because she sought ever more unguidedly "some ever-blooming, ever-burning, ever-piercing joy." At all events she had always, as her creator tells us, and continued to have, "the power of suggesting things much lovelier than herself, as the perfume of a single flower may call up the whole sweetness of spring." So, too, we cannot define the tragedy of Myra Driscoll any more than she could herself. Like herself we speculate: "People can be lovers and enemies at the same time, you know. . . . We were. A man and woman draw apart from that long embrace, and see what they have done to each other. Perhaps I can't forgive him for the harm I did him. Perhaps that's it. When there are children, that feeling goes through natural changes. But when it remains so personal . . . something gives way in one. In age we lose everything; even the power to love." She was not clear about herself and neither are we. But she remains a possession of the imagination even in her strange death alone by the sea and again, as her youth is once more summoned up out of the past by her husband: "We were happy. Yes, happier than it falls to the lot of most mortals to be. . . . Life was hard for her, but it was glorious too." Willa Cather has made us profoundly feel both that hardship and that glory. In doing so she reaches the highest point of her serious and accomplished art.

III

The most notable of American dramatists, Eugene O'Neill, started out as a naturalist in his early one-act plays and in the tragedy "Beyond the Horizon," of which the first tentative afternoon performances early in 1920 marked the memorable beginning of his extraordinary career. Precisely one year later the Provincetown Players presented "The Emperor Jones" at an uptown theater and thus one had *in parvo* and as symbol a picture of O'Neill which the subsequent ten years have thoroughly confirmed. It is the picture of a creative spirit of very uncommon richness and flexibility, especially for America where even the strongest talents are apt to grow rigid in method and to try to repeat the manner and effect of some early triumph. O'Neill has never been content to let well enough alone. He has been a seeker, a groper, a fashioner of form. It is true that he has so far— he is only forty-three—produced no single work that has finality within itself. But a lesser man, dazzled both by so much productivity and at last by so much triumph, would have permitted himself to harden in one of these imperfect molds. O'Neill has never permitted himself to do that. He is still striving; and in that creative striving, rather than in any single performance so far, lies the quality in him that seems to ally him to the major figures in literature.

He is of course, despite his enormous talent, curiously handicapped. He has no felicity; he has not the sweetness that one would expect of his strength. Nor has he the rounded form which can perfectly be combined with an ethically indeterminate ending. Hence neither the spectator's nor the reader's catharsis at the end of any play by O'Neill is final or complete and that leads one to suspect that the creative self-catharsis of the dramatist has been equally imperfect, a circumstance that would go far to account for the rapid change of mood, of dramaturgic method and form, and for the almost fevered productivity already amounting to the equivalent of twenty full-length plays and about to be increased by a trilogy!

Whence comes this imperfection amid so much wealth and vigor, this emotional residuum of void and distaste that O'Neill's plays leave? My criticism may not, of course, be granted; it will certainly not be granted by his closer followers. Yet I have been impressed and stirred by the performances of very many of his plays; I have worked through the entire canon of his works in the study with careful passivity: with more than passivity, with good-will and admiration and the desire to be at once shaken and reconciled as I am, as everyone is, at the conclusion of the major works of the drama. The effect is never single and entire; the catharsis is never complete. What is lacking? An element that is akin to both love and joy—an element allied to zest and relish. There is a sense, a very deep sense, in which the creative artist loves all his characters in their quality of characters within the world of his creative cosmos. He may have loathed their prototypes in life. He relishes the character *qua* character. He devours people because he has an endless creative appetite and relish for them. The snake he has created is as dear to him in this sense as beauty or genius. Now I have the unescapable impression that O'Neill neither loves his kind as a man, a Swiftian indignation being of course only disappointed love, nor enjoys his characters as a creator. He has neither the brooding large love of Dreiser or Hauptmann nor the sharp joyous delight of Shaw, not the bitterness of love outraged of Strindberg, nor even the cold contempt under which a passion of hatred, but still a passion, is held in leash, of such a dramatist as Wedekind. O'Neill's heart is arid toward his creatures. Or, at least, he has not the means of projecting them in a spirit of creative love. Hence there is about all these many people in the plays and about their conflicts something hard and dry; power, in this world of the dramatist's imagination, always has something of violence, the fable always a touch of the coldly arbitrary and intensity at its height is somehow drained of passion. Such were my reluctant conclusions from those early days on when, like every other American concerned over the life of our drama, I hailed—though always with misgivings—the work of Eugene O'Neill. He has, in a high sense, not failed to fulfill the promise of earlier years. He is the chief of American dramatists. Yet those critical conclusions remain unchanged, for the qualities or lack of qualities on which they were based have also remained unchanged in the later plays: in the strong confused symbolism, for instance, of "The Great God Brown," in the fantasy of "Marco Millions," in the enormous creative effort of "Strange Interlude," in the cold constructions of "Dynamo."

The matter may be examined from another angle. There is no love that convinces within the plays and there is, despite superficial impressions to the contrary, little hatred. There is cold physical attraction and there is colder malice—especially the envious malice of parents toward children and the malicious rebellion of the young against the old. There are protestations of love without tenderness and protestations of hatred without heat. Anna Christie and Jim Harris in "All God's Chillun" come nearest to having a heart. Certainly Nina Leeds in "Strange Interlude" has none, nor has Darrell her lover. Their very sensuality is cold. Poor Sam Evans comes near to having human feelings. He is represented with a chill contempt. Who will believe in the love of Michael and Eleanor in "Welded" or in that of Curtis and Martha in "The First Man" or even in that of the patient old Captain —stubborn rather than patient—in "Diff'rent" or in that of either brother for Ruth in "Beyond the Horizon"? Love in these plays is but the voracious aspect of hard egoism and even parental love is, except in one or two instances, oppression and envy. Increasingly and especially in "Strange Interlude" O'Neill has clung to those more superficial aspects of psycho-analysis that seem to bear out—it is the merest seeming to the eye of the imperfectly instructed—this way of perceiving the passions that move mankind. Old Leeds, in "Strange Interlude," prevents Nina from marrying Gordon out of ill-disguised sex-envy; to compensate for that denial of herself to Gordon Nina gives herself with cold indiscriminateness to any wounded soldier who desires her; she in her turn, years later, having a fixation on her son, wants to prevent his marriage at any cost. It is not so simple nor so schematic as that. An older type of neurology is drawn on to provide the doubtful horrors of hereditary madness in the Evans family. But Sam, in fact, remains the sanest of creatures. Is it therefore that he must be made a cuckold? Was the mysterious Mrs. Amos Evans perhaps only impelled by the jealousy of a fixation? "I loved you horribly at that time, Nina—horribly!" Darrell says. Thus do they all love—horribly! Now the world is full of merciless egoism and envy and malice. But no great writer has ever accepted that as a sufficient account of human life. For there is also generous passion and sacrificial love and unfaltering devotion and the

547

sun warms and food delights and even the barren and cruel sea has a magic and a grandeur that it never has in these plays. No one can be a great writer who does not see that other side or, having been tragically deprived of that vision, seeks like Swift or Strindberg to wrest it, as it were, with naked hands from under the very ribs of death. If Eugene O'Neill is a great dramatist he is—so far at least: I emphasize again his comparative youth—the great dramatist of an infinitely little, barren, frigid group and period that vegetates without, symbolically speaking, hope or God in the world. The creatures of the Restoration Comedy were gay; those of O'Neill's plays are somber. They are equally without heart and without true passion. The most authentic human cry in all of O'Neill's plays, the cry that rings truest, is Anna Christie's hard and hopeless cry of fatalism and of moral despair: "Don't bawl about it. There ain't nothing to forgive anyway. It ain't your fault and it ain't mine and it ain't his neither. We're all poor nuts. And things happen. And we just get mixed in wrong, that's all."

This lack of love, both creative and created, this lack of tenderness and warmth, has been partly concealed and partly compensated for by the breadth of O'Neill's intellectual sympathies. He has been steadily on the side of the rude, the simple, the oppressed and rejected. He has been without mercy, as in "The First Man" and "The Great God Brown" and above all, in "The Hairy Ape," to the merely efficient, respectable, stupidly possessive. He has been unfalteringly and perhaps a little unphilosophically on the side of wanderers, outcasts—even of the merely shiftless and the merely unguided. His most concentrated tragic work, the least artificial, the most impassioned is without any question "All God's Chillun Got Wings," which was wrung from him by his imaginative sympathy with the Negro. And next to that the most compelling voice in the plays is the voice of Yank— the symbolical voice of the utterly oppressed. He has substituted social for personal passion and has thus shared in the strength, as he has shared in the weakness of his group and period. It is when he treats purely human and personal conflicts that he is always cold and a little raw, as though he had not quite got to the souls of his people or touched the depth of his own fables, that he remains outside his subjects, almost as though disdainful of a profounder and more impassioned preoccupation.

I shall not dwell on his experiments in dramatic form: the expressionist excursions in "The Emperor Jones" and "The Hairy Ape," the use of symbolical masks in the latter and in "The Great God Brown," the device of the spoken thought, a subtler form of the old "aside," in "Strange Interlude" and "Dynamo." For all these things are or are not justified by the mere test of creative effectiveness and have no independent quality. They have been interesting at their feeblest and striking and illuminating at their strongest. Whether they have not been substitutes for fundamental creative passion is a question which, for the present, withdraws itself from discussion. Nor is it necessary to remark, except in passing, that in nearly all the earlier plays there is the unhappy mark of the mere vulgar theater in the use of coincidences and incredible cross-purposes and sudden unmotivated appearances and disappearances, the worst example of this sort of thing being the dreadful fourth act of

"Anna Christie." For O'Neill's work in the mass, in its totality and in its tireless striving toward other goals, has power and breadth and import enough by this time to render trifling these errors and concessions. It definitely exists, this body of work, with all its lacks and imperfections; it stands out in contemporary literature as something strong, unescapable, formidable. If it cannot compel love, it exacts respect and attention.

It does so by the fact that O'Neill has one of the marks of a great writer. He has created a world of his own and he has peopled his world. I have said everything against the quality and character of this world that had, of necessity, to be said. It is there; it exists. It is allied to such a world as that created by, let us say, Gerhart Hauptmann, by the throng of characters, many of them quite minor who, in their own cold and sordid fashion, wear the unmistakable lineaments of man. Such are Ruth in "Beyond the Horizon" and both Brutus Jones and Henry Smithers in "The Emperor Jones" and Emma Crosby and Benny Rogers in "Diff'rent" and old Carmody and Mrs. Brennan in "The Straw" and Christopherson and Marthy Owen in "Anna Christie" and the Jaysons and Esther Sheffield in "The First Man" and Yank in "The Hairy Ape" and Old Ephraim Cabot in "Desire under the Elms" and the elder Browns and Anthonies in "The Great God Brown" and Shorty and Ella Downey in "All God's Chillun Got Wings" and Charles Marsden and Mrs. Amos Evans in "Strange Interlude" and both the Reverend Hutchins Light and Ramsay Fife in the otherwise cold, violent and mechanical "Dynamo." What a crew! A creature with some rudiments of heart, of spiritual perception, like the girl Lily in "The First Man," strikes one almost as an anomaly. Martha in the same play has both strength and fineness. She is in this respect alone or almost alone among the major characters, who are more likely, like Nina Leeds of "Strange Interlude," to have the selfishness and the cunning, the desirousness and frigidity, the cruelty and sentimentality of the regressive neurotic. What a dreadful crew! But it exists; it is there in its own world and habitat and its creator is therefore a creator of the major order. . . . He has striven; he is still striving. He has moved farther and farther in conception and method from his naturalistic beginnings. In "Dynamo," though upon terms so harsh and barren and perverse, he struggles with a conception that is allied to religion, to God-seeking. He may yet find God, where Euripides and Shakespeare, even Molière and Hebbel found God—in the heart of man. He may yet become a dramatic poet. . . .

Since these lines were written there has appeared the promised trilogy "Mourning Becomes Electra." The work once more bears witness to Eugene O'Neill's sheer power and creative energy. Its success as both play and book confirms almost with the *quod erat demonstrandum* of Euclid all that the analytical psychologists have written concerning the universality of the incest-wish in the heart of man. For if O'Neill has been a little schematic before, he has in this work almost the air of following the text-books. Christine Mannon says to her daughter: "You've tried to become the wife of your father and the mother of Orin!" To her lover, Adam Brant, Christine declares that she fell in love with him because he made her think of Orin, her son. The latter, having killed

551

his mother's lover, cries: "If I had been he I would have done what he did! I would have loved her as he loved her— and killed father, too—for her sake." In the end Orin proposes to his sister Lavinia that *they* commit incest. In brief, Mrs. Mannon has a fixation only on her son; Lavinia on both her father and brother, Orin on both his mother and sister. And why, having really fallen in love with him, did Christine Mannon so bitterly detest her husband Ezra? Because he was unskilful—see the text-books from Stopes to Vandevelde—on their wedding-night. "Whose fault is it? I loved you when I married you! I wanted to give myself! But you made me so I couldn't give! You filled me with disgust!" Shall I be forgiven for saying with all gentleness: *Ça, c'est un peu fort!* It is not for nothing that the great poets have caused the incest-motive, as it is in Hamlet, to be implicit in character and action and hardly ever to impinge upon the waking consciousness. For it is thus that it exists, intertwined with the actions and passions of men. People were surely not so brash and knowing about it in 1865. Nor, except in Bohemian circles, are they now. And even in such circles the matter is handled rather with the touch of that wit who said: "Incest makes the heart grow fonder." No, great works have more of presage and twilight and depend more on the overtones of texture and the implications of beautiful or stirring speech. In "Mourning Becomes Electra" there is once more the harshness and the absence of love, the lack of warmth and goodness or of pity for those who lack these things that disfigures the power and the striving of O'Neill. The trilogy has strength and dramatic energy of movement; it has no tenderness nor pity nor human eloquence of tone. It leaves the position of Eugene O'Neill precisely what it was before and he bids us still, though a little less hopefully, await the days and works to come. . . .

IV

The development of American expression beyond naturalism may best be studied in the poets. Yet what these poets themselves owe to the discipline of naturalism will be apparent in almost every line of their works. Naturalism taught them to see "man and nature and human life" as their predecessors had never permitted themselves to do; it filled their interpretative symbols with substance; it built earth under their feet; it made a psychologist of Edwin Arlington Robinson; it added the tang of daily experience to the work of a spirit originally so elevated and abstract in its moods as William Ellery Leonard; it fills the verses of Vachel Lindsay with the rumor and savor of his country's life. In order to proceed to interpretation poets had first to learn once more to see and to record the thing to be interpreted. This process was a gradual one and can be best observed in the works of Edwin Arlington Robinson.

It has recently been overlooked that Robinson started out in "Children of the Night" with Tennysonian echoes, with ballades and villanelles, with so obvious an imitation of Browning as "Her Eyes" and with certain sonnets not unlike those of, say, Aubrey de Vere. And it has been overlooked because even in those early days he was teaching himself to see character and fate as the Victorians had never permitted themselves to see them and produced the brilliant

553

and popular "Richard Cory," the concrete portrait sonnets "Aaron Stark" and "Reuben Bright" and the significant submission to the discipline of naturalism contained in the admirable lines to George Crabbe. This sound influence may be observed in "Captain Craig" and in "Isaac and Archibald" and in the other blank-verse poems of the period. The ballads and lyrical pieces still often have a Victorian softness and mistiness. Robinson still wrote:

Say the gleam was not for us, but never say we doubted it;

he still wrote:

> Life would have its way with us,
> And I've called it glorious:
> For I know the glory now
> And I read it on your brow.
> You have shown me how.

It is in "The Town Down the River" that one first finds the precision and terseness of speech for which Robinson was increasingly to become known. But the examples of it are as yet few; very many lines go through the mere gestures of poetry and not even the best kind of gesture.

> He dreams of honor and wealth and fame,
> He smiles and well he may;
> For to Vickery once a sick man came
> Who did not go away.

The rewards of the volume are almost if not quite confined to the felicitous and amusing Miniver Cheevy and the pathetic, lavendered lines . . . "we who delve in beauty's lore." . . . "For a Dead Lady," which might, except for the pessimism, have been written by Calverley. The tribute to

Roosevelt with which the volume ends is much like other contemporary tributes. Viereck and Robinson used the same type of rhetoric. It would be a fine point to decide which of them wrote:

> No Nazarite or Nazarene
> Compells our questioning to prove
> The difference that is between
> Dead lions or the sweet thereof.

The poet reached full maturity with "The Man Against the Sky." In this volume are his very best portrait poems: the imaginative "Flammonde," the pathetic and musical "The Poor Relation," "Bewick Finzer" with its well-known close,

> Familiar as an old mistake
> And futile as regret,

and "Veteran Sirens" in which, even more notably than in "Bewick Finzer," observation and wit rise to poetry:

> Poor flesh, to fight the calendar so long;
> Poor vanity, so quaint and yet so brave;
> Poor folly, so deceived and yet so strong,
> So far from Ninon and so near the grave.

Finally the volume contains the two famous pieces, "Ben Jonson Entertains a Man from Stratford" and "The Man Against the Sky." The former poem, still strongly tinged with Browning, is sagacious and even brilliant; the latter is not continuously interesting in either texture or idea, a graver defect in a poet of texture and idea like Robinson than in one who, despite faults of workmanship or lack of logical development, can lift us out of ourselves and beyond his common level by some moment of passion or of rapture, of glory or of fire. The two poems, in addition, give final expression to Robinson's cosmic pessimism, the first in the fine passage, already something of a stock quotation, which ends:

> It's all Nothing.
> It's all a world where bugs and emperors
> Go singularly back to the same dust,
> Each in his time; and the old ordered stars
> That sang together, Ben, will sing the same
> Old stave to-morrow;

the second poem throughout, but especially in the question:

> Are we no greater than the noise we make
> Along our blind atomic pilgrimage
> Whereon by crass chance billeted we go
> Because our brains and bones and cartilage
> Will have it so?

In the context of another question the poet answers: "All comes to Nought." Years later, in "Cavender's House," we find him of the same grim temper and opinion still:

> Was ever an insect flying between two flowers
> Told less than we are told of what we are?

He has not moved from the philosophic Nihilism of his generation, the generation of Bertrand Russell, and is therefore not likely to influence the thought or poetry of the immediate future which is inevitably enlisting under quite other flags.

It is not necessary to go through the later mixed volumes of Robinson. The influence of Browning, tempered by that of Crabbe and by New England shrewdness, persists in the blank-verse pieces; of lyrical portraits there are few; "Dionysus in Doubt," in form and method a companion-piece to "The Man Against the Sky," is admirable in intention, brilliant at moments but reaches in most of its lines neither the sting of wit nor the ardor of poetry. The many later sonnets are never less than gravely well-wrought. They vary from the quite conventional—

> The Lord Apollo, who has never died
> Still holds alone his immemorial reign,
> Supreme in an impregnable domain
> That with his magic he has fortified—

—to such excellent examples of the notable but too rarely found poetic Robinsonian wit as "Karma" and "New England."

It remains to speak of the poet's essays in the epic. These represent in themselves an intellectual and creative effort of a very high order. In the later ones dealing with contemporary life and in all those that treat the Arthurian legends, the influence of Browning is finally transcended and the poet has created, alone among contemporary Americans, a blank verse of his own. The majority of the lines are very slightly end-stopped, which accords well with the sobriety of the poet's mind. All the more effective are harmonies unemphatically interlaced when they occur, as in the beautiful close of "Roman Bartholow":

> He walked away
> Knowing that he had seen for the last time
> The changeless outline of those eastern hills,
> And all those changing trees that flamed along
> A river that should flow for him no more.

But more characteristic is the rhythm and manner that seems slightly to mock the pretensions of poetry, while definitely exemplifying poetry of another kind:

557

"It is not dark," she said, "or not so dark
But that a woman sees if she be careful
Not to fall down these memorable stairs
And break her necessary little neck
At Tristram's feet."

At any rate Robinson has created a style of writing in blank verse that is far more continuously interesting as style, as verse, than that of his lyrical measures. Hence even the later poems of contemporary manners and psychology, like "Roman Bartholow" or "Cavender's House," continually attract the student and lover of poetry despite their cold intricacies and bloodless ingenuities. It is not, be it noted, the presence in these poems of intricacy and ingenuity that is their fatal defect; it is the simultaneous absence of any fusing ardor. The poet has not inner heat enough. The poems are cold. This has nothing to do with subject or method. Lucretius is an intellectual poet, too. But out of his empty universe he wrings the eternal cry:

O genus infelix humanum, talia divis
Cum tribuit facta atque iras adjunxit acerbas!

It is not surprising, then, that the narratives dealing with the Arthurian legends are far more excellent and stirring than the accomplished but dreary novels in verse. For in the legendary poems both story and passion, both man and nature, were ready to the poet's hand. These themes, so often treated and now almost threadbare, did still have a symbolical living value in the consciousness of many men and hence, by using them, Robinson was—like that painter of a Crucifixion used as an example—best able to convey his special qualities. Here his dry and sagacious wit shines. For warmth was already in his matter; and to the heat of the tradition he had the felicity of adding the light of the modern mind. This method of interpreting one's mind and age through symbols of known emotional wealth is, of course, a permanently valid one. Robinson's use of it was the characteristic one of applying the test of common sense and broad reality to the legends. When one remembers the mystical scheme that underlies the "Idylls of the King," the following crucial passage from Merlin will be seen to illustrate Robinson's entire spirit and treatment:

> I'll drink now and be quiet—but, by God,
> I'll have to tell you, Brother Bedivere,
> Once more, to make you listen properly,
> That crowns and orders and high palaces,
> And all the manifold ingredients
> Of this good solid kingdom, where we sit
> And spit now at each other with our eyes,
> Will not go rolling down to hell just yet
> Because a pretty woman is a fool.

This rationalism is, to be sure, not the happiest of poetical moods. Hence it is not surprising to find that "Tristram" is not only the best of Robinson's epical poems but the best of all his works and the one by which he is most likely to be remembered. The legend fired him with its purely human values; he treats these with a fine frankness, so that the picture of Isolt and Tristram by the Cornish shore with the detestable doom that hangs over them is one of unforgettable and tragic beauty. This situation, so thoroughly felt by the poet, wrings from him his best verses:

> I do not think there is much love like ours
> Here in this life, or that too much of it

> Would make poor men and women who go alone
> Into their graves without it more content,
> Or more by common sorrow to be envied
> Than they are now.

The story takes its bitter course. The reconciling element is in the character of Isolt of Brittany, the eternal Gretchen type—

> One must be wise enough, not having all,
> Still to be found among the fortunate—

which Robinson has drawn with great power and great tenderness. With her he wisely closes the story and closing it thus upon her meditations, he achieves a deeper tone than elsewhere and brings into his blank verse those cæsuras symbolizing the break of the human voice under the impact of fate which have always been a characteristic glory of English poetry:

> He had been there,
> She thought, but not for her. He had died there
> But not for her. He had not thought of her
> Perhaps, and that was strange. He had been all,
> And would be always all there was for her,
> And he had not come back to her alive,
> Not even to go again.

That is Robinson's highest reach. "Had he often written thus," Johnson closes his "Life of Gray," "it had been vain to blame, and useless to praise him."

It was for years—practically until the publication of "Two Lives" in 1925—the foolish critical fashion to reproach William Ellery Leonard with conventionality of theme and treatment. His work was never, in fact, as conventional and derivative as a good two-thirds of Robinson's work was until quite recent years. But Leonard's first volume, "The Vaunt of Man," appeared in that *annus mirabilis* of poetic revolt 1912 and he seemed to the hot youths of the moment to resemble too closely the R. W. Gilders and R. U. Johnsons, whom it was their privilege and indeed their duty to detest. The fact is that he resembled these gentlemen as little as possible. For the trouble with them was not their desire to continue the great tradition of English poetry but their utter impotence to do so. Where they failed Leonard, within his limitations, clearly succeeded. For he had both intensity and elevation from the beginning and so had no need, like the late Victorians, to "fake" the one or to ape the other. He spoke with an unwonted largeness of gesture and nobility of tone because his innate mood and spirit were such. He lived in all sincerity within the temper of the high poets and among his earliest verses are many which time is justifying and raising into a new definiteness of outline. Such are the verses on the unhappy setting sail of that "high red liner" of his youth:

> She passed the isles, the leas,
> The green hills, left and right. Behind at home
> The gray towers faded far. The setting sun
> Shot golden lines along our wake of foam,
> The ocean stars rose round us one by one;
> I took my berth to close my eyes and weep;
> I cared for nothing—I was on the deep.

Such, in an even higher degree, are the verses in which he rationalizes his hatred of

> that youth of sallow skin and visage sour

561

who, in college days, first embodied for him the evil and the malice of the world:

> Yet my old hate is but the poet's hate
> Even for the ideal villain of the mind—
> The mind alert forever to create
> The perfect type from every form it find—
> The man himself could enter at my gate
> Like any stranger with his dog behind.

Now when we scrutinize these stirring verses today, it is obvious that the elevation of mood is based upon a naturalistic acceptance of the quite concrete and even the supposedly ignoble details of modern life and that it is controlled by an intellectual integrity and insight unique among American poets since Emerson. Leonard was quite right when, seeking to account many years later for the ill-health of his nerves, he insisted upon the unimpaired sinews of his mind. His intellect has always been a sinewy one and the profound satisfactoriness of his best poetry arises precisely from the blending of his native elevation of mood with a scrupulous, an almost scientific logic. Hence though he addresses the muse, he shows in that very sonnet a prophetic presage of the self-appointment of the artist to his character and mission as the most recent psychological research reveals it and interprets the old mythic notion as his personal sharing in

> The immanent Vigilance, creating still
> The nobler nature, the more bold design.

He loses sight of no reality, whether of the operations of the intellect or of the human scene as it affects him and it is difficult to understand today how any could ever have considered either conventional or remote the poet who wrote

"The Editor" or "Mein Tischgenosse" or "A Hypocrite," with that fine ending wherein moral elevation and homely fact are so admirably blended:

> Eternity itself were scarce enough
> To learn a true man's quality, were he
> Still but the humblest of a peasant stripe;
> But the poor tinsel of your proper stuff
> I mark, established artist though you be,
> With one glance sideways as I fill my pipe.

In brief, the finest of the earlier sonnets such as "The Test," "Success," "The Crisis," are among the finest in the language because they are among the soundest; because their imaginative intensity and moral ardor are guided by that salt of New England wit which also informs the excellent fables either freely invented or retold after Æsop and by that incorruptible mind which kept Leonard freer of war-psychosis than almost any American man of letters. Nor are the earlier poems without their examples of a more sensuous treatment of language or wider imaginative range. Leonard is quite at his best in those companion pieces in octosyllables, "New York Days" and "Urbs Triumphans," which have passages of a Keatsean richness of texture and music:

> Behold in Java and Ceylon
> The silent ages slumber on.
> Their jungles, where the tiger crawls
> By sultry moonlit waterfalls,
> Hide ruined palaces and halls—
> Huge cities, dim, grotesque and damp,
> Where ebon door and ivory lamp
> Had mocked the lightening and the rain
> Ere Tyrian trader coasted Spain.
> They perished by their soma bowls;

They left no hieroglyphs or scrolls;
Their names are lost, and legends tell
The earthquake smote them and they fell.

It was first the domestic tragedy to be narrated later in
"Two Lives," and next the disillusion induced by the World
War that caused a profound change of both mood and
method in Leonard's writing. He addressed himself to the
actual, the concrete alone; he wrote almost wholly in support of those good causes which the war seemed to him to
have left; he concentrated upon the elements of homely
realism and plain nutty New England speech that had always tempered the elevation and moral ardor of his verse
and composed that series of lengthy poems, "The Heretics,"
"The Old Agitator," "The Mountain of Skulls," "Saecla
Ferarum," "The Quaker Meeting House," "Tom Mooney"
and "The Lynching-Bee," which have received their just due
no more than the early sonnets and poems. Not that they
have the perfection of the best among the latter. Far from
it. They have often the air of having been a little prema-
turely composed, a little before the process of poetic gestation was complete; as though they would have been finer,
riper, graver, briefer and so more concentrated and permanent, had the poet been able to put off the writing of them.
They are too full of the agitation of the hour that bred
them; they have not attained the inner poise of creative tranquillity which is quite consonant, it may be said once more,
with the rendering, as subject-matter, of violent disaster and
raging tumult. Nevertheless several of them, especially "The
Lynching-Bee," are among the most continuously exciting of
American poems. In the latter, too, there is once more to be

observed that blending of imaginative splendor with knowledge and intellectual control which make Leonard so satisfactory a poet. The scene and the happenings are rendered with a concreteness of realization that stir one profoundly; the interpretation of the scene and the gestures, drawn from what we know of the interaction of myth and ritual with blood and sex and the immemorial mechanism of expiation by substitution, by the device of the scapegoat, are of a hardihood and exactness that are far to seek in the works of poets who pride themselves so obviously upon the superficial modernity of their verse. Nor are the other poems of this group without their notable passages. The national imagination is not likely to neglect permanently, for instance, the fine account of the Supreme Court's failure to reverse the sentence of imprisonment passed upon Eugene Debs:

> They made report, this row of staunch patricians,
> Unto the bald lone tall man of the plebs;
> They bore no grudge, they took no gold,
> They may have loved him—for they too were old;
> But, seated in their ancient nine positions,
> They sealed the prison sunset years for Debs—
> As vindicators of those stern traditions
> That tore from black Dred Scott his freeman's shirt,
> And locked free child in factory dark and dirt.

There remains Leonard's chief work "Two Lives," which gained immediate recognition upon its final publication. It has been said before but is worth repeating that it forms a third in that group of modern poems, of which the other two are George Meredith's "Modern Love" and Richard Dehmel's "Zwei Menschen," wherein the life of our age, honestly and exactly faced, is raised to the level of high

565

poetry. The attempt to do just that has been frequently made. It was made long ago by Mrs. Browning in "Aurora Leigh"; it has been made by Robinson repeatedly. But Mrs. Browning had little brains and Robinson has little else. Poetry can be produced on a minimum of brains, as we shall see presently in discussing Vachel Lindsay; it can scarcely be produced without fusing passion. In "Two Lives" there are both—brains and passion. The result is a poem almost if not quite great.

Profoundly shaken and swept into utterance as he was, Leonard knew what he was about. He understood the character of the creative process. Friends counseled him to forget his grief and "let the past die." He answered:

> There is, good friends, scant wisdom in this "letting";
> I *am* my past so long as I am I;
> And in a brave reshaping, not forgetting,
> Is my one hope and action not to die:
> The past that might have killed me if it could
> I sternly mold to art and hardihood.

In brief, the measure of the poet's self-catharsis is the measure of the catharsis he can bring to others. That this measure was high in the case of "Two Lives" has been proved by its profound appeal to the best of its contemporaries. That the self-catharsis, though high, was far from complete, is the substance, whether conscious or not, of every just criticism brought against the poem and is born out by the subsequent inner fortunes of the poet himself. The story told in "Two Lives" is disastrous rather than tragic; we do not ultimately consent to it nor to the poet's interpretation of it; we are

566

left with a residuum of confusion and disturbance and dissatisfaction. But it should in all justice be added that the imperfect self-catharsis of every modern poet has to do with our entire metaphysical situation. We have no coherent universe in which to dwell, nor religious certitude by the light of which we can interpret our individual tragedies and sorrows. The poet must be his own god, judge, almost cosmos. Thence arises the lack of wholeness and unity in modern works; thence arise the indeterminate endings in the modern drama since Hebbel and Ibsen; thence is to be derived the fact that "Faust" itself is more fragmentary than the "Divine Comedy" and the plays of Shakespeare than the plays of the Greeks. Sophocles knew his way about his universe and so did Dante. We have become wanderers in a mist. A new cosmology and a new religion can alone breed perfectly achieved works. Thus, for instance, is to be interpreted, as has not been done, Matthew Arnold simultaneously grieving over the loss of religious certitude and his demand for modern works which should be whole, great, entire and his protest against the cultivation of detail and the doctrine of the poetic moment. But, alas, we have only moments; we are— the best of us, but fragments in a fragmentary universe. Who will redeem our chaos unto order? . . . So Leonard's poem must be judged by its best moments, rather than as a whole. And these best moments are very many in the long sweep and argument of his sonnet-stanzas. They are moments of sheer insight into the details of modern life for once fused by the true passion of the poet; they are moments that sum up in simple, magical phrase the whole estate of the modern poet and so of modern man—

Yes, the strongest make
Their music out of thinking and heart-break—;

they are scenes and observations and, as in the magnificent
stanza: "We act in crises . . ." summings up that illustrate
modern life and cleave to its root and core as do the verses
of few poets in any language; they are moments, as in the
half-mystical description of the finding of the eight stalag-
mites in the Bavarian cave which come as near sublimity as
any American poet has ever come:

> For they were eight; and with a flint I smote
> One after other to reverberations,
> And found the octave of the human throat,
> The very scale I found whereby the nations
> Have wrought their pæans and their lamentations,
> Their symphonies and oratorios:
> But what I played was like to none of those;
> O what I played with solemn ululations
> Was not as music in the skiey places
> Of grass and trees: it was a hymn indeed
> Of time and mystery and things that none—
> However sad and lyrical their faces—
> Who have not wholly wandered from the sun
> Can ever hymn or, hearing, ever heed.

I am convinced that the reputation of Leonard's work in
its totality, including his remarkable translations of Empedocles and Lucretius, as well as sundry critical pieces, will
grow while other names now far more in the blaze of noon
will darken and decline. The phenomenon is common and
old. He has not stooped to please; he has had no alliances in
the market-places. Hence toward him as toward others, critics
have assumed the attitudes long ago defined by Johnson:
"Some are too indolent to read anything, till its reputation

568

is established; others too envious to promote that fame which gives them pain by its increase. . . ."

If the incompetence of American criticism is illustrated by its failure to recognize Leonard, it is equally illustrated by its comparative failure to recognize in its true character the both amazing and amusing, the highly significant phenomenon of Vachel Lindsay. For here is a poet who leaped over all the difficulties of modern life or, rather, from the evidence in his work, never encountered them. He has a cosmos, even though it is a Fundamentalist one; he has a religion, even though it is allied with the Anti-Saloon League; he is a patriot who seriously ranks Wilson with Socrates. He beats a tambourine for the Blood of the Lamb and sees the angels, as once did Francis Thompson at Charing Cross, climb up and down Jacob's ladder, between heaven and Springfield, Illinois. The comparison is no idle one. Lindsay has more than a little in common with Thompson, more than a little in common with Blake. He sees visions and believes unbelievable nonsense. He "whoops it up" for Prohibition; his mental processes are therefore, like the peace of God, past understanding. But he has kept the heart of a little child and has written the purest American poetry since Poe! He has written yards of drivel. But that is of no importance. What is of importance to the point of laughter, to the point of tears, is the proof offered by Vachel Lindsay that the poet must believe—even if he believes nonsense. And that again throws a lurid light upon the tragic difficulties of the poets who have minds and cannot believe. But any belief is evidently, from the point of sheer poetry, better than no belief, since it releases vision and music and the eternal child in the heart of man. So, perhaps, poetry is dying, since mankind may be slowly growing up and a religion for mature minds is a thing hard to come by. Meanwhile it has taken a Campbellite and Anti-Saloon Leaguer and hundred-per-cent patriot to write not only the famous set pieces, from "The Congo" down, which have their amazing merits and their definite faults, but this:

> Were I god of the village
> My servants should mate them.
> Were I priest of the church
> I would set them apart.
> If the wide state were mine
> I should live for such darlings,
> And hedge with all shelter
> The child-wedded heart.

And this:

> We shall see silver ships.
> We shall see singing ships,
> Valleys of spray today,
> Mountains of foam.
> We have been long away,
> Far from our wonderland.
> Here come the ships of love
> Taking us home.

And this:

> Our wedding long is over,
> With toil the years fill up,
> Yet in the evening silence,
> We drink a deep-sea cup.
> Nothing the fay remembers,
> Yet when she turns to me,
> We meet beneath the whirlpool,
> We swim the golden sea.

And, above all, this:

> The King of Yellow butterflies
> Now orders forth his men.
> He says, "The time is almost here
> When violets bloom again."
>
> Adown the road the fickle rout
> Goes flashing proud and bold,
> They shiver by the shallow pools
> And whimper of the cold.
>
> They drink and drink. A frail pretense!
> They love to pose and preen.
> Each pool is but a looking-glass
> Where their sweet wings are seen.
>
> Gentlemen adventurers!
> Gypsies every whit!
> They live on what they steal. Their wings
> By briars are frayed a bit.
>
> Their loves are light. They have no house.
> And if it rains today,
> They'll climb into your cattle-shed
> And hide them in the hay.

I have seen none of these verses nor several hundred like them in any anthology nor quoted by any critic. Yet evidently the man that wrote these lines is an English lyrist of almost Elizabethan sweetness and magic and country charm. Let the critic note what Saintsbury used to call the fingering of these verses as well as the tenderness and the delicious fancy. Yet the many poems of this sort, not forgetting the humorous ones like the charming "Dirge for a Righteous

Kitten," are but the by-products, as it were, of this poet's activity. And one could go on quoting almost endlessly from the very Poesque "Last Song of Lucifer" and from the exquisite "Moon-Poems," where again, as in "The Old Horse in the City," Lindsay is so close to other *believing* poets, in this instance to Francis Jammes.

I have accused Lindsay of not using his mind in the contemporary as well as in a more permanent philosophic sense. Let it not be supposed that, any more than Francis Jammes again or Chesterton, he has no insight within his self-imposed limitations. One has only to read the extraordinarily fine lines called "Incense" or the less fine but definitely significant ones called "A Net to Snare the Moonlight," which are subtitled: "What the Man of Faith Said." And again one has but to read the verses, quite worthy of Blake, entitled "The Shield of Faith," or those verses, magnificent variations, again, upon the "Songs of Innocence," "Yet Gentle Will the Griffin Be" or "The Sun Says His Prayers"; Lindsay knows that to the eye of mysticism the universe *can* blossom like a flower, like Tennyson's "awful rose of dawn" within the fiery petals of which wonder and adoration fill the heart of life. It is in this greater mood of his, unvulgarized by the too conscious "folksiness" of his "Calliope" tunes, that he finds love

> stern as the ages and old as Religion,
> With patience its watchword, and Law for its throne.

In this mood he writes out of the heart of his deep compassion for the young of his age:

> Not that they starve, but starve so dreamlessly,
> Not that they sow but that they seldom reap,

> Not that they serve, but have no gods to serve,
> Not that they die but that they die like sheep.

And it is equally out of this mood that he wrings occasionally though never, alas, sustainedly, lines of an imaginative splendor rare in any literature, lines like

> And eagles gigantic, aged and sere,

or

> And revel in the deep palm of the world,

or

> Higher and higher burns the eastern steep,
> Showing the roads that march from every place . . .

In other words, I call attention to the fact, incredibly missed by criticism hitherto, that American Fundamentalism has produced its mystic poet, a poet comparable to the best neo-Catholic poets of the Latin countries and in the direct tradition of Blake and Francis Thompson, and that this poet in Lindsay is the true and lasting poet, rather than the author and reciter of the famous set pieces and finally that this mystical Lindsay is profoundly poetical and has a touch of true magic even when, as is not often the case, he marries his mysticism, usually expressed in verse of traditional contour, to the American folk-rhythms which he has invented:

> Free and proud and mellow jamboree,
> Roar and foam upon the prairie sea,
> Tom turkeys sing the sun a serenade:—
> It is the cross-roads
> Resurrection
> Parade.

The better-known pieces do not fail to retain their interest. "The Congo" remains a profoundly interesting poem; the

573

"Chinese Nightingale" and "Johnny Appleseed" and "The Golden Whales of California" are much less continuously vital. Latterly, too, Lindsay has taken to pouring out this type of poem uncritically. He is always at his best in his mystical mood as in the early "General William Booth Enters Heaven" or the mythopœic "Simon Legree." In his determination to render poetical every common aspect of American folk-life he has gone beyond his own or, in fact, any one's possibilities. Yet it must be admitted that even at his most trivial, as in verses on motion-picture actors, and at his most vulgar, as in "The Drunkard's Funeral," he is never wholly bereft of the poetic touch. But the Lindsay that will count is not in any of these poems, but in the mystical moon and nature verses and in such hours of high imaginative insight as that in which he came upon the secret of John Milton's embodying his dream of beauty and wifehood in the figure of Eve:

> "To justify the ways of God to man"—
> So, self-deceived, his printed purpose runs.
> His love of you is the true key to him
> And Uriel and Michael were your sons.
>
> Your bosom nurtured his Urania.
> Your meek voice, piercing through his midnight sleep
> Shook him far more than silver chariot-wheels
> Or rattling shields, or trumpets of the deep . . .

v

No single thing in modern American literature is more remarkable than the productivity of a group of women in lyrical poetry. I cannot treat them all; there are too many and many are still young. But among the verses of the youngest there is often found that blending of frankness and precision that marks the entire group, that profound though often profoundly troubled willingness to accept and freely to examine their fate and its meaning as women. Among foreign woman lyrists I can think of but one who is in this respect quite comparable to the Americans, namely, Ricarda Hüch. It is noteworthy, too, that these American women, to the quite youngest of the group, to Louise Bogan and Léonie Adams, have been very conservative in respect of form and have depended on their effects for personal meaning and personal music poured into the immemorial and often into the very simplest patterns of English verse. It is perhaps not fantastic to see in this fact the permanent and almost mystical conservatism of women that blessedly remains beneath the rude experiments and violent doctrinal winds of even the most confused and turbulent age.

At the head of this group of women poets stands Edna St. Vincent Millay. She has used no form, hardly a turn of rhythm not consecrated by the long uses of English verse. Yet at her frequent best her voice is entirely her own and more triumphantly so for the associations of long tradition which she had first to resist and then to transmute. Of this method her last book, "Fatal Interview," affords a really matchless instance. The sonnets are unthinkable without Shakespeare's; they are equally unthinkable as anyone's save Edna Millay's. They are not all of an inner perfection to answer the outer one; in not a few the emotion is feigned rather than felt. But of the best of them—of XIV, XXVIII, XXX, XXXI, XXXVII, XLV, XLVII and LI—it may be definitely said that they do not lose when placed beside any sonnets in the language nor when compared with the highest poetry of love and loss in any. It may be pointed out in passing that one can speak in such terms and in such other terms as have been used concerning Robert Frost and William Ellery Leonard and will also be used concerning a handful of poems left by Elinor Wylie, of no prose work by any contemporary American. The novelists very properly and necessarily fill and make to resound the day. The quieter voices of a few poets will be longer heard.

"Fatal Interview" is, of course, Edna Millay's maturest work. But it is significant, especially for an American poet, that her latest work should be her best and should illustrate her mood and method at a point of culmination. That mood of the poet has never varied. She is a pagan with a troubled conscience and a peaceless heart. Brave and strangely though sometimes sordidly beautiful and gallant were those Bohemian days during the war in which the poet gathered her figs from thistles. The revolt against Puritan America was in its bloom and life was to be lived according to another, more burning and more gallant fashion. Alas, in heart and conscience, especially in women's hearts and consciences, there were monitions far older than American Neo-Puritanism. One could not be a pagan without a sob in one's voice and an ache in one's soul and the terror of death was tempered by no slaked thirst of the senses nor any satisfactions of the variable heart. And so this pagan poet is among the most sorrowful, the most plangent of all poets for the simple reason, pointed out by Matthew Arnold long ago, that paganism fails when we are sick and sorry and desolate and afraid of death and dust. And so it is no wonder that one of her most piercing poems "Moriturus" is on that anguished old mediæval theme: *Timor mortis conturbat me* and that in all literature this cry has scarcely been uttered with a more tragic tone:

> Withstanding Death
>   Till life be gone,
> I shall treasure my breath,
>   I shall linger on.
>
> I shall bolt my door
>   With a bolt and a cable;
> I shall block my door
>   With a bureau and a table;
>
> With all my might
>   My door shall be barred.
> I shall put up a fight,
>   I shall take it hard.
>
> With his hand on my mouth
>   He shall drag me forth,
> Shrieking to the south
>   And clutching at the north.

And in a quieter tone she wrote:

> Down, down, down into the darkness of the grave
> Gently they go, the beautiful, the tender, the kind;
> Quietly they go, the intelligent, the witty, the brave.
> I know. But I do not approve. And I am not resigned.

Hence a great anguish comes upon the poet as the iron years march inexorably on:

> I would to God I were quenched and fed
>   As in my youth,

577

From the flask of song, and the good bread
Of beauty richer than truth.

But the flask of song does not endure forever and beauty is
not enough and it is no wonder therefore that the poet cries:

The anguish of the world is on my tongue.
My bowl is filled to the brim with it; there is more than I can
    eat.

One reads these verses of the poet's and remembers in their
gloom earlier ones:

My candle burns at both ends;
    It will not last the night;
But ah, my foes and oh, my friends—
    It gives a lovely light.

or the delightful "Recuerdo" and "MacDougal Street" and
the exquisite four sonnets "Figs from Thistles." The whole
thing in its totality is like a mediæval morality. The pagan
in the heart is always fighting the terrors of mortality. The
pagan invites the old pagan consolations. Corruption may
take the poet; verse remains. It is the sad cold comfort of all
the Latin poets even to Seneca's

Carmina sola carent fato mortemque repellunt.

And so Edna Millay asks:

When shall I be dead?
    When my flesh is withered
And above my head
    Yellow pollen gathered
All the empty afternoon?

and her answer is: "Weep not me, my friend!"

Me, by no means dead
    In that hour, but surely

When this book, unread,
Rots to earth obscurely.

And the lyric plea as it continues rises to a cry of pain:
"Read me, do not let me die!" And again:

Boys and girls that lie
Whispering in the hedges,
Do not let me die,
Mix me with your pledges.

It is a very old cry and it is forever new and late researches
in the structure of the psyche tell us much concerning a
primordial wish for permanence in all human hearts which,
when defeated on the biological plane can never wholly be
satisfied on the plane of art, since in its higher manifestations it needs both methods of expressing itself, even as the
masculine poet needs both wife and muse, both generative
womb and generative heart and is happy and well-balanced
only if he have the good fortune to find that womb and that
heart inhabiting the same body of woman. . . . I offer this
illustration to show how deeply Edna Millay's lyric work
strikes to the root of human life and that the delight taken
in it by men as well as the esteem in which she is justly held
are not accidental. And she speaks especially for the women
of this age who have so often lost the chance or the faith
necessary for expressing their urge to persistence through life
and cultivate barren substitutes and feign to themselves—
without, of course, the poet's genius and justification and
compensatory reward—that the great processes of life are
prosaic and that emptiness is better than fulfillment:

Feed the grape and bean
To the vintner and monger;

579

> I will lie down lean
> With my thirst and my hunger.

This argument could be continued by analyzing such poems as "Humoresque" and "Never May the Fruit Be Plucked" in "The Harp-Weaver" and "Wine from These Grapes"—"stained with these grapes I shall lie down to die!"—from "The Buck in the Snow." But enough has been said to show that the tragic substance of Edna Millay's poetry is both of her time and also timeless, which is the reason why, unlike so many contemporaries, she has not been put to the sterile shifts of mere innovation and experiment but has been able to mold the ancient forms of human verse to her sharp and immediate needs. So much being certain, there is no need here to indulge in mere detailed or textual criticism, saying this poem is better than that and this volume richer than the next. The poet has been at her best often enough to have already assured her place—and she is barely forty—among the major modern lyrical poets of the English language. Nor is this all. Not only is her latest volume, "Fatal Interview," her most perfect; in it, no more troubled by that early Celtic tricksiness and lightness, she strikes a graver tone—a tone that is morally allied to deeper issues than those within the grasp of the exquisite and exquisitely troubled pagan lyrist. And to a larger treatment of such human issues the author of the following noble lines may well yet rise:

> When we that wore the myrtle wear the dust,
> And years of darkness cover up our eyes,
> And all our arrogant laughter and sweet lust
> Keep counsel with the scruples of the wise;
> When boys and girls that now are in the loins
> Of croaking lads, dip oar into the sea,—

And who are those that dive for copper coins?
No longer we, my love, no longer we—
Then let the fortunate breathers of the air,
When we lie speechless in the muffling mould,
Tease not our ghosts with slander, pause not there
To say that love is false and soon grows cold,
But pass in silence the mute grave of two
Who lived and died believing love was true.

Second among the women poets of the period is the late
Elinor Wylie. More detailed accounts of American poetry
would, of course, dwell upon the graceful lyric gift of Sara
Teasdale, the few somber but deep notes of Jean Starr Untermeyer, the precise and poetic psychological notations of
Genevieve Taggard, the candor and clarity of certain quite
early and again quite recent poems of Leonora Speyer, the
emotional richness of Babette Deutsch. To all of these the
anthologist can be juster than the critic who deals with an
entire literature. The latter needs a fairly complete literary
personality to contemplate. And such a one, despite the
meagerness of her output, Elinor Wylie undoubtedly was.
She sacrificed life wholly to art—one has but to read
"Drowned Women," "Self-Portrait," "Confession"—
though she was too deeply human consciously to desire to do
so. It was her fate:

> This little sum of my experience
> Remains the sole contrivance I produce
> To weave this mesh, to colour and confuse
> These ragged syllables with soul and sense.
> I have been put to one supreme expense . . .

She had her reward. Her work is indeed not only slight in
volume; it is also very unequal in quality. But that is be-

cause her aim was not only high but strange. She aimed at complete catharsis and complete objectivizing of the lyric impulse; she was not content even with marble; her desire for permanence was consuming; she wanted what was in sober truth *ære perennius,* more lasting than brass. But her medals were to be graven with a biting tool, not scratched like those of Gautier and other writers of enameled verses. And the tool was first to have drunk the blood of a woman's heart. No wonder that her completely successful poems can be very easily reckoned up. But from "The Eagle and the Mole" and "Madman's Song" on to the magnificent "Address to My Soul" in her last slim volume in which she restated so precisely the intention of her life and art these verses are, in truth, perfect.

> The pure integral form,
> Austere and silver-dark,
> Is balanced on the storm
> In its predestined arc. . . .
>
> Five-petalled flame, be cold.
> Be firm, dissolving star:
> Accept the stricter mould
> That makes you singular.

Nor is their perfection ever a dull or cold perfection as is apt to be the case with poets of this kind. The poems pass easily from the deep human insight of "Simon Gerty" to the wild magic of "King's Ransom" and from the fiery didacticism of "The Eagle and the Mole" to the profound psychological intimacy of her most unforgettable stanzas:

> Now let no charitable hope
> Confuse my mind with images

Of eagle and of antelope:
I am in nature none of these.

I was, being human, born alone;
I am being woman, hard beset;
I live by squeezing from a stone
The little nourishment I get.

In masks outrageous and austere
The years go by in single file;
But none has merited my fear,
And none has quite escaped my smile.

VI

As this record of creative expression in America approaches
its close it must of necessity become more rigidly selective
and leave to the sharper definition of the future the works
of both certain older and certain younger writers. To that
definition and judgment of time I am willing to leave the
shimmering and never unbeautiful effects of Conrad Aiken,
for instance, and the real power as well as the unconvincing
Titanism of Robinson Jeffers; I am willing to leave the bril-
liant-hued poems of Countee Cullen and the piercing Negro
folk-notes of Langston Hughes even as in the novel I must
leave to the judgment of the future the sensitive flights from
naturalism of Glenway Wescott, the tenuous textures of
Elizabeth Madox Roberts, the promising welter of power
of Thomas Wolfe. Nor has so remarkable a stylist and so
incisive a thinker as Maurice Samuel yet given the true
measure of his talent. Hence I shall limit myself to the consideration of a very few figures, not because of the finished
works that these have produced, but because from them

much can be learned concerning the American artist and his creative problems in the age and year in which this page is written.

The disillusion following the World War was deeper than other disillusions because it attained the very bases of human emotion. The more deeply hurt of the younger men refused to select among the more and the less valid of the permanent trends of the human heart but turned wholly against it, limiting their work, in fictional form, to sensuality and adventure, seeking in poetry to substitute the operations of an analytical and next of a synthetic faculty (both aspects of wit in that word's older sense) for the emotions as well as the aspirations that had hitherto characterized practically all literature. To meet this mood came a recently but already strongly rooted tradition in modern French poetry which, brilliantly defined and defended by Paul Valéry, drawn through Mallarmé from Baudelaire, made the aim of poetry a stern pure intellectual exercise, gaining its value for the reader from the apprehension of these intellectual ardors and for the poet, according to Valéry, from the virtue acquired by resistance to all that is facile. "Severe labor in literature manifests itself and operates by rejections—*par des refus.*" Further: "Mallarmé created in France the notion of the *difficult author*" and all good modern poetry must be difficult, because it must derive from intricate intellectual operations alone. Human instinct and with it all that has been known as inspiration must be repudiated. "If I must write, I would infinitely rather write a feeble thing thoroughly conscious and with entire lucidity of mind, than give birth to the most beautiful masterpiece by the favor of a trance or of something outside of myself." Thus Valéry. Now the elementary fallacy involved in this view springs, of course, from a complete and stubborn ignorance of the psychology of the creative process. All the major work of that process, whatever the deliberate aim or method, goes on beneath the flooring of the self-conscious mind and rises into it during the periods of creative ardor, however cold or intellectual that ardor may seem to the poet to be. But this view of literary art as a high and conscious artifice commended itself to those whose disillusion with human emotions and human themes was complete. It is in this spirit and from this point of view that T. S. Eliot returned to Dryden whom "we prize," he writes, "as we do Mallarmé"—note how the theories converge—"for what he made of his material." There speaks by implication the despair of the *material* of poetry, that is, human life and human character and history. Hence Eliot's explanation of disassociation followed by reassociation imposed upon certain seventeenth-century poets; hence the reproach against a later poetry of being "crude," and the dictum, identical with Valéry's "that poets in our civilization, as it exists at present, must be *difficult.*" It all amounts to an involuntary definition of a despair of meaning, to a confession of aridity of heart, of which the proof came in good time through Eliot's flight, paralleled in many periods by those who had pitched their expectations of life too high and could not bear their adolescent disappointment, into the bosom of a fictive father-image and force, in this case Royalism and Anglo-Catholicism.

These considerations define Eliot's character as an artist and account for the falling silent of his poetic voice as well as for the enormous but somewhat waning influence which he exerts upon many of his younger contemporaries. They do not detract from the curious interest of his verse. The earlier verses are the realistic expression of disillusion, of satiety, of low vitality in the exactly seen outer face of life.

And I have known the eyes already, known them all.

Where did that weary rhythm and wearier meaning sound before?

La chaire est triste, hélas, et j'ai lu tous les livres . . .

"I have lost my passion," says a character in one of these poems. And the wretched J. Alfred Prufrock laments:

But though I have wept and fasted, wept and prayed,
Though I have seen my head, grown slightly bald, brought in
    upon a platter.
I am no prophet—and here's no great matter. . . .

From these portraits of arid souls Eliot proceeded to those seven more strictly "metaphysical" poems of his in rich sonorous quatrains in which there is that "development of thought by rapid association which requires considerable agility on the part of the reader." But these poems, whatever mental agility is needed for their reading, have a heavy rhythmic clangor and strange textual charm. Once or twice, too, Eliot, though feigning objectivity, speaks out the aridity of his inner man:

> He knew the anguish of the marrow,
> The ague of the skeleton;
> No contact possible to flesh
> Allayed the fever of the bone.

586

The man who wrote this quatrain is evidently a poet; he is evidently, too, profoundly and tragically sincere. Hence there is no need to revive the controversies that followed the publication of his longest and last poem "The Waste Land." The title sets the theme and tells the story. Civilization is disintegrated and meaning is disintegrated and despair and disillusion stalk the waste land of the world. Now Eliot undertook to delineate this disintegration of thoughts and things and processes by an analogous disintegration of speech and technique. Chaos of the world and the soul is set forth by the learned and calculated chaos of the poem's method. The worm of disillusion has eaten away *form* which is in itself always an act of creative *faith*. He who creates form affirms life, however desolate his meaning, even as the most pessimistic philosophy is still an assertion of the triumph of the human spirit. To a despair so deep that it shatters form and so the world there are two classical issues: suicide or the Catholic Church. Eliot chose the latter. The future will doubtless assign him a definite place among the minor poets and characteristic phenomena of the post-war period. To the youths who cling to him one might say: this is no last word, but one of the oldest. Men not ignoble have gone down before life in other ages and wandered in waste lands and taken refuge in some monastery or hermitage either of the soul or of the body or of both. . . . But the creative imagination is at one with life and its procreative processes and withers both in the desert of despair and in the refuge of blank authority. . . .

Another characteristic stage in the creative problems of the period in America may be usefully and significantly illustrated by the work of such a poet as Mark Van Doren. Even in his first volume there were memorably beautiful things: "Spring Thunder," "Crow," "Marriage." The maturer volumes show the growth of a mystical relationship to nature, quite analogous to Rainer Maria Rilke's, and an equally analogous inner repudiation of urban life. From this union there might arise, as there did in Rilke's case, a poetic vision of a high order. The elements are all present. Mark Van Doren's ultimate ideal, symbolically speaking, is Abraham— pastoral king and patriarch, at one with nature and with life. Van Doren is deterred from his vision and its expression by the metaphysical nihilism so powerfully and poetically projected in the title-poem of "Now the Sky" and still more, one suspects, by those emotional disintegrations and evil sophistications which are held to be the last word of modernity and are probably among the sins and weaknesses that undermined Babylon and made Rome to crumble. Wholeness adequate to his vision is lacking to the poet who wrote "The Crime" and "Disputation" and "Philosopher's Love Songs." From this Nihilism and these emotional sophistries spring in all likelihood that studious understatement and almost furious sobriety that will not let him either wholly embrace his vision or write upon that vision's level. He has been, so far, afraid of both greatness of theme and elevation of speech. Yet the theme is in his soul and in his very bones and he could without doubt write largely and nobly if he would let himself. And that courage toward large and noble work upon large and noble themes must be—unless we are to sink into a long period of futility—the next step in the process of creative speech in America.

588

That being so, there is no need even to name those not ungifted younger poets who, sharing the post-war despair of meaning, offer us shimmering and inextricable patterns of words. It will suffice that here and there appear already on the horizon flickers of courage toward high theme and elevated speech. Thus Hart Crane still pays tribute to a silly fallacy of "modernity" when he writes

> New verities, new inklings in the velvet hummed
> Of dynamos—

as though the machine, that mere intricate tool and extension of the human hand, had had any effect upon the permanent passions or central aspirations of man. But at the same time Crane bursts once more the bonds of disillusion and of frightened murmur and dares to write in that manner which allies to each other the poetic utterances of the ages:

> We danced, O Brave, we danced beyond their farms,
> In cobalt desert closures made our vows. . . .
> Now is the strong prayer folded in these arms,
> The serpent with the eagle in the boughs.

To the reader who has followed this interpretative account of creative expression in America from, let us say, the publication of Franklin's "Autobiography" in 1791 on, it will be very clear that the experiment in human life and human culture which is called America has not been an inarticulate one. If it has sometimes seemed so to be, the reason for that impression was to be sought in the timidity of those historians who closed the chronicle of American art near the beginning and were unwilling to admit that the stream of our literature has broadened and deepened continuously with the increasing years. But such has in truth been the case and especially among the literatures of the twentieth century that of America stands on a level with the strongest and with the richest in creative values. If we have produced no masterpieces of a very high order, if both wholeness and high severity are lacking even to our best works, that is a fate which we share with all but one of the contemporary peoples. And the cause lies, I must be permitted to repeat, in that universal situation of mankind which is in the last analysis a religious and metaphysical one. But the race has passed through other ages of despair; other catastrophes both inner and outer have shattered faith and power in the long course of history; the human spirit has not therefore known any long defeat. It will not now. And in any creative rebirth of the future, whether near or far, America will have her appropriate and splendid share.

INDEX

591

Babbitt, Irving—(*Continued*)
definitions of humanists' theories, 441
negation laws, 434
on realism, 420
reactionism of, 436
"Babbitt," Lewis, 465, 502
as ideal American book, 504
discussed, 510
"Babbitt Warren, The," 502
Bacon, Sir Francis, xii
"Bagatelle," Aldrich, 88
Baker, G. P., 62
Baldwin, Roger, 18
Balzac, Honoré de, xxviii
Bandbox Theater, 389
Banville, Théodore de, 533
"Barbara Frietchie," Whittier, 68
Barchester novels, Trollope, 252
Bard, as exemplified in the short-story writer, 284
environment determines work of, 155
Mark Twain the one American example of the, 217
psychology of the modern, xx
"Barefoot Boy, The," Whittier, 68
Barlow, Joel, 40
Barnum, Phineas T., 103
Bartas, Guillaume du, 39
"Battle Hymn of the Republic," Howe, 80
Baudelaire, Charles Pierre, 154, 584
admiration of Poe, 157
a psychopathic type, 158
"Bay Psalm Book, The," 20
Bazalgette, Léon, 199
Beach, Lewis, 392
Beard, Charles, 355
"Beast in the Jungle, The," James, 264, 269
Beauty, as the aim of literature, 162
ideal of, 535
Platonic idea of, 537
pursuit by transition lyricists, 364
trivial without religion or sex, 533
wholeness of life through, 537
Beer, Thomas, on Crane, 321
Beers, Henry Augustin, 98
"Before Dawn," Hauptmann, 395

Beissel, Johann Conrad, 22
Belasco, David, 63, 313, 330, 389
Bellamy, Edward, 281
Bellay, Joachim du, 535
Benét, William Rose, 374
"Ben-Hur," Wallace, 85, 281
"Ben Jonson Entertains a Man from Stratford," Robinson, 555
Beowulf, xx
"Berenice," 156
Bergson, Henri, 437
"Bernice," Glaspell, 394
Bethlehem Bach festivals, 23
"Better Sort, The," James, 263
Bewett, Hugh, 7
"Bewick Finzer," Robinson, 555
Beyond naturalism, idealistic artist thrown upon his abstract self, 524
in drama, 543-553
inevitability of movement, 523
in poetry, 553-589
new symbols sought, 525
permanent meaning sought, 529
writers typifying, 528-530
"Beyond the Horizon," O'Neill, 543, 547
Bierce, Ambrose, 303, 312
moments of introspective insight, 319
moral sterility of his tales, 318
relation of his life to his art, 317
"Biglow Papers, The," Lowell, 72
Billings, Josh, 216
Biologic causes, superstition of sufficiency of narrow, 324
"Birthplace, The," James, 269
"Black Cat, The," Poe, 165
Blake, William, 572
"Blight," Emerson, 133
"Blithedale Romance, The," Hawthorne, 154, 170, 176
character of, 182
"Bloudy Tenent of Persecution, The," Roger Williams, 13
"Blue Butterfly Day," Frost, 499
Bodenheim, Maxwell, 375, 376
Boehme, Jacob, 21
Bohm, Charles, 315
Boileau, Nicholas, 375

593

594

"Hard-boiled" writers, 518
"Hare Drummer," Masters, 491
Harland, Henry, 268, 283
"Harper's Magazine," 293
"Harp-Weaver, The," Millay, 580
Harris, Frank, 365
Harris, Joel Chandler, 292
Harte, Bret, 222, 235, 275, 282
    formula for the short-story, 284-286
Hartford Wits, 40
Hassgesang, Ernst Lissauer, xx
"Hasty Pudding," Barlow, 40
"Haunted Mind, The," Hawthorne, 179
"Haunted Palace," Poe, 167
Hauptmann, Gerhart, 377, 395, 463, 471, 527, 545
Hawthorne, Julian, 90
Hawthorne, Nathaniel, 6, 62, 154, 236
    as a classic, 185
    as critic and skeptic, 182
    awareness of own limitations, 176
    Emerson's opinion of, 175, 177, 178
    influenced by Brook Farm, 170
    influence of private life on work, 169, 171, 173, 180
    lack of American culture, 194
    married life, 169
    Melville compared with, 186
    nature of his expression, 171
    nature of his romances, 177-180
    neurotic temptation to flee from life, 173
    "sense of guilt" influence, 172, 177
Hawthorne, Mrs., 167
    jealousy of her husband's art, 186
Hay, John, 276
Hayne, Paul Hamilton, level of traditional poetic workmanship, 82
"Hazard of New Fortunes, A," Howells, 247, 249, 254
H. D. (*see* Doolittle, Hilda)
Hearn, Lafcadio, 313, 331
    individualistic style, 348
    rebellion against Western civilization, 347
Hebbel, Friedrich, 86
Hecht, Ben, 402
Hegel, Georg, 118
Heine, Heinrich, 54, 360

Hemingway, Ernest, 346
    gifts of, 518
    human and philosophical note, 520
Henry, O., xxi, 282, 317, 374
    cultural significance, 326
    euphemistic trickery, 328
    influence on life, 329
    influence on the short story, 328
"Herald," New York, 351
"Heretics, The," Leonard, 564
"Her Eyes," Robinson, 553
Hergesheimer, Joseph, 490, 505, 525
    beautiful gesture ideal, 533
    dual personality, 531
    explanation of his works, 533-538
    force of human passion, 533
    search for significant pattern, 532
"Hermann und Dorothea," Goethe, 66
"Hero, The," Emery, 398
"Heroism," Emerson, 127
"Her Own Room," Winslow, 516
Herrick, Robert, 312, 317
    effort to pierce illusions, 468
Hesiod, 377
"Hiawatha," Longfellow, 66, 203
"Hireling and the Slave, The," Grayson, 79
Higginson, Thomas Wentworth, 85
"History of a Literary Radical," Bourne, 418
History of Plymouth Plantation, Bradford, 4
Hoffman, August, 154
Hoffman, Charles Fenno, 49
Hölderlin, Johann, 387
"Holiday," Frank, 403
Holmes, Mary J., 234, 281
Holmes, Oliver Wendell, 97
    failure to achieve distinction, 69
Holz, Arno, 319, 373, 374, 377
"Home Ballads," Whittier, 68
"Home, Sweet Home," Payne, 49
Homer, 377, 462, 496
    influence on Pound, 381
Homosexuality, exemplified in Whitman, 199-201
    in readers and critics, 158
Hooker, Thomas, 8, 9
"Hoosier Schoolmaster, The," Eggleston, 278

603

604

Literature—(*Continued*)
 transition from revery and fantasy
  to observation, 233
 true meaning, xxviii
 wide European audience for Amer-
  ican, 503
"Little Lord Fauntleroy," Burnett, 85,
 281
"Little magazine" trend, 371, 383
"Little renaissance," effect on cul-
 tural aspect of America, 412
"Little Review, The," 383
"Little theater" movement, 393
Little Theater, of Chicago, 389
"Little Women," Alcott, 235
Locke, John, 17
"Lockless Door, The," Frost, 500
Lockwood's school rhetoric, 53
London, Jack, 317
 cult of brutality, 325
 Darwinistic determinism of, 324
 reasons for popularity, 325
"London Life, A," James, 239
Longfellow, Henry Wadsworth, xxi,
 53, 58, 62, 97
 as an educator and pioneer of mod-
  ern scholarship, 64
 as a translator of verse, 64
 Emerson on, 112
 lack of poetic character, 63, 65
"Looking Backward," Bellamy, 281
"Lost Lady, A," Cather, 542
Love, affirmed by Hemingway, 519
 as drawn by O'Neill, 546-548
 as expression of human personality,
  492
 central element of every human activity, 241
 Henry James' incapacity for, 261
 Lindsay's lyrical exposition of, 572
"Love Nest, The," Lardner, 515
"Love's Labour's Lost," Shakespeare,
 136
"Love's Pilgrimage," Sinclair, 471
Lovett, Robert Morss, 303
Lowell, Amy, 314, 374, 377, 379
 later life self-awareness, 385
 sonnets, 385
 warfare for liberation of form, 384

Lowell, James Russell, 60, 70, 97
 as critic, 75
 happy effect of anti-slavery struggle
  on, 71
 on Thoreau's style, 140
 poetic achievement, 73
 polite, Puritanical gentility, 74
Lucretius, ix, xxiii, 246, 347
"Luise," Voss, 66
Lyly, John, 388
"Lynching Bee, The," Leonard, 564
Lyon, Harris Merton, 283
"Lyrical Ballads," Wordsworth, 378
Lyric poetry, 571
 complete objectivizing aimed at,
  582
 productivity of women in, 574-583
"Lyric Year, The," 314, 366

Mabie, Hamilton Wright, xxi, 85, 91,
 299, 418
"MacDougal Street," Millay, 578
"M'Fingal," Trumbull, 40
McKinley, William, 300
"McTeague," Norris, 296
 intensity and concentration of effect,
  322
"Madame de Mauves," James, 236,
 264, 269
"Madman's Song," Wylie, 582
Magazines, 293
 fostering the critical spirit, 417
"Maggie: A Girl of the Street," Crane,
 320
"Magic Mountain, The," Mann, xi,
 506
"Magnolia Cemetery Ode," Timrod,
 81
"Main Street," Lewis, 502
Major, Charles, 296
Mallarmé, Stéphane, 584, 585
"Mamatreya," Emerson, 133
"Mammonart," Sinclair, 469
Man, the total, 455
"Man Against the Sky, The," Robin-
 son, 555
Mangan, James Clarence, 194
"Manhattan Cycle, A," Winslow, 516
Mann, Thomas, xvii, 172, 235, 341,
 506, 507

608

Optimism, 207
   essential to the American spirit, 296
   psychology of the American masses, 286
Orientalism, expressed in Hearn, 348
"Orion," R. H. Horne, 163
"Ormond," Charles Brockdon Brown, 54
Ossian, origins of his form, 203
Others group, 376
"Our Changing Morality," ed. by Freda Kirchwey, 418
"Outbound Road, The," Mulder, 411
"Outlook, The," 299
"Out of the Cradle Endlessly Rocking," Whitman, 211
"Oven Bird, The," Frost, 497
"Over-Soul, The," Emerson, 127

Pacifism, 470
Page, Thomas Nelson, 292, 296
Paine, Thomas, 29
   Deism, 30
   imaginative and philosophic vision, 31
   intellectual descendants, 30
   on Anglo-Saxon nativism, 33
"Painted Veils," Huneker, 354
"Pamela," Richardson, 463
"Pantagruel," Rabelais, 191
Papini, Giovanni, 334
"Paradise Lost," Milton, 171
"Paradiesische Wunderspiel," 22
Parrington, V. L., 180
"Party Dress, The," Hergesheimer, 538
Pastorius, Franz Daniel, xxix, 20
   modest talents, 21
"Patagonia, The," James, 264, 269
"Pathfinder, The," 372
"Pathological," Hearn, 349
Pattee, Fred Lewis, 97
Paulding, James K., 42
Payne, John Howard, 48
Peabody, Sophia (see Hawthorne, Mrs.)
"People of the Abyss," London, 324
"People Round the Corner," Winslow, 516

Penn, William, 20
Pennsylvania, colonial literary traditions, 20-23
Pennsylvania, University of, 25
"Pension Beaurepas, The," James, 264, 269
Periodicals, 351
   essentials of an efficient editor, 284
   lowest denominator group-expression of their age, 311
   of sectionalist period, 293
   part in critical debate, 425
   the "little magazine," 371
Perry, Bliss, 60
Pessimism, 116
   cosmic, 556
   two classical issues to, 587
"Peter Schlemihl," Chamisso, 165
"Phantasus," Holz, 374
Phelps, William Lyon, 155, 446
Philadelphia, in modern fiction, 534
Phillips, David Graham, 303, 317
   cast off sentimental pretenses, 327
   significance, 326
"Philosopher's Love Songs," Mark Van Doren, 588
Philosophy, as expounded by Santayana, 338-342
   divorce of eternal spiritual and moral agreements in America, 337
   new note in literature, 297, 520
   Nietzschean, 539
   of Henry Adams, 343-347
   of pragmatism, 333-335
   of transition era, 331-342
   Oriental trend as compensation, 348
   popular interest in, 337
   supreme interests, 336
"Philosophy of Composition, The," Poe, 162
"Pictorial Review," 63
"Picture Frames," Winslow, 516
"Picture of Dorian Gray," Wilde, 165
"Pierre," Melville, 154, 187, 190
"Pike County Ballads," Hay, 276
Pindar, 202
Pinkney, Edward Coate, 50
"Pit, The," Norris, 322
"Pit and the Pendulum, The," Poe, 165

Pitkin, Walter, 62, 328, 338
Plato, xi, xxiii
  on genius, 461
Poe, Edgar Allan, 44, 49, 154, 236
  a psychopathic type, 154
  as artist, 164
  as poet, 167
  basis of fame, 166, 168
  critical theory, 157, 159, 163, 164
  European estimate of, 158
  fantasy types, 164
  intimately of his time and section, 167
  lack of American culture, 194
  little influence on Bierce, 318
  morbidity, 162
  parentage, 79
  personal legend of greatness, 157
  sources of his art, 156
  theory of "truth," 161
  tragedy of his life, 158
"Poem Outlines," Lanier, 88
"Poems," Poe, 157, 163
Poet, 62
  creative ardor, 585
  defined by Emerson, 128
  experience and expression are one in the modern, xxv
  explanation of term, xviii
  expression a necessity to the, 155
  function of future, 528
  is not inventor, 525
  measure of self-catharsis, 566
  three types of the poetic mind, xix-xxvii
  true business and function of, 65
"Poet, The," Emerson, 123, 127, 136, 417
"Poet, The," Viereck, 366
Poetry, age of tin, 89
  aim as pure intellectual exercise, 584
  belief essential to, 569
  break with genteel tradition, 314
  conditions fostering, 80
  decline of, 235
  despair of the material of, 585
  discipline of naturalism, 553
  folk-expression, 48-54, 100
  foreshadow of the imagists, 321

Poetry—(Continued)
  humor in, 571
  illustration of methods of polite writers, 87
  lyric, 50, 357-366, 436
  manners of expression, xvii
  meaninglessness of later verse of despair, 407
  "metaphysical" strain, 304
  movement beyond naturalism, 553-589
  naturalistic, 488-500
  necessity for verbal and rhythmic expression, 303
  Negro, 583
  of transition era, 301-309, 356-366
  orthodoxy in, 88
  Pennsylvania tradition, 20-23
  Poe's theory, 159
  produced on a minimum of brains, 566
  product of the Revolution, 39
  quality of war verse, 83
  rebirth of diction, 309
  revolt in forms, 373-388
  school of European decadents, 365
  sophistication of unrhythmed, 374
  spiritual revolt in, 372
  the core and spirit of both history and philosophy, xxvi
  use of American vernacular, 307
  verse not the characteristic form of the moderns, xxiv
  verse of colonial New England, 20
  verse the primitive form of, 202
"Poetry: a Magazine of Verse," 314, 383
Pollard, Percival, 316
"Poor Relation, The," Robinson, 555
Pope, Alexander, 39, 375
Porter, Sydney (see Henry, O.)
"Portrait of a Lady, The," James, 267
Pound, Ezra, 370, 372, 375, 376
  a poet of learning, 379, 381
  repudiation of America, 379
Poyas, Catharine Gendron, 79
Pragmatism, 338
  American industrial civilization expressed by, 335
  birth and vindication, 333

615

623

Whittier, John Greenleaf, 73
heritage of love and spiritual courage, 66
insight of, 67
perception of character of poetical process, 68
"Whoever You Are Holding Me Now in Hand," Whitman, 200
"Wide, Wide World, The," Susan Warner, 233
"Widowers' Houses," Shaw, 506
"Wieland," Brown, 54
"Wife of Brittany, The," Hayne, 82
Wigglesworth, Michael, 20
Wilcox, Ella Wheeler, 65
Wilde, Oscar, 158, 160, 205
Wilde, Richard Henry, 50
Wilder, Thornton, 525
"Wilhelm Meister," Goethe, 267
"Will to Believe, The," James, 332
Willard, Emma Hart, 49
Willbrandt, Adolf, 223
"William Wilson," 165
Williams, Roger, 11
enlightened theories, 12
Willis, Nathaniel Parker, 49
Wilson, Augusta Evans, 234, 281
Wilson, Woodrow, 59, 197, 470
"Wine from These Grapes," Millay, 580
"Wings of the Dove, The," James, 264, 266
Winslow, Thyra Samter, 515
Winter, William, 85, 86, 90, 301
Winthrop, John, 7, 8
Wit, 556, 557
Wolfe, Thomas, 583
"Woman's Diary, A," Hearn, 349
Women, American folk-attitude toward, 218-219
as characters in novels, 541
conservatism of, 575
defects of monthly-magazine-made American, 345
Hergesheimer's idea of the eternal woman, 538

Women—(Continued)
renunciation of womanhood by Emily Dickinson, 361
stripped of false superiority, 327
success in lyrical poetry, 574-583
their moral influence in the genteel tradition, 240
tragic error of imitating man, 346
Woodberry, George E., 89, 301
"Woodman, Spare that Tree," Morris, 49
Woodworth, Samuel, 48
Woolson, Constance F., 275, 290, 292
Wordsworth, William, 118, 132, 378, 497
cited, 313
World War era, criticism and protest, 368
crystallization of neo-nationalism, 369
disillusion of, 584-589
historical values hopelessly discredited, 407
intellectual stir in, 410
works introducing the revolt, 371-374
Wright, Harold Bell, 472
a writer of "pious legends," xi
Wylie, Elinor, 576
aim, 582
sacrificed life to art, 581

"Yankee at King Arthur's Court, A Connecticut," Twain, 224, 230
"Yankee Idyll, A," Lowell, 73
"Yellow Book," 268
"Yellow Violet, The," Bryant, 51
"Yet Gentle Will the Griffin Be," Lindsay, 572
Young, Art, 413
Young, Edward, xiv

"Zell," Aikman, 410
Zola, Emile, 319, 472
influence on America, 322-323
"Zwei Menschen," Dehmel, 565

Readers of EXPRESSION IN AMERICA *will be interested in its companion volume*

CREATIVE AMERICA

by the same author. Here, supplementing and completing his original plan for the first book, are the passages of prose and poetry to which he constantly refers. For the full appreciation of his criticism this work is invaluable, as it gives the reader the opportunity to judge for himself the original selections which came under Mr. Lewisohn's consideration.

But this book is more than a supplement of EXPRESSION IN AMERICA, for it gives Americans an ideal treasury of its own prose and poetry. Here are examples of the finest creative work that has been done in the literary history of America. It is a beautiful and a stirring book, a book that Americans may contemplate with pride and satisfaction, since even its more eccentric pages bear witness to the profound reality and the growing articulateness of American civilization.

Among the 120 famous writers appearing in these pages are:

WASHINGTON IRVING	THEODORE DREISER
HENRY D. THOREAU	SHERWOOD ANDERSON
RALPH WALDO EMERSON	SINCLAIR LEWIS
MARK TWAIN	DOROTHY PARKER
EMILY DICKINSON	ERNEST HEMINGWAY
SUSAN GLASPELL	WILLIAM FAULKNER
ELMER RICE	WILLA CATHER
CARL VAN DOREN	EDNA ST. VINCENT MILLAY
T. S. ELIOT	ELINOR WYLIE